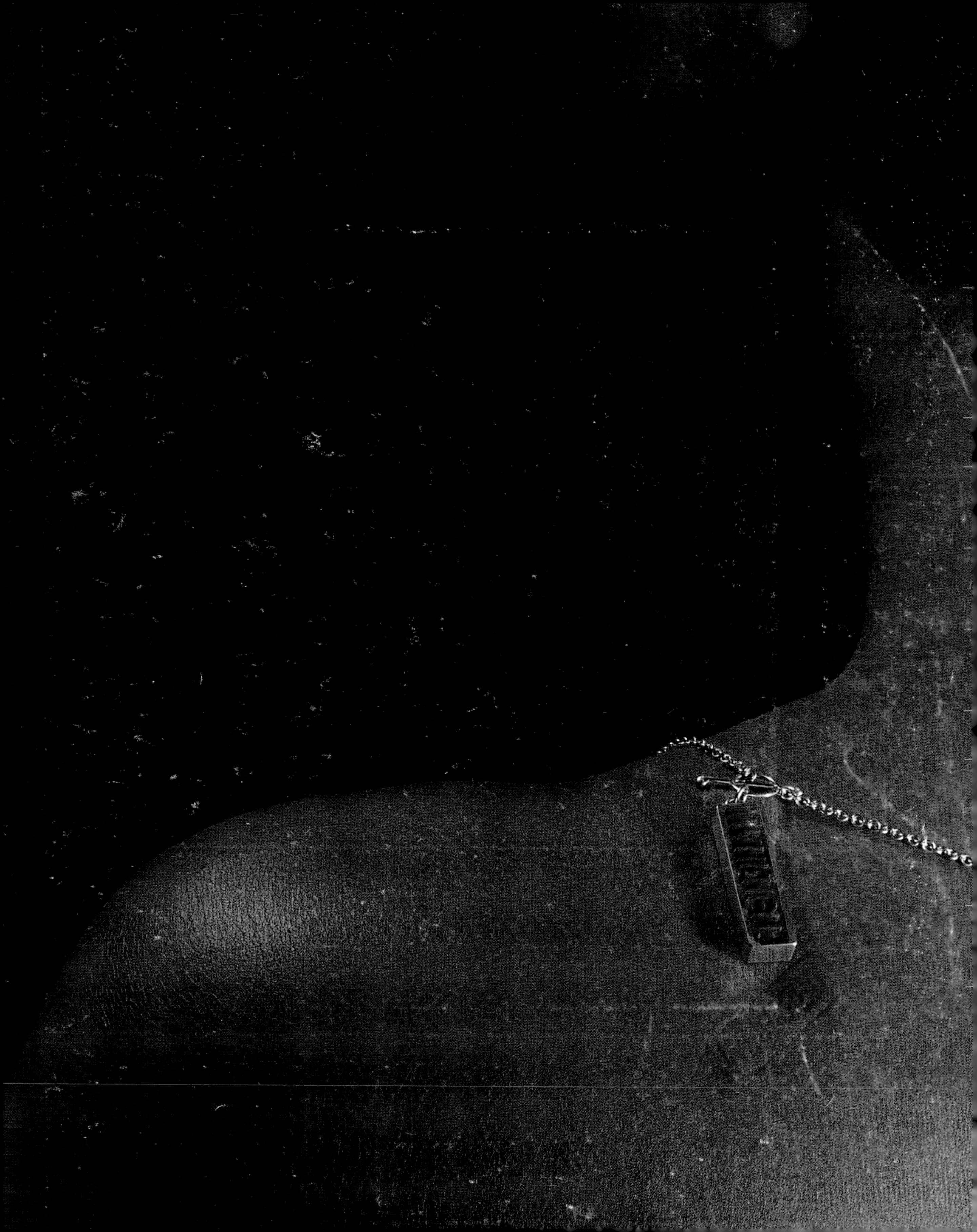

Geschmückte Haut
Decorated Skin
1999/2000

Julia Müllers
Haut-Eindrücke
Anhänger mit Kette
Silber, Gummi
Skin Impressions
pendant with chain
silver, rubber

nicht ohne Schmuck Gerät Produkt

Körpergeschichten
Body Stories
2000/01

Arbeiten von Studierenden, Ehemaligen und Lehrenden aus dem Studiengang Produktdesign, Fachhochschule Düsseldorf

pretty sharp **jewellery implements products**

Works by past and present students and the current staff of the School of Product Design, Düsseldorf University of Applied Sciences

Eva Dufhues
Leibeigene
Körperschmuck
Silberbeschichtete und geschwärzte Grillen, Magnete
Vassals
body jewellery
silver-plated and oxidised cicadas

Insekten am Ohr. An der Übergangsstelle von Körperäußerem und Körperinnerem lösen sie unweigerlich nahezu körperlich spürbare Assoziationen aus.
Insects at the ear. At the transition between the body's outside and inside they cannot but trigger almost physically palpable associations.

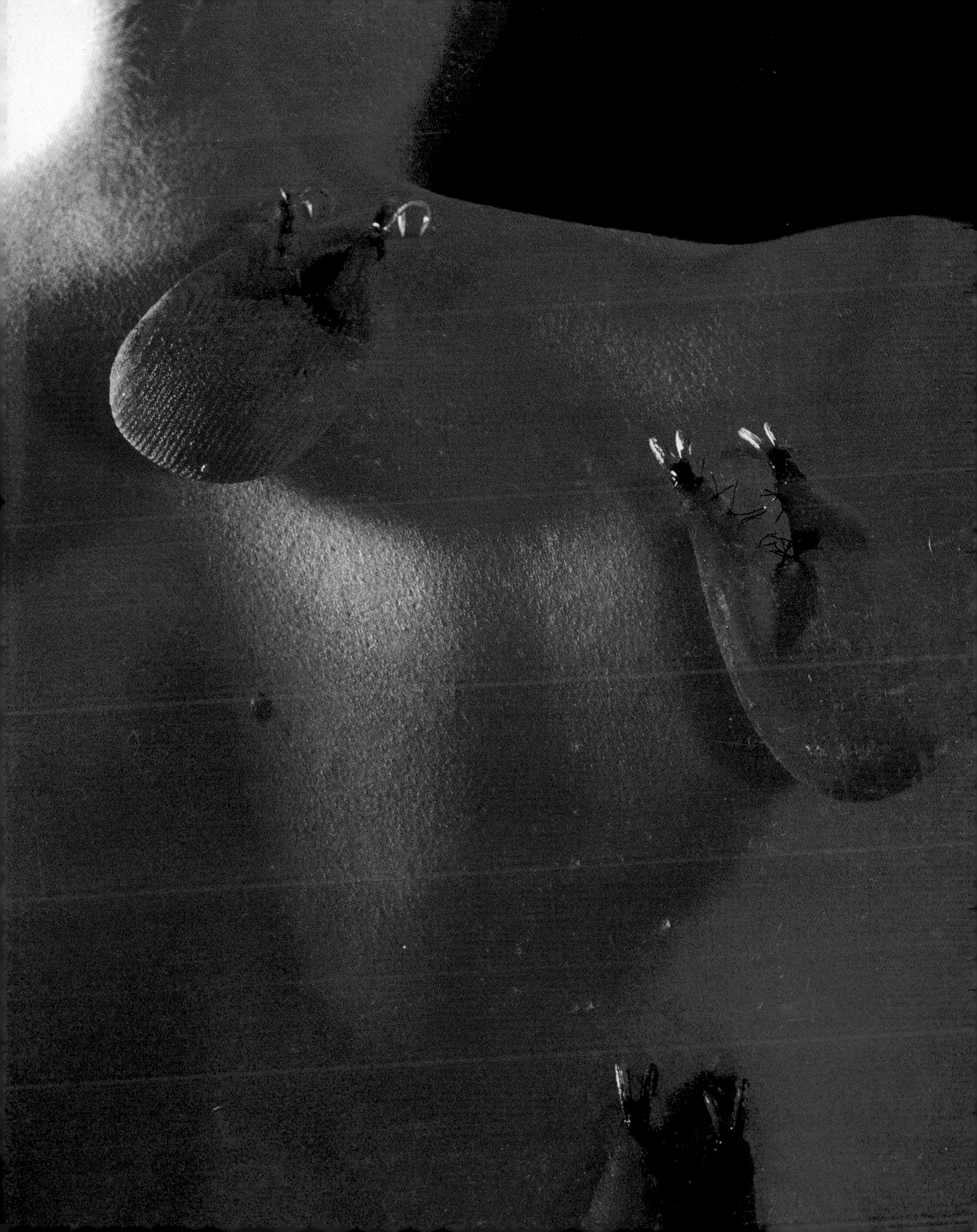

Sabine Staniek Vorwort der Rektorin

Nicole Hanselle
Nackensitzer
Broschen
Latex, Silber, Eisendraht
Nape Sitters
brooches
latex, silver, iron wire

Das Symptom von Sorgen und Ängsten als handhabbares Ding.
A handle on the symptoms of fears and worries.

Sabine Staniek **Foreword by the Rector**

Vor genau 25 Jahren waren Arbeiten aus dem Studienschwerpunkt Schmuckdesign der Fachhochschule Düsseldorf im *Deutschen Goldschmiedehaus Hanau* zu sehen. Zu dieser Ausstellung gab es auch eine kleine bescheidene Veröffentlichung. Es war das erste Mal, dass dieser aus der Werkkunstschule hervorgegangene Schwerpunkt des Fachbereichs Design sich der Öffentlichkeit vorstellte. Die auf dem Titelblatt abgebildete zerknitterte Skizze gibt einen Hinweis darauf, wie dieser Katalog verstanden werden wollte, nämlich als ein Einblick in den Prozess des Lehrens und Lernens sowie als ein Einblick in Arbeiten als Manifestationen dieses Prozesses. Beim Durchblättern fällt auf, dass zu dieser Zeit die Gestaltung von Schmuck als Objekt im Vordergrund stand und die Wechselbeziehung von Schmuck und SchmuckträgerIn kaum thematisiert wurde oder höchstens als technische Problemstellung vorkam. An diesem rührend bescheidenen Zeugnis der Fachhochschule Düsseldorf wird offenbar, wie sehr sich dieser Studiengang in den vergangenen 25 Jahren erweitert und gewandelt hat. Festzustellen ist eine deutliche Erweiterung der Lehrinhalte, denn in dem jetzt vorliegenden Katalogbuch werden die unterschiedlichsten Facetten der Schmuckgestaltung angesprochen, und der tradierte Bereich der Gerätgestaltung ist um Aspekte der Produktgestaltung erweitert. Das Spannungsfeld von Kunst und Design, Schmuck und Produkt, Unikat und Serie, in dem sich Lehrende und Studierende bewegen, wird darüber veranschaulicht. Nicht zuletzt aber sind es die bei Gründung der Fachhochschule eher zufälligen Nachbarschaften zu den anderen Fachbereichen und Studiengängen, die an Bedeutung gewonnen haben. So hat sich besonders die Nähe zu dem größeren Studiengang Kommunikationsdesign immer wieder in studiengangsübergreifenden Projekten niedergeschlagen. Auch dieses Katalogbuch wurde in beispielhafter Weise als interdisziplinäres Projekt des Fachbereichs Design verwirklicht. Er ist damit auch

Körpergeschichten
Body Stories
2000/01

It is now exactly 25 years since works made by the students of the School of Jewellery Design at the Düsseldorf University of Applied Sciences were first exhibited at the *Deutsches Goldschmiedehaus* in Hanau. It was the first public appearance by this department of the Design Faculty, which had been formed from the former College of Arts and Crafts *(Werkkunstschule)*. This original exhibition was accompanied by a modest little publication. The crumpled sketch shown on the cover page gave an indication of the purpose the catalogue, which was intended to provide insights into the process of teaching and learning and the works themselves as a manifestation of this process. Leafing through it now, it is striking that back then the main design focus was on jewellery as an object; the interrelationship between jewellery and its wearer was hardly regarded as an important theme, and when it did arise then only as a technical problem to be solved. This touchingly modest record of the early work of this department of the Düsseldorf University of Applied Sciences clearly illustrates how much the School has grown and developed in the course of the last twenty-five years. The curriculum has become considerably more comprehensive; this new catalogue covers very many different facets of jewellery design, and the program of the traditional silversmithing department now also includes aspects of product design. This also illuminates the field of tension between art and design, jewellery and commercial products, individual works and the series, within which the teachers and students move. And last but not least we can also see the growing importance of other faculties and schools at the university, which has developed to some degree coincidentally as a result of their simple physical proximity. This applies in particular to the close relationship with the larger School of Communication Design, which has borne fruit in a series of inter-faculty

Melanie Halbauer
Leibwächter
Mundschmuck
Gold
Bodyguards
mouth jewellery
gold

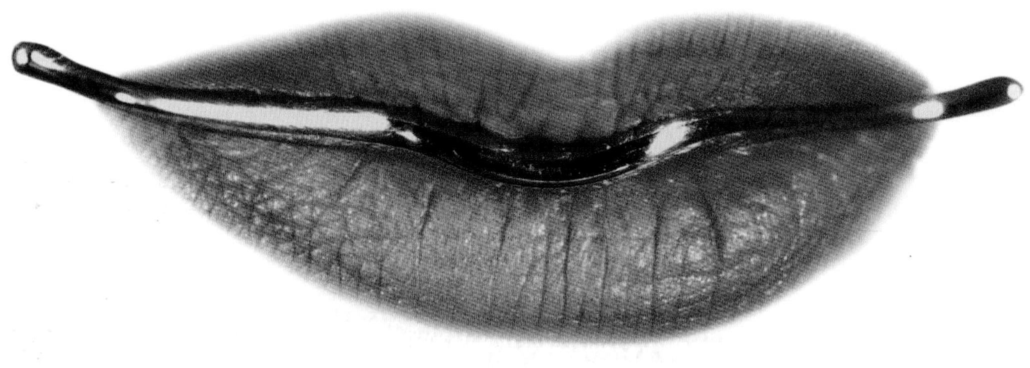

Melanie Halbauer
Leibwächter
Piercing-Schleier
Textilgewebe, medizinischer Stahl
Bodyguards
piercing veil
fabric, surgical steel

Nicht verborgen, sondern verdoppelt. Ein Leibwächter. In seinem Schutz ist Freiheit.
Not hidden, but doubled. A bodyguard. Under his protection is freedom.

ein besonders eindrückliches Beispiel für das interdisziplinäre Potential der Fachhochschule Düsseldorf, das vom Düsseldorfer Schmuckdesign in besonderer Weise verwirklicht wird. Gerne hat die Fachhochschule Düsseldorf wieder die Herausgeberschaft dieses Katalogbuches übernommen, das die Ausstellung im *Deutschen Goldschmiedehaus Hanau* und ihre weiteren Stationen in der *Handwerkskammer Düsseldorf*, dem *Museum für Kunsthandwerk Leipzig/ Grassimuseum (Interim)* und dem *Kestner-Museum* in Hannover begleitet. Dicker und weniger bescheiden als vor 25 Jahren liegt sie jetzt vor. Mit der Übernahme der Herausgeberschaft bringt die Hochschule auch ihre Wertschätzung dieses Studiengangs, dessen Bedeutung weit über Düsseldorf hinausreicht, zum Ausdruck. Als Rektorin der Fachhochschule Düsseldorf ist es mir, gerade vor dem Hintergrund der Profilierung der Hochschule am Standort Düsseldorf, ein besonderes Anliegen, die ganze Fülle und Breite des Beitrages dieses Studiengangs in das Bewusstsein der Öffentlichkeit zu rücken. Diese Ausstellung und das sie begleitende Katalogbuch sind Bestätigung geleisteter Arbeit und Aufbruch zugleich. Deshalb geht an dieser Stelle mein Dank an alle, die sich für das Schmuckdesign am Standort Düsseldorf eingesetzt haben und deren Engagement auch über diese Veröffentlichung sichtbar wird. In der Beschränkung auf die Arbeit der letzten zehn Jahre verdeutlichen Ausstellung und Katalogbuch auch den mit der Berufung von Elisabeth Holder im Jahre 1988 beginnenden Generationenwechsel der Lehrenden und die dadurch bedingten inhaltlichen Veränderungen in der Lehre. So ist zum Beispiel eine stärkere Auseinandersetzung mit gesellschaftlichen Phänomenen einerseits und die Stärkung einer persönlich geführten Auseinandersetzung als Grundlage für die gestalterischen Positionen in Schmuck und Produkt zu beobachten. In guter Nachbarschaft zum Studiengang Kommunikationsdesign erhalten die Studierenden parallel dazu eine

projects. This catalogue, which was produced by the Design Faculty as an interdisciplinary project, is an outstanding example of this. It is also an impressive expression of the interdisciplinary potential of the Düsseldorf University of Applied Sciences in general, and of the Düsseldorf School of Jewellery Design in particular. The Düsseldorf University of Applied Sciences was very happy to act once again as the publisher of this catalogue, which accompanies the exhibition at the *Deutsches Goldschmiedehaus* in Hanau and its subsequent appearances at the *Chamber of Crafts* in Düsseldorf, the *Museum of Applied Arts/Grassimuseum* in Leipzig and the *Kestner-Museum* in Hanover. It is thicker and less modest than its predecessor of 25 years ago. By publishing the catalogue the University is also expressing its appreciation of this School, whose significance extends far beyond Düsseldorf. As the rector of the Düsseldorf University of Applied Sciences it is very important to me to make the entire wealth and breadth of the School's achievements known to the public, especially in connection with the image of the University in Düsseldorf itself. This exhibition and the accompanying catalogue are simultaneously both a confirmation of past achievements and a new beginning. I would thus like to take this opportunity to express my thanks to all the people who have worked to support jewellery design in Düsseldorf, whose commitment is also visible in this publication. In their exclusive focus on the work of the last ten years the exhibition and the catalogue also reflect the arrival of a new generation of teachers, which began with the appointment of Elisabeth Holder in 1988, and the accompanying changes in the curriculum. For example, at the School today one can now observe both a more pronounced examination of social phenomena on the one hand, and a stronger focus on personal search and investigation as the foundation for the

gute Vorbereitung auf wesentliche Aspekte ihrer beruflichen Realität. Dazu gehört es auch, die im Studium entwickelten Arbeiten nach außen zu tragen und zu veröffentlichen. Über die Zusammenarbeit mit dem Studiengang Kommunikationsdesign können hier wichtige Einblicke gewonnen und praxisnahe Erfahrungen gesammelt werden. Die jetzt beginnende Ausstellungsreihe und dieses Katalogbuch sind ein besonders gutes Beispiel für die in den Studiengängen Produktdesign und Kommunikationsdesign gepflegte praxisnahe Ausbildung. In der Zusammenarbeit bei diesem Projekt hat sie zu einem besonders eindrucksvollen Ergebnis geführt. Ich danke allen ganz herzlich, die an diesem umfassenden und in dieser Größe bisher einmaligen Projekt mitgearbeitet und zu seiner Verwirklichung beigetragen haben. Der Ausstellung und dem Katalogbuch wünsche ich die verdiente Aufmerksamkeit.

development of approaches to jewellery and product design on the other. In parallel to this the productive relationship with the School of Communication Design gives the students a good preparation for key aspects of the realities of their chosen profession. This includes the publication and public presentation of the works produced during their course of study. The collaboration with the School of Communication Design provides both valuable insights and the opportunity to gain real-life experience. The series of exhibitions that is now beginning and this accompanying catalogue are a particularly good example of the strong emphasis on practical, real-life training at the Schools of Product Design and Communication Design. Their collaboration on this project has produced particularly impressive results. I would like to express my heartfelt gratitude to everyone who has contributed to the realisation of this comprehensive project, which is the largest of its kind to date, and my hopes that both the exhibition and the catalogue receive the attention they so richly deserve.

Nicola Brand
Atem Körper – Körper Atem
Kleine Körper zum beatmen und beatmet werden.
Latex, PVC-Schlauch, Silber
Breath Body – Body Breath
Small bodies for mutual respiration.
latex, PVC tubing, silver

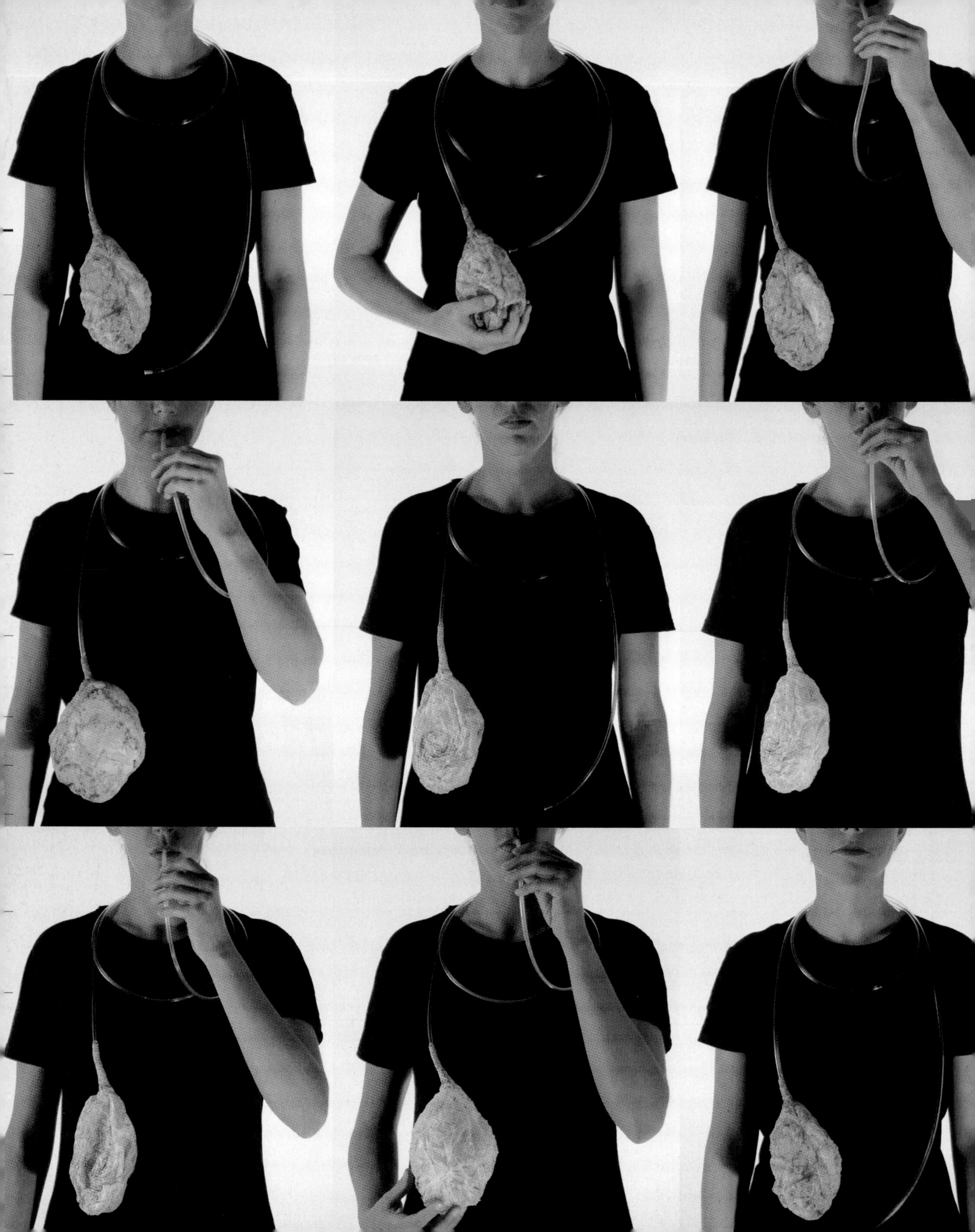

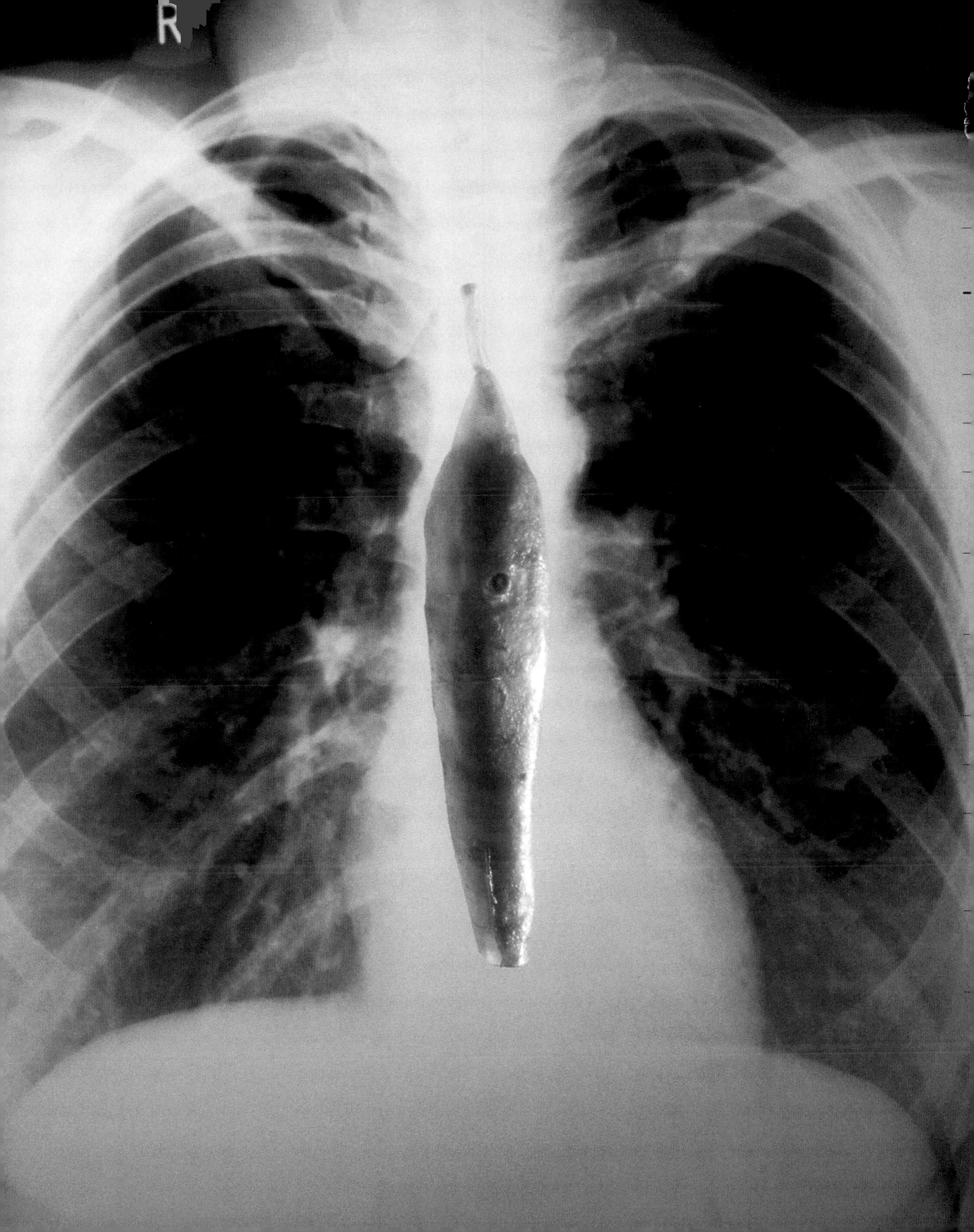
R

Elisabeth Holder Schmuck ist mehr als Zierde

Elisabeth Holder **Jewellery is more than Decoration**

Christiane Wink
After 2000
Parasitäres Implantat
Latex
After 2000
parasitic implant
latex

Der schöne Mensch der Zukunft, körperoptimiert, keine Unterscheidungsmerkmale mehr. Einzig das Körperinnere birgt Raum für Individualität: den Schmuckparasiten, der sich im Körper einnisten kann.

The beautiful person of the future, body optimised, no more distinguishing characteristics. Only inside the body is now space for individuality: for the jewellery parasites that can nest there within.

Ich möchte im folgenden einen Einblick geben in meine Arbeit mit Studierenden. Dazu gehören zunächst einige Reflexionen über meine Auffassung von Schmuck, mein Selbstverständnis als Lehrende und schließlich die in Jahren von mir erarbeiteten methodischen Aspekte der Lehre. Anschließend möchte ich über einen Kurszyklus berichten, der diese Positionen veranschaulichen soll. **Was ist Schmuck?** Alles was am Körper getragen werden kann und vieles, womit sich Menschen gern und unmittelbar umgeben, ist für mich Schmuck. Davon zu trennen sind Objekte der Gestaltung, die wesentlich oder ganz von ihrer Nutzfunktion bestimmt sind. Hier trifft die Bezeichnung Schmuck nicht mehr zu und hier, so meine ich, verläuft auch eine der Grenzen zwischen Kunst und Design. Die Spannweite in meiner Definition von Schmuck birgt sehr unterschiedliche Aussagen, je nachdem ob Schmuck für die Tragbarkeit am Körper konzipiert ist, und damit eine Verbindung mit der Person der Trägerin oder des Trägers eingeht, oder ob Schmuck als ein vom Menschen unabhängiges Objekt gesehen und gemacht wird. In beiden Fällen ist Schmuck weit mehr als nur ein Gegenstand der Zierde, auf die er in der lexikalischen Definition nach wie vor reduziert wird. Schmuck kann schmücken. Er kann schmeicheln, locken und verführen, erinnern und fröhlich machen, aber er kann auch mahnen, nachdenklich stimmen oder provozieren. Schmuck ist also ein höchst vielseitiges Mittel menschlichen Ausdrucks. Wesentlich ist, dass dem Schmuckobjekt in seiner Entstehung so viel mitgegeben wird, dass es aus sich selbst heraus zu sprechen vermag und dass es so zum Träger und Mittler von wie auch immer gearteten Botschaften wird. Eine Überfrachtung von Bedeutungszuweisungen allerdings, die womöglich erst über Erklärungen erschließbar werden, machen ein Schmuckobjekt unlebendig und tot. So viel zu meiner Auffassung von Schmuck, jetzt zu meinem Selbstverständnis als Lehrende. Als Lehrende

Melanie Halbauer
Leibwächter
Handschmuck
Glas
Bodyguards
hand jewellery
glass

I would like to share some insights into my own work with my students. I will begin with some reflections on my understanding of jewellery, my view of my role as a teacher and the methodical approach to teaching that I have developed over the years. I will then describe a cycle of courses that illustrates my general approach. What is jewellery? **Before discussing my own definition, it is important to note that the word for jewellery in my native German, *Schmuck*, has a much broader meaning than its English equivalent. Translated literally, *Schmuck* actually means *decoration* or *ornament*. In the discussions that follow the reader should thus bear in mind that the word used in my original German text is not really *jewellery* but *Schmuck*, with all the associated connotations that are absent in English. In my view, everything and anything that one can wear on one's body, and many of the things people enjoy having around them, can be seen as jewellery. However, I would not go so far as to include design, i.e. objects that are largely or primarily defined by their utilitarian function. This is the point where the term jewellery ceases to apply, and I also believe that this is the demarcating line between art and design. My definition of jewellery thus provides scope for a wide range of expressions, depending on whether the works in question are intended to be worn on the body, thus establishing a relationship with the identity of the wearer, or are designed and produced as independent objects separate from human individuals. In both cases, however, jewellery is much more than the decoration and ornament to which it is still reduced to by its lexical definition. Jewellery can decorate. It can flatter, attract and seduce, stimulate memories and delight. But it can also warn, provoke and make you think. Jewellery, then, is a very versatile medium of human expression. While creating a piece of jewellery the key is to give it so much that it is**

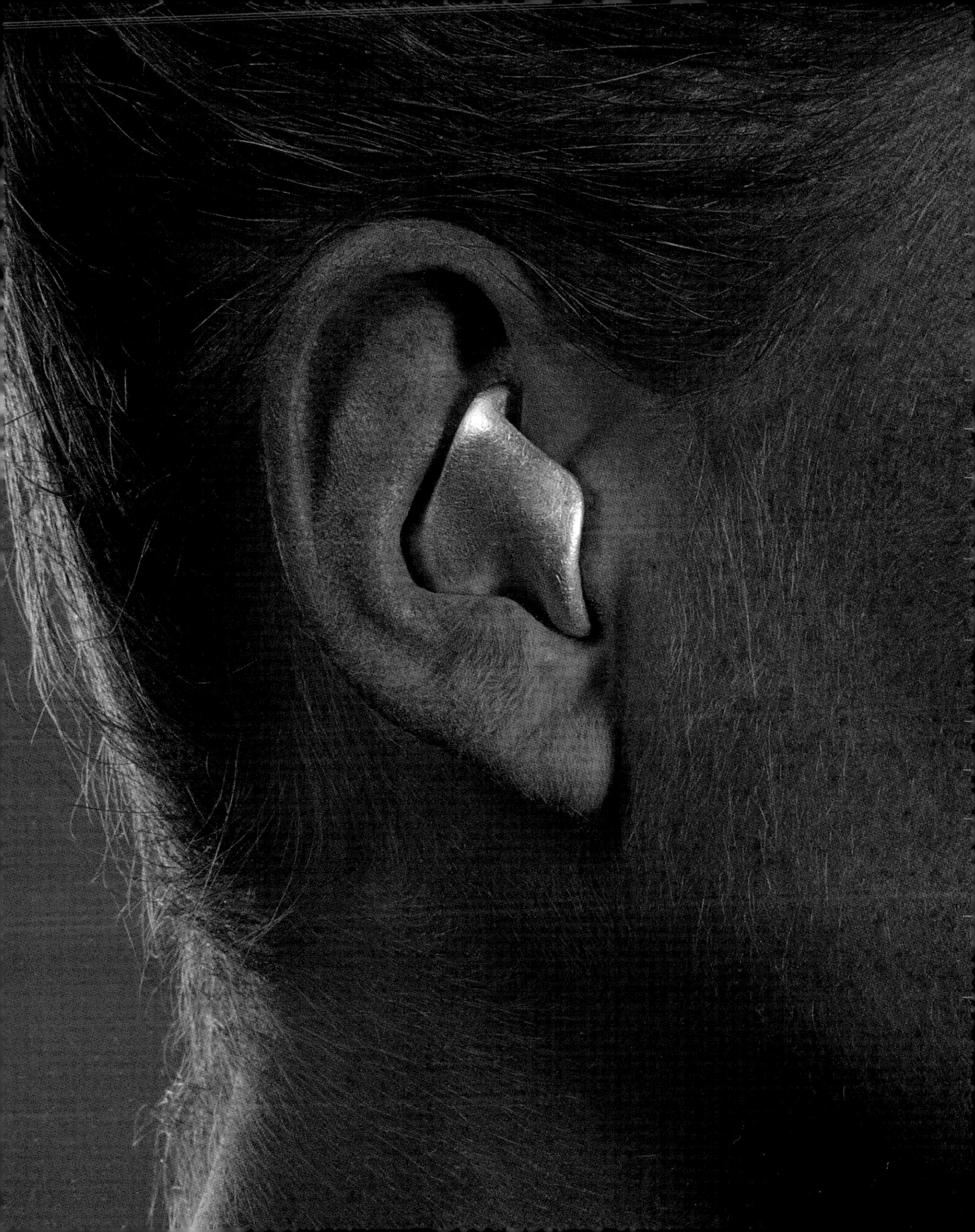

verstehe ich meine Vermittlungsarbeit hauptsächlich als Gruppenarbeit. Zu dieser Position habe ich im Laufe der Jahre gefunden und mich von Einzelbesprechungen als der viel geübten und als probat erachteten Lehrstrategie entfernt. Stattdessen arbeite ich so weit als irgend möglich in und mit der Gruppe, um darüber deren kreatives Potential für jede und jeden Einzelne(n) zu nutzen. Dies entspricht dem Gestaltgesetz, das besagt, das Ganze ist mehr als die Summe seiner Teile. Übertragen auf die Gruppe bedeutet das: Das kreative Potential der ganzen Gruppe geht weit über die Summe der kreativen Möglichkeiten aller einzelnen hinaus. Außerdem hat sich die Gruppenarbeit mit der ihr inhärenten Dynamik als Stärkung für die individuelle Entwicklung der Studierenden erwiesen, die dann ihren Niederschlag in den Arbeiten findet. Die gruppendynamischen Prozesse fördern und provozieren eine größere persönliche Offenheit, und die individuelle Auseinandersetzung mit dem gestellten Thema erfährt darüber eine größere Tiefe. Meine Aufgabe dabei ist, diesen Prozess zu impulsieren und zu steuern. Dies geschieht über langsam immer dichter in das Thema hineinführende Übungen. Wesentlich dabei ist, das gestellte Thema direkt und persönlich erfahrbar zu machen. Dabei wird ein breites Spektrum künstlerischer Methoden herangezogen, die von den klassischen bildnerischen Mitteln des Modellierens mit Ton oder des Malens sowie objekthafter Gestaltungen bis hin zur Einbeziehung assoziativer Techniken und Sprache reichen. Ich rege die Gruppe dabei auch an, das, was die einzelnen Studierenden auf noch weniger bewusster Ebene ausgedrückt haben, zu benennen und damit auf die bewusste Ebene zu heben und der weiteren Bearbeitung zugänglich zu machen. Es hat sich herausgestellt, dass Malen besonders geeignet ist, um spontane Eindrücke und Befindlichkeiten auszudrücken. Verdinglichungen wie Assemblagen oder Objekte eignen sich dagegen besser für die projektive Verarbeitung und den

Mira Leithe
Zuhörer
Ohrstöpsel
Silber
Listeners
ear plugs
silver

able to speak for itself, so that it becomes a container and medium of any messages it is chosen to convey. At the other end of the scale, an excess of assigned meanings – which may even only be accessible through explanation – can make a piece of jewellery lifeless and dead. So much for my understanding of jewellery. I would now like to outline my approach to my role as a teacher. As a teacher I approach my job of imparting knowledge primarily through group work. This is a preference I have developed gradually in years of practise, gradually moving away from the one-to-one meetings that have become established as the accepted teaching method. Instead, I work with and in the group whenever and wherever possible, using its creative potential for every individual member – in keeping with the gestalt principle that the whole is more than the sum of its parts. In terms of the group this means that the creative potential of the entire group goes far beyond the sum of the creative possibilities of all its members. In addition to this I have found that group work, with its inherent dynamics, does a great deal to promote the individual development of the students, and this is reflected in their works. The group dynamics processes promote and provoke more personal openness, and this in turn gives more depth to the students' individual work on the themes they are set. My job is to stimulate and guide this process, which I achieve with exercises that slowly lead the students deeper and deeper into the subject matter. A direct and personal experience of the set theme is crucial. This is achieved with a broad spectrum of artistic disciplines, ranging from the classic mediums of modelling with clay, painting and the creation of three-dimensional objects to the use of associative techniques and language. In the course of this work I encourage the group to identify elements that individual students have expressed on a semi-conscious level, to

ersten Ausdruck eines Anliegens. Innerhalb dieses Prozesses der Auseinandersetzung wird irgendwann eine klare Entscheidung erforderlich, nämlich die, ob die angestrebte Aussage in dem von mir definierten Sinne über das Medium Schmuck möglich ist, oder aber, ob dafür ein deutlich anderes künstlerisches Medium wie z.B.die Installation oder die Performance geeigneter ist. Damit wird auch deutlich, dass für mich als Lehrende die Offenheit für und die Verbindung zu anderen Kunstformen wesentlich ist, um darüber den Studierenden von Schmuckdesign eine erweiterte Basis zu geben. Beispielhaft für meine Lehrtätigkeit möchte ich jetzt drei thematisch eng zusammengehörige Schmuckkurse beschreiben, die sich mit dem übergreifenden Thema des inszenierten Körpers befassten und den Bogen spannten von Tätowierung und Piercing bis hin zu körper- und identitätsverändernden Maßnahmen wie, um ein extremes Beispiel zu nennen, Zungespalten. Nicht immer ist mir die Wahl eines zeitnahen Kursthemas so bewusst. Aber jedesmal dann, wenn ich mit dem angebotenen Thema wieder einmal den Nerv der Zeit getroffen habe, bin ich froh darüber, dass mir dieses für die Aktualität des Lehrangebotes so wichtige Sensorium für Zeitphänomene wieder zu Hilfe gekommen ist. Die Kursthemen des nachfolgend beschriebenen Kurszyklus – *Geschmückte Haut*, *Grenzphänomene von Schmuck* und *Körpergeschichten* – spiegeln auch meinen eigenen Prozess der Annäherung an diese Thematik und mein zunehmendes Verständnis für die mit diesen Phänomenen verbundenen gesellschaftlichen und intrapsychischen Faktoren wieder. In dem ersten Kurs zum Thema *Geschmückte Haut* ging es um hautnahen, auf die Haut rückenden, die Haut beleuchtenden und unter die Haut gehenden Schmuck. Einige Arbeiten seien hier genannt. Julia Müllers entschied sich in ihrer Arbeit für einen sanften Umgang mit der Haut. Sie entwickelte Anhänger und Ringe, die als Stempel fungieren und erst über den

Körpergeschichten
Body Stories
2000/01

verbalise them and lift them to the conscious level, thus making them available for further creative work. I have found that painting is a particularly good medium for the expression of spontaneous impressions and feelings. Objectifications, such as assemblies and objects, are more suited for objective processing and the first expressions of an intention. Sooner or later, as the process of coming to grips with the theme progresses, a time comes for a clear decision: Can the chosen message be expressed in jewellery as I have defined it, or would a very different artistic medium such as installation or performance be more suitable? This also brings up another aspect, namely that it is important for me as a teacher to be open for and able to draw on other art forms in order to be able to provide a broader foundation for my jewellery design students. I would now like to describe three thematically related jewellery courses as an illustration of my teaching work. These courses all dealt with the general subject of body dramatisation, the individual themes ranging from tattooing and piercing to other forms of body and identity alteration such as tongue bifurcation, to name a more extreme example. The choice of a topically relevant course subject is not always as conscious as it was here; but I am always grateful for the sensibility for current phenomena that helps me to come up with topics that tune in to the 'nerve' of the time, as it is very valuable for keeping our course material up to date. The topics of the three courses in this cycle – *Decorated Skin*, *Borderline Phenomena in Personal Adornment* and *Body Stories* – also reflect my own process of getting to grips with the subject matter, and my growing understanding for the social and intra-psychological factors associated with these phenomena. The first course, *Decorated Skin*, dealt with adornment and jewellery on, close to, embellishing, in and beneath the skin. Here are examples of some of

Anne-Sybille Bierbach
Acupuncture
Halsschmuck
Akupunkturnadeln, PVC
Acupuncture
neck ornament
acupuncture needles, PVC

Körper – Grenze. Schmerzen lassen spürbar werden.
Body – Boundary. Pains permitting conscious sensation.

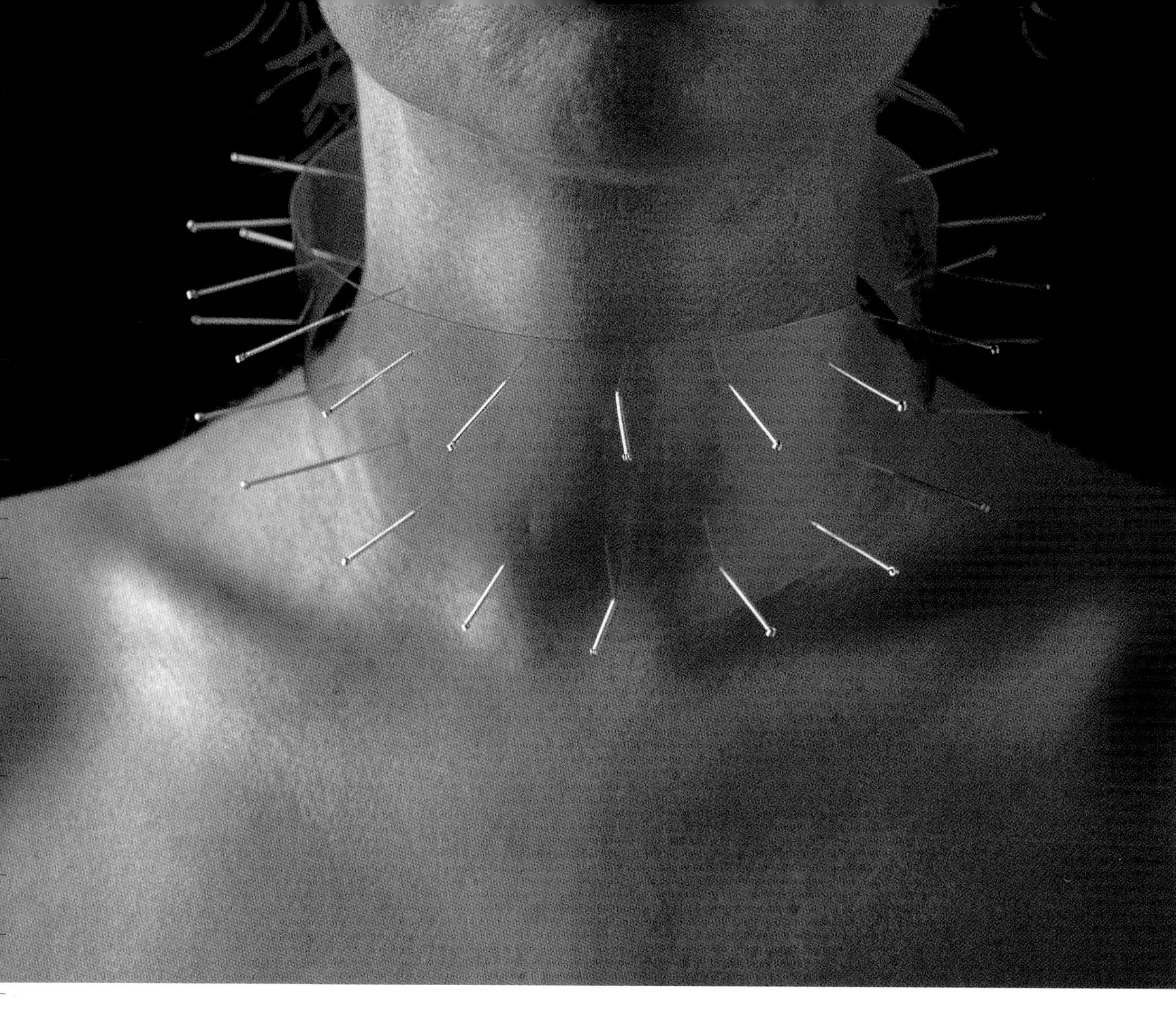

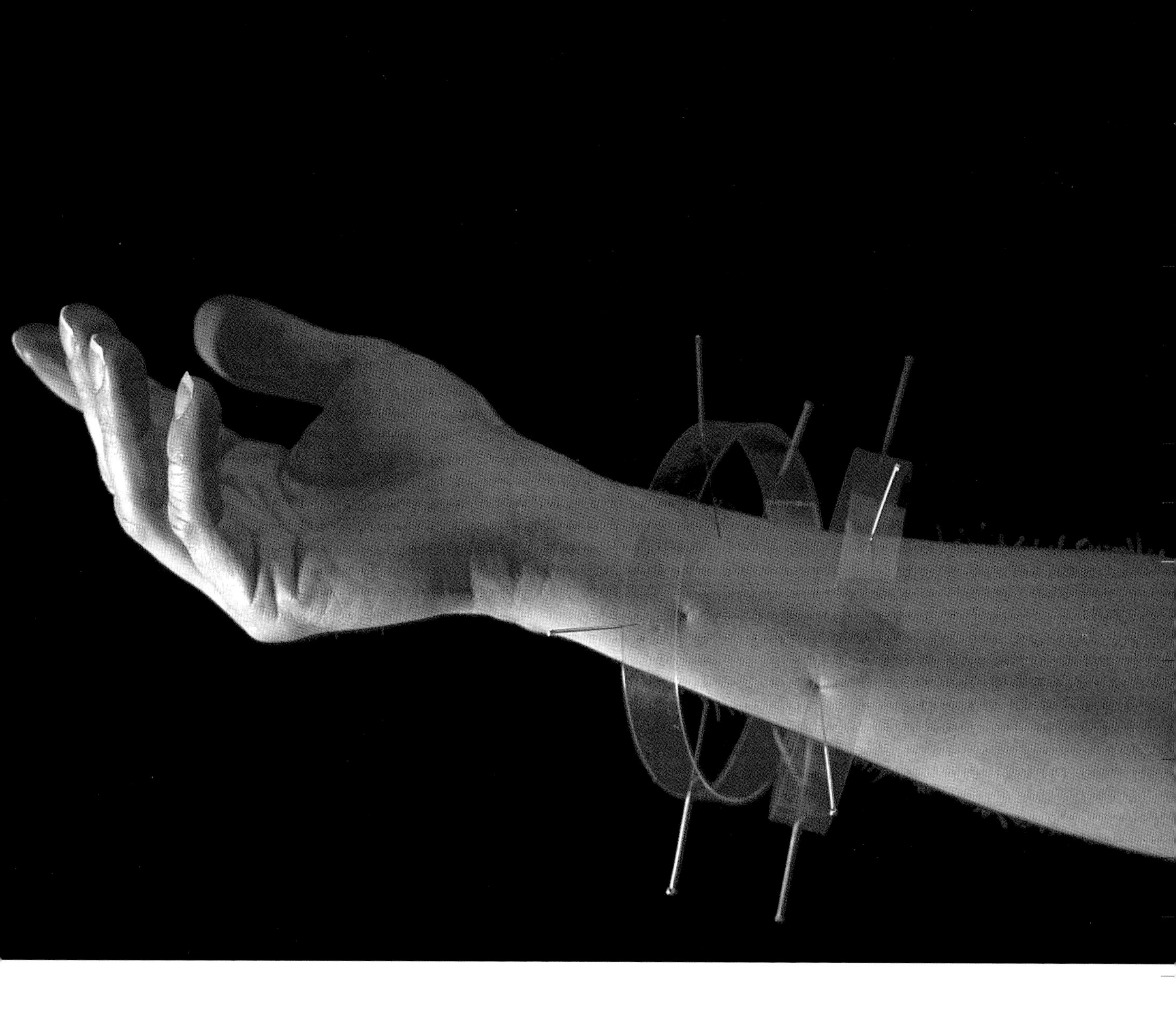

Abdruck in der Haut lesbar werden. Ihre Objekte dienen also als Mittler für die beabsichtigte und nur vorübergehende Schmuckwirkung auf der Haut. In der Auseinandersetzung mit den gesellschaftsfähig gewordenen Phänomenen der Tätowierung und des Piercing – Schmuck, der tatsächlich unter die Haut geht und mit dem Erleiden von Schmerzen verbunden ist – fand Christiane Wink zu ihrer Arbeit. Mit dem Label *Embrace your Demons* will sie neugierig machen auf ein Schmuckstück, das unter einer zunächst harmlos aussehenden Gummimanschette einen Stachel verborgen hält. Andere Studentinnen haben sich der Verletzlichkeit und Anfälligkeit der eigenen Haut besonnen, aber auch ihrer Besonderheit durch Hautmale, Äderchen und Narben. Gerade die individuell gezeichnete Haut, weit ab vom Schönheitsideal der glatten haarlosen und makellosen Haut, führte zu spannenden Schmuckkonzeptionen. So bei Nicola Brand, die ihr Feuermal und ihre Narben auf T-Shirts projizierte oder bei Ariane Hartmann, die ihre Haut selbst zum schmuckwürdigen Material erhob. Sie fotografierte eine erkrankte Hautstelle, sammelte die darauf entstandenen Hautschuppen und brachte beides in ein Schmuckstück ein. Die Ergebnisse des Kurses *Geschmückte Haut* konnten bald danach bei der internationalen Schmuckausstellung *Kunst hautnah* in Wien gezeigt werden, wodurch die Aktualität dieses Themas bestätigt wurde und die Qualität der daraus hervorgegangenen Arbeiten Anerkennung fand. Trotzdem wollte ich nicht bei diesen ersten Ergebnissen stehen bleiben. In dem sich anschließenden zweiten Kurs unter dem Titel *Grenz-Phänomene von Schmuck*, bot ich die Möglichkeit einer Vertiefung in diese Grenzbereiche als Theoriekurs an. Ein wesentlicher Akzent lag auf der Entwicklung des Weges von der Erfahrung, auch eigenleiblicher Erfahrung, mit entsprechenden Materialisierungen und objekthaften Umsetzungen hin zu einem theoretischen Ansatz und schließlich zur Entwicklung einer Schmuckkonzeption.

Anne-Sybille Bierbach
Acupuncture
Armschmuck
Akupunkturnadeln, PVC
Acupuncture
arm ornament
acupuncture needles, PVC

the works produced by the students in the course: Julia Müllers chose a gentle interaction with the skin for her project. She developed pendants and rings that functioned as stamps, whose expression could only be perceived though the impressions they left on the skin. Her objects were thus mediums for the intended and merely temporary decorative effect on the wearer's skin. Christiane Wink found the theme for her project in the investigation of the more and more socially accepted phenomenon of tattooing and piercing. This is jewellery that literally gets under one's skin, and it is also associated with suffering actual physical pain. Her title, *Embrace Your Demons*, was chosen to stimulate curiosity about the work: a piece of jewellery consisting of a seemingly innocuous rubber cuff in which a sharp barb is concealed. Other students investigated the vulnerability and delicacy of their own skin, and also its uniqueness as expressed by birthmarks, fine veins and scars. This work with the individual markings of the skin, moving away from the beauty ideal of smoothness, hairlessness and freedom from blemishes, resulted in some particularly exciting concepts. For example, Nicola Brand projected her strawberry birthmark and scars on T-shirts. Ariane Hartmann actually turned her own skin into a jewellery material by photographing a diseased area of skin, collecting skin scales from the same area and combining both in a piece of jewellery. Shortly afterwards the results of the *Decorated Skin* course were put on show at the international jewellery exhibition *Kunst hautnah* (Art Close to the Skin) in Vienna. In addition to confirming the topical relevance of the theme this exhibition also brought recognition for the high quality of the works produced by the students. Not wanting to stop at these first results I then offered a follow-up theory course titled *Borderline Phenomena in Personal Adornment*, which provided the opportunity

Die Arbeit in der Gruppe erwies sich wieder einmal als besonders hilfreich, um diese Stufen der Entwicklung bewusst zu durchlaufen und sie benennen zu lernen. Der jüngste, mit *Körpergeschichten* überschriebene Kurs traf zufällig mit der Ausschreibung des Forschungswettbewerbs der Körber-Stiftung *Bodycheck* zusammen. Es bot sich also an, den Kurs in Anlehnung an diesen Wettbewerb durchzuführen. Hintergrund dieses sehr anspruchsvollen Kurses war die Tatsache, dass der Körper durch Formen der Körpermodifikation – ein Sammelbegriff für alle körperverändernden Eingriffe Die Schönheitsoperationen, Implantate aus chirurgischem Stahl, die Erzeugung von Schmucknarben, Zungenspalten usw. – als formbares Objekt benutzt wird, und diese Maßnahmen der Körperveränderung und -inszenierung nicht nur äußerlich wirksam sind, sondern zur Erfahrung eines neuen ,Körperselbst' führen. Der Fokus des Kurses richtete sich auf die Erforschung der in einem Spannungsfeld zueinander stehenden Erfahrungs- und Betrachtungsebene unserer selbst: zum einen also auf die sinnlich-leibliche Ebene, die an Körpergrenzen gebunden ist, und zum anderen auf die von außen kommende, betrachtende Ebene, worüber der Körper als Objekt wahrgenommen wird. Um die betrachtende Ebene und die Erfahrungsebene auch spürbar werden zu lassen, nahm diese Phase innerhalb des Kurses einen breiten Raum ein. Dabei spielte das Sich-Einlassen auf entsprechende von mir und zunehmend auch von der Gruppe selbst vorgeschlagene Experimente eine wichtige Rolle. Als Beispiel sei ein Atemexperiment genannt, das die sinnlich-leibliche Erfahrungsebene des ,Körperselbst' ermöglichte. Die Gruppenmitglieder standen in einem verdunkelten Raum im Kreis und waren von Mund zu Ohr mit Rohrabschnitten verbunden, so dass nicht nur der eigene Atem wahrgenommen (Erfahrungsebene), sondern auch der Atem der jeweiligen Nachbarin gehört und auch gespürt werden konnte (Betrachtungsebene). Über

Christiane Wink
Embrace your Demons
Armschmuck
Kautschuk, Schaumstoff, Nadeln
Embrace Your Demons
arm ornament
rubber, foam, needles

Leid und Lust.
Gefahrvoller Schmerz.
Anguish and pleasure.
Hazardous pain.

to take a deeper look at these borderline phenomena. One of the main emphases was on development of the experience path, including personal experience with and through the student's own body, continuing on to physical materialisation, implementation in objects, formulation of a theoretical approach and, finally, development of a jewellery concept. Here too, group work proved to be very effective, helping the students to move consciously through the developmental steps and learn to find verbal expressions for them. As it happened, the scheduling of the most recent of the three courses, *Body Stories*, coincided with a call for entries to the Körber Foundation's *Bodycheck* research competition. It thus seemed a good idea to plan the course around the competition. This very ambitious course was developed from the observation that the body is now being treated as a formable object. A wide range of 'body modifications'– this is the collective term for all body-changing operations like plastic surgery, surgical steel implants, the creation of decorative scars, tongue bifurcation and so on – are now being practised not only to achieve an outward change in the body's appearance but also an experience of a new body and self identity. The course focused on the investigation of the experiential and observational levels of the self, and the tension between these levels – i.e. the sensory/bodily level, which is limited by the physical boundaries of the body, and the level of observation, where the body is seen from without as an object. In order to develop an awareness for these observational and experiential levels we gave a great deal of space to this phase of the course. This awareness was stimulated and intensified with exercises suggested both by me and, increasingly, also by the group members themselves. One good example is a breath experiment that activated the sensory/physical experience level of the body self. In

embrace your demons

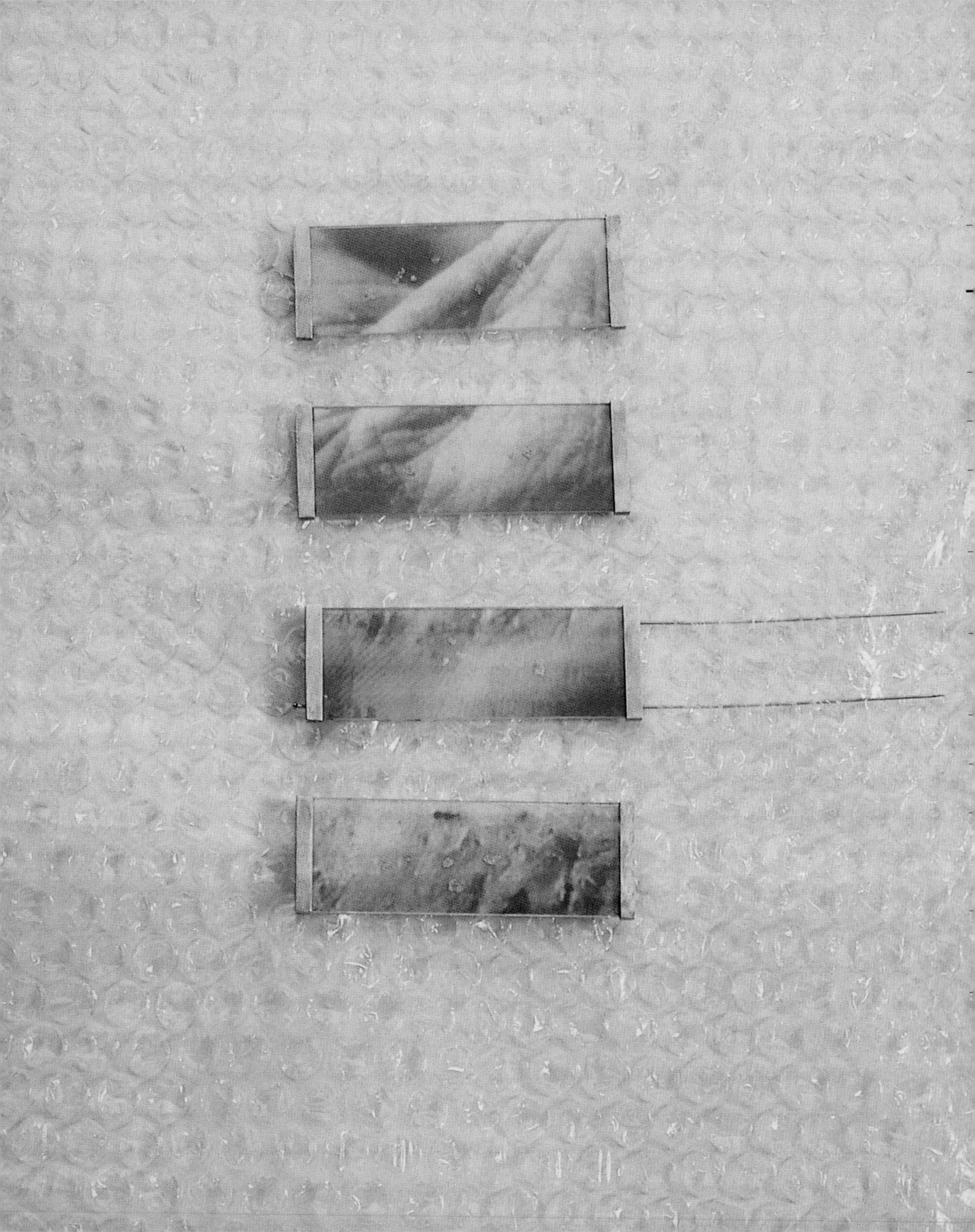

diese Verbindung der beiden Ebenen entstand ein Zirkelschluss, der zu einer die Körpergrenzen erweiternde Erfahrung führte, nämlich ein einziger atmender Körper zu sein. Um die sinnlich-leibliche Erfahrungsebene und die objektivierende Betrachtungsebene in ihrer Beziehung und Wechselwirkung zu begreifen und für jede einzelne Studierende daraus einen Hintergrund für ihre individuelle Gestaltungskonzeption zu entwickeln, bedurfte es vieler solcher zwischen den Ebenen pendelnden Experimente. Die Gruppenmitglieder waren durch diese Vorgehensweise immer wieder bis an die Grenzen ihres individuellen Einlassens gefordert. Die Geduld und das Durchhaltevermögen der Gruppe hat sich aber gelohnt, da jede Studentin zu sehr treffenden Formulierungen ihres individuellen Anliegens fand. Der Untertitel der Wettbewerbsausschreibung *Bodycheck* enthält die Frage, wie viel Körper der Mensch brauche. Diese Frage verwandelte sich über die im Kurs gemachten Erfahrungen in eine nach der Qualität. Körper und Leib wurden als unterschiedliche Qualitäten des Körperselbst erfahren. Und so sind auch die entstandenen Schmuckarbeiten zu verstehen, die ohne Ausnahme zur Auseinandersetzung mit dem Körper und Aspekten der eigenen Leiblichkeit herausfordern. Es sind Arbeiten mit der Kraft zu berühren, zu sensibilisieren, auch ohne Scheu vor der Erzeugung ambivalenter Gefühle. Die Arbeiten von Nicola Brand mit dem Titel *Kleine Körper zum Beatmen* machen das Atmen, eine meist unbeachtet bleibende vitale Lebensäußerung, zum bewussten Vorgang mit meditativem Potential. In dem sanften Pulsieren des Aus- und Einatmens, das gleichzeitig ein beatmen und beatmet werden ist, scheint sich die Grenze zwischen Subjekt und Objekt aufzuheben. Die *Leibwächter* genannten Objekte von Melanie Halbauer bewirken ebenfalls eine Hinlenkung auf die Leiblichkeit. Diese Schmuckobjekte gehen eine ganz innige Verbindung mit dem Körper der Trägerin ein, für die

Ariane Hartmann
Broschen
Silber, Transparentpapier, Hautschuppen
brooches
silver, tracing paper, skin flakes

this exercise the group members stand in a circle in a darkened room with their mouths and ears connected by lengths of tubing. This meant that in addition to experiencing their own breath (experience level) they could also hear (observation level) and feel their direct neighbour's breath. This connection of the two levels created a larger closed circle in which the boundaries of the group members' bodies were expanded and experienced as a single, breathing body. Many more of these inter-level experiments were necessary in order to make the sensual/bodily experience level, the objectifying observation level and their interrelationships really comprehensible, enabling each student to develop a background for their individual design concepts. This methodology repeatedly took the group members to the limits of their individual ability to open up to these experiences. The patience and staying power of the group was worthwhile, however – ultimately, each student managed to produce very apt formulations for their individual concepts. The subtitle of the *Bodycheck* competition consisted of a question, asking how much body a person needs. We applied this question to the experiences made in the course, turning it into a question about quality – about the different qualities and aspects of the 'bodyself'. This was also the context for the messages of the resulting jewellery works, all of which are invitations to examine one's relationship to the body and one's own physicality. They are works with the power to move, to stimulate sensibility and awareness, and they do not shy away from aspects that can generate ambivalent feelings. And this gives them a much broader effect, beyond their own physical limitations. Nicola Brand's works titled *Small Bodies for Respiration* turn breathing – that vital expression of life that normally goes unnoticed – into a conscious process with meditative potential. In the gentle pulsations

sie gemacht sind. So wird beim Anlegen des Mundschmuckes – ein der Lippenkontur eines lächelnden Mundes nachgeformter Golddraht – die seiner Trägerin zunächst von außen auferlegte Haltung des stummen Lächelns auf sie zurückwirken und zu einer das psychische Befinden verändernden Erfahrung führen. Mit ihren Arm- und Halsbändern der Reihe *Acupuncture*, die bestückt sind mit gegen den Körper gerichteten und leichten Schmerz verursachenden Akupunkturnadeln, rückt Anne-Sybille Bierbach die Körpergrenze Haut in das Bewusstsein der Trägerin. Die unter dem Titel *Bio-Ocular Bloodpack* zusammengefassten Arbeiten sind wie eine Steigerung dieser Art von Selbstvergewisserung. Diese Schmuckobjekte werden in den Körper implantiert, an den Blutkreislauf angeschlossen, oder in ihrer harmlosesten Variante nur auf die Haut geklebt und geben so den Blick frei auf das eigene Blut. Die Trägerin oder der Träger kann sich so ganz unmittelbar ihrer bzw. seiner eigenen Lebendigkeit vergewissern. Die *Nackensitzer* von Nicole Hanselle geben den oft unterdrückten Sorgen und Ängsten des Alltags eindrückliche Gestalt. Dieses Schmuckobjekt fungiert als Träger von Projektionen. Als konkret handhabbares Objekt bietet es gleichzeitig andere Möglichkeiten des Umgangs mit solchen im Nacken sitzenden, sich vielfach in körperlichen Symptomen manifestierenden Bedrängnissen. Eva Dufhues hat für ihre Arbeit *Leibeigene* das Ohr, eine höchst empfindliche Übergangsstelle zwischen Körperinnerem und Körperäußerem, als Trageort für Insekten gewählt. Mit dieser Arbeit löst sie in der Phantasie des Betrachters unweigerlich nahezu körperlich spürbare Assoziationen aus, denen sich niemand entziehen kann. Christiane Wink projiziert ihre Arbeit *After 2000 – parasitäres Implantat* in die Zukunft, in der die Körperoptimierung so weit fortgeschritten sein wird, dass sich nach ihrer Vorstellung die einem bestimmten Schönheitsideal unterworfenen Menschen äußerlich

Elgin Fischer
Von der Hand in den Mund
Schalen für Appetithappen
Float-Glas, Email
From Hand to Mouth
canapé dishes
float glass, enamel

of the inhalation and exhalation, which are simultaneously an act of breathing and of being respirated, the borderline between subject and object appears to dissolve. The *Bodyguards* objects created by Melanie Halbauer also focus awareness on the physicality of the body. These jewellery works enter into a very intimate relationship with the body of the wearer for whom they are made. For example, when donned, her 'mouth ornament' – a gold wire construction forming the contours of a smiling mouth – initially gives the wearer the impression of a mute smile imposed from without; but gradually this can also have a feedback effect on the wearer, stimulating an experience of a changed emotional state. Anne-Sybille Bierbach's *Acupuncture* bracelets and necklaces are fitted with small, inward-facing acupuncture needles that generate a slight sensation of pain, heightening the wearer's awareness of the skin as a body boundary. The collection of works in the *Bio-Ocular Bloodpack* series are like an intensification of this kind of self-confirmation: These jewellery objects are implanted in the body, connected to the blood circulatory system or, in the most harmless variation, glued to the skin, providing a view of the wearer's own blood and thus a direct substantiation of her or his physical aliveness. Nicole Hanselle's *Nape Sitter* provides a vivid medium of expression for everyday cares and fears that are all too often suppressed. This jewellery object serves as a medium for projections. At the same time, as a concrete, physical object in its own right, it also opens up other possibilities for dealing with those torments which weigh us down, and which often find expression in physical, bodily symptoms. In her work *Vassals*, Eva Dufhues chose the ear – that highly-sensitive interface between the body's interior and exterior – as the place for wearing insects. Her work stimulates intense, almost physically palpable associations that nobody

Elke Munkert
Suppenschale mit Träger
Glas, Edelstahl
soup bowl with base
glass, stainless steel

Grassi
Grassi
2000/01

kaum mehr unterscheiden werden. Um trotzdem Individualität zu gewährleisten ist sie ins Körperinnere verlegt und kann erzielt werden über den von Christiane Wink konzipierten Schmuckparasiten, der sich im Körper einnisten kann. Durch meine Ausführungen ist sicherlich auch klar geworden, dass ich meine Lehre nicht aus einer Position der Alleswissenden heraus betreibe. Genauso wie die Studierenden auch, und gemeinsam mit ihnen, muss ich mich auf einen Erfahrungs- und Lernprozess einlassen. Die mir zukommende Funktion des Impulsierens, Steuerns und Begleitens bedeutet aber, dass jedes dieser Kurstreffen unter Berücksichtigung des jeweils aktuellen Standes bezüglich Inhalt und Gruppendynamik von mir vor- und nachbereitet sein will. Für den notwendigen Blick von außen suche ich mir immer wieder – wie es für andere Professionen inzwischen selbstverständlich ist – supervisorische Begleitung.

Elgin Fischer
Von der Hand in den Mund
Schalen für Appetithappen
Float-Glas
From Hand to Mouth
canapé dishes
float glass

can withstand. Christiane Wink projected her work, *After 2000 – Parasitic Implant*, into an imagined future where people are so subjected to a specific ideal of beauty that it has become almost impossible to differentiate between individuals by their outward appearance. Individuality is maintained by shifting it to the interior of the body, for example through use of Christiane Wink's *jewellery parasite* that can take up residence inside the body. As these examples have clearly demonstrated, I do not perform my teaching work from an all-knowing stance. Just like my students, I too must be open for the process of learning and experience, embarking on it together with them. At the same time, as the instructor it is also my job to provide impetus, support and guidance, and I am thus responsible for the preparations and follow-up work for each of our meetings as regards both content and group dynamics. In order to obtain the necessary objective perspective from without I also seek regular supervision myself – as is now customary in professions outside the world of teaching.

Anja Oelschlegel
Wippschalen und Becher
Porzellan
tilting bowls and cups
porcelain

Jan-Marc Kutscher
Essbesteck
Edelstahl, hochlegierter
Werkzeugstahl
table cutlery set
stainless steel,
high-alloy tool steel

Herbert Schulze Grassi-Projekt

Kerstin Biesdorf
Vorlegebesteck
versilbertes Messing
knife and fork
serving utensils
silver-plated brass

Herbert Schulze **The Grassi Project**

Die *Grassimesse* wird einmal jährlich als jurierte Ausstellung vom Museum für Kunsthandwerk Leipzig/Grassimuseum veranstaltet und steht in der Tradition der zwischen 1920 und 1941 (in abgeschwächter Form nochmals ab 1949) durchgeführten ebenfalls jurierten Ausstellungen zeitgenössischen Kunsthandwerks. Diese fanden zweimal jährlich statt und waren eine Reaktion auf den gestalterischen Qualitätsverfall der Exponate der zeitgleich stattfindenden *Leipziger Mustermesse*. „Bis zur kriegsbedingten Einstellung kamen hier um die 1500 Kunsthandwerker, Entwerfer, Künstlervereinigungen, Hersteller, Kunstschulen und Vertriebsorganisationen zusammen (...). Das *Grassi* war der Ort, an dem in- und ausländischen Interessenten die neuen Schöpfungen des individuellen Kunsthandwerks und mit zunehmender Tendenz auch der guten Industrieform vorgestellt wurden, an dem sich die Avantgarde der Künstler und Entwerfer begegnete und zu einem Wettbewerb der Moderne antrat." (Dr. Olaf Thormann, Grassimuseum). Die Aussteller der seit 1997 stattfindenden *Neuen Grassi* waren neben einigen Manufakturen und Herstellern überwiegend freischaffende Künstler und Gestalter. Es fehlten vollständig die Design- und Kunsthochschulen. Hier setzte ich an mit meinen beiden Lehrveranstaltungen *Entwurf und Realisation von Bestecken* und *Entwurf und Gestaltung von Gefäßen*. Die in beiden Kursen geforderte Realisation der Entwürfe geschah im Wissen, dass bei der Umsetzung immer noch wichtige entwurfliche Entscheidungen gefällt werden. Mit dieser Forderung eröffnete sich für die Studierenden aber außerdem die Möglichkeit, sich mit den Ergebnissen für die *Grassimesse* zu bewerben und, im Falle der Annahme, wichtige Praxis- und Messeerfahrung sammeln zu können. Die von der Jury akzeptierten StudentInnen bereiteten in den Semesterferien dann die Präsentation ihrer Arbeiten auf der *Grassimesse* im Herbst 2000 vor und ergänzten diese durch selbst gestaltete Drucksachen. Die Qualität der Arbeiten

Simone Nolden
Paragefäße
Knustteller
Metall, Glas, Porzellan
Paravessels
crustplates
metal, glass, porcelain

The *Grassi Fair* is an annual adjudicated exhibition staged by the *Museum of Applied Arts Leipzig/Grassi Museum*. It follows in the tradition of the adjudicated exhibitions of contemporary arts and crafts that were staged from 1920 until 1941 (and also, in a more limited form, from 1949 onwards). These events were staged twice yearly and were a response to the diminishing design quality of the exhibits on show at the *Leipzig Mustermesse* taking place at the same time. "Until the war put an end to it the show was attended by around 1,500 craftspeople, designers, art associations, manufacturers, art schools and sales organisations (...). The *Grassi* was a place where people from Germany and abroad could see the latest creations of individual craftspeople and, as time went on, a growing number of industrial designers as well; a place where the avant-garde of the art and design world came to meet and contend in a modern competition." (Dr. Olaf Thormann, *Grassi Museum).* The exhibitors at the *New Grassi*, which was launched in 1997, were primarily freelance artists and designers, along with a few industrial manufacturers. Design and art colleges were conspicuous by their complete absence. My two courses, *Design and Production of Cutlery Sets* and *Conception and Design of Vessels*, were a direct response to this situation. The actual production of the designs was included in the brief for both courses because I knew that many important design decisions would also take place during the physical realisation process. This requirement also made it possible for the students to submit the results for exhibition at the *Grassi Fair*, and to gain valuable practical and exhibition experience if their works were accepted. The students chosen by the jury worked through the summer holidays to prepare their presentations for exhibition at the *Grassi Fair* in the autumn of 2000, also designing and producing printed materials to

BRAND

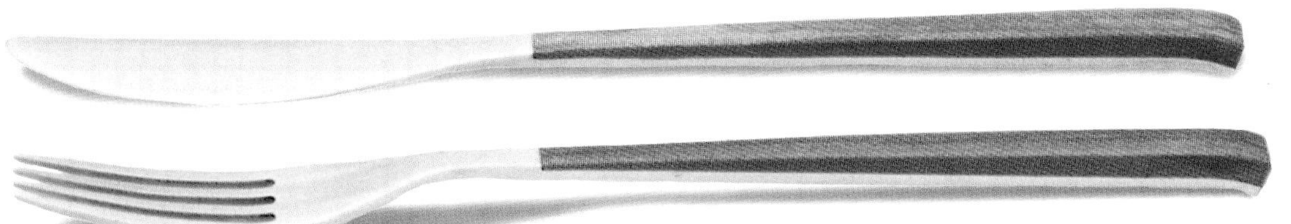

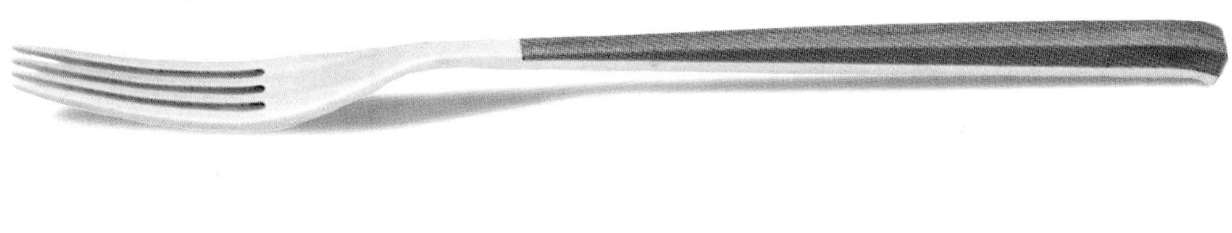

wurde durch die unerwartet guten Verkaufserfolge bestätigt. Als weiteren schönen Erfolg werte ich, dass mit dem Studiengang Produktdesign der Fachhochschule Düsseldorf erstmalig auch wieder eine Designschule auf der *Grassimesse* vertreten war. Da die Themen beider Lehrveranstaltungen nur die Kategorie der zu gestaltenden Gegenstände benannten, blieb reichlich Platz für persönliche Interpretationen. Ein sehr breites Spektrum unterschiedlichster Ansätze war damit vorgezeichnet. Ausgehend von ihren persönlichen Interessen und Analysen historischer und funktionaler Art fanden die Studierenden zu ihrem individuellen Ansatz und später zu ihrem Konzept, das in der kreativen Phase ausgiebig von allen Seiten betrachtet und bearbeitet wurde. Experimente waren ausdrücklich erwünscht. Da es keinerlei Materialvorgaben gab, entstanden Entwürfe für Glas, Porzellan und Metall. Diese offen formulierten Themen spiegeln auch mein Bemühen, den Studierenden so viel Freiraum wie möglich zu geben. Gleichzeitig bin ich bestrebt, die Studierenden zur notwendigen gestalterischen Stringenz anzuhalten. Wieviel Freiraum aber tatsächlich eingeräumt werden kann, ist jeweils abhängig vom Thema, dem zeitlichen Rahmen und der Persönlichkeit des Studierenden. Immer aber ist es mein Ziel, die Sensibilität der Studierenden für die unterschiedlichsten Ebenen des gestalterischen Ausdrucks zu schulen, der bestimmt ist vom Zusammenspiel von Inhalt, Funktion, Form und Material. Alles das zielt letztlich darauf hin, die Absolventinnen und Absolventen zu befähigen, sowohl in der eigenen Werkstatt als auch als angestellter Designer immer wieder Möglichkeiten zu finden, kreative Prozesse in Gang zu setzen und zu formalen und inhaltlichen Lösungen zu gelangen, die Ästhetik und Funktion gleichermaßen berücksichtigen.

Catherine Niegel
Antipastibesteck
Messer, Gabel, Löffel, Schieber, Servierplatte
Olivenholz, Edelstahl
antipasti set
knife, fork, spoon, pusher, serving dish
olive wood, stainless steel

accompany the exhibition. The quality of their work was confirmed by the unexpectedly successful sales at the fair. In addition to this success I also found it very gratifying that it was the Düsseldorf University of Applied Sciences, represented by our product design programme, which achieved the *Grassi Fair* "comeback" for design colleges. The descriptions of both courses only specified the category of the items to be designed, leaving plenty of scope for individual interpretations and ensuring that we would see a broad spectrum of different approaches. Combining their personal interests with historical and functional analyses, the students gradually developed their own approaches and concepts, which they then examined from all sides and processed in the creative phase. Experiments were explicitly encouraged, and since there were no stipulations as regards materials the resulting designs included works in glass, porcelain and metal. The open-ended formulation of the themes also reflects my desire to give the students as much creative freedom as possible. At the same time, I also strive to ensure that the students take care to maintain the necessary design discipline. How much leeway is possible depends on the individual theme, the time frame and the personality of the student. My goal is always to develop the sensibility of the student for the various different levels of design expression, which are determined by the interplay of content, function, form and material. Ultimately, the objective of all this is to empower the course's graduates and make them able to find different ways of getting the creative process working, whether in their own workshops or as employed designers, and to develop design solutions that combine aesthetics and functionality in both form and content.

Alin Boyaciyan
Kinderbesteck
Edelstahl, Buchenholz
children's cutlery set
stainless steel, beech wood

Heike Tries
Für die Kleinen Großen
Kinderbesteck
Edelstahl, Mahagoni
For the Little Big Ones
children's cutlery
stainless steel, mahogany

Mira Leithe
Shirts
Shirts, Wachsperlen, Aluminium
shirts
shirts, wax beads, aluminium

Herman Hermsen Aspekte von Serie

Mira Leithe
T-Shirts
Shirts, Aluminium
t-shirts
shirts, aluminium

Herman Hermsen **Aspects of Serialisation**

Der regelmäßig angebotene *Vier-Themenkurs* ist eine wichtige und grundlegende Begegnung mit elementaren Aufgaben der Formentwicklung. Die intensive und prozesshaft ausgerichtete Auseinandersetzung mit den von mir gesetzten Themen ist damit auch wesentliche Voraussetzung für den an den Erfordernissen der Serienentwicklung orientierten weiterführenden Kurs *Aspekte von Serie*. Aus diesem Grunde möchte ich zunächst den Aufbau des *Vier-Themenkurses* skizzieren. Dieser ist analog zu der Zahl der Themen in vier Phasen gegliedert mit jeweils einer Formentwicklungsaufgabe von zunehmender Komplexität. In der ersten Phase wird eine einfache, auf einer ganz eng gefassten Handlungsanweisung fußende Aufgabe gestellt. Hier gilt es die vielfältigen Möglichkeiten dreidimensionaler Gestaltung zu entdecken, die sich mittels einfacher Eingriffe aus der Fläche entfalten können. Empirisches Arbeiten ohne einen vorgeschalteten Prozess der Ideenfindung oder Festlegung der Zielrichtungen ist dabei gefragt. Die Vorgaben der zweiten Aufgabe sind genau so einfach formuliert, allerdings müssen hier schon eigene Ideen einfließen, um das gegebene Thema sinnvoll bearbeiten zu können. In der dritten Phase dann ist die Themenstellung so, dass Formentwicklung und Ideenentwicklung miteinander verflochten werden müssen. Die vierte Aufgabe beginnt mit der Analyse eines ausgewählten bestehenden Produktes oder Schmuckstücks. Aus den Schlussfolgerungen dieser Analyse und der ebenfalls geforderten kritischen Betrachtung soll das Konzept für ein aussagekräftiges Schmuckstück oder einen Gebrauchsgegenstand abgeleitet werden. Den Studierenden ist dann freigestellt, welchen Entwurf oder welche Idee aus diesen vier unterschiedlichen Aufgabenstellungen sie für die Weiterentwicklung und die Umsetzung in ein repräsentatives Modell aufgreifen. Die Besprechungen mit der Gruppe der Kursteilnehmerinnen und Kursteilnehmer ist an den individuellen Anliegen orientiert. Diese Treffen fordern neben

This *Four-Theme Course*, which is offered on a regular basis, provides an important and fundamental confrontation with the elementary tasks of design development. The intensive, process-oriented work on the themes set by me is thus also an essential preparation for the follow-up *Aspects of Serialisation* course, which focuses on the requirements of serialised production. I would thus like to begin with an outline of the *Four-Theme Course*. It is organised in four phases matching the four themes, each phase involving a design task of increasing complexity. In the first phase the students are set a simple task with very narrowly formulated practical instructions. The objective here is to explore the many possibilities of three-dimensional design that can be developed from the two-dimensional concept through simple actions. What is called for is a direct, empirical approach without pre-set goals or a preparatory brainstorming process. The instructions for the second task are formulated just as clearly as the first, but here the students must also bring their own ideas to bear in order to complete the work on the theme satisfactorily. In the third phase the theme is set so that the development of the design and the underlying ideas must be interwoven with one another. The fourth task begins with the analysis of a selected existing product or piece of jewellery. The students must then apply the conclusions of this analysis and the required critical examination to develop a concept for an expressive piece of jewellery or a consumer item. After this the students are then free to choose one of the designs or ideas from the four first tasks for further development and the production of a representative model. The meetings with the group of course participants focus on the students' individual interests. In addition to the exchange of information these meetings also provide an opportunity for productive discussion and debate within the

Melanie Halbauer
Schattentaucher
Brille
PET
Shadow Diver
spectacles
PET

Karen Kathmann
Männerringe
Silber
men's rings
silver

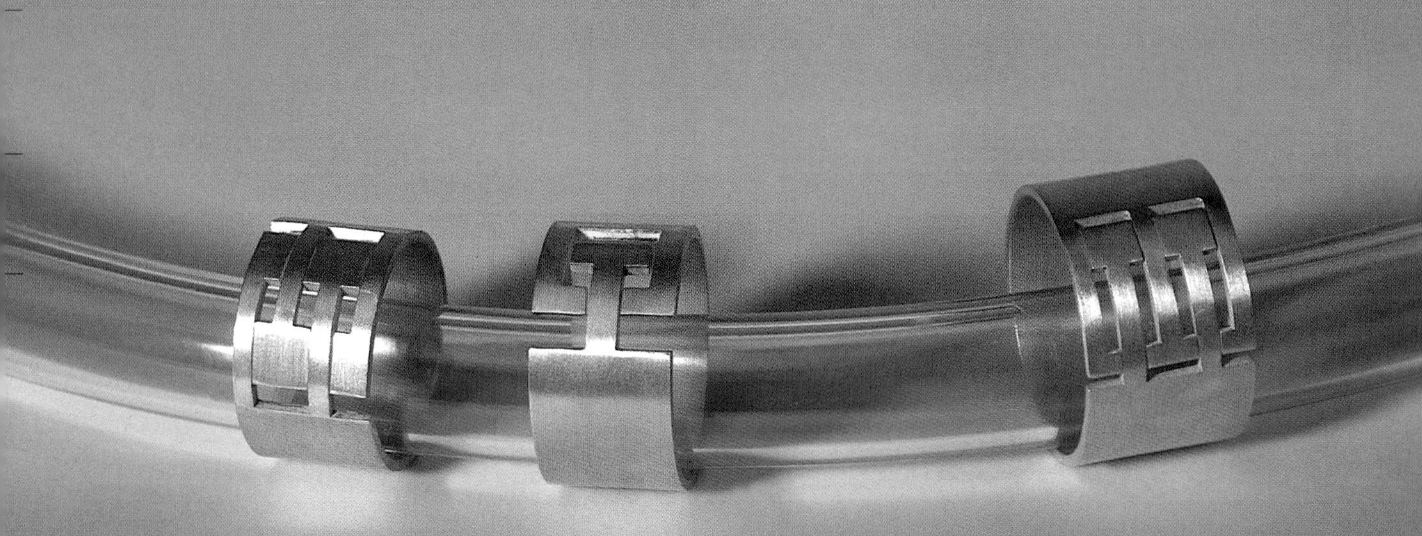

dem Austausch von Informationen auch zu Gruppengesprächen und zur Diskussion heraus. Die Präsentation der Ergebnisse aus allen vier Themenbereichen und des Endergebnisses der zur Weiterentwicklung gewählten Aufgabe gelten als Kursabschluss. Die Betonung liegt damit auf Entwicklung und Prozess, der für wichtiger erachtet wird als die Vorlage eines ausgereiften Endresultates. Die Intention dieses Kurses ist es, die Studierenden an grundlegende Formprobleme bei der Gestaltung von Schmuck und Produkten heranzuführen. Damit ist er zugleich Grundlage für den darauf aufbauenden Kurs *Aspekte von Serie*. Dieser gibt den Studierenden die Möglichkeit einer intensiveren Auseinandersetzung mit der dem Seriengedanken Rechnung tragenden Gestaltung von Schmuck und Produkt. Hier geht es zunächst einmal ganz grundlegend darum, das Bewusstsein der Studierenden für die Gegebenheiten von Serienprodukt bzw. -schmuck und den damit verbundenen Problemen zu schärfen und sich mit den aus diesem Ansatz resultierenden Konsequenzen auseinanderzusetzen und sich darüber Klarheit zu verschaffen, was als Herausforderung angenommen werden kann und was als Beschränkung akzeptiert werden muss. Mit der Entwicklung eines Serienproduktes ist nämlich eine völlig andere, oftmals auch komplexere Problematik gegeben, als dies in der Regel bei der Entwicklung eines Einzelstückes der Fall ist. Darüber hinaus lässt der Begriff Serienprodukt ganz unterschiedliche Interpretationsmöglichkeiten zu. Diese bewegen sich zwischen, ‚Multiple' einerseits und ‚Massenfertigung' andererseits und bestimmen damit ein weiteres Feld der durch den Kurs herausgeforderten Auseinandersetzung. Nach einer genauen Analyse der gestalterischen und technischen Anforderungen, der Realisationsmöglichkeiten und des Marktes, werden die individuellen Konzepte formuliert. Diese können sich sowohl auf eine Schmuckkollektion als auch auf einen Gebrauchsgegenstand beziehen. Der Entwicklungs-

Meike Peters
Halogen-Pendelleuchte
Acryl, Aluminium
halogen suspended lamp
acrylic, aluminium

group. The course is concluded with the presentation of the results of all four phases, and of the task chosen by each student for the in-depth work in the follow-up course. As this structure indicates, the primary emphasis is on development and process, which is seen as more important than a completely finished final product. The intention of this course is to introduce the students to the fundamental problems of form involved in the design of jewellery and products. This also makes the program the preparation for the subsequant courses *Aspects of Serialisation*, which builds on the foundation of the first and gives the students the opportunity to grapple more intensively with the design of jewellery and products intended for serialised fabrication. The initial objective is to sharpen the students' fundamental awareness for the parameters and associated problems of serialised products and jewellery, encouraging them to investigate the consequences of this approach and to understand clearly what can be seen as a challenge and what must be accepted as a limitation. What needs to be understood is that the development of a serialised product involves completely different and often more complex problems than those normally encountered in the production of a one-off piece. Furthermore, the very term serialised product can actually be interpreted in many different ways. These range from 'multiple' at one end of the scale to 'mass-production' at the other, providing broad scope for the work and analysis called for by the course. The individual design concepts are formulated after a thorough analysis of the formal and technical requirements, the possibilities for physical implementation and the market. The same process applies to the development of either a jewellery collection or a consumer product. The goal of the development process is a design that is a balanced and meaningful end product of idea,

prozess zielt auf einen Entwurf, der eine ausgewogene und aussagekräftige Schlussfolgerung aus Idee und gestalterischer Umsetzung, gewähltem Material sowie Konstruktion und Fertigungsmethode bedeutet. Diese hohen Ansprüche zu erfüllen, ist keine einfache Aufgabe. Das trifft insbesondere dann zu, wenn darüber hinaus eine persönliche Aussage oder Stellungnahme in den Vordergrund gestellt wird, die wiederum Voraussetzung ist für signifikante Produkte oder Schmuckstücke. Die skizzierte, dem Entwurfsprozess zugrunde liegende Thematik ist meiner Ansicht nach der des Unikates gleichwertig, jedoch in ihrer gesellschaftlichen Reichweite viel größer. In einem Ausbildungsinstitut wie dem unseren ist es eine wichtige Aufgabe, den Studierenden diese Inhalte differenziert zu vermitteln, um sie dadurch in die Lage zu versetzen, gut und verantwortlich damit umzugehen und sie dabei entsprechend zu fordern und zu fördern.

Britta Göllner
Wandlampe
Stahl
wall lamp
steel

design, selected material, physical construction and production method. Meeting these high standards is no easy task. This applies in particular when one also wishes to communicate a personal statement or perspective, which is always an essential element of significant products and jewellery. I believe that the theme underlying the design process outlined here is equivalent to the development of a one-off piece, but its social scope is much broader. At educational institutions like ours it is important to present the course material to the students in a differentiated fashion, to offer them both support and challenges and to empower them to deal with the material well and responsibly.

NETTO
NETTO
NETTO

Stanislav Braslavsky, Annette Flach
Tütenlampen
Stahl, Aluminium,
Gummischlauch, Plastiktüten
bag lamps
steel, aluminium, rubber tube,
plastic bags

Alin Boyaciyan
Ringset
Silber, blaue Glasfliese
ring set
silver, blue glass tile

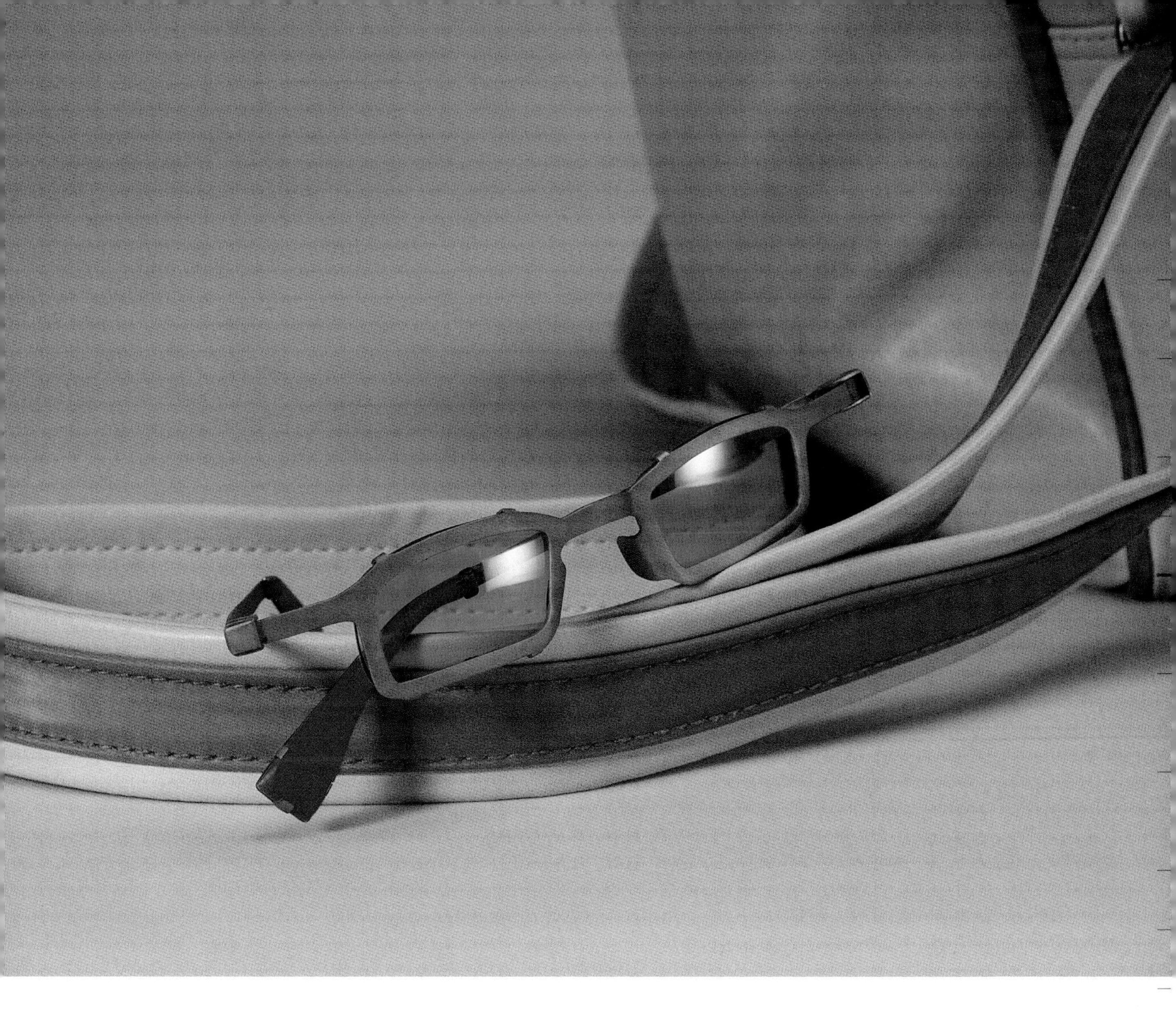

Wolfgang Schepers Kunst versus Design, Design versus Kunst

Bettina Bubel
Brille
Edelstahl, Acrylglas
spectacles
stainless steel, acrylic glass

Wolfgang Schepers **Art versus Design, Design versus Art**

Liebe Leserin, lieber Leser, erlauben Sie mir folgenden ganz persönlichen Einstieg in die Thematik. Im Sommersemester 1992 nahm ich erstmals einen Lehrauftrag an der Fachhochschule Düsseldorf im Fachbereich Design wahr. Ich glaube es war kein Zufall, dass ich damals das Thema *Kunst – Kunsthandwerk – Design – Probleme der Abgrenzung* wählte – nicht nur weil es mich persönlich, eigentlich seit ich am Museum arbeite, beschäftigt, sondern auch, weil ich Reflexionen über das Selbstverständnis der angehenden Schmuck- bzw. Produktdesigner provozieren wollte. Man sollte vielleicht wissen, dass im klassischen Kunstgeschichtsstudium, so wie ich es in den 1970er Jahren absolvierte, Kunsthandwerk überhaupt keine Rolle spielte, ebenso wenig natürlich Geschichte und Theorie des Industriedesigns. Und da kommt man nun plötzlich in den Beruf und ist mit all diesen Fragen und natürlich den Objekten konfrontiert. Zum ersten Mal hält man eine Vase z.B. von Emile Gallé – ist das nun ein Unikat oder ein Serienstück? – in Händen. Sehr schnell wird klar, dass die logische Fortsetzung einer kunsthandwerklichen Sammlung – wie z.B. die des Kunstmuseums Düsseldorf, meiner langjährigen Arbeitsstelle – nur eine Sammlung von Design-Produkten oder präziser von Produktdesign sein kann. Inzwischen zähle ich mich zu den Leitern eines Museums der Angewandten Kunst – auch wenn wir dies noch nicht im Titel deutlich machen. Verschiedene deutsche Spezialmuseen, die auf kunsthandwerklichen Sammlungen des 19. Jahrhunderts basieren, haben sich inzwischen in ‚Museen für Angewandte Kunst' umbenannt, jüngst erst das Museum für Kunsthandwerk in Frankfurt/Main. Letztlich, so glaube ich, tat man dies in eindeutig provokatorischer Absicht. Die Provokation besteht eigentlich darin, dass man mit dem Begriff der Kunst einen Anspruch formuliert, der auf die gleiche Akzeptanz zielt, die Museen der sogenannten ‚freien' Kunst, konkreter der alten und der klassisch modernen Malerei

Anne Kessler
Lockenwicklerringe
mit Feinsilber beschichteter
Kunststoff, Zirkonia
curler rings
plastic coated with refined silver,
zircon

I taught my first course at the design department of Düsseldorf University of Applied Sciences in the summer term of 1992. My choice of subject, *Art, Crafts & Design – Problems of Differentiation* was no coincidence; it is an issue that has interested me for a long time, ever since I started working at the museum in fact, and I also wanted to provoke the students and make them think about their future identities as jewellery and product designers. It is worth mentioning that crafts were completely ignored in the curriculum of the type of traditional art history degree course which I completed in the Seventies. By the same token, the history and theory of industrial design were also conspicuous by their absence. After graduating I started work and found myself confronted with all these questions, and the objects themselves, of course. For example, when I picked up a vase by Emile Gallé for the first time I had to ask myself, is this a one-off piece or a serialised work? It soon became clear that the logical extrapolation of a crafts collection – like the collection at the *Düsseldorf Museum of Art* where I worked for many years – can really only be a collection of design products. Or, to be more precise, a product design collection. I now count myself as one of the curators of a museum of applied art, even though we don't yet express this explicitly in the job title. Several specialised German museums focusing on the crafts collections assembled in the 19th century have now changed their names and started referring to themselves as 'museums of applied art', most recently the *Museum für Kunsthandwerk* in Frankfurt/Main. Ultimately, I believe that the basic intention in making this change was provocative. The provocation is in the use of the term *art*, which formulates a claim to the same acceptance that has long since been accorded to museums devoted to the so-called *free* or *fine* arts, more specifically historical and modern painting in the traditional

schon längst haben. Leider spiegeln dies auch die Besucherzahlen wider, wo doch gerade die auf die ‚nützlichen Künste' orientierten Museen ‚viel näher am Menschen' sind. Um ein Bild zu gebrauchen: Über einen Stuhl, eine Tasse oder ein Besteck zu urteilen, traut sich der Besucher sicher eher zu als über zeitgenössische Kunst kompetent mitzudiskutieren. Aber zurück zum Anfang meines Essays: Damals, im Sommersemester 1992 an der FH Düsseldorf lasen, diskutierten und interpretierten wir gemeinsam Texte u.a. folgender Autoren, die nach meinem Dafürhalten noch immer zu einer historischen Standortbestimmung des Verhältnisses von Kunst und Design nützlich sind: einführend Axel von Saldern (1987), gewissermaßen historisch Gottfried Semper (1851), William Morris (1887), Adolf Loos (1908), Henry van de Velde im Werkbundstreit gegen Muthesius (1914), Walter Gropius (1925), Positionen der Ulmer Hochschule für Gestaltung (Max Bill, Otl Aicher), sowie Texte zum sogenannten *Neuen Design* (Alchimia, Memphis). Sicherlich gibt es noch manche und vor allem immer mehr kluge Texte zu dieser Problematik, aber im Dschungel der Definitionen kann nur die Beschränkung und die historische Determinierung sinnvoll sein. Außerdem möchte ich als ‚Museumsmann' das Thema relativ pragmatisch angehen und lese deshalb den Artikel meines ehemaligen Kollegen Axel von Salden (Direktor des Hamburger Museums für Kunst und Gewerbe) im Katalog *Design – Dasein* (1987) immer wieder gern. Sein Verdienst besteht darin, den Begriff Design auf den Terminus *disegno* der italienischen Renaissance zurückgeführt zu haben.
Der lombardische Maler Giovanni Paolo Lomazzo spricht in seinen Schriften *Trattato dell'arte della pittura* (1584) und *Idea del tempio* (1590) vom *disegno interno* „als (von der) vom Künstler geborenen und von Gott inspirierten idea (... vom) Konzept für das auszuführende Kunstwerk".[1] Im 1588 erschienenen Oxford Dictionary finden wir dann erstmals den noch heute

Julia Stotz
mas ó menos
Salzstreuer und Zuckerstreuer
Glas, Gummi, Edelstahl
mas ó menos
salt shaker and sugar shaker
glass, rubber, stainless steel

sense. Unfortunately, this is also reflected in the visitor attendance figures. The problem is, museums focusing on the 'useful arts' are felt to be much closer to the 'ordinary public'. To provide a simple example, we can be pretty certain that the average visitor would feel much more confident about his or her ability to make a competent contribution to a discussion about the design of a chair, a cup or a piece of cutlery than to one about a work of contemporary art. But I digress. Back in the 1992 summer term at Düsseldorf University of Applied Sciencese we read, discussed and analysed texts by a number of authors who I feel are still useful for establishing an historical overview of the development of the relationship between art and design. They include Axel von Saldern (1987) as an introduction, Gottfried Semper (1851) for a historical background, William Morris (1887), Adolf Loos (1908), Henry van de Velde on the famous *Werkbund Dispute* with Muthesius (1914), Walter Gropius (1925), texts from the Ulm College of Design (Max Bill, Otl Aicher), and texts on the so-called *New Design* (Alchimia, Memphis). Of course there are plenty more and a growing number of intelligent analyses of this issue, but in the jungle of definitions conscious restraint and clarification of the historical context are the only viable solution.
As a 'museum man' who likes to take a relatively pragmatic approach to the subject I still refer frequently and with pleasure to the article by my former colleague Axel von Salden (curator of the Art and Trade Museum in Hamburg), which was published in the catalogue of the *Design – Dasein* exhibition in 1987 (Design – Existence/Being There). His major contribution in this article was to trace the etymology of the term design back to *disegno* in the Italian Renaissance. In his *Trattato dell'arte della pittura* (1584) and *Idea del tempio* (1590), the Lombard painter Giovanni Paolo Lomazzo writes of what he refers to as *disegno interno*

gebräuchlichen englischen Begriff des *design* als „a) Ein vom Menschen erdachter Plan oder ein Schema von etwas, was realisiert werden soll; die erste Konzeption einer Idee, die durch eine bestimmte Handlung in die Tat umgesetzt wird. b) Ein erster zeichnerischer Entwurf für ein Kunstwerk (... oder) ein Objekt der angewandten Kunst, der für die Ausführung eines Werkes verbindlich sein soll."[2] Aufschlussreich erscheint in diesem Zusammenhang der Verweis auf die Designdefinition im Katalog der Züricher Ausstellung von 1983 *Design – Formgebung für jedermann*: „Design wird als ein Vorgang verstanden, der Entwürfe bringt für die Herstellung von Serienprodukten und industrialisierten Methoden und Systemen". Vielleicht doch etwas zu vorschnell fügt von Saldern hinzu: „Diese klare Definition neueren Datums unterscheidet sich prinzipiell nicht von der des 16. Jahrhunderts"[3], übersieht er dabei doch, dass hier die Kategorie der industriellen Produktion eingeführt wird. Hilfreich dürfte also in der Folge die Unterscheidung zwischen Design allgemein und Industriedesign im besonderen sein. Korrekterweise sollte man aber auch noch zumindest zwischen Produktdesign und – etwas altertümlich – Grafikdesign unterscheiden, will man das in den ‚semantischen Griff' bekommen, was z.B. an der FH Düsseldorf gelehrt und studiert wird. Als wir Mitte der 1980er Jahre am Kunstmuseum Düsseldorf begannen, Design zu sammeln, und zwar private Konsumgüter, habe ich die Kriterien des Sammelns auf diesem Gebiet in Anlehnung an Gert Selle folgendermaßen definiert. Wir wollten uns auf „solche Entwurfsverwirklichungen von Technikern und Designern beschränken, die als technische und/oder dekorative Objekte für den privaten Gebrauch und Konsum bestimmt sind".[4] Noch heute stehe ich zu meiner damaligen Feststellung, dass uns in der Museumsarbeit (d.h. beim Sammeln, Bewahren, Forschen und Vermitteln) genau die Dinge interessieren, die „zum Zeitpunkt ihrer erstmaligen Herstellung

Maren Krämer
365 Ösen – Glück
Kette
Silber, roter Samt
365 Links – Happiness
necklace
silver, red velvet

as the "(...) idea inspired by God and given birth to (by the) artist (...) the concept for the work of art to be produced."[1] The definition of the word design in the modern sense appears for the first time in the 1588 edition of the Oxford Dictionary, where in addition to its meaning as a man-made plan or scheme for an idea that is to be realised, it is also described as a definitive draft for the execution of a work of art or crafts.[2] Also instructive in this connection is the reference to the definition of design found in the catalogue of the exhibition *Design – Formgebung für Jedermann* (Design for Everyman) staged in Zurich in 1983: "Design is understood to be a process that produces plans for the manufacturing of seralised products and industrialised methods and systems." Saldern then comments that "This lucid modern definition is not fundamentally different from the one given in the 16th-century."[3] This is perhaps a little hasty, however, as he appears to forget that the definition also introduces the concept of industrial production. In what follows it will thus also be helpful to make a distinction between design in general and industrial design in particular. To be absolutely accurate one should also distinguish between product design and the rather older concept of graphic design, at least if one wants to get a firm semantic grasp of what is actually taught and studied at institutions like Düsseldorf University of Applied Sciences. When we started our design collection at the *Düsseldorf Museum of Art* in the mid-Eighties, focusing on private consumer goods, I defined our collecting criteria as follows, drawing on the principles of Gert Selle: "We want to restrict the collection to the physically realised plans of engineers and designers for technical or decorative objects that were intended for private use and consumption."[4] Today I still hold by the assessment I made then, when I wrote that what interested us in our museum work (i.e. collecting,

365 Ösen Glück

tatsächlich neue physisch funktionale wie psychologisch-ästhetische Gebrauchswerte darstellten bzw. darstellen."[5] Eigentlich könnte alles so einfach sein: Kunst ist Kunst, da nach bürgerlichem Verständnis *frei*, und Design ist Design, da funktionsgebunden und *nützlich* (Hans Wichmann, der ehemalige Leiter der Neuen Sammlung München sprach einmal vom Design als „Kunst, die sich nützlich macht"). Die Geschichte belehrt uns jedoch eines anderen. Genau deshalb studierten wir damals die Texte der Klassiker auf diesem Gebiet. Gottfried Semper reflektiert bereits 1851 sichtlich unter dem Eindruck der Londoner Weltausstellung, der ersten großen Vergleichsschau der Wirtschaftsnationen im Zeitalter des Konkurrenzkapitalismus, das Verhältnis von Kunst zur Industrie oder mit anderen Worten zur Maschine: „Die Maschine näht, strickt, schnitzt, malt, greift tief ein in das Gebiet der menschlichen Kunst und beschämt jede menschliche Geschicklichkeit. Sind dies nicht große herrliche Errungenschaften?"[6] Gleichzeitig warnt er aber vor dem missbräuchlichen Einsatz der Maschine und bereitet die Argumentation der „guten, ornamentlosen Form" – ein Leitsatz späterer Designtheorien – vor. „Wohin führt die Entwertung der Materie durch ihre Behandlung mit der Maschine, durch Surrogate für sie und noch so viel Erfindungen (...). Ich meine natürlich nicht ihre Entwertung im Preise, sondern in der Bedeutung, in der Idee"[7] – womit sich wieder ein Bogen zur Renaissance-Definition des „disegno" als „prima idea" schlagen lässt. Expressis verbis weist er schließlich das „dualistische Trennen der hohen und der industriellen Kunst zurück."[8] Rund eine Generation später formuliert William Morris – vielleicht der wichtigste Vertreter der englischen *Arts and Crafts*-Bewegung, die mit der rückwärtsgewandten Utopie der Wiederbelebung des Handwerks auf die fortschreitende Industrialisierung reagierte – seine *Ziele der Kunst*. „Deshalb ist das Ziel von Kunst die Vermehrung des menschlichen Glücks (...)".[9] Die

Sonja Thiemann
Faulenzerschmuck
Kette, Ohrringe, Ring
Silber
Jewellery for Loungers
chain, earrings, ring
silver

conserving, researching and disseminating information) was precisely "those things which represent, and represented at the time of their first production, genuinely new physical, functional, psychological and aesthetic consumer values."[5] In theory, it could all be so simple: In the public mind art is art because it is *free*, and design is design because it is *functional* and *useful*. (Hans Wichmann, the former curator of *Die Neue Sammlung* in Munich, once referred to design as "art that makes itself useful.") History teaches us a different story, however, and that is why we decided to study the classic texts dealing with this subject. Back in 1851 Gottfried Semper was already reflecting on art's relationship to industry or, in other words, to the machine, when he wrote, "The machine sews, knits, carves, paints, intrudes deeply into the realm of human art and puts all human dexterity to shame. Are these not great and wonderful achievements?"[6] These words also reflect the impressions of the World Exposition in London, which had been the first major event staged in the age of competitive capitalism where the leading industrial nations could compare their achievements. However, at the same time Semper also warns against the misuse of machines, and lays the groundwork for the espousal of the "good, unornamented form", which was to become a basic tenet of later design theories: "Where does it lead, the devaluation of material through its processing by the machine, through surrogates for material and more and more inventions? (...) I am of course not speaking of its devaluation in price, but in its meaning, in the idea"[7] Which brings us back full circle to the Renaissance definition of *disegno* as the *prima idea*. Finally, Semper then makes an *expressis verbis* rejection of the "dualistic separation of higher and industrial art".[8] Around a generation later William Morris – perhaps the most important representative of the British Arts and

Maschine sollte nur zur Erleichterung der menschlichen Arbeit eingesetzt werden. „Treibt er (= der Mensch) aber die Benutzung einer Maschine beim Herstellen von Kunst auch nur einen Schritt weiter, dann handelt er unvernünftig, wenn er die Kunst schätzt und frei ist." Keinesfalls aber dürfe der Mensch zum „Sklaven der Maschine" werden.[10] Offenbar war es noch ein weiter Weg bis zur Akzeptanz industrieller Produktion von formal und funktional gut gestalteten Gebrauchsgegenständen. 1908 formuliert Adolf Loos seine folgenreichen Thesen über *Ornament und Verbrechen* und weist damit weit in die designtheoretische Zukunft, die spätestens seit der klassischen Moderne der 1920er Jahre die klare „sachliche", d.h. ornamentlose Formgebung zur Maxime erhob: „evolution der kultur ist gleichbedeutend mit dem entfernen des ornamentes aus dem gebrauchsgegenstande".[11] Seine „volkswirtschaftliche Begründung" sei noch einmal in Erinnerung gerufen: „Das ornament verteuert in der regel den gegenstand (...). Das fehlen des ornamentes hat eine verkürzung der arbeitszeit und eine erhöhung des lohnes zur folge (...). Ornament ist vergeudete arbeitskraft und dadurch vergeudete gesundheit. So war es immer".[12] Schließlich schlägt er mit dieser an den angewandten Künsten entwickelten Theorie sogar den Bogen zu den sogenannten freien Künsten: „Das fehlen des ornamentes hat die übrigen künste zu ungeahnter höhe gebracht".[13] Hatte es der Deutsche Werkbund 1907 geschafft, Künstler und Industrielle in einer Vereinigung zusammenzuführen, so war man damit noch lange nicht einer Auffassung über die Rolle von Kunst und industriell gefertigten Entwürfen (= Produktdesign). 1914 kulminierten diese Differenzen im sogenannten *Werkbundstreit* zwischen Hermann Muthesius und Henry van de Velde auf der Kölner Werkbundausstellung. Der von Muthesius geforderten „Typisierung" setzte van de Velde den Künstler als „glühenden Individualisten" entgegen, der sich niemals „in eine allgemeingültige

Crafts Movement, which responded to increasing industrialisation with a retrogressively utopian revival of crafts – formulates his stance in his *The Aims of Art*: "Therefore the Aim of Art is to increase the happiness of men."[9] As he sees it, machines should only be used to ease the burdens of human labour. "Carry the machine used for art a step further and he becomes an unreasonable man, if he values art and is free." Morris is adamant that Mankind should never become a "slave to machinery".[10] The acceptance of the industrial manufacturing of formally and functionally well-designed consumer products is clearly still a long way off. In 1908 Adolf Loos then publishes his influential theses in *Ornament and Crime*, pointing far into the future of design theory, when clear and "objective" (i.e. unornamented) design would be elevated to the status of a basic tenet, at the latest with the onset of the classical modern era in 1920s. Loos writes, "Evolution of culture is synonymous with the removal of ornament from everyday commodities."[11] It is also worth recalling his "economic validation" of this stance: "Ornament normally makes the product more expensive... Lack of ornament brings a reduction of working hours and increased pay (...). Ornament is wasted labour and consequently wasted health. It has always been so."[12] Finally, Loos goes so far as to make a connection between this applied arts theory and the so-called 'free arts', with the claim that "The lack of ornament has lifted the other arts to unprecedented heights."[13] Although the *Deutscher Werkbund* (German Association of Craftsmen) succeeds in 1907 in bringing artists and industrial artisans together in a single association, the members are still far from agreement on the roles of art and 'industrially manufactured designs' (i.e. product design). In 1914 these differences culminate in the so-called *Werkbund Dispute* between Hermann Muthesius and Henry van de Velde at the Werkbund Exhibition in Cologne, with

Melanie Halbauer
Stempelring
Silber, Foto, Gießharz, Filz, Stempelgummi
Seal Ring
silver, photo, cast resin, felt, rubber stamp

Flirten. Flüchtiges Berühren und Kontakt aufnehmen.
Flirting. Fleeting touches and establishment of contact.

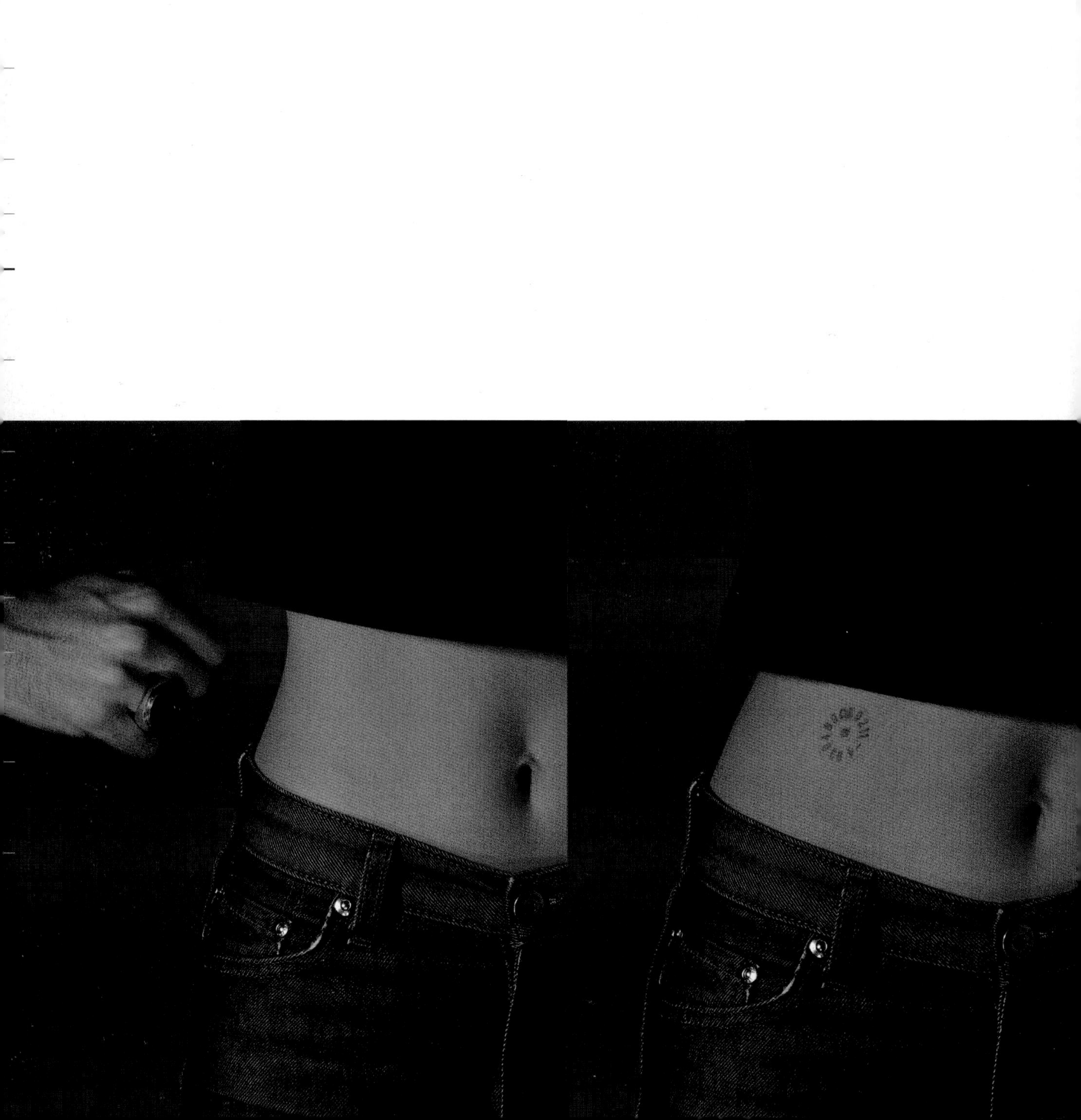

Form hineintreiben" lasse.[14] Was sich hier bereits andeutet, ist die Utopie der klassischen Moderne von allgemeingültigen Lösungen in der Formgebung wie sie beispielsweise durch das Bauhaus vertreten wurde. 1919 unter Walter Gropius gegründet, strebt man zunächst in der Weimarer Zeit eine neue Einheit von „Kunst und Handwerk" an (so Gropius im Manifest von 1919), mit der Übersiedlung nach Dessau 1923 verschieben sich die Ziele in Richtung „Kunst und Industrie eine neue Einheit". 1925 schließlich hat man vollends den „Massenbedarf" im Blick: „Die Lebensbedürfnisse der Mehrzahl der Menschen sind in der Hauptsache gleichartig, Haus und Hausgerät ist Angelegenheit des Massenbedarfs, ihre Gestaltung mehr eine Sache der Vernunft, als eine Sache der Leidenschaft. (...) Die Bauhauswerkstätten sind im wesentlichen *Laboratorien*, in denen vervielfältigungsreife, für die heutige Zeit typische Geräte sorgfältigim Modell entwickelt und dauernd verbessert werden. Das Bauhaus will in diesen *Laboratorien* einen neuen bisher nicht vorhandenen Typ von Mitarbeitern für Industrie und Handwerk heranbilden, die Technik und Form in gleichem Maße beherrschen".[15] Bekanntlich knüpft die nach dem 2. Weltkrieg unter ausgesprochen antifaschistischen Vorzeichen gegründete Ulmer Hochschule für Gestaltung (1953-1968) an die Ideen des Bauhauses an. Erwartungsgemäß existieren auch hier unterschiedliche Auffassungen über das Verhältnis von industrieller Formgebung (Design) zur Kunst. Während die Gründer der Hochschule, Inge Aicher-Scholl und Otl Aicher, an die Utopie einer Ausbildungsstätte für eine neue Generation von Gestaltern glauben, in der Design als umfassende „Zivilisationsarbeit" gelehrt werden soll, versteht sich der erste Direktor der Hochschule, der Schweizer Künstler Max Bill, als künstlerischer Gestalter. Für ihn ist der Entwerfer letztlich ein Künstler.[16] Wegen dieser Differenzen verläßt Bill 1957 schließlich die Schule. Dem über Jahrzehnte hinweg dominierenden

Melanie Halbauer
Brandingringe
medizinischer Stahl, Gold
Branding rings
surgical steel, gold

Zum Zeichen der Liebe.
Schmerzlich, lodernd, lustvoll.
As a sign of love.
Painfully, blazingly, lustfully.

Muthesius calling for "typification" and Van de Velde countering with the concept of the artist as the "passionate individualist" who would never allow himself to be "driven into a standardised form".[14] Here we can already see the beginning of the classical modern era's ideal of generally applicable design solutions, like those advocated by the *Bauhaus School* founded in 1919 by Walter Gropius. During the initial period in Weimar the school strives for a new unity of "art and crafts", as outlined by Gropius in the 1919 manifesto. The move to Dessau in 1923 is then accompanied by a shift in objectives towards "a new unity of art and industry", and by 1925 the focus is firmly on "mass needs": "The daily requirements of most people are fundamentally the same, homes and domestic appliances are mass needs and their design is more a question of reason than one of passion (...). The Bauhaus workshops are basically *laboratories* in which prototypes of industrially-producible appliances typical of the contemporary age are carefully developed and continually improved. In these *laboratories* the Bauhaus wishes to train a new, hitherto unprecedented type of workers for industry and the crafts, workers who will have an equal command of technology and design."[15] The *Ulm College of Design* (1953-1968), which was established after World War II in a pronouncedly antifascist scenario, continued on the theoretical course started by the *Bauhaus School*. Unsurprisingly there were disagreements here too over the relationship between industrial design and art. The college's founders, Inge Aicher-Scholl and Otl Aicher, were committed to the ideal of a training institution for a new generation of designers, where design would be taught as a comprehensive form of "civilization work". In contrast to this, the college's first director, the Swiss artist Max Bill, saw himself as an artist designer. For him the designer was ultimately an artist.[16] In 1957 these

funktionalistisch-asketischen Stil in der Tradition von Bauhaus und Ulm wirken in den 1970er und insbesondere den 1980er Jahren Bewegungen wie das italienische *Radical Design* oder das gesamteuropäische Neue Design entgegen. Der Aufstand gegen das Quadratisch-Praktische, das Ornamentlose und Langweilige der Gestaltung zeigt nun wieder eine größere Nähe zur Kunst. Konzepte, Ideen, formgewordene Manifeste zählen mehr als das perfekte industriegerechte Finish. Der Band 66 (Okt. 1983) des *Kunstforum International* trägt den bezeichnenden Titel *Zwischen Kunst und Design – Neue Formen der Ästhetik*. Der Herausgeber, Rainer Wick, behandelt „Das Ende des Funktionalismus: am Beispiel des Möbeldesign" trendsetzender italienischer Gruppen wie Alchimia und Memphis. Das lange Zeit maßgebliche, Louis Sullivan zugeschriebene Prinzip guten Designs ‚Form follows Function' wird nun umgekehrt: „Die Form geht vor der Funktion."[17] Durch die Theorien der Postmoderne ist plötzlich wieder alles offen: Künstler machen Design, Designer machen Kunst. Das industrielle Serienprodukt tritt zumindest in der öffentlichen Beachtung weit hinter spektakulären Unikaten zurück. Die Fertigungsweise kann mit Fug und Recht als anachronistisch bezeichnet werden, Entwurf und Ausführung liegen ganz im Gegensatz zur Realisierung von Entwürfen des Produktdesign häufig sogar wieder – ganz wie beim klassichen Handwerk – in einer Hand. Selbstverständlich sind auch Ornamente nicht länger tabuisiert. Auch wenn man in den 1990er Jahren eine Hinwendung – oder vielleicht besser eine Rückwendung – zur sogenannten *Neuen Einfachheit* und damit ein Anknüpfen an die formalen Ausprägungen des klassischen Funktionalismus der 1920er Jahre beobachten kann, so zeigt ein Blick in die Kaufhäuser, dass erst nach rund 15 Jahren die ‚Buntheit' von Memphis und Alchimia zur Alltagskultur geworden ist. Ähnliche Phänomene konstatieren wir zuvor für die 1950er Jahre, über die man einmal gesagt

Uta Oeding-Erdel
Transparenz
T-Shirt und Schal
Shirt, Murmeln,
Seidenorganza, Perlen
Transparency
t-shirt and scarf
shirt, marbles,
silk organza, beads

differences then culminate in Bill's departure from the college. In the 1970s, and even more in the 80s, movements like the Italian *Radical Design* and the pan-European *New Design* provide a new counter to the functional and ascetic stylistic traditions of the Bauhaus and Ulm that had dominated the foregoing decades. This rebellion against the square, the practical, the unornamented and the boring in design marks a return to a greater proximity to art. Concepts, ideas and the physical implementation of design manifestos now count more than a perfect and industrially-compatible finish. Volume 66 (Oct. 1983) of *Kunstforum International* bore the telling title *Between Art and Design – New Forms of Aesthetics*. In a leading article titled *The End of Functionalism as Illustrated by Furniture Design*, editor Rainer Wick writes about trend-setting Italian groups like Alchimia and Memphis. The 'form follows function' principle attributed to Luis Sullivan that had been predominant for so long has now been turned on its head. Now it is "Form goes before function."[17] The theories of Post-Modernism have made everything open again: Artists are producing design, designers are making art. The status of mass-produced industrial goods falls far behind that of spectacular, unique works, at least in the estimation of the public at large. This mode of production can justifiably be called an anachronism; in contrast to the product design approach the entire design and manufacturing processes are now frequently once again in the hands of a single person, just as they were in the age of traditional craftsmanship. And, of course, the taboo on ornaments also no longer applies. In the 1990s we see an effective resumption of the formal expressions of the classical functionalism of the 1920s expressed in a perceptible change of direction towards – or perhaps rather a return to – the so-called *New Simplicity*. Despite this, however, a look at the

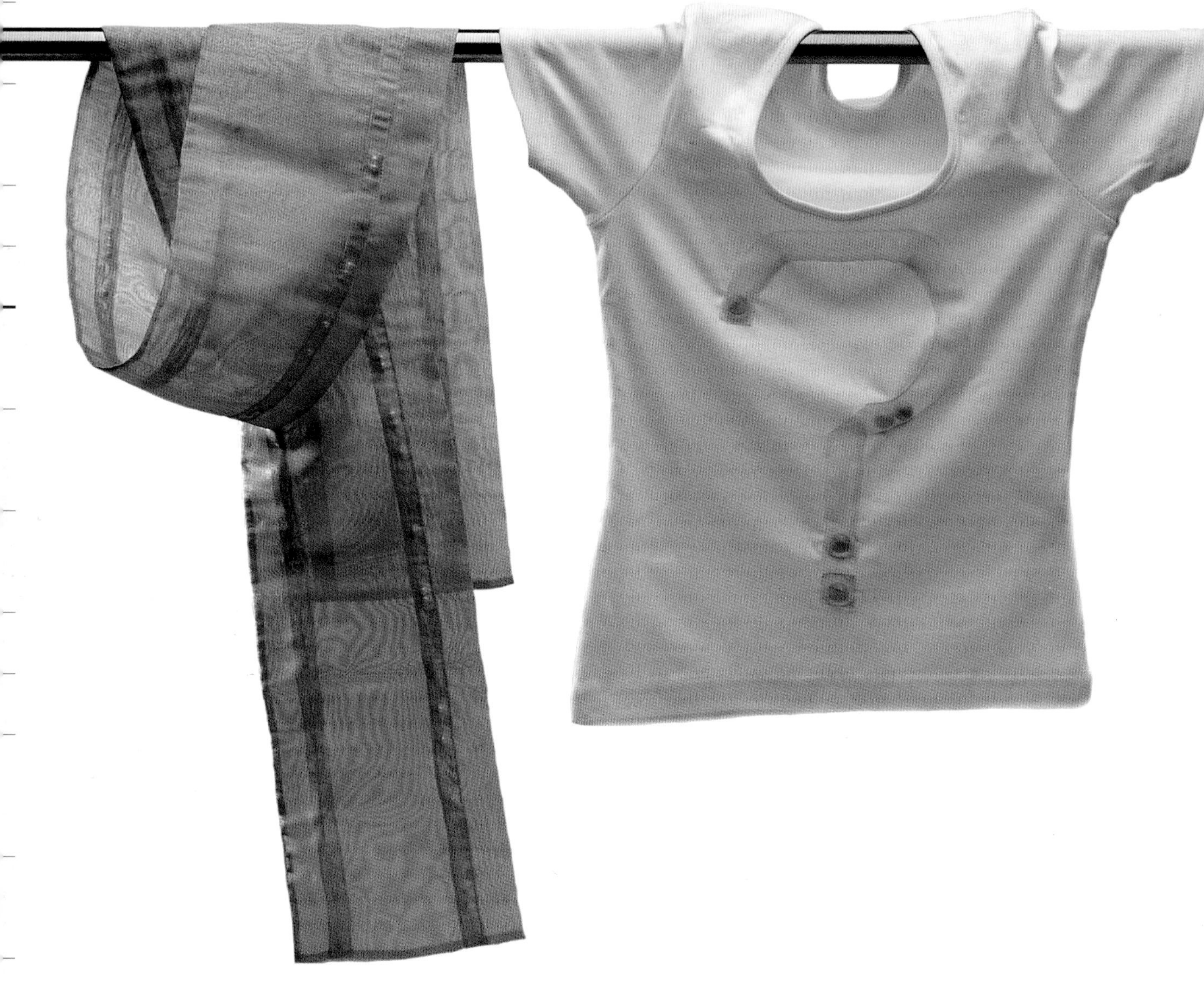

hat, die Tapeten- und Textilindustrie habe mehr für die Verbreitung der abstrakten Kunst getan als jede Kunstausstellung. Hier ist der Fall klar: Design popularisert die Kunst. Heute aber – und das ist das Verdienst der Postmoderne – sind die Grenzen zwischen Kunst und Design wieder fließend. Der kurze historische Rückblick hat gezeigt, wie die beiden Begriffe gewissermaßen oszillieren und in ihrer jeweiligen Bedeutung nur zeitspezifisch fixiert werden können. Von Design würde ich aber immer da sprechen, wo ein Verweis auf Gebrauch, auf Benutzbarkeit im physischen wie psychischen Sinn vorliegt.

1 Axel von Saldern, in: **Design – Dasein**, Ausst. Kat., Museum für Kunst und Gewerbe, Hamburg 1987, S. 9 2 Ebenda 3 Ebenda 4 Wolfgang Schepers, **Designsammlung im Aufbau**, in: Kunstmuseum Düsseldorf, Führer durch die Sammlungen 2, Düsseldorf 1986, S. 124 5 Ebenda 6 Gottfried Semper, **Wissenschaft, Industrie und Kunst. Vorschläge zur Anregung Nationalen Kunstgefühls** (1851), zit. nach: Neue Bauhausbücher 3, ausgewählt und redigiert von Hans M. Wingler, Mainz und Berlin o.J., S. 32 7 Ebenda, S. 37 8 Ebenda, S. 62 9 William Morris, **Die Ziele der Kunst** (1887), zit. nach Volker Fischer/Anne Hamilton (Hrsg.), Theorien der Gestaltung, Frankfurt/Main 1999, S. 15 10 Ebenda S. 16 11 Adolf Loos, **Ornament und Verbrechen**, in: ders.: Sämtliche Schriften in 2 Bänden, hrsg. von Franz Glück Wien/München 1962, S. 277 12 Ebenda, S. 282 13 Ebenda, S. 287 14 Hermann Muthesius/Henry van de Velde, **Werkbundthesen und Gegenthesen** (1914), zit. nach Fischer/Hamilton (s. Anm. 9) S. 36-38 15 Walter Gropius, **Grundsätze der Bauhausproduktion**, in: Neue Arbeiten der Bauhauswerkstätten, Bauhausbücher 7, 1925, hrsg. von Walter Gropius/L. Moholy-Nagy, S. 7 16 Vgl. Wolfgang Ruppert, **Ulm ist tot. Es lebe Ulm**, in: Kursbuch 106, (12/1991), S. 121-125 17 Rainer Wick, **Das Ende des Funktionalismus: am Beispiel des Möbeldesign**, in: Kunstforum International 66 (10/1983), S. 50

displays in the department stores makes it eminently clear that a mere fifteen years have been enough to make the "colourfulness" of Memphis and Alchimia a firmly-established part of mainstream culture. Similar phenomena can also be observed earlier, in the 1950s, about which it has been said that the wallpaper and fabric industries did more for the dissemination of abstract art than any art exhibition. Here we have a clear case of design actively popularising art. Today, however – and this is the achievement of Post-Modernism – the borders between art and design have once again become fluid. This brief historical retrospective has provided a clear demonstration of the oscillating interpretations of these two terms, so that each of them can only be defined clearly within a very specific time-frame. Personally, however, I would always use the term design in connection with utilisation, in both the physical and the mental senses of the word.

1 **Axel von Saldern, in:** Design – Dasein, **exhibit. cat., Museum für Kunst und Gewerbe, Hamburg 1987, p. 9** 2 **Ibid** 3 **Ibid** 4 **Wolfgang Schepers,** Designsammlung im Aufbau, **in: Führer durch die Sammlungen 2, Kunstmuseum Düsseldorf, Düsseldorf 1986, p. 124** 5 **Ibid** 6 **Gottfried Semper,** Wissenschaft, Industrie und Kunst. Vorschläge zur Anregung Nationalen Kunstgefühls **(1851), quote from: Neue Bauhausbücher 3, selected and edited by Hans M. Wingler, Mainz/Berlin (no date), p. 32** 7 **Ibid, p. 37** 8 **Ibid, p. 62** 9 **William Morris,** The Aims of Art **(1887), quoted by Volker Fischer/Anne Hamilton (eds.), in: Theorien der Gestaltung, Frankfurt/Main 1999, p. 15** 10 **Ibid p. 16** 11 **Adolf Loos,** Ornament und Verbrechen, **in: Sämtliche Schriften in 2 Bänden, ed. by Franz Glück, Vienna/Munich 1962, p. 277** 12 **Ibid, p. 282** 13 **Ibid, p. 287** 14 **Hermann Muthesius/Henry van de Velde,** Werkbundthesen und Gegenthesen **(1914), quoted by Fischer/Hamilton (cf. footnote 9) pp. 36-38** 15 **Walter Gropius,** Grundsätze der Bauhausproduktion, **in: Neue Arbeiten der Bauhauswerkstätten, Bauhausbücher 7, 1925, ed. by Walter Gropius/L. Moholy-Nagy, p. 7** 16 **Cf. Wolfgang Ruppert,** Ulm ist tot. Es lebe Ulm, **in: Kursbuch 106, (12/1991), pp. 121-125** 17 **Rainer Wick,** Das Ende des Funktionalismus: am Beispiel des Möbeldesign, **in: Kunstforum International 66 (10/1983), p. 50**

Meike Peters
Vielschichtig
Ringe
Silber
Multi-Layered
rings
silver

Vom Gegenstand zum
Symbol/Zeichen zum Objekt
From Object to
Symbol/Cipher to Object
1999/2000

Judith Sommer
Eine Spur
Strickketten
Silber, Messing, Gummi, Magnete
A Track
knitted chains
silver, brass, rubber, magnets

Einzelbesprechung
für die Bearbeitung individuell
formulierter Themen
Individual Tutorials
1999

Astrid Eckert
Schuppenlampe
Stehleuchte
Stahl, Polypropylen,
Leuchtstoffröhre
Scaly Lamp
standard lamp
steel, polypropylene,
fluorescent tube

Mira Leithe
Spannung – Entspannung
Ansteckschmuck
Gold
Tension – Relaxation
pins
gold

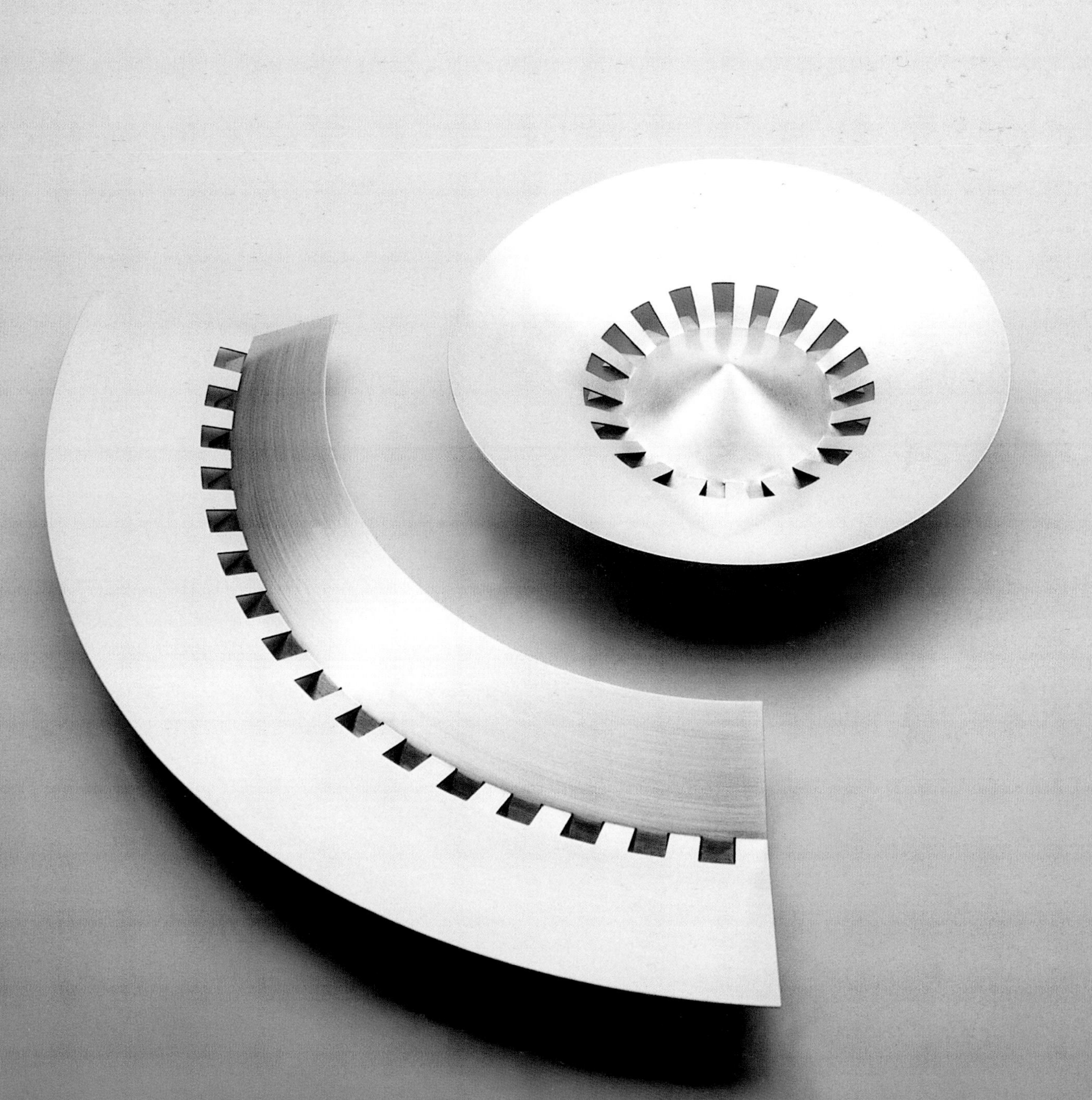

Kurse zwischen 2001 und 1992 Elisabeth Holder, Herman Hermsen, Herbert Schulze, Heike Baschta, Susanne Knapp, Brigitte Tendahl und Petra Weingärtner-Arnold

Michael Boy
Ornament
Obstschalen
Silber
Ornament
fruit bowls
silver

Courses offered between 2001 and 1992 **Elisabeth Holder, Herman Hermsen, Herbert Schulze, Heike Baschta, Susanne Knapp, Brigitte Tendahl, Petra Weingärtner-Arnold**

Kursthemen von Prof. Elisabeth Holder

Schmuck und neue Medien 2001/02. Hinführung zu eigenen Schmuckkonzeptionen auf der Grundlage umfassender Recherchen der aktuellen Entwicklungen im Bereich neuer Medien und der persönlichen Auseinandersetzung damit. **Der Weg vom Objekt in den öffentlichen Raum** 2001/02. Begleitende Arbeiten für das Katalogbuch zur Ausstellung des Studiengangs Produktdesign in den Jahren 2002/03. **Über unsere Köpfe hinweg** 2001. Ein dreitägiger Work-shop zur Entwicklung einer gestalterischen Reaktion auf die drohende Schließung des Studiengangs Produktdesign in Düsseldorf. **Vom Interessensfeld zum Thema zum Objekt** 2001. Der Kurs ist konzipiert für die Identifizierung und Entwicklung eigener gestalterischer Schwerpunkte. **Der Weg vom Objekt in den öffentlichen Raum** 2001. nhaltlich-konzeptionelle und organisatorische Vorarbeiten für das Ausstellungprojekt des Studiengangs Produktdesign. **Politischer Schmuck** 2001. Die Erarbeitung politischer Aussagen und ihre Umsetzung und Verdichtung in einem trag-baren Symbol.

Traditionell weibliche Handwerke und Schmuck 2001/02
Studierende **Dorothee Bach, Alin Boyaciyan, Birgit Bußler, Bettina Bubel, Eva Dufhues, Astrid Eckert, Sigrid Eickhoff, Gisa Elmer, Isabelle Falzarano, Eva Frisch, Melanie Halbauer, Claudia Halder, Danuta Herzog, Karen Hüttner, Karen Kathmann, Anne Kessler, Stefanie Klein, Mira Leithe, Ingrid Micheel, Elke Munkert, Martina Schmitt, Julia Stotz, Heike Tries, Andrea Wagner, Christiane Wink, Nina Wöhlke.** Spinnen, weben, flechten, knüpfen, stricken und sticken, aber auch töpfern sind traditionell von Frauen ausgeübte Handwerke. Sie können als Urformen der Gestaltung begriffen werden. Ziel des Kurses war es, über die Auseinandersetzung und das Experiment mit diesen weiblichen Handwerken zu neuen Aussagen im Schmuck zu gelangen. In den regelmäßigen gemeinschaft-lichen Treffen lag der Fokus auf dem das Unbewußte anregenden Potential dieser Tätigkeiten und den Spuren, die sie als Metaphern in unserer Sprache hinterlassen haben. Aus diesem Tun heraus entwickelten sich die individuellen Ansätze und Gestaltungskonzepte.

Ausformulierungen 2001/02
Studierende **Astrid Eckert, Eva Frisch, Pauline Grootekamp, Claudia Hoppe, Simone Nolden, Bettina Kratz, Simon Wenz.** Dieser Kurs war konzipiert als Fortsetzung für die Teilnehmerinnen und Teilnehmer des Kurses *Aus dem Schatten ans Licht* und des Kurzprojektes *Von einem Interessensfeld zu einem Thema*. Ausgehend von dem gefundenen

Einzelbesprechung
für die Bearbeitung individuell
formulierter Themen
Individual Tutorials
1999/2000

Simon Wenz
Teelichthalter
Edelstahl
tea candle holder
stainless steel

Courses offered by Prof. Elisabeth Holder

ewellery and New Media **2001/02. Systematic development of individual jewellery concepts, building on extensive esearch into current developments in the new media and a personal examination of results.** The Way from the Object to Public Presentation **2001/02. Additional work for the production of the catalogue of the Product Design School's 2002 and 2003 exhibitions.** Over Our Heads **2001. A three-day workshop on the development of a design response to the threatened closure of the Product Design School in Düsseldorf.** From Field of Interest to Theme to Object **2001. The course is conceived to help the students identify and develop their own design focuses.** The Way from the Object to Public Presentation **2001. Preparatory work on the content, concept and organisation of the Product Design School's exhibition project.** Political Jewellery **2001. Development of political statements and their implementation and consolidation in wearable symbols.**

raditionally Female Crafts and Jewellery **2000/01**
Students Dorothee Bach, Alin Boyaciyan, Birgit Bußler, Bettina Bubel, Eva Dufhues, Astrid Eckert, Sigrid Eickhoff, Gisa Elmer, Isabelle Falzarano, Eva Frisch, Melanie Halbauer, Claudia Halder, Danuta Herzog, Karen Hüttner, Karen Kathmann, Anne Kessler, Stefanie Klein, Mira Leithe, Ingrid Micheel, Elke Munkert, Martina Schmitt, Julia Stotz, Heike Tries, Andrea Wagner, Christiane Wink, Nina Wöhlke. **Spinning, weaving, braiding, knotting, knitting, embroidery and also pottery are all crafts that have been traditionally carried out by women. They can be seen as prototypic forms of artistic design. The objective of this course was to arrive at new expressions in jewellery through examination of and experiments with these female crafts. At the regular group meetings the focus was on the potential of these activities to stimulate the unconscious and the impressions they have made on our language in the form of metaphors. This activity then led to the development of individual approaches and design concepts.**

ormulations **2000/01**
Students Astrid Eckert, Eva Frisch, Pauline Grootekamp, Claudia Hoppe, Simone Nolden, Bettina Kratz, Simon Wenz. **This course was designed as a continuation for the students who had participated in the course *From the Shadow into the Light* and the short project *From a Field of Interest to a Theme*. Starting from a selected theme the objective was to conceive, design and realise a larger group of jewellery pieces or objects linked by related thematic content.**

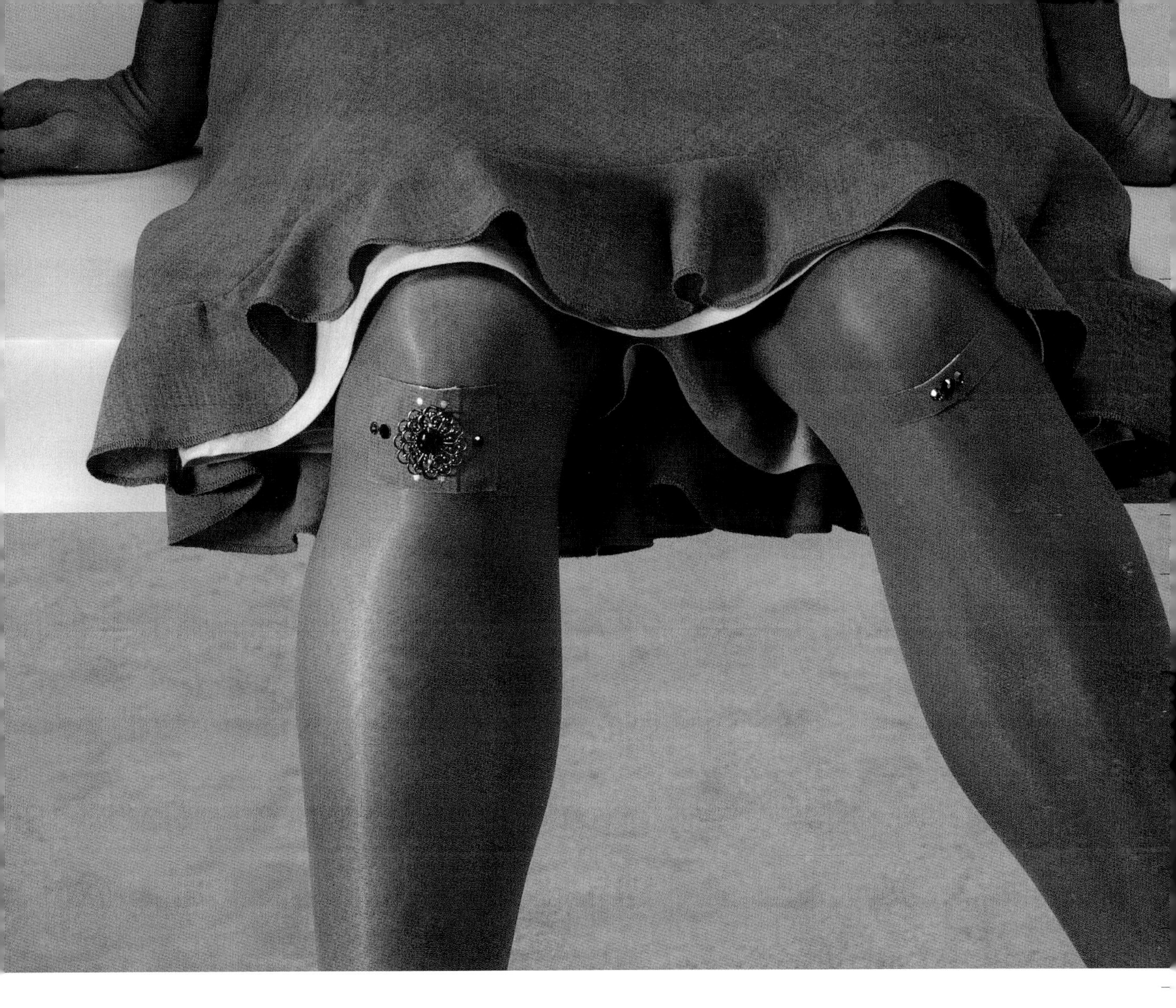

Einzelbesprechung
für die Bearbeitung individuell formulierter Themen
Individual Tutorials
1999

Thema ging es um die Erarbeitung der Konzeption, Gestaltung und Realisation einer größeren inhaltlich zusammengehörigen Gruppe von Schmuckstücken oder Objekten.

Körpergeschichten 2000/01
Studierende **Anne-Sybille Bierbach, Nicola Brand, Eva Dufhues, Melanie Halbauer, Nicole Hanselle, Christiane Wink.** Der Kurs wurde durchgeführt in Anlehnung an den von der Körber-Stiftung ausgeschriebenen Forschungswettbewerb *Bodycheck*, und richtete sich insbesondere an die Studierenden, die sich über vorangegangene Kurse bereits mit dem Thema auseinandergesetzt hatten. In diesem Kurs ging es immer wieder um das Spannungsfeld zwischen dem Körper als formbares Objekt und den unmittelbaren Erfahrungen im ‚Körperselbst'. Durch verschiedenste Inszenierungen konnten diese Pole von unmittelbarem Erfahren und Distanz erfahrbar gemacht werden. Daraus entwickelten sich individuelle Ansätze und Umsetzungen, die als Wettbewerbsbeitrag gebündelt und dokumentiert wurden.

Simone Nolden
Wundschmuckverbände –
Wundschnellschmuck –
Schmuckschnellverbände
Schmuckpflaster
verschiedene Halbzeuge, Strasssteine, Wachsperlen, Glasperlen, Heftpflaster, Silber
Wound Ornament Dressings –
Quick Wound Ornaments –
Ornamental Quick Dressings
ornamental plasters
various semi-finished materials, rhinestones, wax beads, glass beads, sticking plaster, silver

Aus dem Schatten ans Licht 2000
Studierende **Dorothee Bach, Astrid Eckert, Elgin Fischer, Eva Frisch, Danuta Herzog, Claudia Hoppe, Youn Jin Yo, Bettina Kratz, Uschi Magera, Simon Wenz.** Manche unserer Fähigkeiten können sich nicht entfalten sondern führen ein Schattendasein, weil wir sie nicht erkennen oder ihnen mit ablehnender Einstellung gegenüberstehen. Die KursTeilnehmerInnen waren aufgefordert, ihre bisherigen gestalterischen Äußerungen auf entsprechende Urteile und Vorurteile hin zu überprüfen und neu zu bewerten. Das Lieblingsvorurteil oder der Gegenstand der vehementesten Ablehnung wurde zum Ausgangspunkt der Auseinandersetzung genommen und führte zu einer Begegnung mit dem Schattenaspekt. Dieser erwies sich als Dreh- und Angelpunkt der weiteren gestalterischen Arbeit. Die Begegnung mit dem Schatten und die Entdeckung des darin verborgenen positiven Aspektes führte zu einer lustvollen, den kreativen Horizont erweiternden Annahme.

Grenz-Phänomene von Schmuck 2000
Studierende **Anne-Sybille Bierbach, Nicola Brand, Eva Dufhues, Sigrid Eickhoff, Melanie Halbauer, Anne Kessler, Susanne Mayer, Ingrid Micheel, Christiane Wink.** Dieser Kurs bot eine Vertiefung der Beschäftigung mit Grenz-Phänomenen des Sich-Schmückens wie Tätowierung, Piercing usw. Dabei ging es zunächst um die theoretische Auseinandersetzung mit diesen Phänomenen und ihren möglichen Bedeutungen, wobei der Beschäftigung mit Identität

Body Stories **2000/01**
Students Anne-Sybille Bierbach, Nicola Brand, Eva Dufhues, Melanie Halbauer, Nicole Hanselle, Christiane Wink.
This course was a response to the research competition *Bodycheck* staged by the Körber Foundation, and was designed primarily for the students who had already dealt with aspects of the subject in previous courses.
One of the recurrent themes of this course was the tension between the body as a malleable object and one's direct subjective experience in the body itself. A wide range of situations were created to provide an experience of these poles of direct experience and distance. This, in turn, led to the development of individual approaches and implementations that were grouped together and documented as a competition entry.

From the Shadow into the Light **2000**
Students Dorothee Bach, Astrid Eckert, Elgin Fischer, Eva Frisch, Danuta Herzog, Claudia Hoppe, Youn Jin Yo, Bettina Kratz, Uschi Magera, Simon Wenz. **Some of our abilities are unable to develop, leading a shadowy existence, because we reject them or fail to recognise them. The course participants were asked to examine their past artistic work and seek out and re-evaluate judgements and prejudices. The favourite prejudice or object of most vehement rejection was then taken as the starting-point for a development that lead to a confrontation with the shadow principle, which was found to be pivotal for the students' subsequent artistic work. The encounter with the shadow and the discovery of the positive aspect hidden within it led to a pleasurable acceptance that broadened the creative horizons.**

Borderline Phenomena in Personal Adornment **2000**
Students Anne-Sybille Bierbach, Nicola Brand, Eva Dufhues, Sigrid Eickhoff, Melanie Halbauer, Anne Kessler, Susanne Mayer, Ingrid Micheel, Christiane Wink. **This course provided a more in-depth treatment of borderline phenomena in the realm of personal adornment such as tattooing, piercing etc. It started with a theoretical examination of the phenomena and their possible interpretations, placing a strong emphasis on the question of identity. This extensive reflective section was then followed by the systematic development from theoretical analysis to practical concept.**

Characters as Mediums for Meaning between Ornament and Writing **2000**
Students Gisa Elmer, Isabelle Falzerano, Britta Göllner, Mira Leithe, Judith Sommer, Sonja Thiemann, Simon Wenz.

ein großes Gewicht zukam. Im Anschluß an diesen ausführlichen reflektorischen Teil ging es dann um die Entwicklungsschritte von der theoretischen Auseinandersetzung hin zur Konzeption.

Einzelbesprechung für die Bearbeitung individuell formulierter Themen **Individual Tutorials** 1996

Zeichen als Bedeutungsträger zwischen Ornament und Schrift 2000
Studierende **Gisa Elmer, Isabelle Falzerano, Britta Göllner, Mira Leithe, Judith Sommer, Sonja Thiemann, Simon Wenz.** Ausgangspunkt bildeten jahrtausendealte an der Nahtstelle von Ornament und Schrift stehende Zeichen, deren Bedeutung uns unbekannt ist oder bestenfalls vermutet werden kann. Gemeinsame Experimente mit den Ausdrucksmöglichkeiten solcher Zeichen dienten dem Versuch einer Annäherung an die möglichen bezeichnenden Bedeutungsgehalte und das den Zeichen innewohnende Potential in Richtung Ornament und in Richtung Schrift. Schließlich wurden die grundlegenden Bedeutungen der *Sprache* dieser Zeichen auch für Schmuck erkundet und daran anknüpfend Gestaltungskonzepte entwickelt.

Geschmückte Haut 1999/2000
Studierende **Nicola Brand, Kirsten Grünebaum, Ariane Hartmann, Anne Kessler, Nicole Langen, Julia Müllers, Gülten Tapan, Nicole Unterseh, Christiane Wink.** Nachdem das Ohrloch lange Zeit die einzige akzeptierte Form des Piercings war und Tätowierungen hauptsächlich bei Seefahrern und gesellschaftlichen Randgruppen vorkamen, haben Tätowierungen und Piercings heute Kultstatus. Der Kurs bot den Rahmen für die Auseinandersetzung mit diesen und anderen hautnahen Phänomenen des Sich-Schmückens, aus dem heraus ein eigenes Schmuckkonzept entwickelt wurde. Die Ergebnisse konnten auf Einladung in der Ausstellung *Kunst hautnah* im Wiener Künstlerhaus gezeigt werden.

Er-Findungen oder Nützliches für den Alltag 1999/2000
Studierende **Susanne Augenstein, Dorothee Bach, Kerstin Biesdorf, Astrid Eckert Babette Egerland, Eva Dufhues, Claudia Halder, Anja Heinemeyer, Stefanie Klein, Heike Köhler, Maren Krämer, Susanne Mayer, Ingrid Micheel, Catherine Niegel, Uta Oeding-Erdel, Meike Peters, Martina Schmitt.** Kleine, sich im alltäglichen Tun störend oder als Irritation bemerkbar machende Probleme waren Anlass und Anreiz für eigene Erfindungen. Aus einer Vielzahl solcher vorher identifizierter und gesammelter Probleme wurden gemeinsam mehrere Themen abgeleitet, die dann von kleinen Teams bearbeitet wurden. Entwickelt wurden ein Müllsammelbehältnis für das Auto, ein Orientierungssystem für die Handtasche, veränderbare Vasen, Halterungen für die Lesebrille und eine variabel einsetzbare Transportkiste für das Fahrrad.

The starting-point for this course were millennia-old characters on the borderline between ornament and writing, whose meaning is either completely unknown to us or can only be guessed at. Joint experiments were carried out to investigate the potential of such characters for expression and find an approach to their possible *characteristic* meaning, along with the characters' innate ornamental potential and moving towards the function of writing. Finally the basic meaning of the *language* of these characters for jewellery was also investigated and this was followed by the development of design concepts.

Uli Biskup
leicht und groß
Schale
Wellpappe
Light and Large
bowl
corrugated cardboard

Decorated Skin **1999/2000**
Students Nicola Brand, Kirsten Grünebaum, Ariane Hartmann, Anne Kessler, Nicole Langen, Julia Müllers, Gülten Tapan, Nicole Unterseh, Christiane Wink. **For many years earrings were the only acceptable form of piercing, and the use of tattoos was restricted mainly to sailors and groups on the fringes of society. Today piercing and tattoos have acquired a cult status. The course offered a framework for an investigation of these and other types of body decorations, on the basis of which a personal jewellery concept was developed. The results of this course were shown by invitation at the Künstlerhaus in Vienna, in an exhibition titled *Kunst hautnah* (Art Close to the Skin).**

Inventions or Useful Items for Everyday Life **1999/2000**
Students Susanne Augenstein, Dorothee Bach, Kerstin Biesdorf, Astrid Eckert Babette Egerland, Eva Dufhues, Claudia Halder, Anja Heinemeyer, Stefanie Klein, Heike Köhler, Maren Krämer, Susanne Mayer, Ingrid Micheel, Catherine Niegel, Uta Oeding-Erdel, Meike Peters, Martina Schmitt. **Small problems experienced as annoyances or irritations in everyday life provided the inspiration and motivation for a series of personal inventions. A large number of such problems were identified and collected and then several crystallised themes were developed by small teams. The resulting inventions included a rubbish container for use in cars, an organisation system for women's handbags, variable vases, holders for reading glasses and a variable transport box for bicycles.**

From Object to Symbol/Cipher to Object **1999/2000**
Students Britta Göllner, Ina Leppin, Sylvia Kleine-Börger, Susanne Mayer. **This course was part of a two-term project with supplementary activities designed to provide insight into the genesis of culture and art. The brief was to select an object with a high level of individual significance and then find a symbolic expression for it**

Vom Gegenstand zum Symbol/Zeichen zum Objekt
From Object to Symbol/Cipher to Object
1999/2000

Vom Gegenstand zum Symbol/Zeichen zum Objekt 1999/2000
Studierende **Britta Göllner, Ina Leppin, Sylvia Kleine-Börger, Susanne Mayer.** Dieser Kurs war Teil eines über zwei Semester angelegten Projektes mit sich ergänzenden Angeboten, die Einblick gaben in die Entstehung von Kultur und Kunst. Für einen gewählten Gegenstand mit hoher individueller Signifikanz sollte ein zeichenhafter Ausdruck gefunden werden, der die Bedeutsamkeit dieses Gegenstandes symbolisierte. Anschließend wurde dann versucht, den gefundenen zeichenhaften Ausdruck wieder objekthaft umzusetzen.

tot 1998/99. Leben und Sterben berühren sich im Erschrecken angesichts von Tod. Der Unfalltod von Birgit Straube, Studentin des Studiengangs Produktdesign und Diplomandin, war Anlass für das fach- und semesterübergreifende Projekt *tot* mit einer für alle gemeinsamen Vortrags- und Veranstaltungsreihe. Für die TeilnehmerInnen dieses Kurses lautete die Frage: Können Berührungsmomente von Leben und Sterben über den Umgang mit Material ausgedrückt werden und gibt es die Möglichkeit einer objekthaften Umsetzung?

Schmuck für dich 1998/99
Studierende **Sigrid Eickhoff, Regina Freistadt, Verena Gosebrink, Melanie Halbauer, Sylvia Kleine-Börger, Silke Lazarevic, Nicole Unterseh.** Es wird in der zeitgenössischen Schmuckszene wenig geübt, ein Schmuckstück für eine bestimmte Person zu machen und diese Person in den Mittelpunkt zu stellen. Dies war Anlass für die Themenstellung und Konzeption dieses Projektes, das den Studierenden Raum bot, sich bei der Entwicklung des Schmuckstücks auf die jeweilige Empfängerin oder den jeweiligen Empfänger einzulassen. Die fertigen Arbeiten waren das Ergebnis des inneren oder äußeren Dialogs mit der gewählten Person.

Stationen auf dem gestalterischen Weg 1998. Die periodisch geforderten gestalterischen Umsetzungen werden in der Betrachtung zum Gegenüber. Die Konfrontation damit macht den kreativen Prozess bewusst und die reflexive Auseinandersetzung möglich.

Perlen-Schätze, Hommage an eine Schenkung 1997, 1997/98
Studierende **Melanie Backes, Ariane Hartmann, Anja Heinemeyer, Katja Kempe, Ina Leppin, Anne Mersmann, Gülten Özdemir, Stefanie von Scheven, Barbara Schwab, Ulrike Scheer, Heike Tries, Nicole Unterseh, Susanne Winckler, Anke Wolf.** Dieser Kurs schloss sich an ein im Sommersemester 1997 durchgeführtes interdisziplinäres

Britta Göllner
Objekte
Silber, Kupfer, Wolle, Email, Glasperlen
objects
silver, copper, wool, enamel, glass beads

Streben. Von dunkelgrobem Dickicht über feine, lichte Klarheit hin zu etwas Neuem.
Striving. From darkly coarse thicket through fine, light clarity to something new.

encompassing and communicating the object's importance. The final step was then to take the developed symbolic expression and turn it back into an object.

Dead **1998/99. Meeting of living and dying in the shock at the confrontation with death. The accidental death of Birgit Straube, final-year student at the School of Product Design, gave the impetus for the interdisciplinary, multi-term project *Dead* with a programme of lectures and events open to everyone. The following question was posed to the course participants: "Can moments of meeting between living and dying be expressed through work with material, and is objective embodiment of this possible?"**

Jewellery for You **1998/99**
Students Sigrid Eickhoff, Regina Freistadt, Verena Gosebrink, Melanie Halbauer, Sylvia Kleine-Börger, Silke Lazarevic, Nicole Unterseh. **Making a piece of jewellery for someone else, placing the entire focus on this one individual, is something that is not generally practised all that much. The theme and concept of this project were a response to the observation that this is a common omission in the contemporary jewellery scene. It gave the students the space required to concentrate on the recipient for whom they were developing the piece of jewellery. The completed works were the result of the students' internal or actual dialog with the selected person.**

Milestones on the Designer's Path **1998. Objective examination of the designs that the students are required to translate into physical projects at regular intervals. This confrontation with the objective, physical embodiments of their work increases awareness for the creative process, enabling a reflective investigation.**

Bead Treasures, Homage to a Bequest **1997, 1997/98**
Students Melanie Backes, Ariane Hartmann, Anja Heinemeyer, Katja Kempe, Ina Leppin, Anne Mersmann, Gülten Özdemir, Stefanie von Scheven, Barbara Schwab, Ulrike Scheer, Heike Tries, Nicole Unterseh, Susanne Winckler, Anke Wolf. **This course built on an interdisciplinary project completed in the summer term of 1997 titled *Homage to a Bequest – Beads by the Ton*. The project focused on the special origin and the bequest of the beads, how they were transported to the university and the theme of beads' potential as primeval symbols of decoration and instruments of design. The subsequent course held during the winter term then developed and elaborated the findings gained during the previous term. Works based on the bequest were shown to the public in two weekend**

Projekt an mit dem Thema *Hommage an eine Schenkung – tonnenweise Perlen*. Dabei war es um die besondere Herkunft und Schenkung der Perlen gegangen, ihren Transport bis zur Fachhochschule, sowie um eine Annäherung an das Potential der Perle als Ursymbol des Schmückens und Mittel der Gestaltung. In dem sich anschließenden Kurs im Wintersemester ging es um eine Weiterentwicklung und Ausarbeitung der im vorigen Semester gewonnenen Ansätze. Unter dem Titel *Perlenflut* wurden die Arbeiten aus dem Fundus der Schenkung bei zwei Wochenendaktionen in Nimwegen und Ahaus in die Öffentlichkeit gebracht. Der Druck einer Dokumentation sowie Ausstellungen im Glasmuseum in Wertheim und im Museum für Glaskunst in Lauscha beschlossen das Projekt.

Vom Raum zur Fläche zum Körper 1996/97. Schmuckkonzeptionen auf der Grundlage der Erfahrungen und Erkenntnisse individuell-definierter Raumsituationen und -gegebenheiten und ihrer Überführung in Fläche und Körper. **Generalprobe** 1995/96. Bearbeitung eines selbst gewählten Themas nach den Regeln einer Diplomarbeit. **Widmung und/oder Vermarkung** 1995. In Zusammenarbeit mit Karin R'hila. Schmuckgestaltung im Spannungsfeld von inhaltlichen Aussagen und ökonomischen Überlegungen. **Zurückblickend ein Ziel ins Auge fassen** 1994/95. In Zusammenarbeit mit Karin R'hila. Die Verwirklichung eigener Entwürfe und die Entwicklung der dafür angemessenen Strategien für ihre Veröffentlichung. **Weg von der Abstraktion, hin zur direkten Erfahrung** 1994/95. Über Experimente und Übungen zu einem neuen Zugang zu den geometrischen Grundformen Quadrat, Kreis, Dreieck und den damit in Beziehung stehenden Liniengefügen und Körpern finden. **Schmuckbestimmungen** 1994. Schmuckkonzeptionen abgeleitet von dem Wechselspiel zwischen Schmuckstück und Schmuckträgerin. **Das kann ich nicht, das liegt mir nicht, das ist nicht meins – oder doch?** 1994. Ein Kurs zur persönlichen Auseinandersetzung mit und Neubewertung von negativ besetzten gestalterischen Positionen. **Schmuck für Hand, Hals und Ohr** 1993/94. Gestaltung eines dreiteiligen Schmuckensembles für den Christian-Bauer-Wettbewerb 1994. **Vorsicht Schmuck** 1993/94. Konzeption und Realisation einer Schmucksonderschau auf einer Fachmesse für gestalterische Tätigkeiten in Freizeit und Beruf. **Nur ein Stein** 1993. Die Betonung der thematischen Aussage und ihre Formulierung als Feststellung, Frage oder Ausruf war bestimmend für die individuelle Schmuckkonzeption. **Fokus** 1993. Schmuckkonzeptionen abgeleitet aus dem Fundus eigener Fotografien. **Der rote Faden** 1993. Fortführung der Ideen und Ansätze aus dem Kurs *Schmuckskizzen*. **Ringe** 1992/93. Gestaltung von Ringen einer bestimmten Gattung, wie z.B. Freundschaftsring, Siegelring, Trauerring usw. **Schmuckskizzen** 1992/93. Übungen und Improvisationen zur Entwicklung von Schmuckideen.

presentations in Nimwegen and Ahaus under the title *Inundation of Beads*. The project was rounded off with the publication of a printed documentation and exhibitions at the Glass Museum in Wertheim and the Museum of Glass Art in Lauscha.

Elgin Fischer
Burgenringe
Ringe
Silber, Email, Zuchtperlen, Feinsilber
Castle Rings
rings
silver, enamel, cultured pearls, refined silver

From Space to Surface to Body **1996/97. Jewellery concepts on the basis of experience of and insights into individually defined space situations and conditions and their translation to surface and body.** Dress Rehearsal **1995/96. Work on a theme chosen by the student subject to the requirements for a degree thesis.** Dedication and/or Marketing **1995. In collaboration with Karin R'hila. Jewellery design in the tension between artistic content and economic considerations.** Looking Back, Focusing on an Objective **1994/95. In cooperation with Karin R'hila. Realisation of the students' own designs and development of suitable strategies for their publication.** Away from Abstraction and Towards Direct Experience **1994/95. Experiments and excercises to find a new access to the basic geometric forms – square, circle and triangle – and the complexes of lines and bodies related to them.** Jewellery Objectives **1994. Jewellery concepts drawn from the interaction between the jewellery and its wearer.** "I can't do that, I'm not good at it, it's not my forte – or is it?" **1994. A course providing an opportunity for a personal investigation and re-evaluation of negative design stances and assumptions.** Jewellery for Hand, Neck and Ear **1993/94. Design of a three-piece jewellery set for the 1994 Christian Bauer Competition.** Caution, Jewellery **1993/94. Design and production of a special jewellery exhibition for presentation at a trade fair for hobby and professional design work.** Just One Stone **1993. Development of an individual jewellery concept with an emphasis on the course theme, interpreted as a statement, question or exclamation.** Focus **1993. Jewellery concepts drawing on a collection of own photographs.** The Leitmotif **1993. Continuation of the initial ideas and proposals developed in the Jewellery Sketches course.** Rings **1992/93. Design of special types of rings, such as a friendship ring, a seal ring, a mourning ring etc.** Jewellery Sketches **1992/93. Exercises and improvisation for the development of jewellery ideas.**

Elgin Fischer
Prinzessin auf der Erbse
Ringe
Silber, Email, Zuchtperlen, Feinsilber
Princess on a Pea
rings
silver, enamel, cultured pearls, refined silver

Ornament and Form **1992**
Students Michael Boy, Petra Borgmann, Martina Czunczeleit, Anuka Eichbaum, Pia Iavaroni, Malte Meinck, Christiane Schneider. **This course provided an alternative to the contemporary understanding of ornament as decoration or a decorative motif. Ornament was not originally a superfluous accessory or addition, but rather a way of identifying and giving symbolic expression to holistic aspects of reality. Ornament can thus also be understood as the**

Ausformulierung
Formulations
2000/01

Ornament und Form 1992
Studierende **Michael Boy, Petra Borgmann, Martina Czunczeleit, Anuka Eichbaum, Pia Iavaroni, Malte Meinck, Christiane Schneider.** Der heute gängigen Definition von Ornament als Verzierung oder Verzierungsmotiv wurde eine andere Auffassung gegenübergestellt. Ornament war ursprünglich nicht Aufsatz oder entbehrliche Zutat, sondern Möglichkeit, Aspekte der Welt in ihrer Ganzheit zu erkennen und symbolhaft darzustellen. Damit ist Ornament auch eine bestimmten Gesetzmäßigkeiten folgende, sichtbar gemachte Ordnung. Im Kurs wurden die Möglichkeiten ausgelotet, die den Gestaltern heute im Umgang mit Ornament offenstehen und daraus individuelle Ansätze und Konzepte entwickelt. Aus den Entwicklungsreihen gewonnene Erkenntnisse wurden dann auf konkret fassbare Gegenstände angewandt.

Kursthemen von Prof. Herman Hermsen

Einzelbesprechungen für die Bearbeitung individuell formulierter Themen
Dieser Kurs findet jedes Semester statt und hat zum Ziel, die Schwerpunktbildung im Studium zu fördern und zu unterstützen. Es wird großen Wert darauf gelegt, dass die Studierenden ihre Interessensbereiche selbst benennen und daraus das zu erforschende und zu erarbeitende Thema selbst ableiten und formulieren. Dieses Angebot kann entweder zur Vertiefung von erarbeiteten Inhalten aus vorherigen Lehrveranstaltungen genutzt werden oder für die Erarbeitung komplett neu formulierter Themen. In beiden Fällen kann es um Entwicklungen gehen, die sich am Unikat orientieren, oder sie können auf eine Auseinandersetzung mit der Serienthematik zielen.

Für *inpetto* 2001/02. Gestaltung von Schmuck für die Kollektion von *inpetto* zur Präsentation auf der Inhorgenta 2002 in München. **Eine Ausstellung an vier Orten** 2001/02. Gestaltung der Ausstellungsarchitektur für die Ausstellung des Studiengangs Produktdesign in den Jahren 2002 und 2003.

Intensivprojekt 2001
Studierende **Susanne Augenstein, Isabel Falzarano, Elgin Fischer, Annette Flach, Tanja Hartmann, Claudia Hoppe, Jan-Marc Kutscher, Julia Müllers, Andrea Wagner, Simon Wenz.** Die Themen für zwei von der Galerie V&V und der Galerie RA geplante Ausstellungen wurden den Teilnehmerinnen und Teilnehmern dieses zweiwöchigen Intensiv-

visual expression of an underlying order that follows certain fundamental principles. The course examined the options available to modern designers, moving from there to the development of individual approaches and concepts. The findings of the development processes were then applied to concretely comprehensible objects.

Courses offered by Prof. Herman Hermsen

Individual Tutorials
This course is offered every term. Its goal is to support and promote the development of a focus for each student's course of study. Every effort is made to encourage the students to specify their own special areas of interest, and then to clarify and formulate the subject they wish to study and develop on the basis of these interests. The tutorials can be used either to go deeper into subjects covered in previous courses or for the development of completely new themes. In both cases the work can focus on the development of either one-off pieces or an examination of serialisation themes.

inpetto **2001/02. Design of jewellery for the *inpetto* collection for exhibition at the Inhorgenta 2002 in Munich.**
An Exhibition in Four Locations **2001/02. Design of the architecture for the exhibition of the product design school for 2002 and 2003.**

Intensive Project **2001**
Students Susanne Augenstein, Isabel Falzarano, Elgin Fischer, Annette Flach, Tanja Hartmann, Claudia Hoppe, Jan-Marc Kutscher, Julia Müllers, Andrea Wagner, Simon Wenz. **The participants in this two-week intensive project could choose their subjects from the themes of two exhibitions planned by Galerie V&V and Galerie RA. The third option was a free choice of subject by the students themselves. Over the two weeks the following themes were developed by the students, working in teams of between two and four: Development of alternatives to the standard name badges for company staff members, symposium participants, exhibitors at trade fairs and exhibitions etc. Masks as hand jewellery. Storage containers that can be hoisted up to the ceiling.**

Simone Nolden
Das Händchen das die Mutter schlägt, das wird im Himmel abgesägt
Halsschmuck
Silber, Puppenärmchen,
Perlen, Fotoätzung, Email, Schiefer,
Schmetterlinge
The little hand that strikes Mother will be sawn off in Heaven
neck ornament
silver, doll arm, beads,
photo engraving, enamel, slate,
butterflies

Kindheit ist kein Kinderspiel.
Childhood is no child's play.

projektes zur Wahl gestellt. Das dritte Thema war ein von den StudentInnen frei gewähltes Thema. Die in dem zweiwöchigen Intensivprojekt in Teams von zwei bis vier Studierenden bearbeiteten Themen waren wie folgt gefasst: die Entwicklung von Alternativen zu den gängigen Namensschildern für Firmenmitarbeiter, Symposionsbesucher, Aussteller auf Messen usw. Masken als Handobjekte. Zur Decke hochziehbare Aufbewahrungsbehälter.

Vier Themen
Dieser Kurs wird regelmäßig für Studierende des Grund- und Hauptstudiums angeboten und dient der Vorbereitung auf komplexere Themen der Schmuck- und Produktgestaltung im Kontext serieller Überlegungen. Der Kurs folgt immer dem hier skizzierten gleichen Grundschema. Es werden vier nacheinander bekannt gegebene Themen bearbeitet, wobei den Studierenden für jedes Thema durchschnittlich zwei Wochen Bearbeitungszeit zur Verfügung stehen. Im Anschluß daran wählen die Studierenden eines der vier Themen zur weiteren Vertiefung und Entwicklung. Am Schluss stehen Modelle oder Prototypen, die aus der konzeptionellen und gestalterischen Auseinandersetzung mit der jeweiligen Funktionsart oder Produktart erwachsen sind.

Aspekte von Serie 2001
Studierende **Dorothee Bach, Alin Boyaciyan, Stanislav Braslavskij, Bettina Bubel, Astrid Eckert, Gisa Elmer, Elgin Fischer, Annette Flach, Eva Frisch, Melanie Halbauer, Tanja Hartmann, Danuta Herzog, Claudia Hoppe, Karen Hüttner, Karen Kathmann, Ingrid Micheel, Catherine Niegel, Meike Peters, Julia Stotz.** Dieser Kurs war ein weiterführendes Angebot für diejenigen Studierenden, die ihre im vorigen Semester erarbeiteten Themen vertiefen und weiterentwickeln wollten. Er war aber auch offen für alle Studierenden, die an einer intensiven Auseinandersetzung mit der Serienthematik interessiert sind und denen an der mit der geplanten Ausstellung verbundenen Praxiserfahrung gelegen ist.

Aspekte von Serie 2000/01
Studierende **Birgit Bußler, Gisa Elmer, Isabel Falzarano, Danuta Herzog, Anne Kessler, Meike Peters, Regina Quaring, Sonja Thiemann.** Ziel dieses Kurses war die Gestaltung von Schmuck oder Produkten (z.B. Geräte oder Gefäße), die von der Idee und deren Entwicklung für die Herstellung in einer kleinen Auflage und einer günstigen Preiskatagorie geeignet sind. Unter dem Titel *Aspekte von Serie II* sollen die Ergebnisse in einer reisenden Ausstellung der Öffentlichkeit präsentiert werden. Ähnlich wie bei dem ersten Ausstellungsprojekt dieser Art wird eine Gruppe von

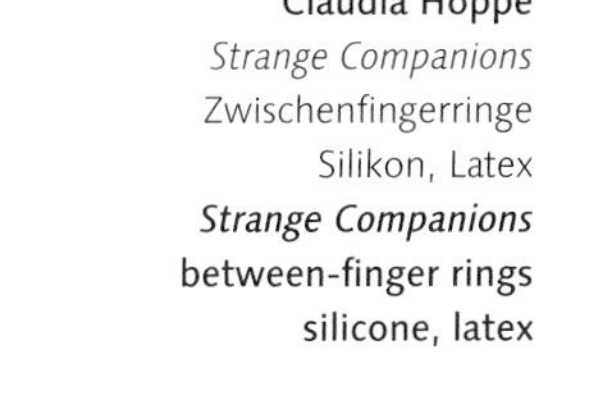

Four Themes
This course, which is offered regularly for the students in the basic and main curricula, serves as preparation for more complex themes of jewellery and product design within a serialised production framework. The course always follows the same basic outline: Four themes are specified by the instructor one after the other, and the students are given an average of two weeks for the development of each theme. After this the students each choose one of the four themes for more in-depth development and exploration. The final result of the course are models or prototypes that are the product of the conceptual and design work on the individual functions or products.

Claudia Hoppe
Strange Companions
Zwischenfingerringe
Silikon, Latex
Strange Companions
between-finger rings
silicone, latex

Aspects of Serialisation **2001**
Students Dorothee Bach, Alin Boyaciyan, Stanislav Braslavskij, Bettina Bubel, Astrid Eckert, Gisa Elmer, Elgin Fischer, Annette Flach, Eva Frisch, Melanie Halbauer, Tanja Hartmann, Danuta Herzog, Claudia Hoppe, Karen Hüttner, Karen Kathmann, Ingrid Micheel, Catherine Niegel, Meike Peters, Julia Stotz. **This course, which was a follow-up to the winter term, was a supplementary option for the students who wanted to develop and deepen the themes they had worked on during the previous term. It was also open for all students interested in a more in-depth treatment of serialised production, and who wanted to profit from the experience that could be gained from participating in the planned exhibition.**

Kleine Wegbegleiter. Immer dabei, machen sie es sich überall bequem, im Knopfloch, zwischen den Fingern oder einfach in der Tasche.
Small companions. Always there, they make themselves comfy everywhere – in the buttonhole, between the fingers or just in a pocket.

Aspects of Serialisation **2000/01**
Students Birgit Bußler, Gisa Elmer, Isabel Falzarano, Danuta Herzog, Anne Kessler, Meike Peters, Regina Quaring, Sonja Thiemann. **The objective of this course was the design of jewellery or products such as appliances or vessels whose concept and development made them suitable for serialised production in small quantities at a reasonable price. The results are to be shown in public in a travelling exhibition titled *Aspects of Serialisation II*. As in the first exhibition project of this type, a group of students will take on responsibility for the entire conception and organisation of the exhibition, including the production of the exhibition catalogue, which will also provide valuable additional experience.**

Intensive Project **1999/2000**
Students Susanne Augenstein, Sybille Bierbach, Kerstin Biesdorf, Nicola Brand, Birgit Bussler, Astrid Eckert, Isabel Falzarano, Elgin Fischer, Verena Gosebrink, Melanie Halbauer, Tanja Hartmann, Katja Kempe, Heike Köhler, Maren

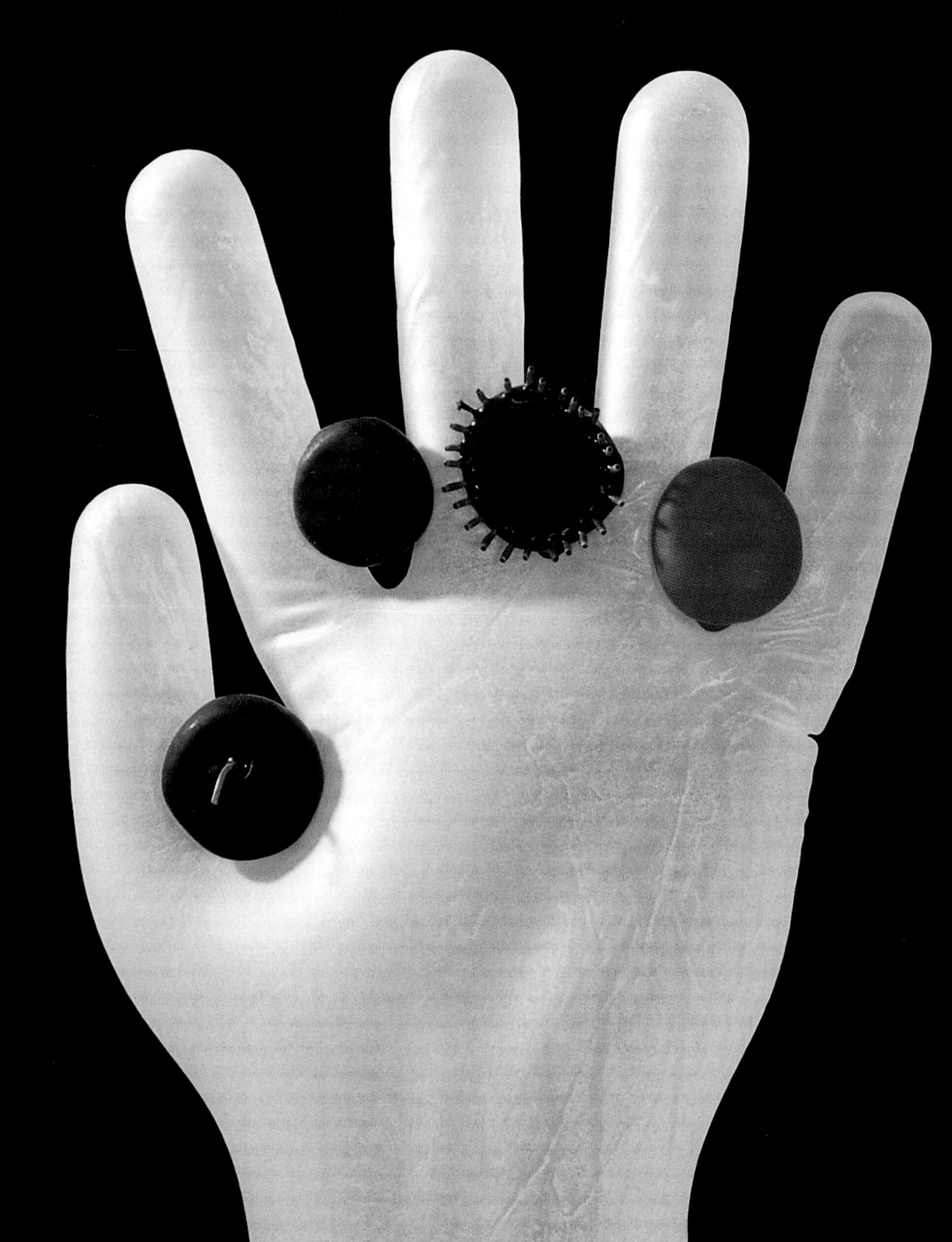

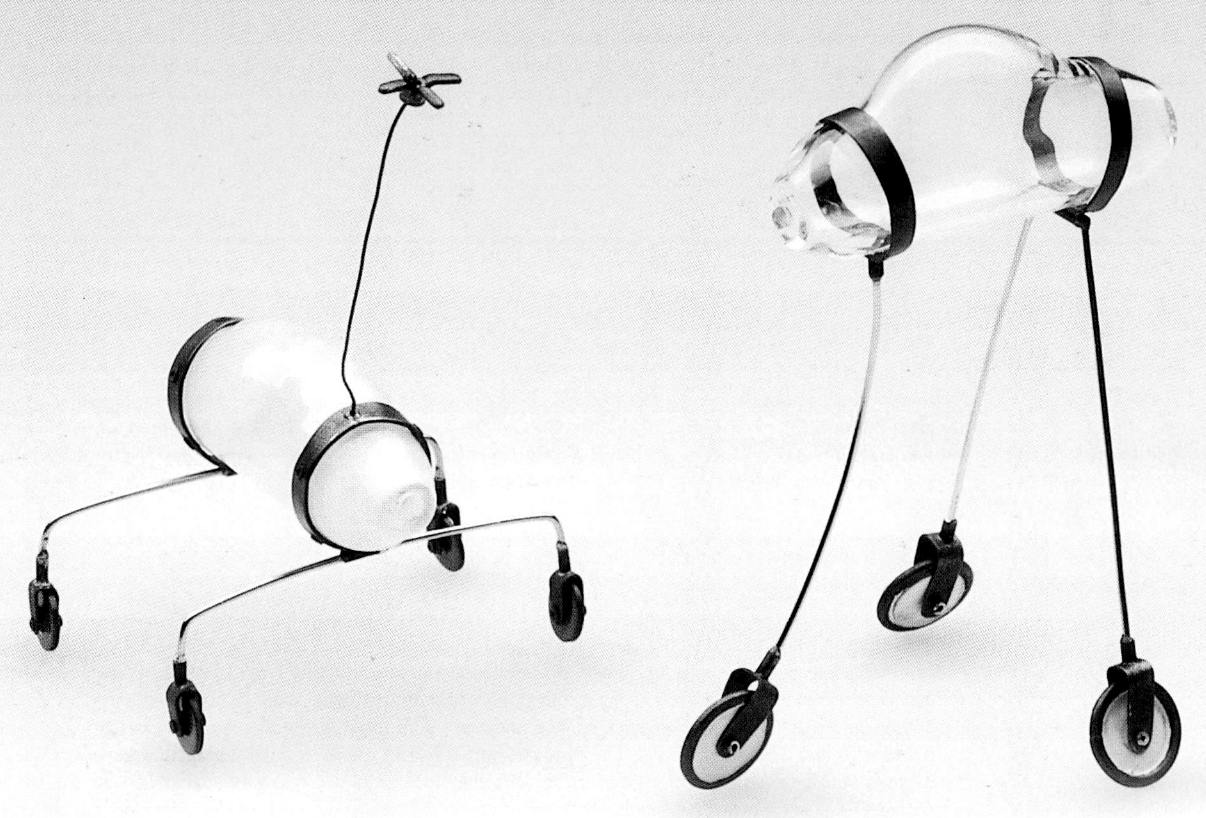

Studierenden mit der Konzeption und Organisation der Ausstellung einschließlich des dafür vorgesehenen Kataloges betraut sein und darüber wichtige Praxiserfahrung sammeln können.

Intensivprojekt 1999/2000
Studierende **Susanne Augenstein, Sybille Bierbach, Kerstin Biesdorf, Nicola Brand, Birgit Bussler, Astrid Eckert, Isabel Falzarano, Elgin Fischer, Verena Gosebrink, Melanie Halbauer, Tanja Hartmann, Katja Kempe, Heike Köhler, Maren Krämer, Jan Marc Kutscher, Nicole Langen, Julia Müllers, Catherine Niegel, Simone Nolden, Regina Quaring, Monica Seitter, Sonja Thiemann, Heike Tries.** Bei diesem zweiwöchigen Intensivprojekt waren die in kleinen Teams zu erarbeitenden Themen vorgegeben. Die erste Woche war vorgesehen für Brainstorming, kritische Reflexion, Ideenfindung, Konzeptformulierung und Entwurf, die zweite Woche war der Realisation der Modelle und Prototypen vorbehalten. Die Aufgabenstellungen – *Schmuck für eine Gala*, *Kronleuchter*, *Liegestuhl* und *Accessoires, ein Set* – waren so formuliert, dass sie extravagante Lösungsvorschläge geradezu herausforderten.

Produkt wie ein Gedicht, Schmuck wie ein Gedicht 1999/2000
Studierende **Birgit Bußler, Sigrid Eickhoff, Gisa Elmer, Elgin Fischer, Kirsten Gronenber, Melanie Halbauer, Stefanie Klein, Heike Köhler, Bettina Kratz, Mira Leithe, Ingrid Micheel, Elke Munkert, Uta Oeding-Erdel, Anja Oelschlegel, Monica Seitter, Judith Sommer, Sonja Thiemann, Anke Wolf.** Ausgangspunkt für diesen Kurs war ein von den Studierenden gewähltes Gedicht, mit dem sie sich indentifizieren und verbunden fühlen konnten. Er zielte auf die Entwicklung von Schmuckstücken oder Gebrauchsgegenständen, die sich dadurch auszeichnen, dass man sich gerne damit umgibt. Über die Auseinandersetzung mit dem Gedicht, die Interpretion der Inhalte und die Einfühlung in die durch das Gedicht vermittelten Stimmungen sollten die Studierenden zu der sie inspirierenden Quelle für eigene Gedanken, Abstrahierungen, Assoziationen und Metaphern finden. Bei der Ideenentwicklung galt es, die vorläufig gezogenen Schlussfolgerungen in einem Prozess der ständigen Reflexion immer wieder neu zu überprüfen. Die Ideen zu konkretisieren, ohne sie jedoch auf zu direkte und plakative Weise umzusetzen und ohne den persönlichen Inhalt und die Poesie zu verlieren, war dabei die große und interessante Herausforderung.

Experimenteller Schmuck aus unedlen Materialien 1999
Studierende **Susanne Augenstein, Sybille Bierbach, Kerstin Biesdorf, Nicola Brand, Birgit Bußler, Eva Dufhues, Sigrid Eickhoff, Elgin Fischer, Tanja Hartmann, Katja Kempe, Stefanie Klein, Maren Krämer, Bettina Kratz, Nicole Langen,**

Bettina Kratz
Objekte
Glas, Flüssigkeiten, Kupfer, Silber
objects
glass, fluids, copper, silver

Von Phantasie beflügelt wagen sie sich in die Welt.
Given wings by fantasy they venture out into the world.

Krämer, Jan Marc Kutscher, Nicole Langen, Julia Müllers, Catherine Niegel, Simone Nolden, Regina Quaring, Monica Seitter, Sonja Thiemann, Heike Tries. **In this two-week intensive project the students developed the defined themes working in small teams. The first week was devoted to brainstorming, critical reflection, searching for ideas, formulation of concepts and drafting the designs. In the second week the models and prototypes were then produced. The descriptions of the themes – *Jewellery for a Gala, Candelabra, Reclining chair and Set of Accessoires* – were consciously formulated to provoke extravagant solutions.**

Jewellery Like a Poem, Product Like a Poem **1999/2000**
Students Birgit Bußler, Sigrid Eickhoff, Gisa Elmer, Elgin Fischer, Kirsten Gronenber, Melanie Halbauer, Stefanie Klein, Heike Köhler, Bettina Kratz, Mira Leithe, Ingrid Micheel, Elke Munkert, Uta Oeding-Erdel, Anja Oelschlegel, Monica Seitter, Judith Sommer, Sonja Thiemann, Anke Wolf. **The starting-point for this course was a poem selected by each student, one that they could identify with and that had a personal significance for them. The objective was to develop jewellery or everyday products the outstanding feature of which was to be that people would enjoy having them around. The idea was that the students should use their work on the poem, interpret its meaning and tune in to the mood it communicated, and then use the results as inspiration for their own thoughts, abstractions, associations and metaphors. They were asked to approach the development of their ideas as a process of continuous reflection, re-examining their initial conclusions again and again. The main and most interesting challenge was to find concrete expression for their ideas while avoiding being too direct and literal, and without losing sight of their personal meaning and the poetry itself.**

Experimental Jewellery Made of Non-precious Materials **1999**
Students Susanne Augenstein, Sybille Bierbach, Kerstin Biesdorf, Nicola Brand, Birgit Bußler, Eva Dufhues, Sigrid Eickhoff, Elgin Fischer, Tanja Hartmann, Katja Kempe, Stefanie Klein, Maren Krämer, Bettina Kratz, Nicole Langen, Catherine Niegel, Uta Oeding-Erdel, Meike Peters, Gülten Tapan, Sonja Thiemann, Christiane Wink. **The goal of this course was to develop unconventional jewellery concepts using non-precious materials. The brief was to formulate the concepts on the basis of an intensive examination of current trends in the fine arts, applied arts or cultural and social phenomena, and then express them in a small group of jewellery pieces. These works could be planned either as one-off pieces or as serialised products. The presentation of the work was planned as an exhibition, for which an adequate number of shop-window dummies were made available.**

Catherine Niegel, Uta Oeding-Erdel, Meike Peters, Gülten Tapan, Sonja Thiemann, Christiane Wink. Dieser Kurs hatte die Zielsetzung, unkonventionelle Schmuckkonzepte auf der Basis von unedlen Materialien zu entwickeln. Die Konzepte sollten nach einer intensiven Auseinandersetzung mit zeitgenössischen Strömungen in der bildenden und der angewandten Kunst oder mit kulturellen und gesellschaftlichen Phänomenen formuliert werden und in einer kleinen Gruppe von Schmuckstücken Ausdruck finden. Die Stücke konnten ebenso als Unikat wie als Serienprodukt konzipiert werden. Für die Präsentation in Form einer Ausstellung wurden den Kursteilnehmerinnen und -teilnehmern eine ausreichende Zahl von Schaufensterpuppen zur Verfügung gestellt.

Produkt wie ein Gedicht, Schmuck wie ein Gedicht
Product Like a Poem, Jewellery Like a Poem
1999/2000

Serienreif 1999. Entwicklung von Schmuck oder Produkt für die serielle Herstellung mit eigenem oder vorgegebenem Thema. **Thema Nummer eins** 1998/99. Schmuck oder Produkt zu einem aktuellen Thema **Nearly famous** 1998/99. Erarbeitung der Ausstellungskonzeption für eine Wanderausstellung. **Maroc – Völkerverständigung durch Design** 1998. *Marokko-Projekt* in Zusammenarbeit mit Herbert Schulze und Petra Weingärtner-Arnold: Entwicklung von Ideen für Gebrauchsgegenstände zur Fertigung durch marokkanische Kunsthandwerker. **Bescheidenheit** 1998. Gestaltung von Schmuck oder Produkten als Verkörperung dieses Begriffs oder als Ausdruck einer diesem Begriff zugrundeliegenden Haltung. **Mein Ding** 1997/98. Ein Angebot zur Definition des eigenen gestalterischen Schwerpunkts. **Eine Imagekampagne für den Blutspendedienst des DRK** 1997. Ein Projekt in Zusammenarbeit mit Herbert Schulze und Prof. Philipp Teufel, Studiengang Kommunikationsdesign. **Eine Lampe von A-Z** 1997. Von der Idee bis zum Prototyp. **Wettbewerbsthemen als Kursthema** 1996/97. In Zusammenarbeit mit Herbert Schulze. *Die Mitte der Tafel,* Gestaltungswettbewerb für Tafelschmuck, Klingenmuseum Solingen und Gesellschaft für Goldschmiedekunst. *Türbeschläge,* Innovationswettbewerb der Firma HEWI Metall. *Handsäge,* Designwettbewerb der Firma Schneider und Klein. **2000+** 1996/97. Schmuckvisionen: wie es sein könnte, sollte oder müßte. **26+4** 1996. Entwicklung einer Schmuckkollektion und Erarbeitung der Ausstellungskonzeption für eine Wanderausstellung. **Hochaktuell** 1995/96. Schmuck zu einem frei gewählten, gegenwartsbezogenen gesellschaftlichen Thema. **Die Kunst der Serie** 1995. Entwurf und Realisation von Serienschmuck in Anbindung an einen Gestaltungswettbewerb. **Für Küche und Tischkultur** 1995. Bearbeitung des Themas eines europäischen Design-Wettbewerbes. **Gut sortiert** 1994/95. Eine Obstschale für bestimmte Früchte. **Eine persönliche Aussage** 1994/95. Schmuck-Gedanken-Ideen-Stücke. **Gestaltung eines Tee- oder Kaffeeservices** 1994/95. In Zusammenarbeit mit Herbert Schulze. **Sechs Themen, ein Produkt** 1994. Ausarbeitung eines Entwurfs aus dem Fundus der zu den gestellten Themen entwickelten Ideen. **Wollte immer schon mal, bin aber noch nie dazu gekommen...**

Monika Seitter
Königskinder
Anhänger
Aluminium, Plüsch, Gummi, Papiercollagen, Folie, Kunststoff
Royal Children
pendants
aluminium, plush, rubber, paper collages, foil, plastic

Seifenopern blubbern ganz modern lieblich schöne Märchen.
Soap operas gabbling oh so modernly sweetly pretty fairy tales.

Ready for Production **1999. Development of jewellery or products for serialised production from an own or pre-set theme.** Theme No. 1 **1998/99. Jewellery or products based on a contemporary theme.** Nearly Famous **1998/99. Development of a concept for a travelling exhibition.** Maroc – International Understanding through Design **1998. *Morocco Project* in collaboration with Herbert Schulze and Petra Weingärtner-Arnold: Development of design concepts for products for production by Moroccan craftspeople. See the *Maroc* chapter for full details.** Modesty **1998. Design of jewellery or products as an embodiment of this concept or an expression.** My Thing **1997/98. An opportunity to define your own design focus.** Image Campaign for the German Red Cross Blood Donor Service **1997. A project in collaboration with Herbert Schulze and Prof. Philipp Teufel, School of Communication Design.** A Lamp from A to Z **1997. From the initial idea to the prototype.** A course based on competition themes **1996/97. In cooperation with Herbert Schulze. *The Centre of the Table,* design competition for table decoration staged by the Solingen Knife Museum and the Goldsmithing Society. *Door Fittings,* innovation competition staged by the HEWI Metall company. *Hand Saws,* design competition staged by the Schneider und Klein company.** 2000+ **1996/97. Jewellery Visions: How it Could, Should or Must Be.** 26+4 **1996. Development of a jewellery collection and a concept for a travelling exhibition.** Highly topical **1995/96. Jewellery based on a freely-selected contemporary social theme.** The Art of Serialisation **1995. Design and production of serialised jewellery for a design competition.** For Kitchen and Table Culture **1995. Work based on the theme of a European design competition.** Well Ordered **1994/95. A Fruit Bowl for Specific Fruits.** A Personal Statement **1994/95. Jewellery-Thoughts-Ideas-Pieces.** Design of a Tea or Coffee Service **1994/95. In cooperation with Herbert Schulze.** Six Themes, One Product **1994. Production of a draft design based on the pool of ideas developed for the set themes.** "I always wanted to but I never got around to it..." **1994. Work on individual themes.** AufSehen (Exciting Vision) **1994. Joint course offered together with Elisabeth Holder and Herbert Schulze covering the staging of the design competition for innovative spectacle frames by the NiGuRa Optik and Mazuchelli Optivnova companies.** The Connecting Link **1993/94. Design of a linked chain on the basis of elementary studies in form.** Aspects of Serialisation **1993/94. Development of serialised jewellery and a concept for a travelling exhibition.** Light Design **1993/94. Development of a project proposal submitted by the AEG company for students of the Schools of Design and Architecture.** Own Choice **1993. Design of a consumer product or utensil selected by the student.** Exemplary **1993. Development of a jewellery collection with a common form or design principle.** Mirrors in Jewellery, Jewellery Mirrored **1992/93. Development of concepts for the use of mirrors and the implementation of the concept of reflection in jewellery.** Serialisation through Repetition **1992/93.**

Ausformulierung
Formulations
2000/01

Astrid Eckert
Ringe
Porzellan
rings
porcelain

es
waren
Zwei
königskinder
die
hatten
so
einander
Lieb
"ach liebster könntest du schwimmen,so schwimm doch herüber zu mir!"
drei kerzlein will ich anzünden und die sollen leuchten zu dir

Produkt wie ein Gedicht, Schmuck wie ein Gedicht
Product Like a Poem, Jewellery Like a Poem
1999/2000

1994. Bearbeitung von eigenen Themen. **AufSehen** 1994. Gemeinsam mit Prof. Elisabeth Holder und Herbert Schulze angebotener Kurs für die Durchführung des Gestaltungswettbewerbs der Fimen NiGuRa Optik und Mazuchelli Optivnova für Produktinnovationen bei Brillenfassungen. **Das bestimmte, bindende Glied** 1993/94. Gestaltung einer gegliederten Kette auf der Grundlage elementarer Formstudien. **Aspekte von Serie** 1993/94. Entwicklung von Serienschmuck und Erarbeitung der Ausstellungskonzeption für eine Wanderausstellung. **Lichtgestaltung** 1993/94. Bearbeitung eines Projektvorschlages der Firma AEG für Studierende der Fachbereiche Design und Architektur. **Nach eigener Wahl** 1993. Gestaltung eines frei gewählten Gebrauchsgegenstandes. **Mustergültig** 1993. Entwicklung einer Schmuckkollektion auf der Basis eines gemeinsamen Form- oder Konstruktionsprinzips. **Spiegel im Schmuck, Schmuck gespiegelt** 1992/93. Entwicklung von Konzepten für die Verwendung von Spiegeln und die Anwendung des Prinzips der Spiegelung im Schmuck. **In Serie durch Wiederholung** 1992/93. Schmuckgestaltung unter Ausschöpfung aller Interpretationsmöglichkeiten des Themas. **Form und Zweck mit Laune** 1992. Redesign oder Neuentwurf eines selbstgewählten Produktes. **Halsschmuck** 1992. Eine Kette aus Gliedern, die eine Geschichte erzählen.

Kursthemen von Herbert Schulze

Rapid Prototyping 2001/02. Ein Projekt in Zusammenarbeit mit Prof. Martin Nachtrodt, Fachbereich Maschinenbau. **Außer Betrieb – oder wenn die Schrift in Urlaub ist** 2001. Kursangebot in Zusammenarbeit mit Prof. Roland Henß, Typografie. Buchstaben als Formvorlagen für freie Arbeiten. **Liturgisches Gerät: Gestaltung einer Mesusa** 2001/02. Das Thema des internationalen Gestaltungswettbewerbs des Spertus Institute of Jewish Studies in Chicago, USA, wurde als Kursthema ausgegeben und bearbeitet. Die Kursreihe *Liturgisches Gerät*, näher beschrieben im gleichnamigen Kapitel, soll in loser Folge fortgesetzt werden. **13. Silbertriennale** 2000/01. Entwurf und Realisation von Gerät und Gefäß zur Beteiligung an der Silbertriennale.

Entwurf und Realisation von Bestecken 1999/2000, 2000
Studierende **Alin Boyaciyan, Annette Flach, Danuta Herzog, Jan Marc Kutscher, Heike Tries.** Die Studierenden sollten sich mit den besonderen Bedingungen von Bestecken auseinandersetzen und auf der Basis dieser Erkenntnisse neue Gestaltungsansätze für Besteck formulieren. Die engere Aufgabenstellung und die Aufteilung von Entwurf und

Claudia Hoppe
Glücksstrudel
Broschen
Geschwärztes Silber, vergoldetes Silber,
Whirl of Happiness
brooches
oxidised silver, gold-plated silver

Jewellery design based on an exhaustive interpretation of the set theme. Cheerful Form and Function **1992. Redesign or new design of a product selected by the student.** Necklace **1992. A chain made of links that tell a story.**

Courses offered by Herbert Schulze

Rapid Prototyping **2001/2002. A project in collaboration with Prof. Martin Nachtrodt, Mechanical Engineering Faculty.** Out of Service, or When Script is on Holiday **2001. In collaboration with Prof. Roland Henß, Typography. Letters as Foundation for Artistic Works.** Liturgical Equipment: Design of a Mezuzah **2001/2002. The theme of the international design competition organised by the Spertus Institute of Jewish Studies in Chicago, USA, was set as the subject of a course. The course series *Liturgical Equipment*, which is described in more detail in the chapter of the same name, is to be continued on an irregular basis.** 13th Silver Triennial **2000/2001. Development of silversmith's work for participation in the Silver Triennial.**

Designing and Producing Cutlery **1999/2000, 2000**
Students Alin Boyaciyan, Annette Flach, Danuta Herzog, Jan Marc Kutscher, Heike Tries. **The students were asked to study and analyse the special features and requirements of cutlery design and to use their findings as the foundation for the formulation of new cutlery design approaches. The restriction of the theme and the division of design and production phases into two semesters also made it possible for the students from the basic curriculum to participate in this course, which was designed as part of the *Grassi Project*.**

Designing and Building Vessels **1999/2000, 2000**
Students Susanne Augenstein, Kerstin Biesdorf, Gisa Elmer, Elgin Fischer, Eva Frisch, Mira Leithe, Elke Munkert, Catherine Niegel, Anja Oelschlegel, Julia Stotz, Simon Wenz. **The brief here was to design dinner table vessels. There were no further specifications as regards theme or design; experiments were expressly encouraged. An additional term was allowed for the professional production of the designs. The results were then the foundation for applications for participation at the *Grassi Fair* in Leipzig.**

Realisation auf zwei Semester erlaubte auch Studierenden des Grundstudiums, sich an diesem als Bestandteil des *Grassi-Projektes* angebotenen Kurs zu beteiligen.

Entwurf und Realisation von Gefäßen 1999/2000, 2000
Studierende **Susanne Augenstein, Kerstin Biesdorf, Gisa Elmer, Elgin Fischer, Eva Frisch, Mira Leithe, Elke Munkert, Catherine Niegel, Anja Oelschlegel, Julia Stotz, Simon Wenz.** Es sollten Gefäße aus dem Umfeld des *Gedeckten Tisches* entwickelt werden. Diese Aufgabe war an keine weiteren Vorgaben hinsichtlich Thema und Material geknüpft, Experimente waren ausdrücklich erwünscht. Für die professionelle Umsetzung der Entwürfe war ein weiteres Semester vorgesehen. Die Ergebnisse waren Grundlage für die Bewerbung zur Teilnahme an der *Grassimesse* in Leipzig.

Liturgisches Gerät: Gestaltung eines Toramantels 1999
Studierende **Sylvia Kleine-Börger, Heike Tries.** Das Thema des internationalen Gestaltungswettbewerbs des Spertus Instiute of Jewish Studies in Chicago, USA, wurde zum Kursthema. Siehe auch das Kapitel *Liturgisches Gerät*.

Das Fest 1999. Konzeption und Planung eines Festes zu einem bestimmten Thema oder die Gestaltung eines Accessoires für ein Fest, z.B. Schmuck oder Tischgerät. **Liturgisches Gerät für einen bestehenden Kirchenraum** 1998, 1998/99. Gestaltungswettbewerb der evangelischen Kirchengemeinde Niestetal bei Kassel. Siehe auch das Kapitel *Liturgisches Gerät*. **Entwurf eines Accessoires aus Silber** 1998. Gestaltungswettbewerb der Firma Deumer.

Maroc – Völkerverständigung durch Design 1998
Studierende **Susanne Augenstein, Kerstin Biesdorf, Nicola Brand, Isabelle Falzerano, Verena Gosebrink, Tanja Hartmann, Anne Kessler, Sylvia Kleine-Börger, Heike Köhler, Maren Krämer, Silke Lazarevic, Uschi Magera, Julia Müllers, Catherine Niegel, Regina Quaring, Ulrike Scheer, Britta Schmicking, Monika Seitter, Sonja Thiemann, Anke Wolf.** *Marokko-Projekt* in Zusammenarbeit mit Prof. Herman Hermsen und Petra Weingärtner-Arnold. Entwicklung von Gestaltungskonzepten für Gerät und Gefäß zur Fertigung durch marokkanische Kunsthandwerker. Ausführliche Projektbeschreibung im gleichnamigen Kapitel.

Gefäßgestaltung 1998. Gestaltung einer Kanne für die Fertigung in Silber. **12. Silbertriennale** 1997/98. Entwicklung und Fertigung von Silberschmiedearbeiten zur Beteiligung an der Silbertriennale. **Schmuckes Gefäß** 1996/97.

Produkt wie ein Gedicht,
Schmuck wie ein Gedicht
Product Like a Poem,
Jewellery Like a Poem
1999/2000

Liturgical Equipment: Design of a Thora Covering **1999**
Students Sylvia Kleine-Börger, Heike Tries. **The theme of the international design competition organised by the *Spertus Institute of Jewish Studies* in Chicago, USA was made the subject of the course. Further details can be found in the *Liturgical Equipment* chapter.**

The Party **1999. Concept and planning for a party with a specific theme, or design of an accessory for a party, such as decoration or tableware.** Liturgical Equipment for an Existing Church Room **1998, 1998/99. Design competition organised by the Protestant Parish of Niestetal near Kassel. Further details can be found in the *Liturgical Equipment* chapter.** Design of a Silver Accessory **1998. Design competition staged by the Deumer company.**

Maroc – International Understanding through Design **1998, 1998/99**
Students Susanne Augenstein, Kerstin Biesdorf, Nicola Brand, Isabelle Falzerano, Verena Gosebrink, Tanja Hartmann, Anne Kessler, Sylvia Kleine-Börger, Heike Köhler, Maren Krämer, Silke Lazarevic, Uschi Magera, Julia Müllers, Catherine Niegel, Regina Quaring, Ulrike Scheer, Britta Schmicking, Monika Seitter, Sonja Thiemann, Anke Wolf. ***Morocco Project* in collaboration with Prof. Herman Hermsen and Petra Weingärtner-Arnold. Development of design concepts for utensils and vessels for production by Moroccan craftspeople. See the *Maroc* chapter for full details.**

Design of Vessels **1998. Design of a Jug for production in silver.** 12th Silver Triennial **1997/98. Development of silversmith's work for participation in the Silver Triennial.** Jewellery/Vessel **1996/97. The concepts inherent in the association sequence *jewellery – ornamental – vessel – ornamental vessel – jewellery/vessel* were used as a starting-point for the design of a wide variety of objects born of the contrasts and contradictions between jewellery/ornaments and vessels.**

Liturgical Equipment **1996/97**
Students Simone Nolden, Sylvia Kleine-Börger, Stefan Schmotz, Katharina Schwabe. **Design competition staged by the Liturgisches Institut Trier (Trier Liturgical Institution). The competition theme was made the subject of a course in which the students were asked to design and produce an item of equipment used in the Catholic liturgy. This competition provided the impetus for the *Liturgical Equipment* course series, which is described in detail in the chapter of the same name.**

Stefanie Klein
Tränen
Kette
Glas
Tears
necklace
glass

Diese Tränen sind schwer.
Sie gründen tief, tief in dir;
Werden tiefer – trittst du hinein
Sie überfließen dich und du gehst
unter. Hab keine Angst; hast du diese
Tränen geweint, sind sie leicht.
These tears weigh heavy.
They root deep, deep within you;
Deepening – and you enter.
They overflow you and you go under.
Have no fear; once have wept them,
they are light, these tears.

Produkt wie ein Gedicht, Schmuck wie ein Gedicht
Product Like a Poem, Jewellery Like a Poem
1999/2000

Die in der Assoziationskette *Schmuck – Gefäß, Schmuckes Gefäß, Schmuckgefäß* liegende Begrifflichkeit ist Ausgangspunkt für die Gestaltung unterschiedlichster Gegenstände aus dem Spannungsfeld zwischen Schmuck und Gefäß.

Liturgisches Gerät 1996/97
Studierende **Simone Nolden, Sylvia Kleine-Börger, Stefan Schmotz, Katharina Schwabe.**
Gestaltungswettbewerb des Liturgischen Instituts Trier. Mit der Aufgabe, ein Gerät aus der katholischen Liturgie zu entwerfen und zu realisieren wurde das Thema des Wettbewerbs zum Kursthema. Dieser Wettbewerb war impulsgebend für die Kursreihe *Liturgisches Gerät*. Diese ist im gleichnamigen Kapitel näher beschrieben.

Einzigartiges 1995/96. Gestaltung von Objekten oder Gerät zu einem selbstgewählten Thema. **Farbmittel Email** 1995. Entwurf und Fertigung von Gerät unter Berücksichtigung einer späteren farblichen Gestaltung durch Email. **Vorlegelöffel** 1993/94. Gestaltung eines Löffels zum Servieren von Speisen mit pastöser oder fester Konsistenz. **Präsente** 1993/94. In Zusammenarbeit mit Prof. Gerhard Meussen, Kommunikationsdesign. Entwicklung von repräsentativen Geschenken und *Giveaways* der FH Düsseldorf. **Bewahrendes** 1993. Gestaltung von Gefäßen zur Umsetzung des Begriffes *Bewahrendes* im konkreten wie im übertragenen Sinne seiner Bedeutung. **Leuchten ohne Elektrizität** 1993. Entwicklung eines elektrizitätsunabhängigen Leuchters für den Innen- oder Außenbereich. **Gestaltung eines Großschachspiels** 1992. In Zusammenarbeit mit Prof. Hans Rothweiler, Plastisches Gestalten. **Gerätgestaltung** 1992. Alles, nur keine Kannen.

Kursthemen von Lehrbeauftragten

Schluss mit dem Papierkrieg, hinein in die Realität 2001/2002. Lehrende **Heike Baschta.** Konzeption und Umsetzung des Messeauftritts von *inpetto* auf der Inhorgenta 2002 in München. **Ortszeit Düsseldorf** 2001/2002. Lehrende **Karin Hoffmann.** Designkonzepte zum Thema Armbanduhr. Entwicklungen für den Firmenpartner M&M in Zusammenarbeit mit *inpetto.* **Formendiebe** 2001. Lehrender **Wolfgang Lieglein.** Vom Plagiat zur Neuinterpretation. ***inpetto*** 2001. Lehrende **Heike Baschta.** Konkretisierung des Konzeptes einer Manufaktur für Schmuck und Produkt. **Zwischenraum** 2000/01. Lehrende **Heike Baschta.** Konzeption einer Manufaktur für Schmuck und Produkt. **Produktdesign** 2000. Lehrender **Paul Schudel.** Ein Gebrauchsgegenstand für den privaten Bereich.

Stefanie Klein
Blut
Kette
Theaterblut, Kunststoff
Blood
necklace
theatre blood, plastic

Von Leben umschlungen.
Entwined in life's embrace.

Unique **1995/96. Design of objects or products with a theme selected by the student.** Enamel for Colour **1995. Design of products including design of the later application of coloured enamel.** Serving Spoon **1993/94. Design of a spoon to serve pasty and solid foods.** Gifts **1993/94. In collaboration with Prof. Gerhard Meussen, Communication Design. Development of representive gifts and give-aways for the Düsseldorf University of Applied Sciences.** Preservation **1993. Design of vessels that embody the term *preservation* in both the concrete and the metaphoric senses.** Lamps without Electricity **1993. Development of a non-electrical lamp for interior or exterior use.** Design of a large-scale chess set **1992. In collaboration with Prof. Hans Rothweiler, Three-dimensional Design.** Design of Utensils **1992. Anything but pots and jugs.**

Courses offered by Guest Lecturers

Out of the Paperwork and Into Reality **2001/2002. Instructor** Heike Baschta. **Conception and implementation of a trade fair presentation for *inpetto* at the Inhorgenta 2002 in Munich.** Local Time Düsseldorf – Design Concepts for Watches **2001/2002. Instructor** Karin Hoffmann. **Developments for M&M Partners in collaboration with *inpetto*.** Design Thieves **2001. Instructor** Wolfgang Lieglein. **From plagiarism to reinterpretation.** inpetto **2001. Instructor** Heike Baschta. **Consolidation of a concept for a jewellery and product workshop.** Interspace **2000/2001. Instructor** Heike Baschta. **Concept for a jewellery and product workshop.** Product Design **2000. Instructor** Paul Schudel. **A consumer product for private use.**

Intent and Purpose – Developing Serialised Jewellery **2000**
Instructor Heike Baschta. **Students** Astrid Eckert, Meike Peters, Dorothee Bach, Sigrid Eickhoff, Susanne Mayer, Melanie Halbauer, Uta Oeding-Erdel, Birgit Gödert, Verena Gosebrink. **Intent stands for the definition of a design standpoint with regard to a personal theme. The question was, "What is jewellery for me?" The final product documents the current answer and the designer's approach to the medium of jewellery. Purpose is expressed in a prototype. It is the development of the Intent under the conditions imposed by serialised production methods. A serialised jewellery product is created for a specific market and the needs of a defined target group, and through this the designer finds his or her relationship to the question of Intent. The objective of the course is to experience the tension between personal intent and imposed purpose. Awareness of the student's personal**

Was es will und was es soll – Entwicklung von Serienschmuck 2000
Lehrende **Heike Baschta.** Studierende **Astrid Eckert, Meike Peters, Dorothee Bach, Sigrid Eickhoff, Susanne Mayer, Melanie Halbauer, Uta Oeding-Erdel, Birgit Gödert, Verena Gosebrink.** Was es will steht für die Definition eines gestalterischen Standpunkts zu einem persönlichen Thema. Die Frage war: „Was ist Schmuck für mich?" Das Endprodukt dokumentiert die derzeitige Antwort und den Anspruch des Gestalters an das Medium *Schmuck*. Was es soll stellt sich dar in einem Prototypen. Er ist die Weiterentwicklung von *was es will* unter den Bedingungen serieller Herstellungsmethoden. Im Hinblick auf einen bestimmten Absatzmarkt und die Bedürfnisse einer speziellen Zielgruppe ist ein Serienschmuck entstanden, in dem sich sein Gestalter durch den Bezug zum *was es will* wiederfindet. Das Ziel des Kurses ist die Erfahrung der Spannung zwischen dem Wollen und dem Sollen. Wichtig ist das Bewusstsein um das eigene gestalterische Spektrum: die Größe des eigenen kreativen Freiraums und die Bereitschaft zu Konzessionen an die Verkäuflichkeit.

Produkt wie ein Gedicht, Schmuck wie ein Gedicht
Product Like a Poem, Jewellery Like a Poem
1999/2000

Männerschmuck 1999/2000
Lehrende **Petra Weingärtner-Arnold.** Studierende **Nicola Brand, Birgit Bußler, Verena Gosebrink, Maren Krämer, Julia Müllers, Meike Peters, Regina Quaring, Sonja Thiemann, Christiane Wink.** Ziel des Männerschmuckprojektes war die Entwicklung einer *Schmuckwelt für Männer* mit einer neuen Material- und Formsprache. Modern. Selbstbewusst. Kulturell. Beflissen. Dynamisch.

Wie aus Eimern gießen 1999. Lehrende **Katja Korsawe.** Arbeiten mit Gusstechniken in Metall, Keramik und Glas.
Das ungleiche Paar 1999. Lehrende **Brigitte Tendahl.** Entwicklung von zwei aufeinander bezogenen Schmuckstücken.
Made of Glass 1998/99. Lehrende **Katja Korsawe.** Glasobjekte aus Pâte de Verre.

Wabi-sabi 1998
Lehrende **Susanne Knapp.** Studierende **Eva Dufhues, Isabelle Falzerano, Verena Gosebrink, Claudia Hoppe, Michaela Huber, Ina Leppin, Regina Quaring, Britta Schmicking, Andrea Wagner, Christiane Wink.** Wabi-sabi kommt aus Japan und ist eine Philosophie der Bescheidenheit. In seiner umfassendsten Ausprägung ist Wabi-sabi eine Form der Lebensführung. Enger gefasst kann es die Schönheit vergänglicher und unvollständiger Dinge, die Schönheit anspruchsloser und schlichter Dinge, aber auch die Schönheit unkonventioneller Dinge bezeichnen. In diesem Kurs waren die Studierenden aufgefordert, ihr Wabi-sabi zu finden, daraus Schmuckkonzepte abzuleiten und

design spectrum is important: the extent of one's own creative scope and the willingness to make concessions in the interest of marketability.

Men's Jewellery **1999/2000**
Instructor Petra Weingärtner-Arnold. **Students** Nicola Brand, Birgit Bußler, Verena Gosebrink, Maren Krämer, Julia Müllers, Meike Peters, Regina Quaring, Sonja Thiemann, Christiane Wink. **The objective of the men's jewellery project was the development of a *male jewellery world* with a new language of material and form. Modern. Self-confident. Cultural. Keen. Dynamic.**

Casting Around **1999. Instructor** Katja Korsawe. **Casting techniques for metal, ceramics and glass.** An Unmatched Pair **1999. Instructor** Brigitte Tendahl. **Development of two related pieces of jewellery.** Made of Glass **1998/99. Instructor** Katja Korsawe. **Glass objects made of pâte de verre.**

Wabi-sabi **1998**
Instructor Susanne Knapp. **Students** Eva Dufhues, Isabelle Falzerano, Verena Gosebrink, Claudia Hoppe, Michaela Huber, Ina Leppin, Regina Quaring, Britta Schmicking, Andrea Wagner, Christiane Wink. **Wabi-sabi is a Japanese term for a philosophy of simplicity and understatement. In its most comprehensive expression wabi-sabi is a lifestyle. More narrowly defined it can mean the beauty of transient and imperfect things, the beauty of unassuming and plain things, but also the beauty of unconventional things. In this course the students were encouraged to find their own wabi-sabi, and to develop and realise jewellery concepts on the basis of it.**

Small Spaces **1998. Instructor** Brigitte Tendahl. **Development of jewellery pieces with a focus on the spatial and three-dimensional aspects.** Maroc – International Understanding through Design **1998, 1998/99. Instructor** Petra Weingärtner-Arnold. ***Morocco Project* in collaboration with Prof. Herman Hermsen and Herbert Schulze. Development of design concepts for jewellery for production by Moroccan craftspeople.** Pawing the Ground Before the House **1997/98. Instructor** Katja Korsawe. **Jewellery with enamel.** Product Design **1997/98. Instructor** Paul Schudel. **A small product for the home.** New Ideas for Cultured Pearls **1997/98. Instructor** Petra Weingärtner-Arnold. **Design competition for jewellery with cultured pearls, staged by the Gellner company in Wiernsheim.** Caution, Fragile **1996/97 Instructor** Brigitte Tendahl. **Jewellery for one or more characters in the**

Elgin Fischer
Gürteltaschen
Nylon, handgewickelte Glasperlen
Belt Bags
nylon, hand-wound glass beads

„Der Fachverkäufer – welchen Berg von Kühle trägt er durch diese Hitze."
"The sales clerk – what a mountain of coolness does he carry through this heat."
Haiku von Bashō, *Haiku, japanische Gedichte*, ins Deutsche übersetzt von Dietrich Krusche, München 1999, S. 72

Produkt wie ein Gedicht, Schmuck wie ein Gedicht
Product Like a Poem, Jewellery Like a Poem
1999/2000

diese umzusetzen. **Kleine Räume** 1998. Lehrende **Brigitte Tendahl.** Entwicklung von Schmuckstücken mit dem Hauptmerkmal der Räumlichkeit bzw. Dreidimensionalität. **Maroc – Völkerverständigung durch Design** 1998, 1998/99. Lehrende **Petra Weingärtner-Arnold** *Marokko-Projekt*: Entwicklung von Schmuckideen zur Fertigung durch marokkanische Kunsthandwerker. Ausführliche Beschreibung im gleichnamigen Kapitel. **Scharren vor dem Haus** 1997/98. Lehrende **Katja Korsawe.** Schmuck mit Email. **Produktdesign** 1997/98. Lehrender **Paul Schudel.** Ein kleines Produkt für den Wohnbereich. **Gestaltungswettbewerb der Firma Gellner, Wiernsheim für Schmuck mit Zuchtperlen** 1997/98. Lehrende **Petra Weingärtner-Arnold.** **Vorsicht zerbrechlich** 1996/97. Lehrende **Brigitte Tendahl.** Schmuck für eine oder mehrere Figuren des Films *Haut – Bas – Fragile* von Jaques Rivette. **Schmuck für die Sinne** 1996, 1996/97. Lehrende **Petra Weingärtner-Arnold.** Entwicklung der Schmuckkonzeptionen zum vorgegebenen Thema bis zur Produktionsreife. Ein semesterübergreifendes Projekt in Zusammenarbeit mit der Firma Niessing, Vreden. **Auf Biegen und Brechen** 1996/97. Lehrende **Elke Hackner.** Von Material- und Bearbeitungsversuchen mit Metall und Email zum Schmuckobjekt. **FrauenPortraits** 1995/96. Lehrende **Karin R'hila.** Ausstellungskonzepte für Museen, Galerien oder Kulturinstitute und erhöhte Marktpräsenz über Editionen und Serien.

Schmuck mit Steinen 1995
Lehrende **Brigitte Tendahl.** Studierende **Petra Brenner, Nicoletta Cammilleri, Ursula Dey, Astrid Heininger, Anja Heinemeyer, Michaela Huber, Henriette Junkers, Heike Kähler, Uta Krüsselmann, Alexander Loose, Ortrun Meinhard, Cordula Möwes, Helena Pichler, Britta Schmicking, Birgit Straube, Susanne Winckler.** Bei der Auseinandersetzung mit dem Thema *Steine im Schmuck* wurden tradierte Vorstellungen hinterfragt, wonach kostbare Steine nur edel gefasst und in Verbindung mit teurem Material gedacht werden können. Über den Einsatz alternativer Materialien und Fasstechniken sowie Auseinandersetzungen inhaltlicher Art konnte der Blick frei werden für unkonventionelle Lösungen.

Frucht ohne Kern 1995/96. Lehrende **Uta Feiler.** Gefäßemail. **Beflügelt** 1994. Lehrende **Brigitte Roos.** Gestaltung von Kopfbedeckungen. **Zugvögel** 1994. Lehrende **Uta Feiler.** Bearbeitung des Themas mit spezifischen emailtechnischen Vorgaben. **Pâte de verre** 1993/94. Lehrende **Helen Aitken-Kuhnen.** Schmuckgestaltung mit der Technik des Pâte de verre. **A rose is a rose is a rose...** 1993. Lehrende **Alexandra Bahlmann.** Kette und Halsschmuck als Ergebnis von Reihung. **Gestaltungswettbewerb** 1992/93. Lehrender **Paul Schudel.** Gestaltungswettbewerb der Firma M&M zur Gestaltung und Realisation von Uhren am Körper, an der Kleidung, auf dem Tisch. **Takara Bune**

Melanie Halbauer
Seelsorge
Broschen
Geweihter Stahl, vergoldetes Silber, Foto
Pastoral Care
brooches
blessed steel, gold-plated silver, photo

film *Haut – Bas – Fragile* by Jaques Rivette. Jewellery for the Senses **1996/97. Instructor** Petra Weingärtner-Arnold. **Development of jewellery concepts on a set theme, up to readiness for production. A multi-term project in collaboration with the Niessing company in Vreden.** Of Bending and Breaking **1996/97. Instructor** Elke Hackner **From material and working experiments with metal and enamel to a jewellery object.** Portraits of Women **1995/96. Instructor** Karin R'hila. **Exhibition concepts for museums, art galleries or culture institutes, enhancing market presence with editions and series.**

Jewellery with Stones **1995**
Instructor Brigitte Tendahl. **Students** Petra Brenner, Nicoletta Cammilleri, Ursula Dey, Astrid Heininger, Anja Heinemeyer, Michaela Huber, Henriette Junkers, Heike Kähler, Uta Krüsselmann, Alexander Loose, Ortrun Meinhard, Cordula Möwes, Helena Pichler, Britta Schmicking, Birgit Straube, Susanne Winckler. **This examination of the subject of stones in jewellery questioned the traditional belief that precious stones must always be presented in precious settings and combined with expensive materials. The use of alternative materials and setting techniques and a critical analysis of aspects of content helped the students to become open for unconventional solutions.**

Fruit without Stones **1995/96. Instructor** Uta Feiler. **Enamel vessels based on the theme.** Given Wings **1994. Instructor** Brigitte Roos. **Design of head coverings.** Birds of Passage **1994. Instructor** Uta Feiler. **Work expressing this theme using specific enamel techniques.** Jewellery with Pâte de Verre **1993/94. Instructor** Helen Aitken-Kuhnen. **Jewellery design utilizing the technique of pâte de verre.** A rose is a rose is a rose... **1993. Instructor** Alexandra Bahlmann. **Chains and necklaces based on sequencing.** Product Design **1992/93. Instructor** Paul Schudel. **Design competition staged by the M&M company, design and production of clocks/watches for the body, clothing and table.** Takara Bune or the Treasure Ship **1992/93. Instructor** Isabel Beyermann. **Cult vessels made of enamel in combination with other materials.** A Passion for Recycling **1992/93. Instructor** Hermann Becker. **Design of recycling containers for households, offices and public places.** Salome **1992. Instructor** Egon Kuhn. **Concept for an exhibition.**

oder das Schatzschiff 1992/93. Lehrende **Isabel Beyermann.** Kultgefäße aus Email in Kombination mit anderen Materialien. **Sammelleidenschaft** 1992/93. Lehrender **Hermann Becker.** Gestaltung von Sammelcontainern für Haushalt, Büro oder den öffentlichen Raum. **Salome** 1992. Lehrender **Egon Kuhn.** Konzeption für eine Ausstellung.

Produkt wie ein Gedicht,
Schmuck wie ein Gedicht
Product Like a Poem,
Jewellery Like a Poem
1999/2000

Workshops

Körperbefragungen 2000. Lehrende **Susanne Hammer.** Entwicklung körperbezogener Schmuckkonzepte. **Eine Kette für Düsseldorf** 1999/2000. Lehrender **Ted Noten.** Entwicklung ortsbezogener Arbeiten. **Rituale** 1999. Lehrende **Dinie Besems.** Schmuck und Objekt mit ritueller Funktion. **Crystallizing Ideas** 1998/99. Lehrende **Diana Hobson.** Einführung in die Technik des Pâte de verre. **Mokume Gane** 1997. Lehrende **Birgit Laken.** Schmuck aus Metalllaminaten. **A Synthesis of Dots.** 1995/96. Lehrende **Jaqueline Mina** Schmuckgestaltung mit der Technik der Granulation. **Equilibre** 1994. Lehrende **Johanna Dahm.** Schmuck oder Objekt zum Thema *Gleichgewicht*.

Workshops

Body Polls **2000. Instructor** Susanne Hammer. **Development of body-oriented jewellery concepts.** A Chain for Düsseldorf **1999/2000. Instructor** Ted Noten. **Development of locale-oriented works.** Rituals **1999. Instructor** Dinie Besems. **Jewellery and objects with ritual functions.** Crystallising Ideas **1998/99. Instructor** Diana Hobson. **An introduction to pâte de verre work.** Mokume Gane Jewellery **1997. Instructor** Birgit Laken. **Jewellery made of metal laminates.** A Synthesis of Dots **1995/96. Instructor** Jaqueline Mina. **Jewellery design using the granulation technique.** Equilibre **1994. Instructor** Johanna Dahm. **Jewellery or object on the theme *Equilibrium*.**

Anja Oelschlegel
Bauschmantel
Frühstücksbeutel, Kunstfell
Bustle Dress
sandwich bags, artificial fur
Foto: Dirk Hansen, Köln

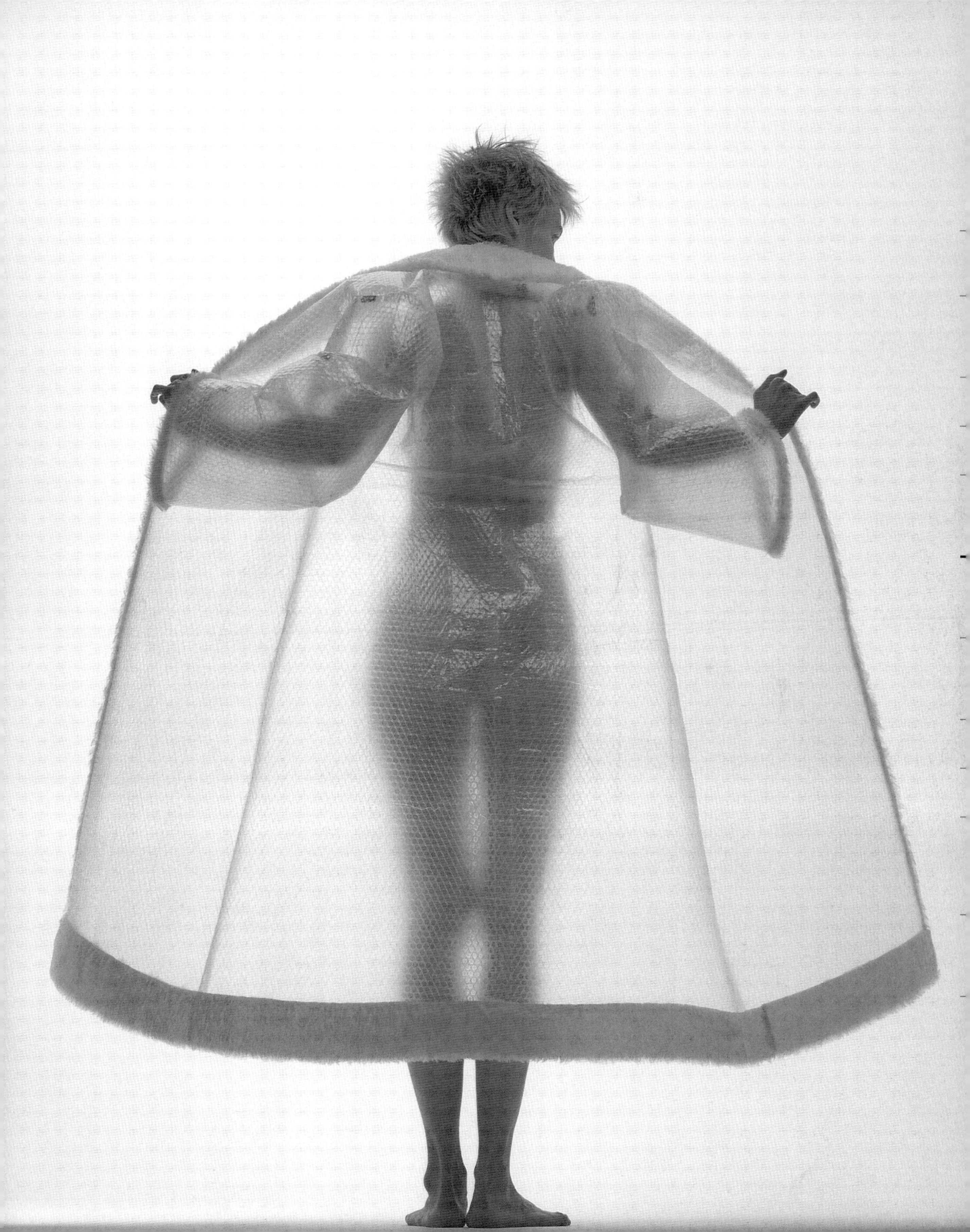

Produkt wie ein Gedicht,
Schmuck wie ein Gedicht
Product Like a Poem,
Jewellery Like a Poem
1999/2000

Anja Oelschlegel
Morgenmantel
Luftpolsterfolie, Kunstfell
Dressing Gown
bubble film, artificial fur
Foto: Dirk Hansen, Köln

Verena Gosebrink
Ringe und Gussformen
Silber, Holz
rings and casting moulds
silver, wood

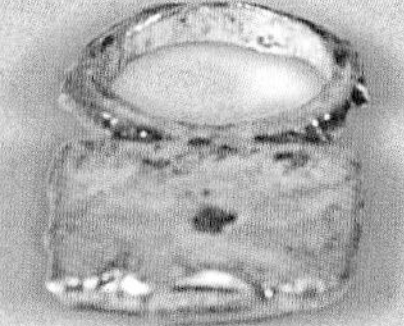

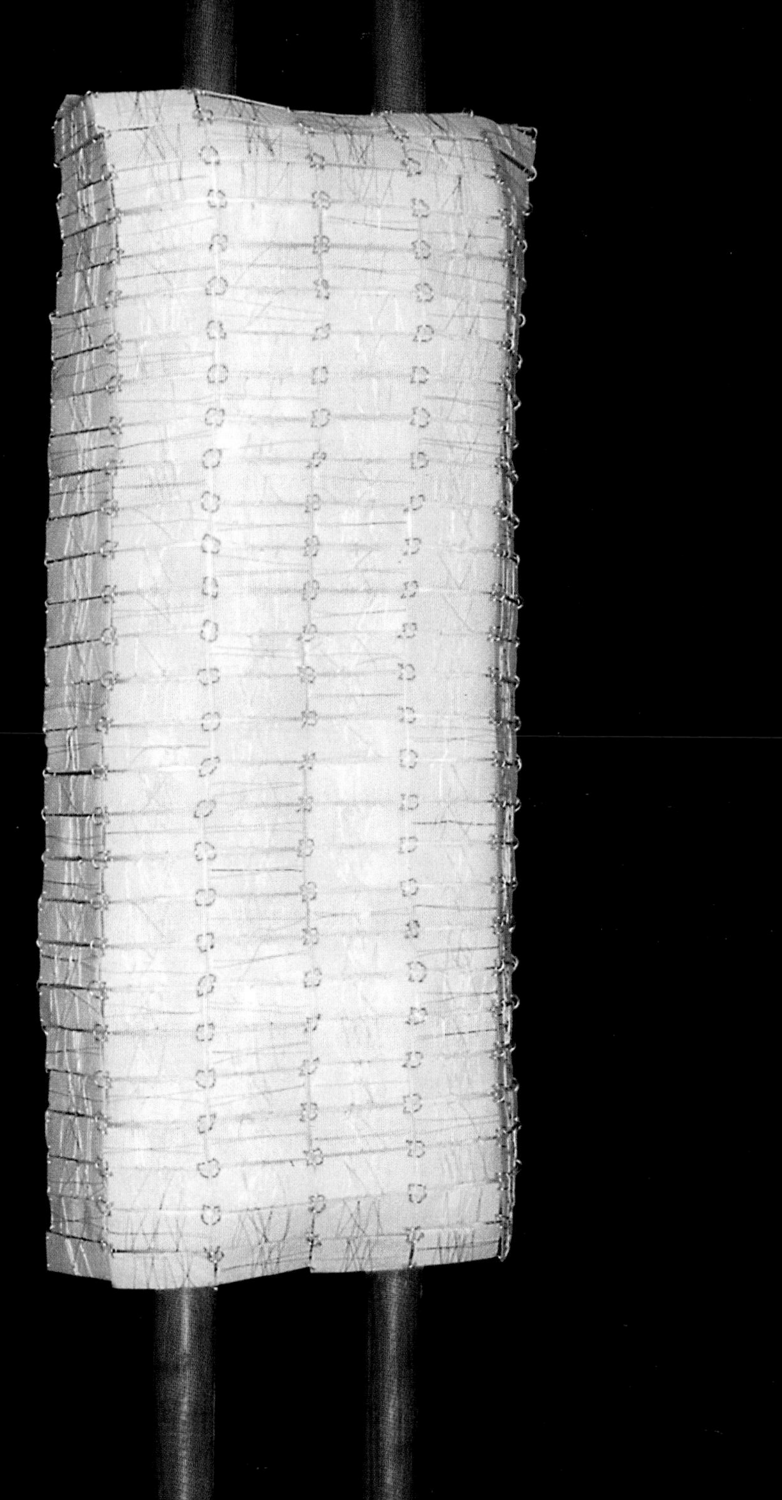

Liturgisches Gerät
Gestaltung eines Toramantels
Liturgical Equipment
Design of a Thora Covering
1999

Heike Tries
Thora-Mantel
Vliesstoff, Silber
torah cover
fleece fabric, silver

Die Gestaltung von Liturgiegefäßen hatte in den 50er und 60er Jahren ihre letzte Blütezeit. Neu gegründete Gemeinden, sowie Gemeinden, die ihre durch den 2. Weltkrieg erlittenen Verluste ersetzen mussten, trugen zu dem großen Bedarf an kirchlichem Gerät bei. Um diesen zu decken, wurde auf Katalogware zurückgegriffen, die sich vornehmlich aus Repliken und schlecht gestalteten Serienprodukten zusammensetzte. Der Anteil individuell gefertigter Liturgiegefäße ging immer weiter zurück und wurde schließlich fast völlig verdrängt. Der Bedarf an individuell gefertigtem Sakralgerät in den 80er und 90er Jahre war dann verschwindenend klein, dementsprechend war die Gestaltung von Liturgiegefäßen an der Fachhochschule Düsseldorf auch jahrelang von untergeordneter Bedeutung. Dies änderte sich gegen Ende der 90er Jahre, als das Liturgische Institut in Trier anläßlich seines 50jährigen Jubiläums den internationalen Wettbewerb *Liturgiegefäße* ausschrieb. Diese Initiative führte zu einer intensiven Beschäftigung mit dem Thema. Drei bis zum Endresultat durchgeführte Studienarbeiten und eine Diplomarbeit waren die von Düsseldorfer Studierenden eingereichten Wettbewerbsbeiträge. Eine Anfrage der evangelischen Kirchengemeinde Niestetal führte zur Ausschreibung eines zweiten Wettbewerbes für die Gestaltung von Liturgiegefäßen und, nach der eingehenden Beschäftigung mit der katholischen Liturgie, zur willkommenen ergänzenden Beschäftigung mit der in der evangelischen Kirche gebräuchlichen Liturgie. Während zuvor aus dem gesamten Kanon der *Vasa sacra et non sacra* geschöpft werden konnte, waren die Vorgaben im zweiten Wettbewerb wesentlich genauer: Weinkanne, zwei Abendmahlkelche, Becher, Brotschale und Reinigungsgefäß sollten gestaltet werden. Selbstverständlicher Bestandteil beider Gestaltungsaufgaben waren präzise analytisch-konzeptionelle Vorarbeiten zur Vermeidung gestalterischer Beliebigkeiten. Eine weitere Vertiefung des für Silberschmiede so

Traditionell weibliche
Handwerke und Schmuck
Traditionally Female
Crafts and Jewellery
2000/01

The design of liturgical vessels experienced its last flowering in the 50s and 60s. New parishes and parishes that needed to replace items destroyed during the War generated lively demand for new church equipment. As a result, most parishes ordered standard catalogue items, most of which were replicas and poorly-designed, mass-produced products. The number of individually-built liturgical vessels decreased continually, and they were finally almost completely supplanted by the mass-made goods. In the 80s and 90s the demand for individually-produced liturgical equipment was minute, and consequently the design of liturgical equipment was also disregarded at the Düsseldorf University of Applied Sciences for a number of years. This changed towards the end of the 90s when the *Liturgical Institute* in Trier organised a *Liturgical Equipment Design Competition* to mark its 50th anniversary. This initiative generated lively fresh interest in the subject. Four entries were submitted by students at the university in Düsseldorf, consisting of three completed thesis projects and one diploma dissertation. A query from the Protestant parish in Niestetal then led to the organisation of a second liturgical vessels design competition. After the intensive work on the Catholic liturgy this provided a welcome opportunity for a complementary study of the liturgy used in the Protestant Church. While in the first competition the students had been able to draw on the entire canon of *vasa sacra et non sacra*, the brief of the second was much more precise: The contestants were asked to design a wine cruet, two communion chalices, beakers, a ciborium and a finger bowl. The rules for both contests emphasised precise, analytical preparations and concepts to rule out subjective and uninformed designs. A further opportunity to go deeper into this field of work, which is extremely interesting for silversmiths, was provided by the *Torah Cover*

Stefanie Klein
Zwang
umhäkeltes Hundehalsband
Leder, Nieten, Garn
Compulsion
dog collar with crotcheted cover
leather, studs, yarn

Geschönt und gemildert,
doch geführt und gegängelt.
Prettified and cushioned,
led and controlled.

HASSLICH
NEUGIER 16
OFFEN
KALT
FAUL
WUTEND
VERDAMMT
TOT

interessanten Arbeitsfeldes bot der vom Spertus Institute of Jewish Studies ausgelobte Wettbewerb *Gestaltung eines Toramantels*, der die Einarbeitung in eine wiederum andere Ausprägung des Glaubens und der Liturgie erforderte. Zwei Studierende erreichten die Endrunde des Wettbewerbes und konnten ihre Arbeiten in Chicago präsentieren, und eine der Arbeiten wurde sogar mit dem dritten Preis ausgezeichnet. Dieser schöne Erfolg zeigt, wie gut sich die Studierenden in die ihnen eher fremden und fernen kultischen Gebräuche eingefühlt haben und darüber zu gestalterisch bedeutungsvollen Aussagen gekommen sind. Er zeigt aber auch, dass das liturgische Gefäß wieder zum lohnenden Bereich gestalterischer Aufmerksamkeit geworden ist.

Stefanie Klein
Freiheit
Halskette, gehäkelt
Silber, Garn
Freedom
necklace, crotcheted
silver, yarn

Gefühle befreien.
Feelings liberate.

***Design Competition* staged by the *Spertus Institute of Jewish Studies*, which called for study and analysis of the liturgy and expressions of yet another different faith. Two students reached the finals of this competition and were able to present their works in Chicago, one of which actually won the third prize. This very gratifying success demonstrates how well the students were able to tune in to religious practices that were actually quite alien to them, and to produce designs with meaningful messages. In addition to this, it also shows that liturgical vessels are now once again a worthwhile field of design.**

Melanie Halbauer
Trinkgefäß
Porzellan
**drinking vessel
porcelain**

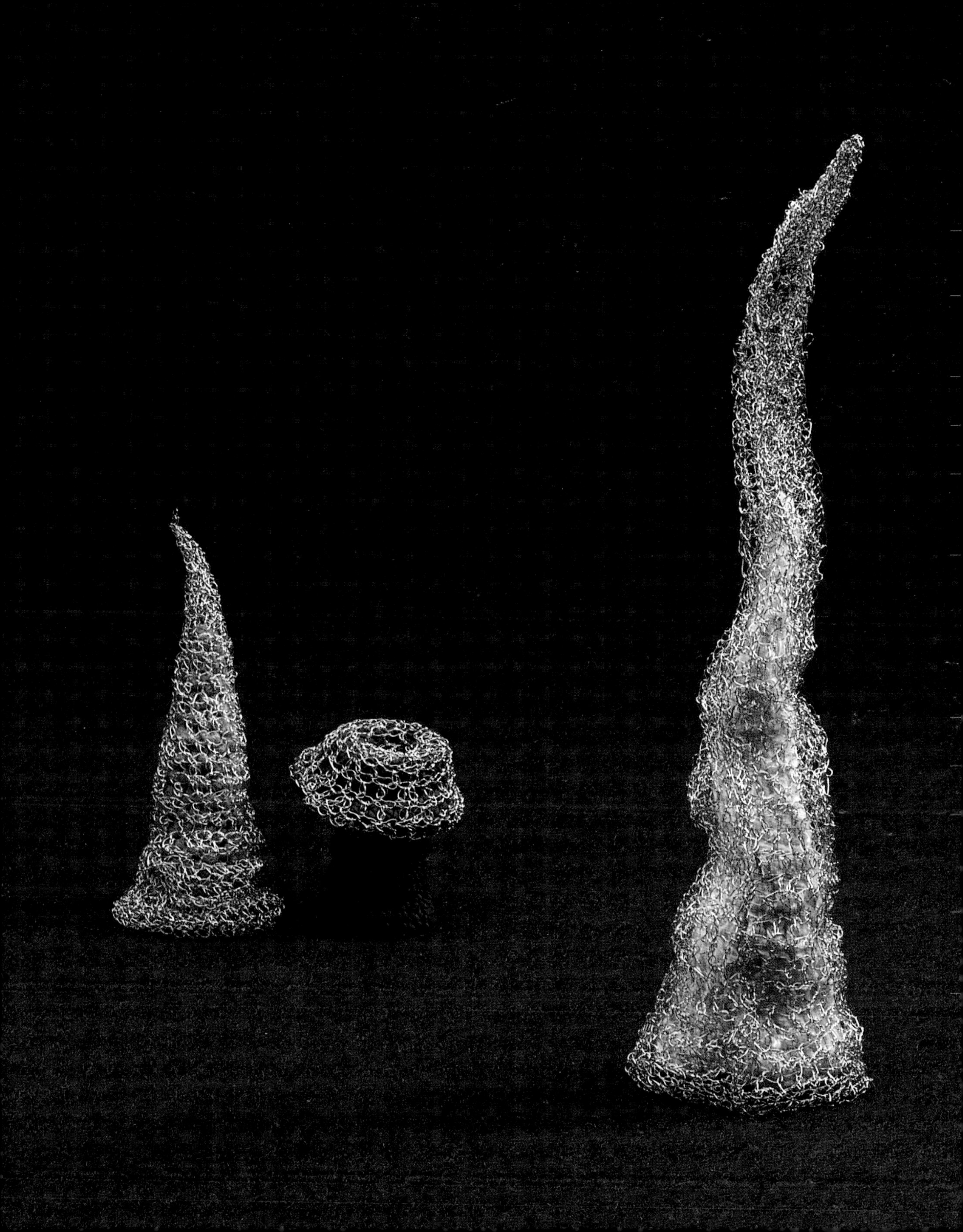

Traditionell weibliche
Handwerke und Schmuck
Traditionally Female
Crafts and Jewellery
2000/01

Nina Wöhlke
Der Schein trügt
Fingerlinge
Kupfer, Silber, Eisen, Wolle, Nylon,
Gummi, synthetische Steine
The Appearance is Deceptive
fingerlings
copper, silver, iron, wool, nylon,
rubber, synthetic stones

Sigrid Eickhoff
Energiekollektoren
Brosche, Glasring, Kupferring, Ohrringe
Kupfer, Email, Glas
Energy Collectors
brooch, glass ring, copper ring, earrings
copper, enamel, glass

ANFANG

Traditionell weibliche
Handwerke und Schmuck
Traditionally Female
Crafts and Jewellery
2000/01

Gisa Elmer
Der rote Faden
Ring, Anhänger
Silber, Garn
Red Thread – The Leitmotif
ring, pendant
silver, thread

Karen Kathmann
Ringe
Plastik, Filz, Nicki, Vlies,
Füllstoff, Glasperlen, Garn
**rings
plastic, felt, velour, fleece,
filling, glass beads, yarn**

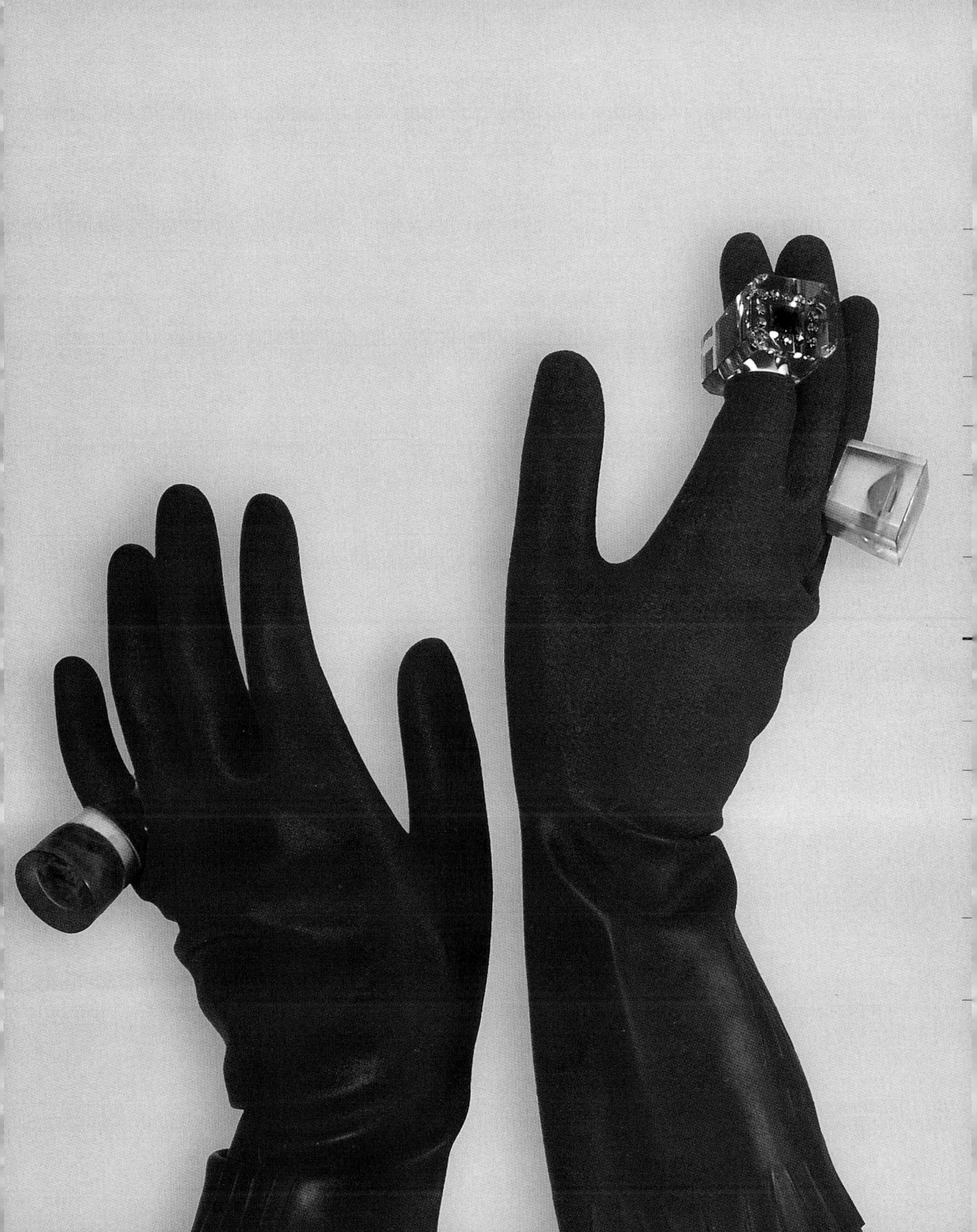

Birgit Straube
Ringe
Epoxydharz, Steine
rings
epoxy resin, stones

Perlen-Schätze,
Hommage an eine Schenkung
Bead Treasures,
Homage to a Bequest
1997, 1997/98

Katja Kempe
Perlenrausch
Armreif
Glasperlen
Intoxication of Beads
armlet
glass beads

Perlen-Schätze,
Hommage an eine Schenkung
Bead Treasures,
Homage to a Bequest
1997, 1997/98

Elisabeth Holder Einige Gedanken zur Arbeit mit Perlen
Geschrieben im Jahre 1998, anlässlich der Ausstellung im Glasmuseum Wertheim mit Arbeiten aus den Perlen der Schenkung von Anton van Eyk

Katja Kempe
Perlenrausch
Ringe
Glasperlen
Intoxication of Beads
rings
glass beads

Elisabeth Holder **Few Thoughts on Working with Beads**
Written in 1998 for the exhibition of works with the beads from the Anton van Eyk bequest, at the Wertheim Glass Museum

Perlen – *beads* wie sie im Englischen genannt werden können, um sie von pearls, den Meeres- und Süßwasserperlen zu unterscheiden – sind ganz einfach strukturiert. Sie sind nicht mehr als ein kleines Ding mit Loch. Ihre Vielfältigkeit erhalten sie erst durch Farbe, Größe und Material. Darüber faszinieren und berühren sie. Die Perle selbst lässt sich nicht verändern. Sie kann letztlich nur immer wieder neu gereiht und über Rhythmus, Metrik, Farbe und Größe spielerisch variiert werden. Der gestalterische Wille und das sonst geübte konzeptionell-analytische Vorgehen, das Anfang und Ende kennt, müssen beim Umgang mit der Perle zunächst aufgegeben werden. Die Perle kennt nur das Prinzip der Wiederholung, dem zu gehorchen zu einer Erfahrung von fast meditativem Charakter führt. Die Perle fordert dazu auf, sich diesem Geschehen zu überlassen und rührt damit an das Unbewusste. Aus diesem Nährboden des Schöpferischen entsteht wie von selbst Neues. Es erfordert Mut, sich dieser Herausforderung auszusetzen und sich von gewohntem Denken und geübtem Vorgehen zu lösen. Alle die sich auf die Auseinandersetzung mit der so schlicht strukturierten Perle einlassen, werden mit den Grenzen konfrontiert, die diese dem Formwillen der Schmuckgestalterinnen und Schmuckgestalter setzt.

Männerschmuck
Men´s Jewellery
1999/2000

Regina Quaring
Schlicht, dezent, unauffällig
Broschen für Männer
Aluminium, Magnete
Plain, Discreet, Inconspicuous
brooches for men
aluminium, magnets

Verena Gosebrink
Zwei Seelen
T-Shirts
Shirts, Textildruck,
Edelstahl, Magnete
Two Souls
t-shirts
shirts, fabric print,
stainless steel, magnets

Beads and pearls are the epitome of simplicity – viewed objectively they are nothing more than small objects with holes through them. Their great variety comes from their colours, their sizes and their material. And yet they have the capacity to fascinate and move us. The bead itself is not open to change. It can only be placed in ever-new arrangements, achieving variety through rhythm, metre, colour and size. When working with beads one must first abandon the designer's will and one's customary conceptual and analytical approach. Beads know only the principle of repetition, and submitting to this principle is an experience with an almost meditative character. Beads challenge one to abandon oneself to this process, and in this they touch our subconscious. In this fertile, creative soil the new arises almost of its own accord. It needs courage to take up this challenge and let go of customary ways of thinking and well-practised methods. Nobody who is willing to be open for this interaction with beads in the simplicity of their structure can avoid coming up against the limitations that they impose on the jewellery designer's will to impose form.

Christiane Wink
Stay Cowboy
Pistole mit Halfter
Gießharz, Leder, Holz
Stay Cowboy
pistol with holster
cast resin, leather, wood

Sonja Thiemann
Clip-it
Broschen
Aluminium, eloxiert
Clip-it
brooches
anodised aluminium

Männerschmuck
Men's Jewellery
1999/2000

Petra Weingärtner-Arnold Schmuck nur für Männer

Julia Müllers
Schmuck für den neuen Mann
Ketten mit Anhänger
Silber, Kupfer, Messing, Perlen aus Glas, Hämatit, Granat, Türkis
Jewellery for the New Man
chains with pendants
silver, copper, brass, beads made of glass, hematite, garnet and turquoise

Nicola Brand
Schmuck für Aussteiger und Weltreisende
Männerschmuck
Kokosfaser, Leinengarn, Latex, Fundstücke
Jewellery for Drop-Outs and World Travellers
men's jewellery
coconut fibre, linen, latex, found objects

Meike Peters
Die Ferse des Achilles
Ketten, Ringe
Eisen, Edelstahl
The Heel of Achilles
chains, rings
iron, stainless steel

Petra Weingärtner-Arnold **Jewellery for Men**

Nicola Brand
Schmuck für Aussteiger und Weltreisende
Männerschmuck
Kokosfaser, Leinengarn, Latex
Jewellery for Drop-outs and World Travellers
men's jewellery
coconut fibre, linen garn, latex

Das Schmuckbedürfnis der Männer führt ein Schattendasein. Wenn es nach der Schmuckindustrie ginge, müssten sie sich mit Krawattennadeln, Manschettenknöpfen und Reverssteckern begnügen. Entsprechend war es das Anliegen des Projektes, die sich hinter dem kargen Angebot der Schmuckindustrie verbergenden Stereotyen Vorstellungen zu identifizieren, zu hinterfragen und zu durchbrechen. Das Projekt zielte damit auch auf die Erforschung einer neuen Material- und Formensprache von Schmuck für Männer. Die Erarbeitung der individuellen Ansätze, Ideen und Konzepte für Männerschmuck erfolgte vor dem Hintergrund weiterer intensiver Recherchen. Diese umfassten geschichtliche, psychologische, kulturelle und gesellschaftliche Themen ebenso wie Themen der Bereiche Lifestyle und Bekleidung. Als Zielgruppe wurden Männer zwischen 20 und 50 Jahren gewählt mit den Zuschreibungen *Modern. Selbstbewusst. Kulturell. Beflissen. Dynamisch.* Geschmückt wurde der neue Mann: In Balance zwischen Beruf, Familie und Freizeit. Manchmal Held, manchmal Abenteurer. Seiner Männlichkeit bewusst. Sensibel, spielerisch, phantasievoll. Harte Schale, weicher Kern. Die Grenzen waren offen – von experimentell bis tragbar – alles war erlaubt. Obwohl Schmuck überwiegend an Stellen wie Ohr, Hals, Arm und Finger, getragen wird, steht er doch auch in einer engen Beziehung zur Kleidung. Deshalb sollte besonders der Anzug, die Berufskleidung des Mannes, auf neue Tragemöglichkeiten von Schmuck untersucht werden. Die Firma Dressmaster in Herne war Partner für den Austausch von Ideen und Diskussionspartner bei der Bewertung der entwickelten Schmuckkonzepte und der fertigen Arbeiten.

Men's interest in jewellery leads a shadowy existence. If it was left to the jewellery industry they would have to make do with tie pins, lapel pins and cufflinks. The motivation of this project was thus to identify, question and break through the stereotypical beliefs underlying the meagre product lines offered by the jewellery industry. The specific objective was the investigation of a new language of material and form in jewellery for men. The development of the individual approaches, ideas and concepts to and for men's jewellery took place on the foundation of intensive, in-depth research, which covered historical, psychological, cultural and social themes and themes relating to lifestyle and clothing. The chosen target group encompassed men between 20 and 50 with the attributes *Modern. Self-confident. Cultural. Keen. Dynamic.* Jewellery to ornament *The New Man* – in equilibrium between profession, family and leisure. Sometimes a hero, sometimes an adventurer. Aware of his masculinity. Sensitive, playful, imaginative. Hard shell, soft at core. The boundaries were open – from experimental to wearable – everything was allowed. Although jewellery is mainly worn in places like the ears, neck, arms and fingers it is also closely associated with clothing. A focus was thus placed on investigation of the suit, men's work attire, to identify its potential for new ways of wearing jewellery. The *Dressmaster* company in Herne provided valuable input here, acting as our partner for the exchange of ideas and meeting with us to discuss and evaluate the developed jewellery concepts and the finished works.

Verena Gosebrink
Ummantelter Kern
Anhänger
Porzellan, Filz
Coated Core
pendant
porcelain, felt

Susanne Augenstein
Halsschmuck mit Verpackung
Silikon, Glassteine
neck ornament with packaging
silicone, glass beads

Maren Krämer
Müllermilch
Kette, Ringe
bedruckter Kunststoff
Müller Milk
necklace, rings
printed plastic

Experimenteller Schmuck
aus unedlen Materialien
**Experimental Jewellery Made
of Non-precious Materials**
1999

Meike Peters
Kette, Ring
Spontex-Schwamm, Edelstahl
**chain, ring
Spontex sponge, stainless steel**

Er-Findungen oder
Nützliches für den Alltag
Inventions or Useful
Items for Everyday Life
1999/2000

Eva Dufhues, Anja Heinemeyer,
Steffi Klein, Ingrid Micheel
Brillenhalter
Edelstahl
spectacles holder
stainless steel

Experimenteller Schmuck
aus unedlen Materialien
Experimental Jewellery Made
of Non-precious Materials
1999

Anne Kessler
Sylvester
Ringe
eloxiertes Aluminium, Zinn
New Year's Eve
rings
anodised aluminium, tin

Ringorakel. Verwandelt
zur Erinnerung.
Ring oracle. Transformed
for remembrance.

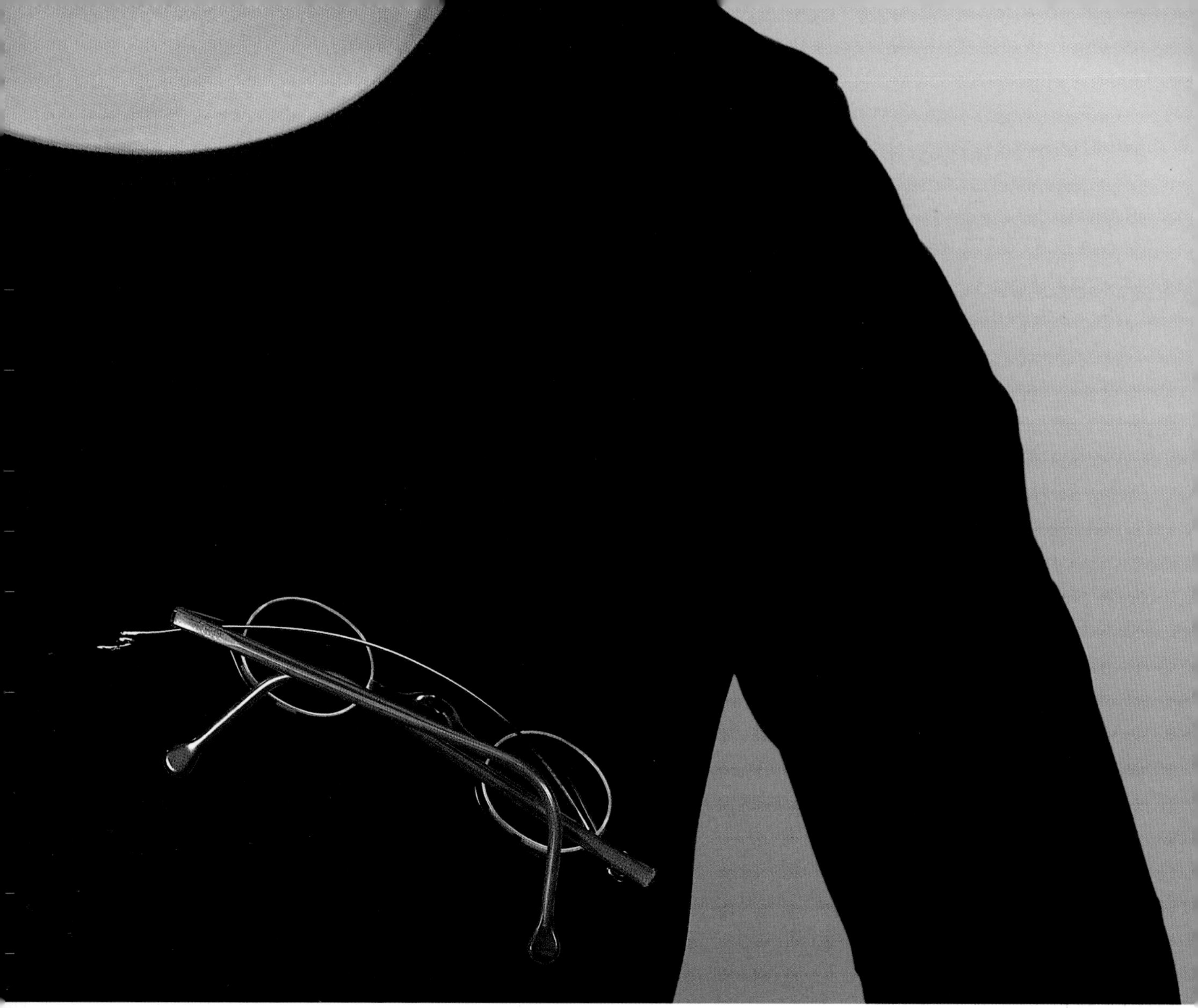

1999

1999

2000

Er-Findungen oder
Nützliches für den Alltag
Inventions or Useful
Items for Everyday Life
1999/2000

Eva Dufhues, Anja Heinemeyer,
Steffi Klein, Ingrid Micheel
Brillenhalter
Edelstahl
spectacles holder
stainless steel

Er-Findungen oder
Nützliches für den Alltag
Inventions or Useful
Items for Everyday Life
1999/2000

Astrid Eckert, Babette Egerland,
Claudia Halder, Susanne Mayer,
Uta Oeding-Erdel
Variable Vasen
Silikon, verschiedene
andere Materialien
variable vases
silicone, various other materials

Er-Findungen oder
Nützliches für den Alltag
Inventions or Useful
Items for Everyday Life
1999/2000

Astrid Eckert, Babette Egerland,
Claudia Halder, Susanne Mayer,
Uta Oeding-Erdel
Variable Vasen
Silikon, verschiedene
andere Materialien
variable vases
silicone, various other materials

Nicola Brand, Heike Köhler
Accessoires für eine Partynacht
Taschen
Roter Satin, Lurex-Stoff, Kordel
Accessories for a Night Out
bags
red satin, Lurex, cord

**Isabelle Falzarano, Maren Krämer,
Julia Müllers**
Rocktasche
Organza, Naturseide
skirt bag
organza, natural silk

Monika Seitter
Kreisel
Holz, blattvergoldet, Gummi
spinning top
wood gilded with gold leaf, rubber

Maroc – Völkerverständigung
durch Design
**Maroc – International
Understanding through Design**
1998

Herbert Schulze Maroc — Völkerverständigung durch Design

Nicola Brand
Gewürzgefäße
Silber, Porzellan
spice containers
silver, porcelain

Herbert Schulze **Maroc — International Understanding through Design**

Anke Wolf
Brunnengefäß
Schale
Messing, versilbert
Well Vessel
bowl
silver-plated brass

In den Jahren 1998 und 1999 wurde an der Fachhochschule Düsseldorf von den Fachbereichen Architektur und Design ein semesterübergreifendes Projekt durchgeführt. Dieses Projekt, vom Deutsch-Marokkanischen Freundeskreis initiiert und vom Marokkanischen Ministerium für Handel, Wirtschaft und Kunsthandwerk unterstützt, wurde kurz und bündig *Marokko-Projekt* genannt. Studierende der beiden Fachbereiche waren dabei aufgefordert, sich im Rahmen eines Wettbewerbs mit der Gestaltung von marokkanischem Design und Kunsthandwerk zu beschäftigen. Hintergrund dieser Initiative war die Tatsache, dass marokkanisches Kunsthandwerk und Design auf dem europäischen Markt auf großes Interesse stieß. Mit diesem offenen Gestaltungswettbewerb, war nicht nur der Wunsch verbunden diesen Trend aufzugreifen und zu verstärken, sondern es verband sich damit die Vorstellung, dass ein solches Projekt auch der Völkerverständigung dienen könne. Zu Beginn des Sommersemesters 1998 wurde es offiziell durch einen Vertreter der marokkanische Botschaft eröffnet und im Folgenden ständig durch Mitglieder des Deutsch-Marokkanischen Freundeskreises begleitet. Ein Lichtbildervortrag gab Studierenden und Lehrenden ersten Einblick in die Kultur, Architektur und Landschaft Marokkos. Es folgten Filmvorführungen, Museumsbesuche unter fachkundiger Führung usw. Damit sollten die an dem Projekt Beteiligten vertiefende Einblicke in das kulturelle Leben, die architektonischen Schätze und die landschaftlichen Ausprägungen eines ihnen wenig vertrauten Landes erhalten. Gleichzeitig dienten diese Aktivitäten der Vorbereitung auf die ebenfalls vorgesehenen Exkursionen nach Marokko, waren Grundlage für die Festlegung der Themenbereiche und die Erarbeitung erster Konzepte. Im Studiengang Innenarchitektur wurde mit dem Thema *Gestaltung eines Paravents* eine für alle Studierenden gleiche Aufgabe vorgegeben, während in den Studiengängen Kommunikationsdesign und

In 1998 and 1999 a multi-semester design project was staged in the faculties of architecture and design at Düsseldorf University of Applied Sciences. The project, which was organised as a competition, was initiated by the *German-Moroccan Friends Association* and supported by the Moroccan Ministry of Trade, Commerce and Crafts. Named simply the *Morocco Project*, the basic idea was to give students in both faculties the opportunity to do some in-depth work with Moroccan design and crafts. Among other things it was a response to the great interest in Moroccan design, arts and crafts on the European market. In addition to taking up and supporting this trend it was also hoped that the competition would help to promote international understanding. The project was officially opened by a representative of the Moroccan embassy at the beginning of the 1998 summer term, and members of the *German-Moroccan Friends Association* provided ongoing advice and support throughout. First a slide show was staged to give the students and their teachers a basic introduction to the culture, architecture and landscape of Morocco. This was followed by film screenings, museum visits with expert guides and so on. All these activities were designed to give the project participants deeper insights into the cultural life, architectural heritage, landscape and scenery of a country that was very new to them. They also served as preparation for visits to Morocco and as a foundation for the definition of the project themes and the development of initial concepts. All the students in the interior design course had the same task, namely to design a paravent screen. The students in the communications design and product design courses did work in photography, jewellery and appliances and were able to choose their own subjects. The range of the product design students' works was very broad, encompassing jewellery, jugs, spice containers, perfume

Maroc – Völkerverständigung durch Design
Maroc – International Understanding through Design
1998

Ulrike Scheer
Couscous-Besteck
Edelstahl
couscous cutlery set
stainless steel

Uschi Magera
Broschen
Messing
brooches
brass

Heike Köhler
Couscous-Schale
Edelstahl, Porzellan
couscous-dish
stainless steel, porcelain

Maroc – Völkerverständigung durch Design
Maroc – International Understanding through Design
1998

Produktdesign, die sich mit den Bereichen Fotografie, Schmuck und Gerät beteiligten, die Studierenden ihr Thema frei wählen konnten. Bei den Studierenden von Produktdesign war die Bandbreite der Entwürfe sehr groß. Sie umfasste Schmuck, Kannen, Gewürzbehältnisse, Parfümflakons, Besteck, Leuchten, Kleidung und Taschen. Durch die im Frühjahr und Herbst 1998 durchgeführten Exkursionen bot sich allen Studierenden die Möglichkeit, ihre theoretischen Erkenntnisse und Konzepte vor Ort zu überprüfen und im Lande selbst weitere Recherchen durchzuführen. Die unterschiedlichen Gestaltungsansätze, an ganz unterschiedlichen einheimischen kunsthandwerklichen Bereichen mit den ihnen typischen Techniken und Materialien anknüpfend, legten den Besuch entsprechender Werkstätten und Produktionsstätten nahe. Vom Deutsch-Marokkanischen Freundeskreis wurde ein entsprechendes Besuchsprogramm in den Städten Rabat, Fes, Marrakesch, Essaouira und Casablanca zusammengestellt. Bei einem Besuch des Ministeriums für Handel, Wirtschaft und Kunsthandwerk in Rabat konnten sich Studierende und Lehrende sowohl über die Situation des Kunsthandwerks in Marokko als auch über die Aus- und Weiterbildungsmöglichkeiten der marokkanischen Kunsthandwerker informieren. Gleichzeitig bot dieser Besuch die Gelegenheit zur Vorstellung der beiden gestalterischen Fachbereiche der Fachhochschule Düsseldorf und nicht zuletzt zu einer ausführlichen Vorstellung der im Rahmen des *Marokko-Projektes* erarbeiteten Gestaltungskonzepte. Diese Auseinandersetzungen zu Hause in der eigenen Hochschule, und besonders die Erfahrungen vor Ort im Kontakt mit den Menschen Marokkos, war für alle Teilnehmerinnen und Teilnehmer dieses Projektes eine große Bereicherung. Die dadurch gewonnenen Einblicke und Einsichten in eine bis dahin fremde Kultur haben zu einer ganz neuen Sicht von Land und Leuten geführt. Am Ende des Wintersemesters und ein Jahr

Verena Gosebrink
Ringe
Silber, Gold
rings
silver, gold

Britta Schmicking
Ringe
Silber, Kupfer
rings
silver, copper

Isabelle Falzerano
Ringe
Silber, Bronze
rings
silver, bronze

bottles, cutlery, lamps, clothing and bags. In the spring and autumn of 1998 the students travelled to Morocco, where they were able to compare their theoretical learning with the reality in the country itself and carry out their own research to deepen their understanding. In view of the variety of both the design approaches and the techniques and materials of the Moroccan arts and crafts involved, it also seemed advisable to visit some of the local workshops and studios where the products were actually made. The *German-Moroccan Friends Association* thus organised a tour programme in Rabat, Fès, Marrakech, Essaouira and Casablanca. This programme also included a visit to the Ministry of Trade, Commerce and Crafts in Rabat, where the students and teachers were able to learn about the current situation of the Moroccan arts and crafts sector and the training options available for Moroccan craftspeople. At the same time the visit also provided an opportunity to introduce the two design faculties of Düsseldorf University of Applied Sciences to the ministry officials, who were also given a comprehensive presentation of the design concepts drawn up in the *Morocco Project*. All this work, both at the college in Düsseldorf and even more so in combination with the experiences in Morocco and the contact with the people there, was greatly enriching for all the project participants. It provided valuable insights into a formerly foreign culture, giving everyone a completely new understanding of the country and its people. At the end of the winter term, one year after the opening ceremony, the works created during the project were put on show in a foyer exhibition for open day at Düsseldorf University of Applied Sciences. This interesting project was then concluded with the official judging and the award of prizes for the best works.

nach der festlichen Eröffnung konnten die realisierten Arbeiten dieses Projektes zum Tag der offenen Tür in einer Foyerausstellung im Gebäude der Fachhochschule Düsseldorf gezeigt werden. Die Jurierung und Prämierung der besten Arbeiten aus allen Bereichen bildete den Abschluss dieses interessanten Projektes.

Catherine Niegel
Flacons
Silber, Acrylglas
flacons
silver, acrylic glass

Sonja Thiemann
Tasche
Messing, Stoff
bag
brass, fabric

Kerstin Biesdorf
Teekanne
Tombak, versilbert, Acrylglas
teapot
**silver-plated garnet gold,
acrylic glass**

Christina Karababa
Tatoo-Ringe
Silikon, Silber
tatoo rings
silicone, silver

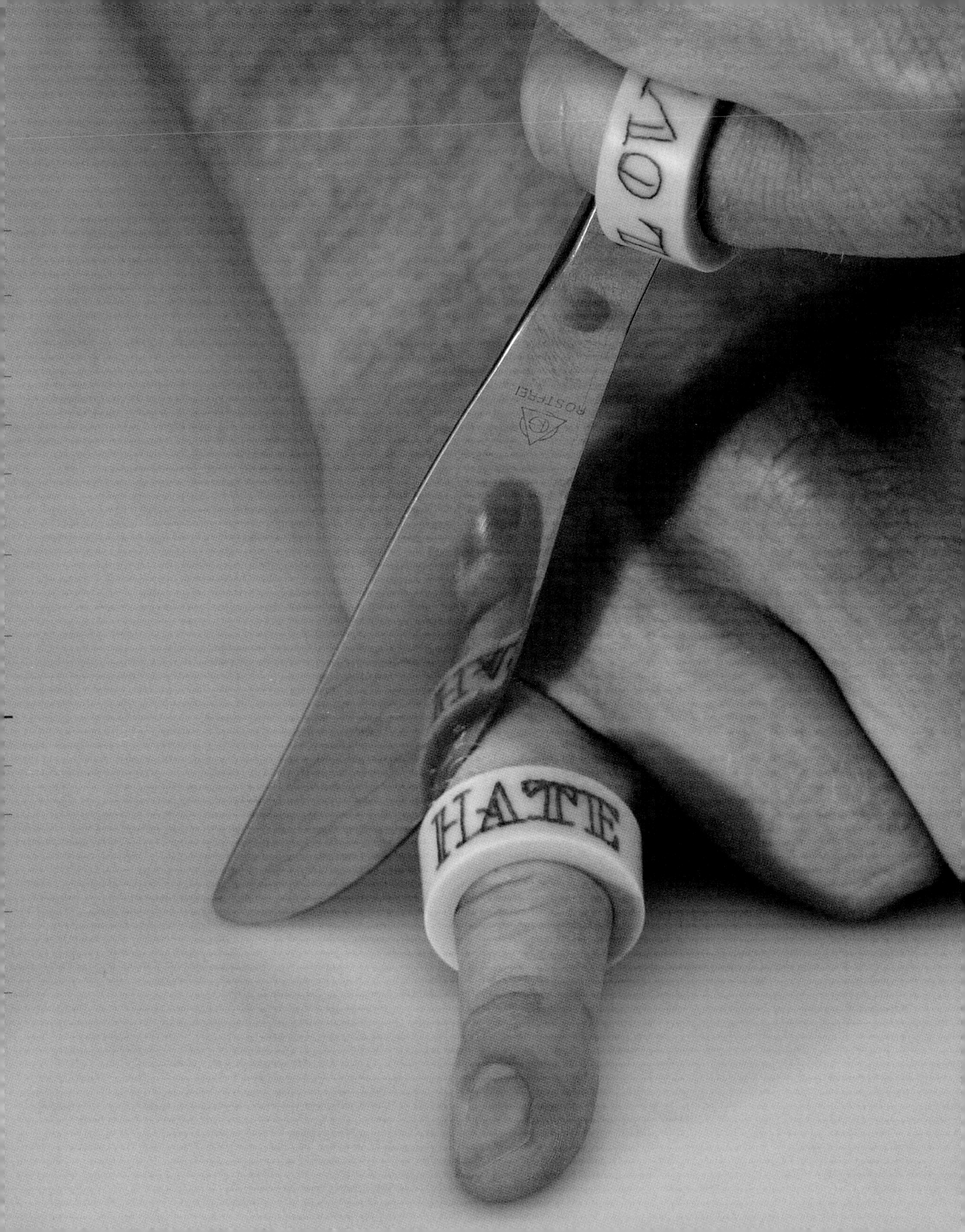
ROSTFREI
HATE

TEMPIC
QUARTZ

Heike Baschta inpetto – weniger als wirklich aber mehr als eine Vision

Gisa Elmer
Rahmen-Broschen
Silikon, Silber
frame brooches
silicone, silver

Heike Baschta **inpetto – less than real but more than a vision**

Nicole Hanselle
Armbanduhr
Fahrradschlauch
wristwatch
bicycle inner tube

Wir haben eine Idee. Wir nennen sie *inpetto*. Es ist eine Entwicklungs-, Produktions- und Vertriebsstätte zugleich. Wir konzipieren Schmuckkollektionen und Produktsortimente. Hier probieren wir die neusten Möglichkeiten der Herstellung und produzieren alles Ausgereifte in Serie. Und hier stellen wir unsere Entwicklungen aus. Wir beziehen Räume im Zentrum der Stadt. Von dort aus möchten wir mit Leuten in Kontakt treten, die interessiert sind und unsere Kollektionen kommentieren. Dann wissen wir, ob wir den Schmuck und die Produkte in unser Messeangebot aufnehmen können, um sie dem Fachhandel anzubieten. Wir sind Vermittler zwischen Studenten und Herstellern. Gute Produkt- und Schmuckkonzepte brauchen nicht in der Schublade zu verschwinden. Denn wir haben Kontakt zu denen, die solche Konzepte brauchen und kaufen möchten. Wir werden aktiv in der Öffentlichkeitsarbeit. Und dank freundlicher Unterstützung aus dem benachbarten Studiengang Kommunikationsdesign lernen wir, unsere Philosophie des Gestaltens nach außen zu kommunizieren. Gleichzeitig fordert uns die wirtschaftliche Seite von *inpetto*, dass wir uns in der Buchhaltung schulen, Kosten-Nutzen-Rechnungen erstellen können und einen Finanzierungsplan im Auge behalten. Wir wachsen heran zu einem starken Team aus lauter gestalterischen Persönlichkeiten, die auch nach dem Diplom lebensfähig sind.   In unserer Vision werden die Kollektionen und Sortimente von *inpetto* den Markt beeinflussen. ‚Vielfalt von hoher Designqualität' ist unser Motto und damit stehen wir in der kommerziellen Markenflut zunächst alleine. Aber es wird die Fragen „Wie sieht es aus, und was macht es her?" zukünftig wandeln in: „Was bedeutet es, und passt es zu mir?"   Schöne Aussichten: denn wir werden eines Tages als junge UnternehmerInnen besser vorbereitet auf einen Markt treffen, dem ein in unserem Sinne geprägtes Schmuck- und Produktverständnis eigen ist.   Ist das zu schön, um wahr zu sein?   Wir arbeiten daran,

Ingrid Bartesch-Schek
Dirndl-Ring
Silber, Garn
dirndl ring
silver, yarn

We have an idea. We call it *inpetto* – an Italian phrase used colloquially in German to refer to something that one has in reserve, or "up one's sleeve". This is going to be our combined development centre, production workshop and sales outlet, where we will design jewellery collections and product lines. It will be a place where we can try out the latest production methods, turn out finished, serialised products and exhibit our creations. We are going to move into premises in the city centre. From there we will make contact with people who are interested and willing to provide feedback on our collections. Then we will know whether we can include the jewellery and products in our exhibition line and offer them to commercial dealers. We are mediators between students and manufacturers. Good product and jewellery ideas don't need to gather dust in the cupboard. We have contacts to people who need those ideas and are willing to pay for them. We are going to be active in public relations. And with the kind support from our colleagues in the communications design department we are learning how to communicate our own philosophy of design to our audience. At the same time, the economic aspects of *inpetto* are motivating us to learn accounting, how to perform cost-benefit analyses and keep an eye on our finance plan. We are growing, becoming a strong, integrated team of capable design personalities who are going to be at home in the real world after graduation.   Our vision is that the collections and product lines of *inpetto* are going to influence the market. "Diversity of high-quality design" is our motto, and initially we are going be pretty much alone with it in the flood of the commercial market. But in the course of time it will help to transform the question "How does it look and what impression does it make?" into "What does it mean and is it right for me?"   It's an attractive prospect – as young entrepreneurs we will be

Regina Quaring
Kabelbinder-Ringe
Silber, synthetische Steine
cable tie rings
silver, synthetic stones

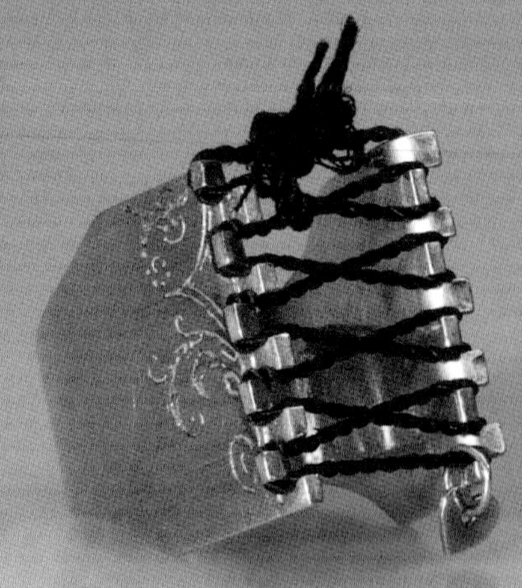

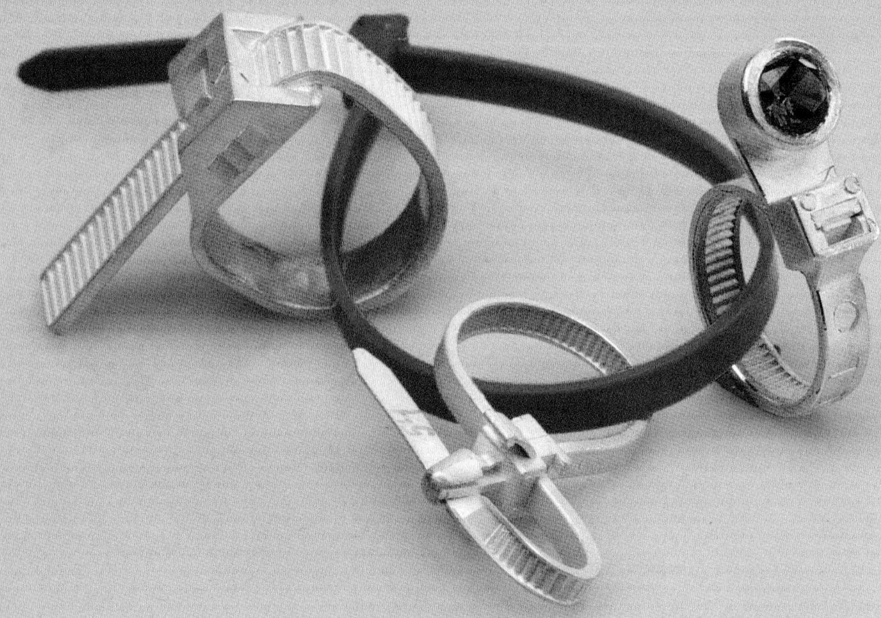

COMPANY

unsere Idee der Realisation ein Stückchen näher zu bringen. *inpetto* ist nun ein Jahr alt. Es steht immer noch nicht auf eigenen Beinen, aber es ist gefestigt in seiner Konzeption, es gibt schon Partner an seiner Seite, und Schmuck wird es auch bald zeigen. Und wir – wir haben durch diese Arbeit schon viel erlebt, was uns niemand mehr nehmen wird!

Mentorin **Prof. Elisabeth Holder.** Projektleitung **Heike Baschta.** Team **Sandra Schulte, Ingrid Micheel, Julia Muellers, Alin Boyaciyan, Andrea Blaschke, Britta Göllner, Meike Peters, Maren Krämer, Claudia Halder.** Grafik **Prof. Philipp Teufel, Felix Lemcke, Markus Brand.**

Renate Pukis
Clip-Ring
Gold, synthetischer Stein
clip ring
gold, synthetic stone

Ingrid Micheel
Flös
Flaschenöffner-Ring
Edelstahl
Flös
bottleopener ring
stainless steel

better prepared to cope with a market that has accepted a jewellery and product philosophy that we have helped to form. Is this all too good to be true? Step by step, we are working to turn our idea into a concrete reality. *inpetto* is now a year old. It is not yet standing on its own feet, but the concept rests on a solid foundation, we already have partners and soon we will also be able to present the first jewellery. And as far as we are concerned – the wealth of experience that this work has already given us is something that nobody can take away!

Mentor Prof. Elisabeth Holder. **Project Coordinator** Heike Baschta. **Team** Sandra Schulte, Ingrid Micheel, Julia Muellers, Alin Boyaciyan, Andrea Blaschke, Britta Göllner, Meike Peters, Maren Krämer, Claudia Halder. **Graphics** Prof. Philipp Teufel, Felix Lemcke, Markus Brand.

Sommer 2000 Aus einem Bedürfnis wächst eine Idee – im Studium sollen kreative Lernprozesse von der Vorbereitung auf reales Marktgeschehen begleitet werden. **September 2000** Die Manufaktur im Zwischenraum – ein Arbeitsname für das geplante Forum zwischen Hochschule und freiem Markt. Ein Team von Studenten unter der Leitung von Heike Baschta erarbeitet ein Konzept und spürt mögliche Geldgeber auf. **Februar 2001** Erster Tag der offenen Tür bei *inpetto* – die Idee hat nun einen Namen. Das nächste Ziel ist definiert: eine Rechtsform. Gerne mit einem Partner; doch der ist noch nicht in Sicht. **März 2001** Das *inpetto*-Team wächst. Arbeitsfelder für die Zukunft werden definiert: Herstellung und Vertrieb von Schmuck und Kleinprodukten, Designdienstleistung, Kulturstandort. **Juli 2001** Zweiter Tag der offenen Tür bei *inpetto* – Kontakte werden geknüpft. Ein Partner aus der Schmuck und Uhrenbranche möchte *inpetto* bei seiner Arbeit unterstützen – M&M Uhren GmbH, Düsseldorf. **September 2001** Für *inpetto* arbeiten mehrere Teams: Planung eines Messeauftritts auf der Inhorgenta, Schmuck- und Uhrenfachmesse in München, im Februar 2002. Erstellen einer eigenen Schmuckkollektion unter der Leitung von Prof. Herman Hermsen. Begleitung der Zusammenarbeit mit M&M durch Karin Hoffmann. **Januar 2002** *inpetto* wird gemeinnütziger Verein. **Februar 2002** Messeauftritt von *inpetto* auf der Inhorgenta in München.

Summer 2000 **A need gives rise to an idea – creative learning processes in the course of study at the university should be accompanied by preparation for participation in the real-life market.** September 2000 **Workshop in the Inter-Space – the working title for the planned forum between the university and the free market. A team of students led by Heike Baschta draws up a concept and locates potential sponsors.** February 2001 **First open day at *inpetto* – the idea now has a name (*inpetto* is an Italian phrase used colloquially in German to refer to something that one has in reserve, or *up one's sleeve*). The next objective is also defined: Establishment as a legal entity. Ideally with a partner, but a potential candidate has yet to be found.** March 2001 **The *inpetto* team is growing. Fields of activity are defined: Production and sale of jewellery and small products, design services and general publicity work, including exhibitions, lectures and seminars.** July 2001 **Second open day at *inpetto* – new contacts are established. M&M Uhren GmbH from Düsseldorf, a company from the jewellery and watch industry, offers to support *inpetto* in its work.** September 2001 **Several teams are now working for *inpetto*: Planning for a presentation at the Inhorgenta jewellery, watches and clocks fair in Munich in February 2002. Production of an original jewellery collection under the direction of Prof. Herman Hermsen. Coordination of the collaboration with M&M by Karin Hoffmann.** January 2002 ***inpetto* is registered as a non-profit organisation.** February 200 **Presentation by *inpetto* at the Inhorgenta in Munich.**

Elisabeth Holder
1992
Maltese Square
Schmuckobjekt
Zink, Silber, Edelstahl
Maltese Square
jewellery object
zinc, silver, stainless steel

Barbara Maas Die neue Generation der Lehrenden: Elisabeth Holder, Herman Hermsen und Herbert Schulze

Elisabeth Holder
1992
Maltese Square
Schmuckobjekt
Zink, Silber, Edelstahl
Maltese Square
jewellery object
zinc, silver, stainless steel

Barbara Maas **The New Generation of Teachers: Elisabeth Holder, Herman Hermsen and Herbert Schulze**

Schmuckgestalter werden in Düsseldorf seit 1947 ausgebildet, zunächst an der *Meisterschule für das gestaltende Handwerk*, dann an der *Werkkunstschule* und schließlich an der 1971 neugegründeten *Fachhochschule*. Zu den großen Lehrpersönlichkeiten der Vergangenheit gehörten der angesehene Pädagoge und Fachlehrer der Metallklasse Karl Schollmayer, der Silberschmied Paul Georg Schminder und die bekannte Emailkünstlerin Lili Schultz, die 1958 von der legendären Burg Giebichenstein in Halle an der Saale an den Rhein wechselte. Von ihr übernahm 1965 Sigrid Delius, eine Schülerin der renommierten Schmuckmacherin und Leiterin der Goldschmiedeklasse an den Kölner Werkschulen Elisabeth Treskow, die Werkgruppe Email. Sie lenkte seit ihrer Ernennung zur Professorin im Fachbereich Design an der Fachhochschule die Geschicke des Studienganges, der vor allem in den ersten drei Jahren wichtige inhaltliche Umgestaltungen erfuhr. Gemeinsam mit ihrem Kollegen, dem international bekannten ‚Schmuckingenieur', Kinetiker und Wegbereiter des variablen Schmuckes Friedrich Becker – er hatte 1956 die Nachfolge von Karl Schollmayer angetreten und bis 1982 als Professor an der Fachhochschule unterrichtet – übte sie mit ihrem beispielhaften Engagement prägenden Einfluss auf den schmuckkünstlerischen Nachwuchs aus. Gegen Ende der 80er Jahre übernahm mit Herbert Schulze, Elisabeth Holder und dem Niederländer Herman Hermsen eine neue Generation die Lehrtätigkeit im Fachbereich Produktdesign mit seinen Schwerpunkten Schmuck, Email und Gerät bzw. Produktgestaltung. Der 1953 in Düsseldorf geborene Herbert Schulze hatte nach einer Lehre als Gürtler und Metalldrücker von 1974 bis 1978 an der Fachhochschule Düsseldorf im Fachbereich Design seine Ausbildung zum Diplom-Designer erhalten, bevor er zum Nachfolger seines ehemaligen Lehrers Paul Georg Schminder ernannt wurde. Neben seiner Tätigkeit an der Fachhochschule Düsseldorf führten ihn Lehraufträge als

Courses of study in jewellery design have been offered in Düsseldorf since 1947, first at the *Meisterschule für das gestaltende Handwerk*, then at the *Werkkunstschule* and most recently at the new *Fachhochschule* (University of Applied Sciences) opened in 1971. Many great teachers have contributed to these courses over the years, including the widely-respected educator and head of the metalwork faculty Karl Schollmayer, the silversmith Paul Georg Schminder and the famous enamel artist Lili Schultz, who left the legendary Giebichenstein Castle in Halle on the Saale river in 1958 to come to the city on the Rhine. In 1965 Schultz' position as head of the enamel department passed to Sigrid Delius, a student of Elisabeth Treskow, the celebrated jeweller and head of the goldsmithing faculty at the *Kölner Werkschulen*. Following her appointment as professor of design at the Fachhochschule, Delius took on responsibility for the jewellery design programme and initiated a number of important changes in the curriculum in the three years that followed. She was deeply committed to her work, and together with her colleague, the internationally famous jewellery engineer Friedrich Becker, she had a profoundly formative influence on the prospective jewellers in her care. Becker, kinetic artist and pioneer of variable jewellery, had succeeded Karl Schollmayer in 1956 and continued to work as professor at the University of Applied Sciences until 1982. The late Eighties saw the arrival of a new generation of teachers – Herbert Schulze, Elisabeth Holder and the Dutchman Herman Hermsen – at the product design faculty, which now had three main departments: jewellery, enamel and product design. Herbert Schulze was born in Düsseldorf in 1953. Following an apprenticeship in brass ornament making and metal spinning he studied at Düsseldorf University of Applied Sciences from 1974-1978. After graduating with a degree in design he was then appointed

Elisabeth Holder
1999
Einschreibungen
Armschmuck
Feinsilber, Nylon
Inscriptions
arm ornament
refined silver, nylon

Elisabeth Holder
1999
Einschreibungen
Armschmuck
Feinsilber, Gummifaden, Silber
Inscriptions
arm ornament
refined silver, rubber band, silver

Elisabeth Holder
2001
Hexenbesen
Ring
Silber mit Stahlkern, Magnet
Witch's Broom
Ring
Silver with steel core, magnet

Gastdozent an die Fachhochschule für Gestaltung nach Pforzheim und an die Kunsthochschule nach Tallinn. 1989 erhielt Herbert Schulze den Staatspreis des Landes Nordrhein-Westfalen im Bereich Metall. Er ist mit seinen Arbeiten u.a. im Bauhaus-Museum in Dessau, im Deutschen Goldschmiedehaus Hanau, im Leipziger Grassimuseum und in der Sammlung Torsten Bröhan vertreten. Mit Elisabeth Holder wurde 1988 eine besonders im englischsprachigen Raum weithin bekannte Schmuckkünstlerin zur Professorin für Schmuckdesign an die Fachhochschule Düsseldorf berufen. Nach Abschluss ihrer Goldschmiedelehre hatte die gebürtige Sindelfingerin an der Staatlichen Zeichenakademie Hanau, der Fachhochschule Düsseldorf und dem Royal College of Art in London studiert, wo sie von 1985 bis 1988 auch als Dozentin tätig war. Nach insgesamt zehnjährigem Englandaufenthalt kehrte sie an ihre Alma Mater nach Düsseldorf zurück und ist heute im Bereich Schmuckdesign für das Gestalten von Unikaten zuständig. Seit 1998 ist sie zudem Mitglied im Präsidium der Gesellschaft für Goldschmiedekunst e.V. in Hanau und hält in ihrer Eigenschaft als Jurorin und externe Prüferin weiterhin engen Kontakt zur Schmuckszene in Großbritannien. Einzelausstellungen der Schmuckkünstlerin waren in der Electrum Gallery in London, dem Schmuckforum Zürich sowie dem Jewelerswerk in Washington D.C. zu sehen. Ihre Arbeiten befinden sich in der Art Gallery of Western Australia in Perth, im Victoria and Albert Museum in London, im Royal Museum of Scotland, im Schmuckmuseum Pforzheim sowie im Museum für Kunstgewerbe Berlin, um nur einige zu nennen. 1992 erhielt das Team Holder/Schulze Verstärkung durch die Berufung des holländischen Produktdesigners Herman Hermsen zum Professor für Produktdesign und Serienschmuck. Zuvor hatte Hermsen, nach seinem Studium an der Akademie der Bildenden Künste in Arnheim und einer vierjährigen Tätigkeit als Assistent bei Emmy van

Elisabeth Holder
2001
Hexenbesen
Nadel
Geschwärztes Silber mit Stahlkern, Magnet
Witch's Broom
pin
oxidised silver with steel core, magnet

Gebündelte Konzentration und widerspenstige Eigenwilligkeit.
Focused concentration and wilful idiosyncrasy.

as the successor of his own former teacher, Georg Schminder. In addition to his work at Düsseldorf University of Applied Sciences Schulze also had stints as a guest lecturer at the Design College in Pforzheim and the Art College in Tallinn. In 1989 he was awarded the North Rhine-Westphalia State Prize for metalwork. His work is on show at the *Bauhaus Museum* in Dessau, the *Goldschmiedehaus* in Hanau, the *Grassi Museum* in Leipzig, the Torsten Bröhan Collection and elsewhere. The jewellery artist Elisabeth Holder, whose work is particularly well known in Great Britain, became professor of jewellery design at Düsseldorf University of Applied Sciences in 1988. She originally hails from Sindelfingen. After completing her goldsmith's apprenticeship she studied at the *Staatliche Zeichenakademie* in Hanau, the University of Applied Sciences in Düsseldorf and the *Royal College of Art* in London, where she also worked as a lecturer from 1985 until 1988. After a total of ten years in England she returned to her alma mater in Düsseldorf, where she is now responsible for one-off pieces in the jewellery design department. In 1998 she also became a member of the governing committee of the *Society for Goldsmiths' Art* in Hanau. She also maintains close contact with the jewellery scene in Great Britain in her capacity as a juror and external examiner. Exhibitions of her jewellery art have been shown at the *Electrum Gallery* in London, the *Schmuckforum* in Zurich and the *Jewelerswerk* in Washington D.C. Her work is also on show at many leading museums, including the Art Gallery of Western Australia in Perth, the *Victoria and Albert Museum* in London, the *Royal Museum of Scotland*, the *Jewellery Museum* in Pforzheim and the *Museum of Applied Art* in Berlin. In 1992 the Holder and Schulze team received reinforcement in the person of the Dutch product designer Herman Hermsen, who became professor of product design and serialised jewel-

Leersum und Gijs Bakker, Produktdesign an der Hochschule für Bildende Künste in Utrecht und, von 1990 bis 1992, Produkt- und Schmuckgestaltung an der Akademie der Bildenden Künste in Arnheim gelehrt. Herman Hermsen war mit Einzelausstellungen in der Galerie RA in Amsterdam, bei Marzee in Nijmegen und Spektrum in München vertreten. Seine Arbeiten findet man in privaten und öffentlichen Sammlungen in den Niederlanden, Großbritannien, Deutschland, Kanada und den USA, darunter im Stedelijk Museum Amsterdam und im Londoner Victoria and Albert Museum. Die drei Lehrenden prägen mit ihrer künstlerischen Persönlichkeit und ihrer jeweiligen Lehrauffassung auf unterschiedliche Weise den Fachbereich und seine Studierenden. Die von Herbert Schulze an sein eigenes Schaffen wie auch an das seiner Studierenden angelegten strengen Gestaltungsmaßstäbe werden gemildert durch das Bemühen, den Nachwuchs in seinen Begabungen zu fördern und ihn bei der Suche nach eigenständigen Lösungen zu unterstützen. Herman Hermsen ist es eher ein Anliegen, die seiner Meinung nach häufig allzu angepassten deutschen Studenten ein wenig aufzurütteln und sie zur Rebellion zu ermuntern, zum Experimentieren, zu Grenzüberschreitungen. Sein Ziel ist es nicht, wie er selber treffend formuliert, „Nutzpflanzen zu züchten, sondern Unkraut, Wildwuchs". Nicht die perfekte Beherrschung des Goldschmiede-Handwerks hat für ihn vorrangige Bedeutung, sondern die Gestaltungsabsicht, für die es dann gilt, die optimale technische Lösung zu suchen. Auch Elisabeth Holder geht es nicht allein um die Vermittlung von Fachkenntnissen, wenngleich sie großen Wert legt auf eine der Gestaltungsidee angemessene, sorgfältige handwerkliche Umsetzung. Die für ihre undogmatische und einfühlsame Haltung bekannte Lehrerin möchte die angehenden Schmuckdesignerinnen und -designer anregen, sich auf Entdeckungen einzulassen, sich persönlich einzubringen und darüber möglichst

lery. After his course of study at the College of Art in Arnheim and a four-year spell as assistant to Emmy van Leersum and Gijs Bakker, Hermsen had taught product design at the College of Art in Utrecht and, from 1990–1992, product and jewellery design at the College of Art in Arnheim. Exhibitions of his work have been staged at *Galerie RA* in Amsterdam, *Marzee* in Nijmegen and *Spektrum* in Munich. His work can also be seen in private and public collections in the Netherlands, Great Britain, Germany, Canada and the USA, including the *Stedelijk Museum* in Amsterdam and the *Victoria and Albert Museum* in London. Each of the three teachers has an individual artistic personality and educational approach, each contributing different facets and qualities to the department and its students. The strict artistic standards that Herbert Schulze imposes on both himself and his students are counterbalanced by his commitment to developing the individual talents of his charges, and by his efforts to help them find their own unique solutions. Herman Hermsen's focus is more on stirring up his, as he sees them, often all-too conformist German students, and on encouraging them to rebel, experiment and break away from conventions. His goal, as he himself so aptly puts it, is "to cultivate wild growth and weeds rather than standard agricultural crops." His priority is not perfect mastery of the goldsmith's craft but rather the design idea itself, for which one must then find the best possible technical solution. Elisabeth Holder is also not exclusively interested in the mere communication of technical skills, even though she sets great store by the development of the scrupulous craftsmanship needed to realise the artistic idea. Known for her sensitive and undogmatic style, Holder encourages her budding jewellery designers to be open for new discoveries, to give of themselves in their work and to use the medium of jewellery for the expression of universal

Herman Hermsen
1981/1998
Charis
Stehleuchte
Aluminium, Stahl, Messing
Charis
standard lamp
aluminium, steel, brass
Foto: Fotostudio Hans Döring, München
Hersteller: ClassiCon, München

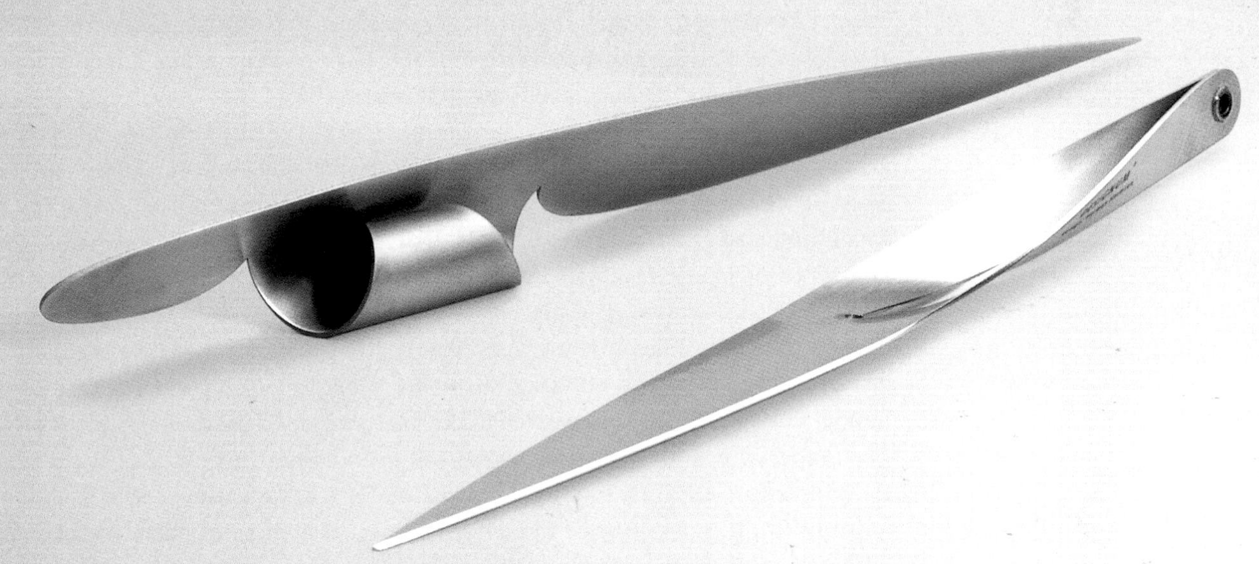

zu allgemeingültigen Aussagen im Schmuck zu gelangen. Elisabeth Holder hat keine fertigen Antworten parat; die von ihr betreuten angehenden Schmuckkünstler und -künstlerinnen geraten aber darüber ins Schwärmen, wie sie – durchaus mit einer gewissen Nachdrücklichkeit – die richtigen Fragen zu stellen weiß, die den Weg zu eigenen Erkenntnissen ebnen und die Individualität des Einzelnen fördern. Die Pluralität in der Lehrauffassung setzt sich fort im künstlerischen Selbstverständnis der drei Dozenten. Trotz der Beanspruchung durch die Lehrtätigkeit kann jeder von ihnen ein substantielles Werk vorweisen, das in seiner künstlerischen Eigenart den Studierenden Orientierungsmöglichkeit und Reibungsfläche zugleich bietet. **Poetische Abstraktionen oder Über die Kunst des Weglassens. Schmuck von Elisabeth Holder** Leicht macht er es einem nicht, der Schmuck von Elisabeth Holder: keine weich fließenden Formen, nichts Üppiges, kein strahlender Glanz des Metalls oder magisches Funkeln farbiger Steine, wenig dem Auge und der Hand Schmeichelndes. Auch die verführerische Aura unterkühlter Erotik, die so manches Designerschmuckstück umgibt, die Archaik überdimensionaler Formate, die Gesprächigkeit figurativer Darstellung sucht man vergebens. Weder machen die Arbeiten durch aggressive, scharfkantige Provokation auf sich aufmerksam, noch locken sie mit der anmutigen Zartheit filigraner Kostbarkeit. Still und scheinbar selbstgenügsam liegen die kargen, matt schimmernden Schmuckobjekte aus Metall vor einem, kaum dazu angetan, das Herz zu entflammen, geschweige denn Gelüste des Berührens oder Besitzens zu wecken. So viel Sprödigkeit, Zurückhaltung, Distanziertheit, so wenig Bemühen, zu gefallen oder einen Effekt zu erzielen – nimmt es da wunder, wenn sich die Sinne enttäuscht, ja gelangweilt abwenden? Nun mögen die Sinne nicht sogleich gefangen genommen werden von Elisabeth Holders verhaltenen, unprätentiösen Kreationen, der Verstand indes fühlt sich allemal

Herman Hermsen
1992
Fontana
Brieföffner
Edelstahl
Fontana
letter opener
stainless steel
Foto: Ans Dekkers, Arnheim
Hersteller: Designum

Herman Hermsen
1992
Swift
Brieföffner
Edelstahl
Swift
letter opener
stainless steel
Foto: Ans Dekkers, Arnheim
Hersteller: Designum

messages. Elisabeth Holder does not deliver stock answers; but the prospective jewellery artists in her care are enthusiastic about her ability, which she exercises with a certain degree of emphatic vigour, to pose just the right questions – questions that enable the students to make their own discoveries and develop their own individuality. The plurality expressed in the three's approach to teaching is continued in their own artistic work. Despite the demands of their teaching duties, each of them has produced a substantial and idiosyncratic oeuvre that gives the students both orientation and a source of positive friction. Poetic Abstraction or the Art of Leaving Things Out – Jewellery by Elisabeth Holder **The jewellery of Elisabeth Holder doesn't make it easy on the beholder: there are no gently flowing forms, no opulence, no brilliant gleaming of metal or magical glittering of coloured stones, little to indulge the hand or the eye. One searches in vain for the seductive aura of subdued eroticism found in some designer art, the archaism of over-dimensioned formats or the loquacity of figurative representations. These works do not draw attention to themselves with aggressive, sharp-edged provocation, nor do they beckon with the graceful delicacy of precious filigree finery. With their matte gleam, these austere jewellery objects lie before one quietly and with seeming modesty, hardly looking as though they might be able to awaken the fire of passion in the heart, let alone the desire to touch or possess. Confronted with so much aloofness, reservation and distance, so little effort to please or create an effect – is it any surprise when the senses first turn away in disappointment, even boredom? However, even though our senses may not be immediately captivated by Elisabeth Holder's reticent, unpretentious creations, they certainly do exercise a pull on the mind. Our intellect demonstrates a willingness to open to them, plumb their possible**

von ihnen angezogen. Er ist bereit, sich auf sie einzulassen, mögliche Bedeutungen auszuloten, Nuancen zu erkunden, Geheimnisse zu entschlüsseln. Diese intellektuelle Herangehensweise von Seiten der Betrachterin oder des Betrachters mag eine untypische Reaktion auf die angewandte Kunst sein, aber unter der Prämisse, dass Schmuck nicht nur von Schmücken kommt, sondern dass er auch Bedeutungsträger sein kann, erscheint ein derart ‚kopflastiges' Herantasten der Trägerin oder des Trägers durchaus nicht abwegig.

Elisabeth Holders Schmuck ist komplexer, als er auf den ersten flüchtigen Blick erscheinen mag. Die Künstlerin arbeitet von Anfang an in Werkgruppen, welche ein bestimmtes Grundmotiv variieren und durch prozesshaftes Vorgehen erschließen. Ein frühes Beispiel hierfür stellt eine Reihe von runden Broschen aus Silber und Stahl dar, die 1980 während ihrer Zeit in England entstanden sind. Die Broschen sind beinahe identisch und weisen lediglich minimale Abweichungen in den reliefartigen Erhöhungen im Zentrum des ansonsten schmucklosen Rundes auf. Rein formal entstehen diese Abdrücke durch die unterschiedlichen Rahmen, über die das hauchdünne Silber gespannt ist. Ein Ergebnis systematischer Formvariation oder Ausdruck verschlüsselter Zeichenhaftigkeit? Ungefähr zehn Jahre später finden sich auf einer ruhigen ovalen Silberbrosche zwei zarte, eckige Abdrücke – *Impressions* –, die rätselhaften Chiffren gleichen. Erst wenn man erfährt, dass es einen dazugehörigen Ring, eine Kombination aus Quadrat und Dreieck, gibt, erklären sich die Spuren: Ringspuren auf einer Brosche, zwei Schmuckobjekte – oder sollte man besser sagen Subjekte? –, die in Beziehung zueinander stehen, miteinander kommunizieren, obwohl sie unterschiedlicher in der Form nicht sein könnten.

In seiner minimalistischen Formgebung, die sich im Wesentlichen auf geometische Grundelement wie Kreis, Quadrat, Dreieck und Linie konzentriert, mag der Holdersche Schmuck zwar spröde anmuten, er strahlt aber

Herman Hermsen
1996
Zapp
Bücherkette
Fotos, Kunststoff,
Silber, Fluoritperlen
Zapp
book chain
photos, plastic, silver,
fluorite beads
Foto: Ans Dekkers, Arnheim

meanings, explore nuances, decipher secrets. This intellectual approach on the part of the beholder may be an atypical response to applied art, but given the premise that jewellery can transport meaning as well as being mere decoration, it actually seems quite reasonable the wearer should choose such a cerebral way of coming to grips with the work.

Elisabeth Holder's jewellery is actually more complex that one might imagine at first glance. The artist always uses the medium of a series within which she varies and explores a basic motif in a process of development. One early example of this is a series of round brooches made of silver and steel produced in 1980 during her period in England. The brooches are virtually identical, with only minimal variations in the relief-like elevations in the centre of the otherwise unadorned circle. In purely formal terms, these impressions are created by the differences in the frames on which the paperthin silver is stretched. The result of a systematic variation in form, or perhaps an expression of encrypted semiotics? Around ten years later, on a quiet oval silver brooch, we find two delicate, angular *Impressions* with the character of mysterious ciphers. These marks only make sense when we learn that there is a matching ring, in the form of a combination of a square and a triangle. Impressions of a ring on a brooch, two jewellery objects – or better, subjects – that have a relationship with one another, communicate with one another, although their individual forms could hardly be more different.

In its minimalist form, which is essentially restricted to a basic geometrical element like circle, square, triangle or line, Holder's jewellery may appear reserved, but it by no means has the unfriendly coldness of a more technological aesthetics, nor is it inaccessible in its introversion. On the contrary; an openness for experiments in relating is one of its foremost characteristics. She only rarely produces an isolated piece. Her works do

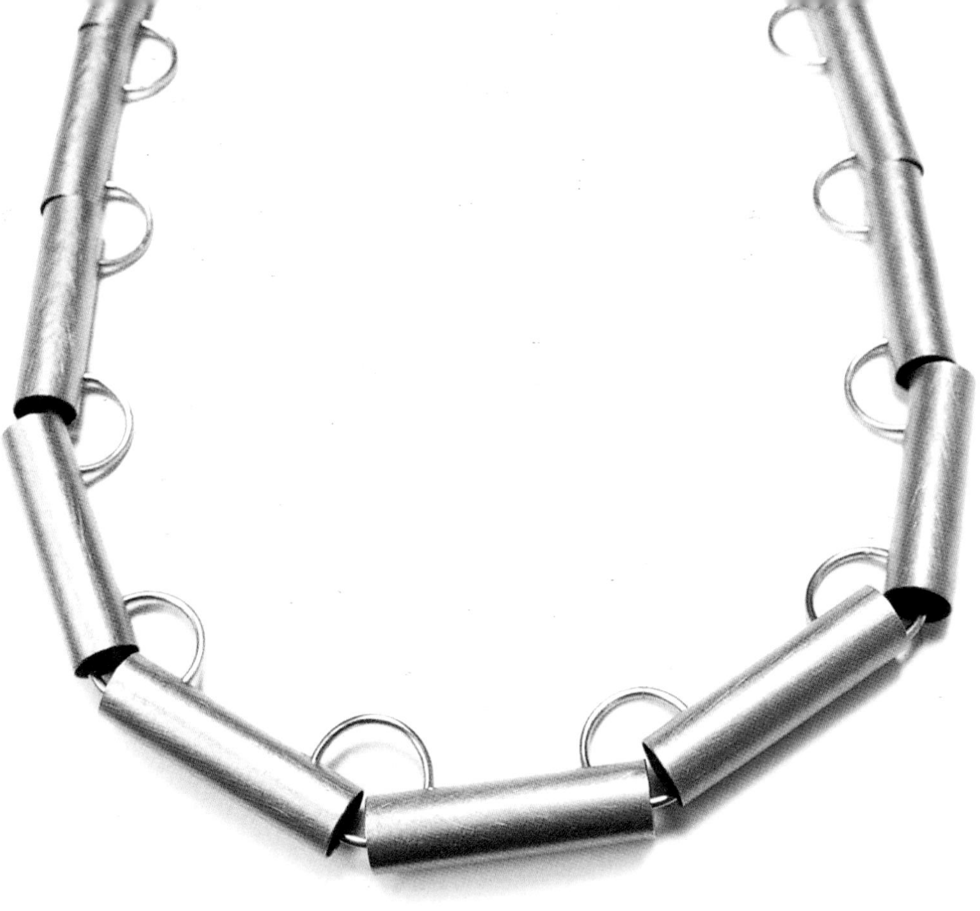

Herman Hermsen
1997
Röhrchenkette
Silber, Gold
Tubelet chain
Silver, gold
Foto: Ans Dekkers, Arnheim

keineswegs die abweisende Kälte einer technisch geprägten Ästhetik aus oder ist in seiner Introvertiertheit unzugänglich. Im Gegenteil, ihm ist eine Offenheit für Experimente des In-Beziehung-Setzens eigen. Nur selten steht ein Stück für sich allein. Nicht festgefügt, starr und endgültig präsentieren sich die Arbeiten, sondern beweglich, mehrteilig, variabel, ja unvollendet und ergänzungsbedürftig. Es ist an der Trägerin bzw. dem Träger, mögliche Beziehungsvarianten zu erkennen oder spielerisch zu erproben, durch Kombination und Hinzufügung am Gestaltungsprozess teilzunehmen und dem Schmuckstück eine individuelle Deutung zu verleihen. Die Werkgruppe *Gardenpieces* etwa, die aus den 90er Jahren datiert, greift ein wiederkehrendes Thema des zeitgenössischen Schmuckschaffens der Avantgarde auf und wandelt es ab, nämlich Schmuck aus Fundstücken. Anders als ihre frühen Ringe aus geschliffenen Bruchstücken viktorianischer Kacheln, wie man sie in Londoner Hauseingängen findet, sind die *Gardenpieces* weniger Arbeiten *aus* Fundstücken, sondern *für* Gefundenes. Die äußerst reduziert gestalteten Klemm-Ringe und Anhänger aus zwei lose durch einen Gummifaden miteinander verbundenen rechteckigen Silberplatten sind als Behältnisse konzipiert und dienen dem temporären Bewahren von Nichtigkeiten, seien es Scherben, Federn, Papier, Zweige oder Blätter. Durch diese Hinzufügungen der Trägerin werden die asketischen, kühlen Metallbehältnisse in ganz persönliche Schmuckstücke von poetischem Potential verwandelt. Ausgangspunkt für die Serie war eine Ausstellung zum Thema Duftschmuck, im Rahmen derer Elisabeth Holder einfache, breite Manschettenarmreife aus Doublé mit parfümierten Ästchen durchsteckte bzw. mit zur Innenseite hin getragenen Lavendelsachets versah. So entstand ein spannungsvolles Wechselspiel von organisch gewachsenem, unregelmäßigem Fundmaterial und handwerklich präzise bearbeitetem Metall, von Natur und Konstruktion, von

Herman Hermsen
1994
Mäander
Ringe
Gold
Meanders
rings
gold
Foto: HP Hoffmann Agentur, Düsseldorf
Hersteller: Niessing

Eheringe. Mäandrierende Bänder, mit Bewegungsspielraum verbunden.
Wedding rings. Meandering bands, linked with room for movement.

not present themselves as fixed, rigid and finalised, but rather as mobile, multi-part and variable, even unfinished and in need of completion. It is up to the wearer to identify possible variations in relationship, to discover them by playful experiment, to participate in the design process and give the piece an individual meaning through combination and addition. The *Garden Pieces* series for example, which dates from the 90s, takes up and transforms a frequent theme of contemporary avant-garde jewellery – the use of *objets trouvés*. In contrast to her earlier series of rings incorporating polished fragments of Victorian tiles of the type still found in the doorways of London houses, the *Garden Pieces* are made for rather than of *objets trouvés*. With a design of extremely reductionist simplicity, the clip rings and pendants made of two rectangular silver plates loosely connected by a rubber band are conceived as containers for the temporary keeping of trifles like pottery shards, feathers, paper scraps, twigs or leaves… These additions by the wearer transform the cool, ascetic metal containers into very personal jewellery suffused with poetic potential. The point of departure for this series was an exhibition of 'fragrance jewellery', for which Elisabeth Holder took simple, broad, rolled gold bracelets and pierced them with perfumed twigs or installed little sachets of lavender on the inside surfaces. The result was an exciting interaction of the organic irregularity of found materials with the precise craftsmanship of the worked metal, of nature with construct, of the fragmentary and coincidental with meticulously-created form. Beyond the sparse language of the jewellery and the reduction of form to the essential, another characteristic feature of these works is their autonomous existence, independent of the human body. It is not that this jewellery aspires to the status of the object. Rather, the object is the starting-point from

Bruchstückhaftem oder Zufälligem und formgebender Genauigkeit. Abgesehen von der kargen Schmucksprache und der auf das Wesentliche reduzierten Form ist eine vom menschlichen Körper unabhängige, eigenständige Existenz ein weiteres charakteristisches Merkmal der Arbeiten. Nicht, dass die Schmuckstücke nach Objekthaftigkeit strebten, sie entstehen vielmehr aus dem Objekt heraus. Der Bezug zum Körper und Tragen ergibt sich erst in einem zweiten Schritt, ist sekundär: tragbare Objekte eben. Dies gilt insbesondere für die beiden Werkgruppen *Divided Squares* und *Divided Squares Revisited*. Zu letzterer zählen die sogenannten *Schlüssel Ringe*, eine systematisch-konzeptuell entwickelte Serie von mehrteiligen Ringsets, bei denen die möglichen Teilungslinien eines Quadrates als in den Raum ragende, lineare Ringköpfe in unterschiedlicher Kombination am Finger getragen werden. Die *Schlüssel Ringe* können in gewissem Sinne als Endpunkt rationaler Formexerzitien verstanden werden, in denen ein variantenreiches Thema endgültig auf den Punkt gebracht wird. Neben der methodisch-strengen und der spielerisch-experimentellen Seite des Werkes von Elisabeth Holder gibt es auch noch die meditative, aus dem Unbewussten schöpfende. Ein Schlüssel zum Verständnis einer ganzen Reihe von Arbeiten ist die neolithische Baukunst in ihrer Zeichenhaftigkeit und ihrem Verzicht auf den rechten Winkel. Die Künstlerin nähert sich der neolithischen Architektur auf dem Wege der Meditation und Intuition und übersetzt ihre so gewonnenen Einsichten in zeichenhaften Schmuck. Das *Maltese Square* beispielsweise, eine Arbeit aus dem Jahre 1992, verweist auf steinzeitliche Kultstätten auf Malta. Auch in diesem Fall steht das Objekt wiederum im Vordergrund: Wir nehmen ein aus unterschiedlich großen Quadern und Stäben zusammengeschobenes Quadrat wahr, dessen Binnenzeichnung eine von freier Hand gezogene Gitterstruktur erkennen lässt. Wie in der Megalith-Tempelarchitektur hat

which the piece of jewellery eventually evolves. The relationship to the human body and the act of wearing arises in the next step, it is secondary – these are wearable objects. This applies in particular for the two series *Divided Squares* and *Divided Squares Revisited*. The latter includes the *Key Rings*, a systematically developed conceptual series of ring sets, in which the possible bisection lines of a square are projected into space as linear ring heads, worn on the finger in a variety of combinations. In a sense, the *Key Rings* can be seen as the end product of rational spiritual exercises with form, in which a rich and varied theme has been reduced to its final essence. The methodical strictness and playfully experimental side of Elisabeth Holder's work is counterbalanced by another, more meditative aspect drawing on the realm of the unconscious. Neolithic architecture, in its symbolism and eschewal of right angles, can be taken as a key to a whole succession of her works. The artist approaches Neolithic architecture on the path of meditation and intuition, translating the insights gained into symbolic jewellery. The *Maltese Square*, for example, a work dating from 1992, is a reference to the Stone Age temples found on Malta. Here too, the object occupies the foreground. It impinges on our awareness as blocks and rods of varying sizes grouped together to form a square, within which is a pattern in which we identify a grid structure drawn freely by hand. As in megalithic temples, each element has its own idiosyncratic shape and fit, the delicate curvatures, depressions and bulges of which give them an almost *baroque* verve that sets them apart from the precisely-worked, sharply-delineated stone blocks of occidental architecture. Well-structured, the *Maltese Square* rests in itself, exuding an aura of harmony and balance. The different colours of the chemically-tinted zinc, silver and steel lend it subtle nuances. The square reminds one a little of the

Herbert Schulze
1989
Mokkakanne
Silber, Edelstahl,
anodisiertes Aluminium
coffee pot
silver, stainless steel,
anodised aluminium

Konstruktive, klare Linien mit
kleinen Abweichungen.
Vorwitzig hier und lautlos
entschwebend da.
Constructive, clear lines with
small deviations.
Cheeky here, soundlessly drifting
away there.

jedes Element eine individuelle Passform, die sich von der in der abendländischen Architektur vorherrschenden kantigen Schärfe exakt gearbeiteter Werksteine dadurch unterscheidet, dass die Quader zarte Wölbungen, Ein- und Ausbuchtungen, ja einen geradezu ‚barocken' Schwung aufweisen. Wohlgefügt ruht das *Maltese Square* in sich, Harmonie und Ausgewogenheit ausstrahlend. Die verschiedenen Materialfarben des chemisch gefärbten Zinks, des Silbers und Stahls verleihen ihm eine subtile Nuancierung. Das Quadrat erinnert ein wenig an die Bodenskulpturen des Minimal Art-Bildhauers Carl Andre, der aus dem Zusammenspiel zwischen Skulptur und Umgebung eigenständige Orte entwickelte, deren Eigentümlichkeit er übrigens mit den Jahrtausende überdauernden Wirkungen steinzeitlicher Kultstätten verglich. Die Ruhe und Geschlossenheit des *Maltese Square*, seine harmonische Ordnung sind jedoch nicht von Dauer. Sie werden beim Übergang vom Objekt zum Schmuckstück aufgelöst, und zwar durch die Trägerin, die einzelne Elemente aus dem geordneten Zusammenhang der Fläche löst, um sie an einem Halsreif aufzureihen. Regelmäßige Lochbohrungen an den Seitenteilen der Quader und Stäbe lassen unterschiedliche Winkel bei der Aufreihung zu, so dass die Teilchen buchstäblich aus dem Lot geraten und in eine neue Beziehung zueinander gesetzt werden. Eine schier unendliche Fülle an Kombinationsmöglichkeiten tut sich auf und fordert zu spielerisch-schöpferischem Umgang heraus. Elisabeth Holders Schmuck ist linear, aber nicht geradlinig; er ist still, konzentriert und unaufdringlich, aber nicht stumm; von strenger Anmutung, enthält er gleichzeitig das Element des Spielerischen; seine Formen sind schmucklos, puristisch und komprimiert, aber nicht klinisch glatt oder von kalter Perfektion; er ist nicht dekorativ, sondern eher zeichenhaft; er verzichtet auf Ornamentales, dennoch schmückt er; er ist zugleich nüchtern und voller Poesie; dort, wo er systematisch aus einem Konzept heraus entwickelt

floor sculptures by minimalist sculptor Carl André, who creates new spaces from the interplay of sculpture and environment. Interestingly, André himself has associated the peculiar quality of these spaces with the atmosphere of Stone Age religious sites that has survived down through the millennia. The peace and unity of the *Maltese Square*, its harmonious order, are not lasting, however. They become dissolved in the transition from object to jewellery – by the wearer, who extracts the individual elements from the well-ordered context of the plane to string them together on a necklace. Regular holes drilled in the sides of the blocks and rods permit them to be strung together at a variety of angles, so that the elements are literally taken out of true and placed in a new relationship with one another. A virtually infinite range of possible combinations opens up, inviting playful and creative interaction. Elisabeth Holder's jewellery is linear, but not straight; it is quiet, concentrated and unobtrusive, but not dumb; it is of strict demeanour, but embodies at the same time an element of the playful; its forms are unembellished, purist and compressed, but not clinically smooth or of cold perfection; it is emblematic rather than decorative; it eschews the ornamental, and yet it ornaments; it is simultaneously sober and replete with poetry; even where it develops systematically from a conceptual idea it is quite willing to permit itself deviations from the same. Its material is metal: silver with a matte gleam, subtly-tinted zinc, bronze, steel, sometimes gold, more often rolled gold – all materials that are not easily formable and exercise resistance to being worked, for which any excess of desire to impose a design is alien. Holder's jewellery does not dominate its wearer, but it does demand receptivity to its qualities. It eludes rapid conquest but permits approach. And it is the wearer who releases and elevates it from the status of a mere object. The Search

Herbert Schulze
1990/1999
Teekanne mit Stövchen
Silber, Laborglas, Ebenholz
Auflage 8+1
teapot with warmer
silver, laboratory glass, ebony
in an edition of 8+1
Foto: Walter Klein, Düsseldorf

wird, erlaubt er sich durchaus Abweichungen von demselben; sein Werkstoff ist das Metall: matt schimmerndes Silber, subtil gefärbtes Zink, Bronze, Stahl, manchmal Gold, öfter Doublé – alles, was nicht leicht formbar ist und bei der Bearbeitung Widerstand leistet; ein ‚Zuviel' an Gestaltungswille ist ihm fremd. Der Holdersche Schmuck dominiert seine Trägerin nicht, verlangt aber, dass man sich auf ihn einlässt. Einer raschen Vereinnahmung entzieht er sich, Annäherung indes lässt er zu. Und erst die Trägerin oder der Träger erlöst ihn aus seiner reinen Objekthaftigkeit.

Auf der Suche nach neuen Lösungen. Schmuck- und Produktdesign von Herman Hermsen Herman Hermsens Liebe gilt dem Produkt, insbesondere den Leuchten. Schon anlässlich der Präsentation seiner Examensarbeiten im Jahre 1979 an der Kunsthochschule in Arnheim schlug sich sein ‚Lampenfieber' in einer Reihe von stark funktionsbezogenen und überwiegend flexibel konstruierten Beleuchtungskörpern von minimalistischer Gestaltung nieder. Häufig bleibt die eigentliche Lichtquelle sichtbar, wird geradezu bloßgelegt statt sich unter einem betulichen Lampenschirm zu verstecken. So wird eine nackte, kopfgespiegelte Glühbirne an einen schlichten beweglichen Stab montiert, den ein roher Bleiklotz beschwert: Le Corbusierscher Brutalismus im Lampendesign sozusagen. Auch bei der Tischlampe *ACB* – hinter diesem technisch anmutenden Kürzel verbirgt sich ein durchaus poetischer Titel *Along Came Bette* – reduziert sich das Design auf das Wesentliche. Vom einfachen Aluminiumfuß ragt das runde Rohr empor, an dessen Ende die Glühbirne angebracht ist. Auf ihr balanciert eine runde Aluminiumscheibe in verwegen schrägem Neigungswinkel – eine Reminiszenz an die extravagante Hutmode der Hollywoodstars vergangener Tage, wie der Titel des Teiles impliziert! Aus jüngster Zeit stammt der Entwurf einer Stehleuchte für die Firma *ClassiCon*. Das 1990 gegründete Unternehmen produziert Reeditionen von Klassikern im Möbel- und Leuchtendesign,

Herbert Schulze
2001
Teekanne
Silber, Ebenholz
teapot
silver, ebony
Foto: Walter Klein, Düsseldorf

for New Solutions – Jewellery and Product Design by Herman Hermsen **Herman Hermsen's love is for the product, in particular lamps. His 'lamp fever' was already clearly apparent in the diploma projects he presented in 1979 at the Art College in Arnheim, which consisted of a series of severely functional and largely flexible light fittings with a minimalist design. In his work the actual light source is often visible, is consciously laid naked rather than being concealed behind a twee lampshade. For example, he mounts a naked, mirror-head light bulb on a plain, mobile rod weighted with a block of raw lead: Le Corbusier brutalism in lamp design, so to speak. The design of his *ACB* table lamp – a technical-sounding acronym that actually stands for the rather poetic moniker *Along Came Bette* – is also reduced to the absolute minimum. The bulb is mounted in a round tube rising up from a plain aluminium base; and atop the bulb balances an aluminium disc at a brash angle reminiscent of the elegant hats worn by Hollywood stars of yesteryear – as the title implies.**

One of his more recent works is a standard lamp design for *ClassiCon*, a company established in 1990 that produces re-releases of classical furniture and lamps, including both works by people like Eileen Gray and creations of younger designers that have the potential to be the classics of tomorrow. Christened *Charis*, Herman Hermsen's standard lamp rises up like a slim stele to a height of over two metres. It is fitted with two swivelling reflector sections made of brushed, anodised aluminium that can be adjusted in relation to one another for a wide variety of lighting effects – a versatile solution of unassuming elegance.

The search for innovative solutions is not restricted to the design of lamps, furniture and consumer items like bowls, vases, trays and letter-openers. It is also apparent in Herman Hermsen's approach to his jewellery work, which is clearly influenced by the requirements

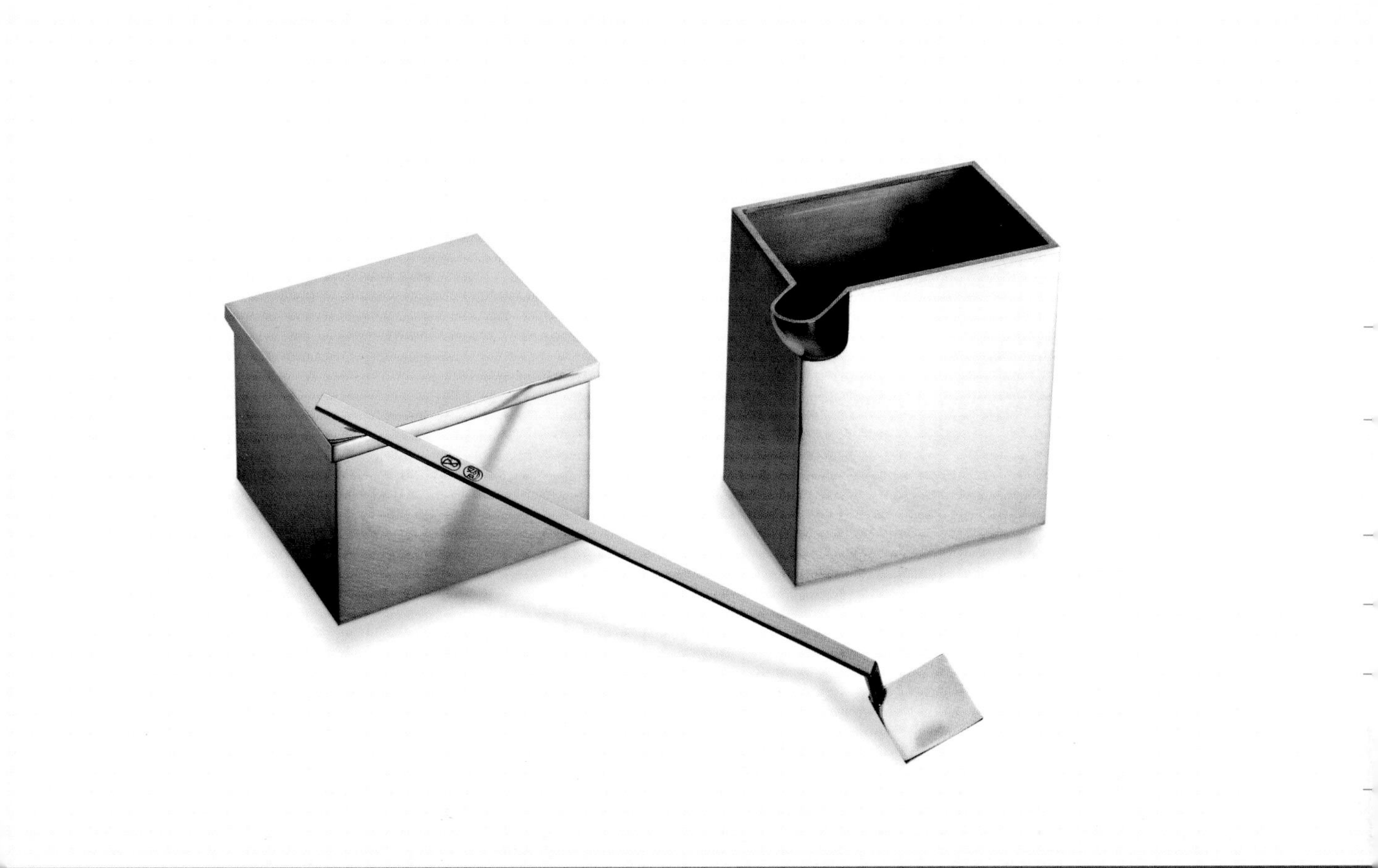

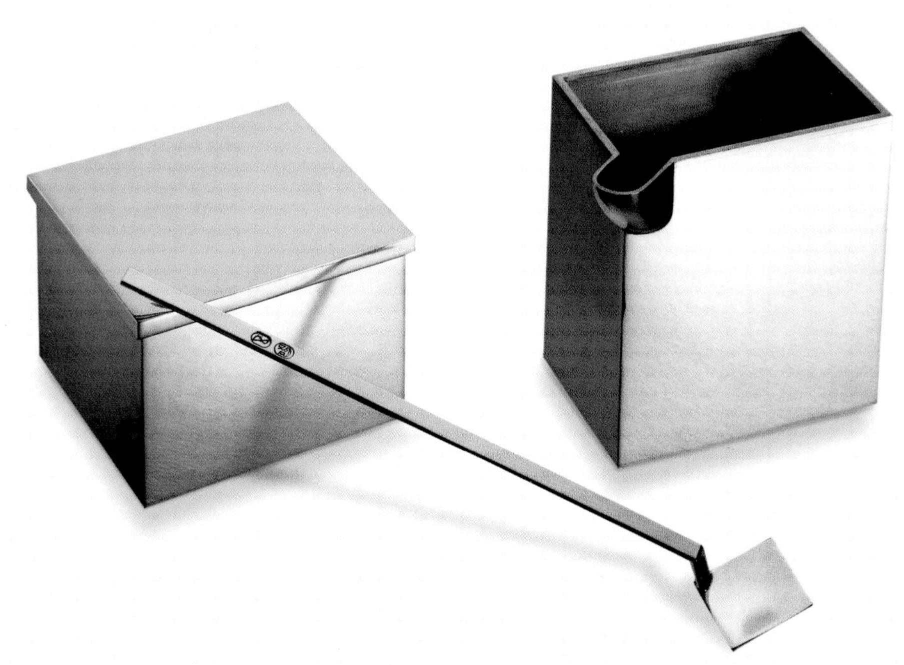

Herbert Schulze
2001
Sahnegießer, Zuckerschale, Zuckerlöffel
Silber
cream jug, sugar bowl, sugar spoon
silver
Foto: Walter Klein, Düsseldorf

u.a. von Eileen Gray, aber auch von jüngeren Designern, die das Zeug zum Klassiker von morgen haben. Einer schlanken Stele gleich ragt die Leuchte *Charis* von Herman Hermsen über zwei Meter in die Höhe. Mit ihren beiden drehbaren Reflektor-Profilen aus gebürstetem eloxierten Aluminium können – je nach Stellung der Profile zueinander – unterschiedliche Lichteffekte erzeugt werden – eine variable Lösung von schlichter Eleganz. Die Suche nach innovativen Lösungen beschränkt sich nicht auf das Leuchtendesign oder die Gestaltung von Möbeln und Gebrauchsartikeln wie Schalen, Vasen, Tabletts und Brieföffner, sondern bestimmt auch Herman Hermsens Herangehensweise an den Schmuck. Letztere ist geprägt von den Erfordernissen und den Erfahrungen im Umgang mit dem Produktdesign. Während seiner Studienzeit fertigte Hermsen nur ein einziges Schmuckstück: eine die Augen spiegelnde Klammer aus verchromtem Messing für die Nasenwurzel. Ein irritierendes, eher verunzierendes denn schmückendes Objekt, welches herkömmlichen Schmuckauffassungen gründlich widersprach. Erst im Anschluss an das Studium fand eine intensivere Auseinandersetzung mit der Schmuckgestaltung statt und während der Zeit als Assistent von Emmy van Leersum erfolgte eine quasi autodidaktische Aneignung der Grundlagen des Handwerkes. Eine klassische Gold- und Silberschmiedeausbildung absolvierte Hermsen nicht. Herman Hermsen macht Schmuck wie ein Produktdesigner, was sich einerseits in seiner Vorliebe für Serienschmuck, zum anderen in der auf äußerste Reduktion gerichteten Gestaltungsabsicht manifestiert.
Mit seiner Auffassung, dass ein aussagekräftiges, gut gestaltetes Schmuckstück nicht nur einer einzigen, womöglich besonders wohlhabenden Käuferin zugänglich gemacht oder wegen seines materiellen Wertes in einem Tresor weggeschlossen werden sollte, steht Hermsen ganz in der niederländischen Tradition eines ‚demokratischen' Schmuckverständnisses, wie es von

Herbert Schulze
1993/1999
Schalen
Silber
bowls
silver

of and experience from the disciplines of product design. During his student days Hermsen only created one piece of jewellery, a clip made of chrome-plated brass, designed to be worn at the base of the nose so that it reflected the eyes. Marring the wearer's appearance rather than flattering, it was a disconcerting work that ran directly counter to established jewellery concepts. It was only after graduation that Hermsen embarked on a more intensive involvement with jewellery design, acquiring the necessary grounding in the craftsmanship autodidactically during his period as Emmy van Leersum's assistant. He never received any formal training as a goldsmith or silversmith. Herman Hermsen approaches jewellery as a product designer. This is manifested both in his partiality for serialised jewellery and in the extreme reductionism of his designs. Hermsen believes that an expressive, well-designed piece of jewellery should not be a one-off piece destined for and accessible to only a single, wealthy buyer, and possibly even locked away from sight in a safe because of its extreme material value. This stance places him firmly in the Dutch tradition of 'democratic jewellery' propagated since the Seventies by artists like Emmy van Leersum and Gijs Bakker. In his opinion the rationale of serialised jewellery is absolutely equal in value to that of the one-off pieces. Just like unique works, jewellery produced in series cannot have significance if it does not embody an individual message imparted to it by the designer. Many of the Dutchman's jewellery works are like cryptic, provocative commentaries on themes that include both jewellery itself and social criticism. In particular the early, minimalist works created in the Eighties, made of colourfully-painted steel wire, aluminium and plastic, with a linearity reminiscent of architectural drawings, are experiments in form that negate or lampoon established ideas of jewellery rather than attempting to be wearable, let

Emmy van Leersum und Gijs Bakker seit den 70er Jahren propagiert worden war. Seiner Meinung nach ist die dem Serienschmuck zugrunde liegende Thematik der des Unikates absolut ebenbürtig. Auch im seriell gefertigten Schmuck könne kein signifikantes Stück entstehen, sofern die Form nicht eine inhaltliche, individuelle Aussage des Entwerfers verkörpere. Zahlreiche Schmuckobjekte des Niederländers kommen hintersinnigen, provokanten Kommentaren von teilweise schmuck- und gesellschaftskritischer Relevanz gleich. Vor allem die frühen minimalistischen Arbeiten der 80er Jahre aus farbig lackiertem Stahldraht, Aluminium und Kunststoff, die in ihrer Linearität an Architekturzeichnungen erinnern, sind eher gängige Schmuckvorstellungen negierende oder persiflierende Formexperimente, als dass sie sich an der Tragbarkeit oder gar am Aspekt des Schmückens orientierten. Da gibt es den sperrigen Kopfschmuck aus signalrot lackiertem dünnen Stahldraht, der – über den Ohren befestigt – kantig und abweisend in den Raum hineinragt und den Kopf der Trägerin zum Sperrbezirk erklärt. Oder die zweiteiligen Drahtbroschen, die recht ‚unbroschenhaft' daherkommen, sind sie doch eines ihrer wichtigsten Funktionsmechanismen, nämlich der Broschierung, beraubt. Sie halten durch ausgeklügelt simples Stecken an der Kleidung. Ohrringe aus rotem Kunststoff in Form von Mündern werden einfach über die Ohrläppchen gezogen, die einem dann sozusagen frech die Zunge aus dem geöffneten Mund am Ohr herausstrecken. Und beim *Strahlenkranz für die säkularisierte Madonna* ruhen überdimensionale, stark farbige Glassteine – in graues PVC gefasst – wie ein verrutschter Heiligenschein auf den Schultern der Trägerin; die technische Herausforderung bei diesem Stück lag übrigens in dem Verfahren, die Steine in Kunststoff zu betten. Starke monochrome Farben, reduziertes Design, unedle Materialien, intelligente neuartige Verschlusslösungen und eine kritische Auffassung von Schmuck charakterisieren die

Ina Leppin
2000
Ein Hauch von ...
Pusteblumenschale
PVC, Löwenzahnsamen
A breath of ...
dandelion bowl
PVC, dandelion seeds

alone decorative. For example an unwieldy head ornament made of thin steel wire painted signal red, which, when worn, projects defensively into surrounding space, clearly defining the head of the wearer as an off-limits zone. Or his two-piece wire brooches, which he made decidedly un-broochlike by eliminating the clasp, thus robbing them of their most elemental function; instead, they were kept in place on the clothing by an extremely simple method of fastening. Then there are earrings made of red plastic in the shape of mouths to be slipped over the earlobes, looking then as though they were cheekily sticking out their tongues with the wearer's ears. And in the *Halo for the Secularised Madonna* oversized, brightly-coloured glass stones set in grey PVC rest on the shoulders of the wearer in a construction like a halo that has slipped out of place; the technical challenge of this piece lay in the process required for setting the stones in the plastic. Strongly monochromatic colours, reduced design, nonprecious materials, intelligent and novel fastening solutions and a critical attitude to jewellery are the characteristics of the works of his first decade, which were developed as prototypes and then serialised with marked success. It was refreshing, unconventional, carefree jewellery, work of the zeitgeist destined for a young audience.
Herman Hermsen is anything but a dogmatist, and in his more recent works the aspect of adornment is now playing an increasingly important role, along with the theme of balance between technical construction and design. He has also extended his pallet of materials, now using silver, gold, pearls and synthetic and precious stones as well. His works continue to formally reductionist, but pure experiments in form are retreating increasingly into the background. In the early Nineties he produced a series of gold jewellery pieces in which the brooch pin or fastening was simply sawn out of the material and turned back,

Auf den zweiten Blick erschließt sich in Ruhe und Besinnung ein Hauch, der die Dinge in Bewegung setzt.
On second glance, in quiet contemplation, one discerns a subtle breath that sets things in motion.

Ina Leppin
2000
Ein Hauch von ...
Pusterohr-Ring
Edelstahl, Silber, Glas, Löwenzahnsamen, Styropor
A breath of...
blowpipe ring
stainless steel, glass, silver, dandelion seed, Styrofoam

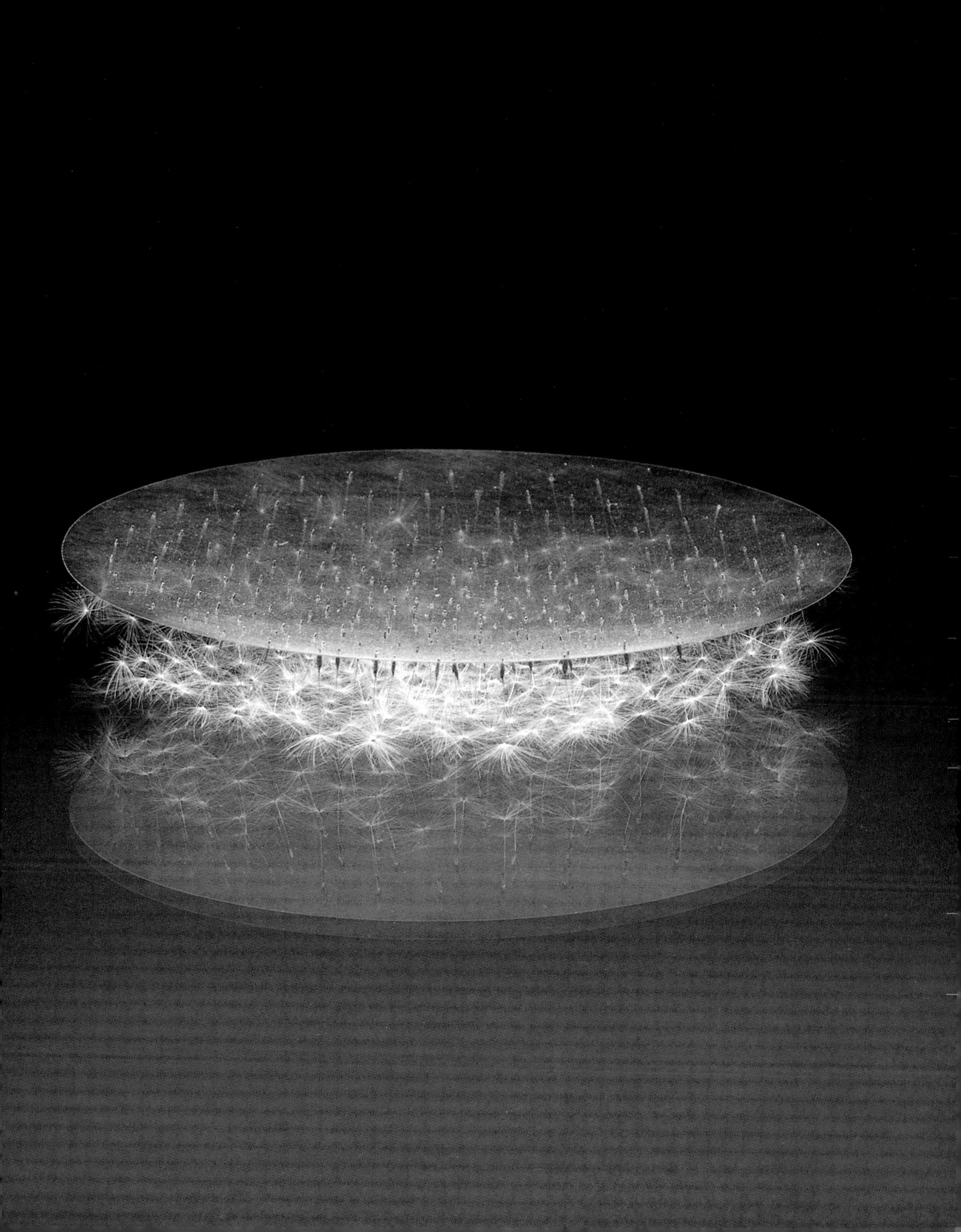

Stücke der ersten Dekade, die als Prototypen entwickelt überaus erfolgreich in Serie gingen. Es war ein erfrischend unkonventioneller, unbekümmerter, vom Zeitgeist geprägter Schmuck für ein junges Publikum. Nun ist Herman Hermsen fürwahr kein Dogmatiker und so spielt bei seinen neueren Arbeiten neben dem Thema der Balance von technischer Konstruktion und Gestaltung zunehmend der Aspekt des Schmückens eine Rolle. Auch die Palette der verwendeten Materialien hat sich erweitert und umfasst neuerdings Silber und Gold, Perlen, synthetische und edle Steine. Nach wie vor sind die Arbeiten formal stark reduziert, aber reine Formexperimente treten zusehends in den Hintergrund. Anfang der 90er Jahre entsteht eine Serie von Schmuckstücken aus Gold, bei der die Broschierung bzw. die Befestigung aus der Fläche gesägt und nach hinten geklappt wird. Die Grenze zwischen Dekor und Funktion verwischt sich, indem die Funktion der Befestigung sichtbar gemacht und gleichzeitig als dekoratives Element verwendet wird. Bei den für die Ehering-Kollektion der Firma Niessing entworfenen *Mäanderringen* greift Hermsen eines der klassischen Ornamente der Antike auf. Mittels Laserstrahl wird die Zierkante in der Mitte des Edelmetallbandes um den ganzen Ring herumgezogen, hat aber nicht nur schmückenden, sondern gleichzeitig konstruktiven Charakter. Sie teilt den Ring in zwei Teile, die mit einem gewissen Bewegungsspielraum dauerhaft miteinander verbunden bleiben: eine gelungene Metapher für den Bund der Ehe. Ende der 90er Jahre entstehen mithilfe von Fertigungsprinzipien, die dem Maschinenbau entlehnt sind, Silberringe mit Schmucksteinen von bestechend klarem Design und kühler Erotik. Zwei Rohrabschnitte von gleichem Durchmesser und gleicher Länge werden an den Berührungspunkten verlötet, wobei ein Rohrabschnitt als Ringschiene fungiert, der andere, in dessen Tiefe der von zwei Sprengringen gehaltene facettierte Stein glitzert, als Ringkopf. In einer Weiterent-

Ina Leppin
2000
Ein Hauch von ...
Pusteblumenschale
PVC, Löwenzahnsamen
A breath of...
dandelion bowl
PVC, dandelion seeds

clouding the division between decoration and function by making the fastening function visible and using it simultaneously as a decorative element. In his *Meander Rings* collection of wedding rings created for the Niessing jewellery company Hermsen took up one of the classic ornaments of antiquity. A laser beam was used to inscribe the meander around the entire circumference of the precious metal band. In addition to its decorative function, this pattern was also structural, actually dividing the ring into two parts that could move slightly in relation to one another while still remaining permanently bonded – a successful metaphor for the bond of marriage. At the end of the Nineties he used production methods borrowed from mechanical engineering to create a series of silver rings set with decorative stones that shone with strikingly clear design and cool eroticism. Two lengths of tube of the same diameter and length were soldered together at the point of abutment. One functioned as the ring proper, the other as the ring head, with a faceted stone held in place by two snap rings glittering within its depths. In a further development of this series Hermsen designed rings made of a metal strip twisted in the form of the figure eight with a channel in the centre, in which the stone rested, within the smaller loop. The colours of transparent stones have played a greater role throughout all his work in recent years. In the series *Jewelry for Oneself* they are often found in pendants in which the stone is only visible to the wearer. Among his most recent works is a series of variable necklaces with the expressive title *Zapp*, which can be seen as an investigation of the topical theme of 'image overload'. The necklaces consist of small, square books with seven pages each, containing laminated photo clippings that can be turned like the pages of a ring binder for ever-changing configurations. The themes of the photo-stories are generally

wicklung dieser Serie entwarf Hermsen Ringe aus einem Metallstreifen mit mittiger Riefe, die in der kleineren Rundung des zu einer Acht gebogenen Bandes den Stein fixiert. Die Farbigkeit transparenter Steine spielt insgesamt eine größere Rolle in den letzten Jahren. Im Rahmen der Werkgruppe *Schmuck für sich* werden sie häufig zu Anhängern verarbeitet, bei denen der Stein allein für die Trägerin sichtbar ist. Als eine Auseinandersetzung mit dem Thema ‚Bilderflut' kann man die aus jüngster Zeit datierenden variablen Halsketten mit dem vielsagenden Titel *Zapp* deuten. Die Colliers bestehen aus kleinen quadratischen, jeweils siebenblättrigen Büchern, deren laminierte Fotoausschnitte wie die Seiten eines Ringbuches umgeklappt werden können und zu immer neuen Konfigurationen führen. Die Themen der Bildergeschichten sind meist beliebig: Tiere, Pflanzen, der Arbeitstag südamerikanischer Goldgräber, Landschaften, Hautstrukturen oder Mineralien. Einzelheiten sind aus der Distanz nicht erkennbar, wahrgenommen wird eine bunte Vielfalt flüchtiger Eindrücke. Erst ein näheres Hinsehen bringt Aufschluss und kann gelegentlich Irritationen auslösen, wie etwa eine Auftragsarbeit mit Ausschnitten von Erotika. Herman Hermsens Anliegen ist es, neue technische Lösungen und eine innovative Formgebung im Serienschmuck mit inhaltlichen Aussagen zu verbinden. Er würde sicherlich dem Heisenbergschen Diktum zustimmen, das besagt: „Wo kein Inhalt mehr zur Gestaltung drängt, hilft es nicht, neue Formen zu erfinden". Damit setzt er sich wohltuend von so manch seelenlosem Designerschmuckstück ab und beweist, dass serielle Fertigung und künstlerischer Anspruch sich nicht ausschließen müssen. **Klassisch modern – harmonisch exzentrisch: Gerät von Herbert Schulze** Weitgehend frei von einengenden Vorgaben individueller Auftraggeber und fernab den Bedingungen des Marktes und des industriellen Produktionsprozesses formuliert Herbert Schulze in seiner Werkstatt selbstbestimmt Gestaltungsideen

Ina Leppin
2000
Ein Hauch von ...
Schnurrhaarringe
Edelstahl, Silber,
Katzenbarthaare, Styropor
A breath of...
cats' whiskers rings
stainless steel, silver,
cats' whiskers, Styrofoam

arbitrary: animals, plants, South American gold-diggers at work, landscapes, close-ups of skin structures or minerals. Seen from a distance no details are visible, one only perceives a colourful flood of fleeting impressions. The actual images only become discernible when one moves closer, and this can also lead to occasional surprises, for example in the case of a commissioned work with erotica clippings. Herman Hermsen's objective is to combine new technical solutions and innovative forms with artistic statements in the medium of serialised jewellery. He would no doubt agree with Heisenberg's dictum: "Where there is no content impelling the unfolding of design it will not help to invent new forms." In this his work is a welcome contrast to the soullessness of much designer jewellery, proving that serialised production and artistic standards do not have to be mutually exclusive. Classically Modern, Harmoniously Eccentric – Product Design by Herbert Schulze Herbert Schulze formulates his design ideas in metal in the freedom of his own workshop, largely unrestricted by the demands of individual clients and far from the impositions of the market and the industrial manufacturing process. His seminal influences include the Scottish designer Christopher Dresser, an early proponent of the language of functional form in the 19th century, whose work was characterised by the aesthetics of clear lines and transparent construction, and Jan Eisenloeffel, whose early works in the Netherlands at the turn of the century laid the foundation for modern design. However, in contrast to these two silversmiths, both of whom at least occasionally produced or flirted with the production of serialised works, Herbert Schulze only makes one-off pieces, in which he sometimes integrates elements made of industrial glass. Seen together, his works constitute an oeuvre of

in Metall. Zu seinen Vorbildern zählen der schottische Designer Christopher Dresser, ein früher Vertreter der funktionalen Formensprache im 19. Jahrhundert, dessen Arbeiten sich durch die Ästhetik klarer Linien und die Transparenz im konstruktiven Aufbau auszeichnen, sowie Jan Eisenloeffel, der in den Niederlanden mit seinem Frühwerk um die Jahrhundertwende die Grundlagen für eine sachlich-moderne Formgebung legte. Im Unterschied zu den beiden genannten Silberschmieden, die sich zumindest zeitweise auf die Gestaltung von Serienprodukten konzentrierten bzw. damit liebäugelten, fertigt Herbert Schulze ausschließlich Unikate, in die er gelegentlich Elemente aus Industrieglas integriert. Die Arbeiten fügen sich zu einem Werk von bemerkenswerter Homogenität, welches mit seiner komprimierten, konstruktiven Formensprache an die Tradition des Bauhauses anknüpft. Im Zentrum des Schaffens steht die durch funktionale und ergonomische Erfordernisse bestimmte Korpusware, klassisches Gebrauchsgerät von bestechender Eleganz. Versuche freiplastischer Natur, die die Kaffeekanne oder Zuckerdose um jeden Preis in den Rang eines Kunstwerkes erheben wollen, sind ihm ebenso fremd wie bizarre Materialexperimente. Dennoch erschöpfen sich die handwerklich präzisen Arbeiten nicht in reiner Funktionalität, sondern lassen Raum für poetische Assoziationen. Schulze gestaltet prozesshaft allein aus dem Material heraus, ohne vorgefertigtes Konzept oder detaillierte Entwurfszeichnungen. Eine kurz nach Beendigung des Studiums entstandene Mokkakanne von handschmeichlerischer Qualität, mit der er 1980 auf der 6. Silbertriennale in Hanau vertreten war, weist grundlegende Merkmale Schulzescher Gestaltung auf, wie die ostentative Betonung der Funktionselemente und die formale Integration des Deckels. Eine ungewöhnliche Grifflösung unterstreicht die kompakte Geschlossenheit des Gefäßkörpers: Wie ein Mantel legt sich das Nussbaumholz um einen Teil des silbernen Kannenkorpus, umgreift

Anne Mersmann
2000
Hautstruktur
Armreifen
Bedrucktes Aluminium
Skin Structure
armlet
printed aluminium

Markenzeichen Haut. Identität spüren und nach außen tragen.
Trademark: Skin. Sensing and outward presentation of identity.

striking homogeneity, with a condensed, constructive form language that draws on the traditions of the Bauhaus. His main focus is on classic consumer items of remarkable elegance, their forms defined by functional and ergonomic requirements. Free sculpture experiments aimed at elevating the coffee pot or sugar bowl to the status of art at any cost are just as alien to him as bizarre experiments with materials. Nevertheless, his precisely-crafted works are by no means restricted to mere functionality, they also leave room for poetic associations. Schulze's design approach is to draw entirely on the material itself in an active process, without a planned concept or detailed drawings. The hand-pleasing coffee pot created shortly after his graduation and exhibited at the 6th Silbertriennale in Hanau in 1980, already provides a good example of the hallmark Schulze design features, including the marked emphasis of the functional elements and the formal integration of the lid. An unusual handle solution underlines the compact unity of the pot's body: the walnut wood encloses part of the silver pot like a mantle, grasping it while simultaneously being grasped by the hand of the user. The structure of the vessel is only interrupted by the short tube of the spout at the upper edge, which projects cheekily upwards, giving the work a decidedly puckish note. A pot with a similar handle solution, created in 1989 as part of a series titled *60 Degrees*, won the prestigious North Rhine-Westphalia State Prize for Handicrafts. At the end of the Eighties Herbert Schulze started combining hand-forged metal frames with vessels made of industrial glass to produce teapots and wine decanters. One of his most striking creations is a teapot with an integrated silver tea strainer rising up like a cylindrical column within the bulging glass belly of the pot. The teapot and matching warmer stove have an off-centre stand at

ihn quasi und lässt sich gleichzeitig selber von der Hand des Benutzers umgreifen. Die Statik des Korpus wird allein durch die am oberen Rand ansetzende, kurze Röhre der Schnaupe gebrochen, die sich keck in die Höhe reckt und dem Teil eine recht vorwitzige Note verleiht. Eine Kanne mit ähnlicher Grifflösung, die 1989 im Rahmen der Werkgruppe *60 Grad* entstand, wurde mit dem begehrten Staatspreis des Landes Nordrhein-Westfalen für das Kunsthandwerk ausgezeichnet. Ende der 80er Jahre begann Herbert Schulze, handgeschmiedete Metallfassungen mit Gefäßkörpern aus Industrieglas zu Tee- und Weinkannen zu fügen. Besonders prägnant ist eine Teekanne mit silbernem Teesieb, das säulenähnlich im Innern des bauchigen Glaskolbens emporragt. Teekanne und Stövchen haben einen dezentralen, seitlich verlagerten Stand aus Silber und Ebenholz, der gleichzeitig als Griff konzipiert ist. Trotz asketischer Formreduzierung haftet dem Gerät nichts Labortechnisches an; vielmehr scheint es von der Aura alchemistischer ‚Zauberküchen' umgeben. Über die bloße Profanität des Gebrauchsgegenstandes hinaus geht auch eine Reihe von zentrisch-exzentrischen Schalen mit verschobenem Mittelpunkt, deren nach innen gezogener, unterschiedlich breiter Rand einerseits den Eindruck massiver Dickwandigkeit vermittelt, andererseits aber eine unerhört elegante Dynamik erzeugt: Die Schalen scheinen zu rotieren und man wartet förmlich darauf, dass sie sich jeden Augenblick in die Lüfte erheben und lautlos entschweben. Themen wie *Quadrat* oder *Dinner for Two* haben Herbert Schulze zu weiteren Arbeiten inspiriert. In der zweiten Hälfte der 80er Jahre widmet er sich dem Typus der Kanne mit kugeligem Korpus. Die meist abgeflachten sphärischen Gefäßkörper zeichnen sich durch die Betonung der Gieß- und Haltefunktion aus. So endet bei einer Kanne das Vierkantrohr der überlangen Tülle mit aufgesetzter goldener Niete in Höhe des doppelwandigen Henkelbogens, der die Kurvatur des Kannenkorpus

one side, made of silver and ebony, which doubles as a handle. Despite the ascetic reductionism of its forms there is nothing of technical lab ware in this teapot. It seems rather to be surrounded by the aura of an alchemist's magical kitchen. A series of bowls with eccentrically off-centre midpoints also goes beyond the profanity of the consumer object. With their turned-in edges of differing widths they manage to convey both an impression of thick-walled solidity and an unprecedentedly elegant dynamism: the bowls appear to rotate and one almost expects them to rise up into the air and float away silently. Themes that have inspired other works by Herbert Schulze include *Square* and *Dinner for Two*. In the second half of the Eighties he started focusing on pots with globular bodies. The main characteristic of these works, most of which have a body consisting of a flattened sphere, is the emphasis of the functions of pouring and holding. In one pot, for example, the square tube of the over-long spout ends in an applied golden rivet at the same height as the double-walled bow of the handle, which echoes the curvature of the pot body and also bears two small golden rivets that loosen up the reductionism of the strict overall composition. In another spherical pot the eccentric arc of the handle is made of transparent Plexiglas tubing. An architectural effect is achieved in another teapot whose full, round body, the base of which is seemingly flush with the supporting surface, is carried by the right angle formed by the greatly-projecting handle and the buttress-like, angular spout stretching out before. On closer examination, the flushness of the base turns out to be an illusion; the pot actually has three legs with which it stands firmly planted on the foundation of constructive reality. Herbert Schulze's works exhibit refined simplicity and timeless elegance. The traditional materials of the silversmith, the clear forms of strict

Anne Mersmann
2000
Hautidentität
T-Shirts
Baumwolle, Leselupen
Skin Identity
t-shirts
cotton, reading magnifiers

IDENTITAET

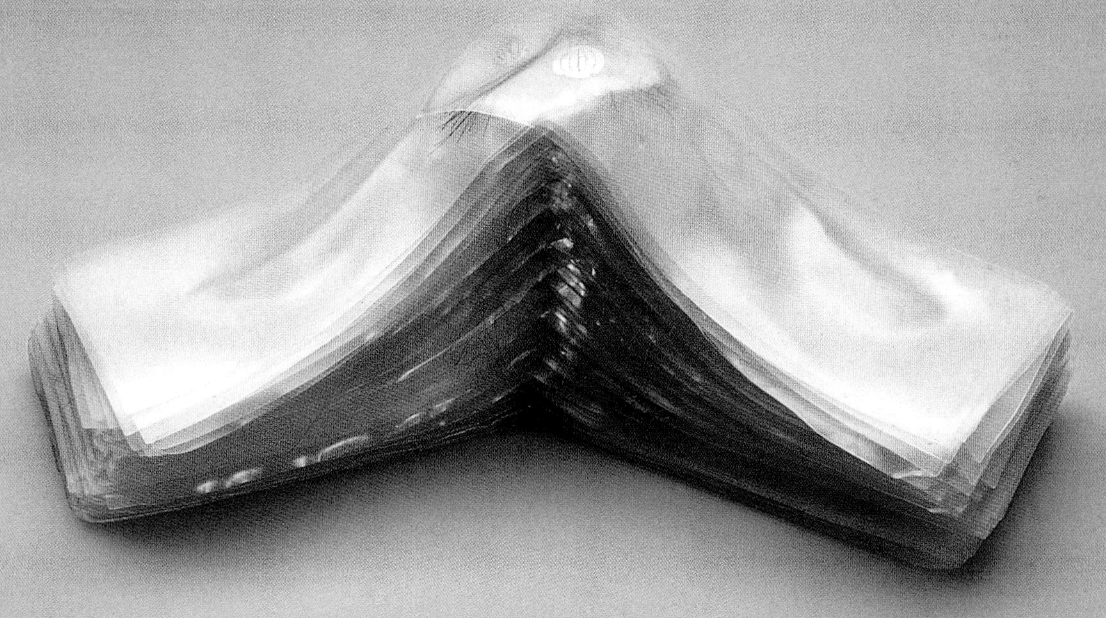

Anke Wolf
2000
Weg-Begleitung
Bauchschmuck mit Handschalen
Silber, Seide
Travel Companion
belly ornament with hand bowls
silver, silk

nachzeichnet und ebenfalls zwei kleine goldene Nieten aufweist, welche die Reduziertheit der strengen Gesamtkomposition auflockern. Bei einer anderen Kugelkanne besteht das exzentrische Kreisbogensegment das Griffes aus transparentem Plexiglasrohr. Von architektonischer Anmutung erweist sich eine Teekanne, deren scheinbar bodenflüchtiger, vollrunder Korpus vom rechten Winkel des weit herausragenden Henkels und der pfeilerartig vorgelagerten, kantigen Schnaupe getragen wird. Bei genauerem Hinsehen entpuppt sich die Bodenflüchtigkeit allerdings als Illusion: die Kanne steht gewissermaßen mit drei Beinen fest auf dem Boden der konstruktiven Realität. Herbert Schulzes Arbeiten sind von edler Schlichtheit und zeitloser Eleganz. Die traditionellen Materialien des Silberschmiedens, klare, designstrenge Formen und ausgewogene Proportionen machen sie zu Klassikern des modernen Gerätes. Klassiker mit kleinen Abweichungen allerdings, die den Arbeiten einen ganz eigenen Charakter verleihen.

Anke Wolf
2000
Handweg
Objekt
Wachs mit Kupfer, Blattgold
und Haare
Hand Path
object
wax with copper, gold leaf
and hair

Miteinander. Objekte einzigartiger Geschichten gemeinsamer Wege.
Together. Objects embodying unique stories of shared journeys.

design and their harmonious proportions make them classic examples of modern products. Classics, however, with small deviations from the norm that give them their own, very idiosyncratic character.

Susanne Winckler
2000
Trümmerring
Ring
Eisen, Gold
Rubble Ring
ring
iron, gold

Susanne Winckler
1999
Dämmerung
Schale mit Gedeck
Blei, Glas, Spiegel, Folie, Filz, Stoff
Twilight
bowl with cover
lead, glass, mirror, foil, felt, fabric

Sich in die Dämmerung versenken,
in ein Zwischenreich des
Erinnerns und Vergessens,
in eine Welt der Wünsche,
Träume und Sehnsüchte.
To immerse oneself in the twilight,
in a realm between
remembrance and forgetting,
in a world of wishes,
dreams and longings.

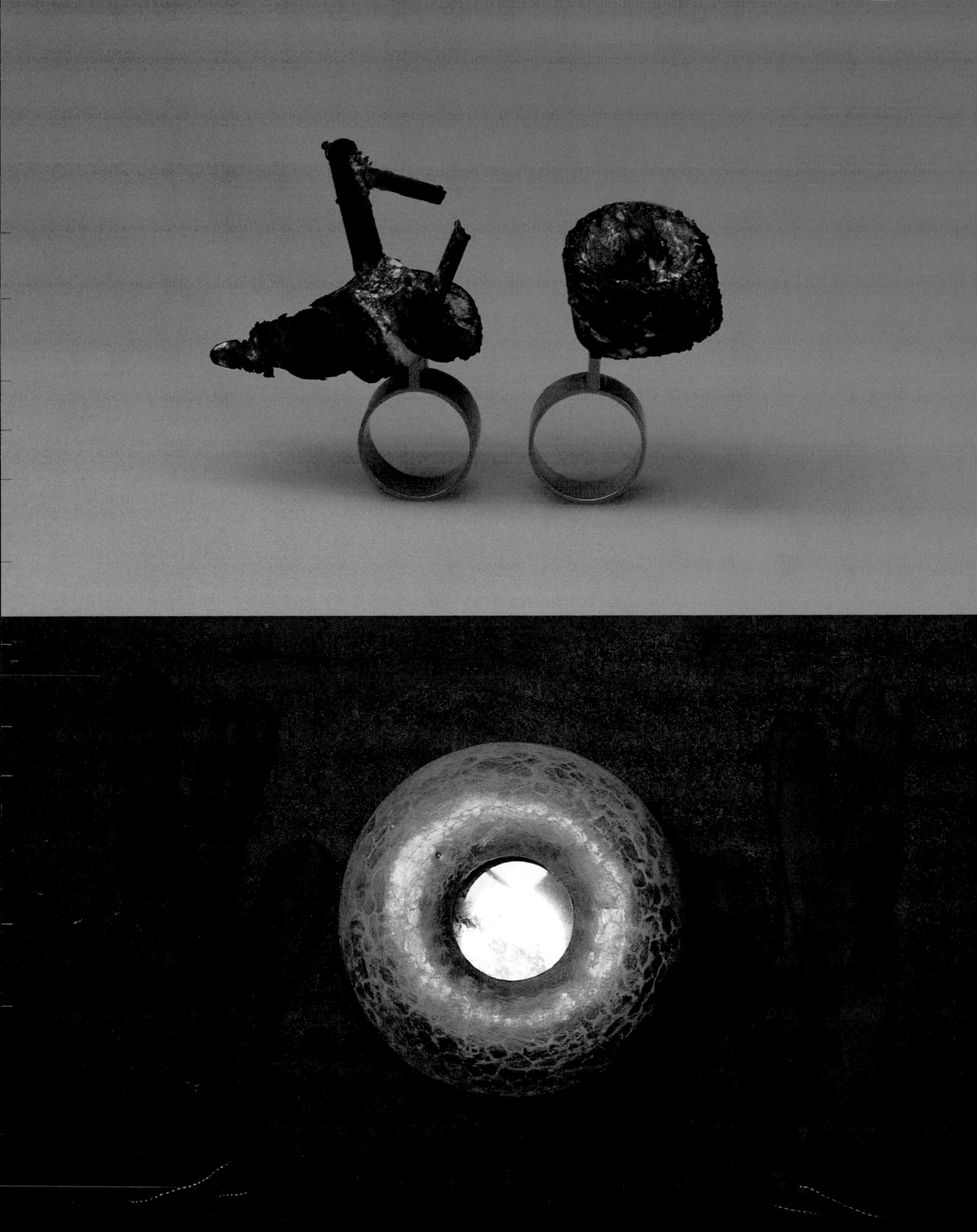

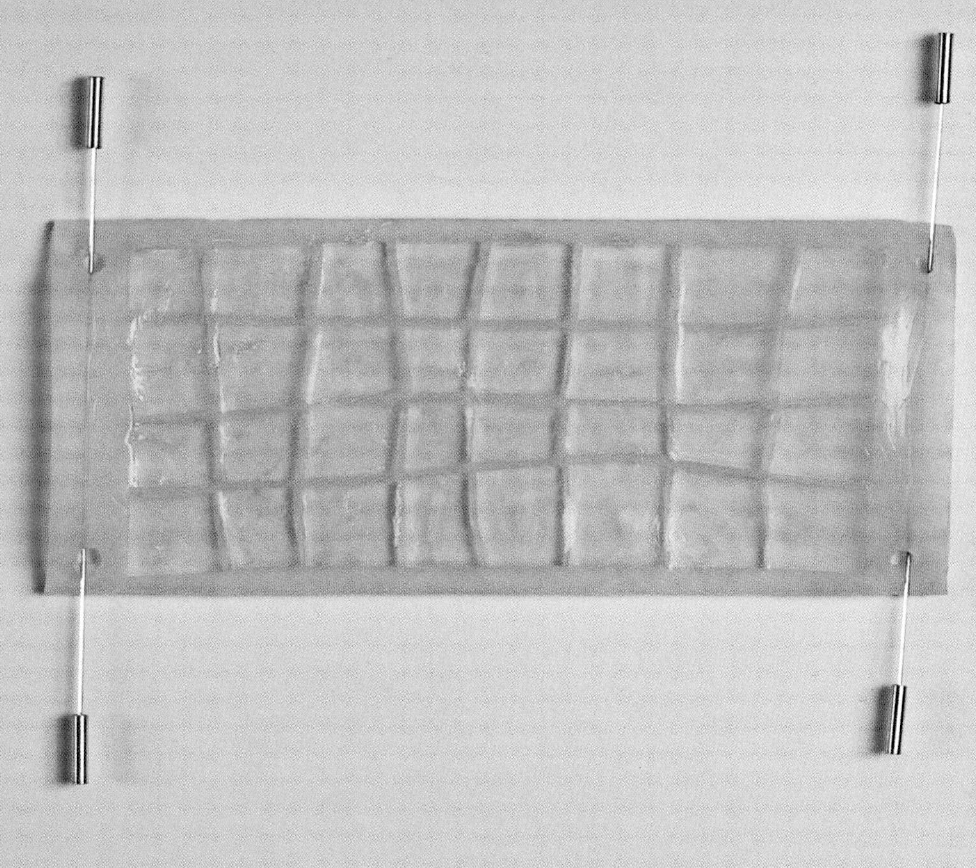

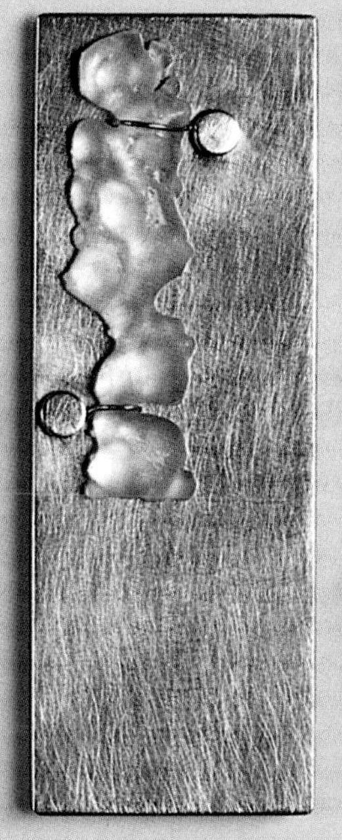

Heike Kähler
1998
Elastisches Rechteck
Ansteckschmuck
Glas, Silikon, Edelstahl, Silber
Elastic Rectangle
brooch
glass, silicone, stainless steel, silver

Mittendrin und danach Victor Malsy, Professor für Editorial Design, im Gespräch mit Studierenden, Absolventinnen und Lehrenden über die Realitäten von Studium und Beruf und das damit verbundene Wünschen und Hoffen

Heike Kähler
1999
Ansteckschmuck
Glas, Silber, Edelstahl
brooches
glass, silver, stainless steel

„Denn weder die Hülle noch der verhüllte Gegenstand ist das Schöne, sondern dies ist der Gegenstand in seiner Hülle. Enthüllt aber würde er unendlich unscheinbar sich erweisen."
"For it is neither the cover nor the covered object that is beautiful, but rather the object in its covering. When uncovered it would be revealed to be infinitely unremarkable."
Walter Benjamin, *Illuminationen*, hier: *Goethes Wahlverwandtschaften*, Baden-Baden 1955, S. 141

In the Thick of it and Thereafter **Editorial design professor Victor Malsy talks to students, graduates and teachers about the realities of designers' student and professional lives, and their hopes and wishes**

Victor Malsy In diesem Gespräch wollen wir Ihnen, liebe Leserin und lieber Leser, Einblick in die Lebenssituation der angehenden bzw. im Beruf stehenden SchmuckgestalterInnen geben. Wir wollen über den Unterschied zwischen Studium und Beruf, zwischen akademischer Theorie und Arbeitsrealität, zwischen Traum und Wirklichkeit berichten. Beginnen wir mit einer kurzen Vorstellungsrunde. **Uli Biskup** Nach meiner Ausbildung zur Goldschmiedin habe ich 1989 mit dem Studium begonnen. Sechs Jahre später wurde meine Tochter Louisa geboren. Für mich als Alleinerziehende hat sich das Studium dadurch verlängert und ich habe erst 1997 Diplom gemacht. Seit 1999 führe ich gemeinsam mit einer Kollegin eine Werkstatt und Galerie. Da man davon nicht leben kann, verkaufe ich meine Arbeiten auch über andere Galerien und gebe nebenher Kurse an einer Bildungsstätte für Kunst und Theater. **Hilde Janich** Früher war ich Lehrerin und habe vier Jahre lang an einer Hauptschule unterrichtet. Danach wechselte ich und wagte mit einer Goldschmiedelehre den Neuanfang. Von 1987 bis 1992 habe ich dann Schmuckdesign studiert. Seither bin ich freiberuflich als Schmuckdesignerin tätig. **Anne Mersmann** Ich habe von 1994 bis 2000 studiert und arbeite heute freiberuflich. Mit fünf anderen Schmuckschaffenden aus Köln habe ich mich zu einer Werkstattgemeinschaft zusammengeschlossen. Wie schon während meines Studiums beteilige ich mich an Ausstellungen und Messen. Um in meiner Arbeit als Schmuckdesignerin keine zu großen Kompromisse machen zu müssen, arbeite ich nebenberuflich. **Monika Seitter** Ich habe im Februar 2001 meine Diplomprüfung abgelegt und mich unmittelbar danach selbständig gemacht. Jetzt hoffe ich, mich so etablieren zu können, dass ich keinen Nebenjob annehmen muss. Mein Studium war recht breit angelegt und schloss u.a. Kurse in Kommunikationsdesign mit ein, was mir jetzt beruflich von Nutzen ist. **Susanne Winckler** Zuerst habe ich eine Ausbildung zur Silber-

Martin Pittig
1999
Nährhafter – das Mädchen und die Blume
Fingerapplikation
Rose, Stecker, Hochfrequenzstecker, Silber, Pflaster
Nutritious – The Girl and the Flower
finger application
rose, pin, high-frequency connector, silver, sticking plaster

Victor Malsy **We staged this discussion to provide you – our readers – with some insights into the lives of jewellery design students and professionals. Among other things we are going to talk about the difference between studying and working, between academic theory and the working world, between the dream and the reality. We will begin with a brief round of introductions.** Uli Biskup **After training as a goldsmith I started the university course in 1989. My daughter Louisa was born six years after that. Being a single mother meant that I needed more time to finish the course, and I didn't graduate until 1997. Since 1999 I've been running a workshop and gallery together with a colleague. That doesn't generate enough income to live from though, so I also sell my work through other galleries and teach courses at an adult education centre for art and theatre.** Hilde Janich **I used to be a teacher, I taught at a secondary modern school for four years. Then I decided to risk a new beginning and started an apprenticeship as a goldsmith. After that I studied jewellery design, from 1987 until 1992. Since then I've been working as a freelance jewellery designer.** Anne Mersmann **I studied from 1994 until 2000 and now I'm also working as a freelance. I've joined up with five other jewellery makers, we've formed a workshop cooperative. I show my work at trade fairs and exhibitions, just as I did while I was a student. I also have another part-time job to ensure that I don't have to make too many compromises in my work as a jewellery designer.** Monika Seitter **I took my diploma exams in February 2001 and set up on my own directly after that. Now I hope that I can establish myself well enough so that I don't have to take on a part-time job. My course of study was quite wide-ranging. Among other things it included courses in communication design, which I now find helpful in my work.** Susanne Winckler **I originally trained as a**

„Ein Mädchen hatte eine Blume, die es über alles liebte und hegte. Doch einmal musste es lachen und die Blume begann zu welken, denn sie vertrug nur Stille. Da trennte es sich den Daumen ab und setzte die Blume an seiner Stelle ein, denn es dachte, sein Blut würde sie nähren."
"A girl had a flower that she loved and cared for above all. But she had to laugh and the flower began to wilt, for it could bear naught but silence. And so she cut off her thumb and planted the flower in its place, thinking that her blood would nourish it."
Gerhard Rühm
Knochenspielzeug, Märchen, Fabeln und Liebesgeschichten,
Düsseldorf 1995

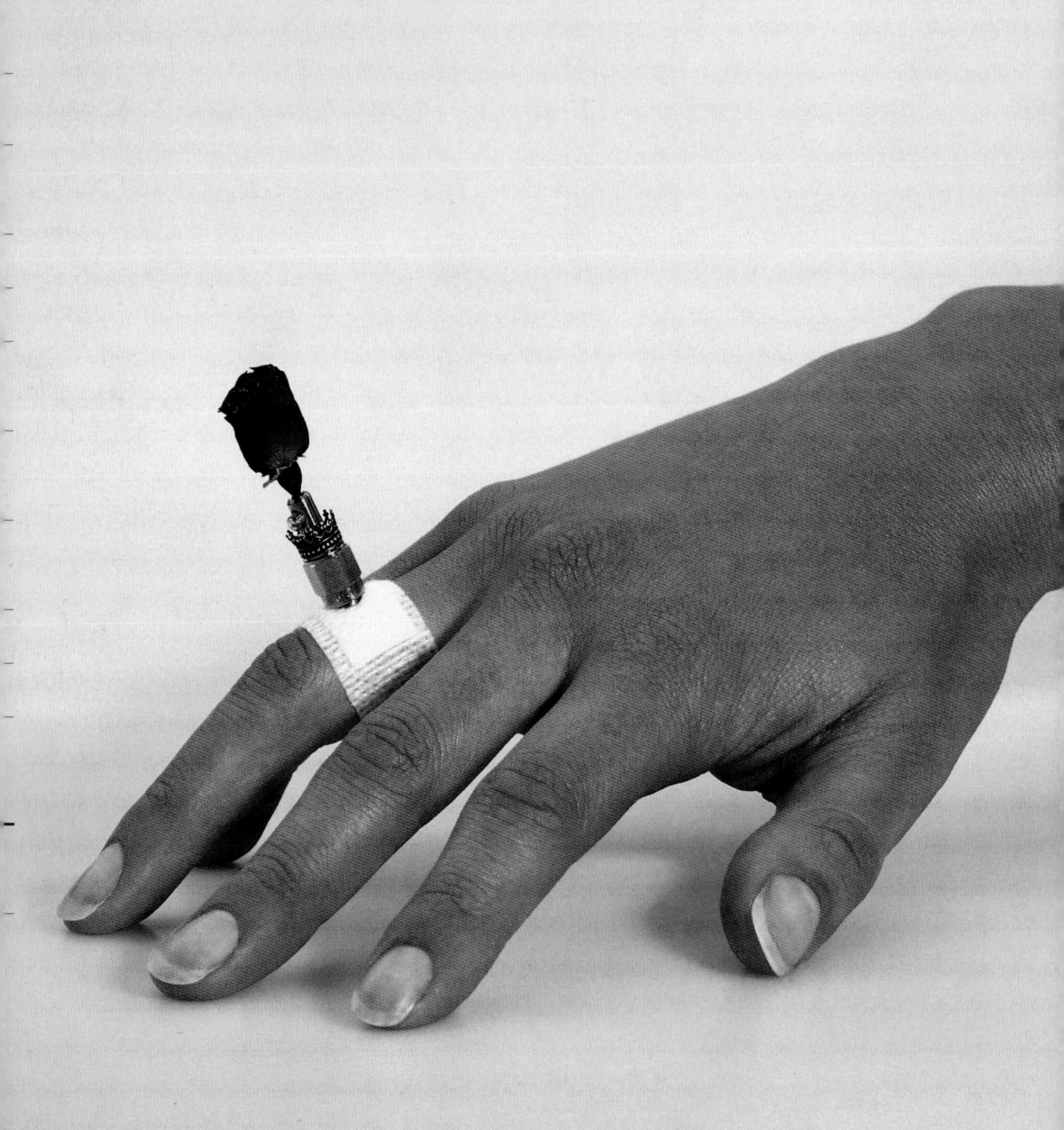

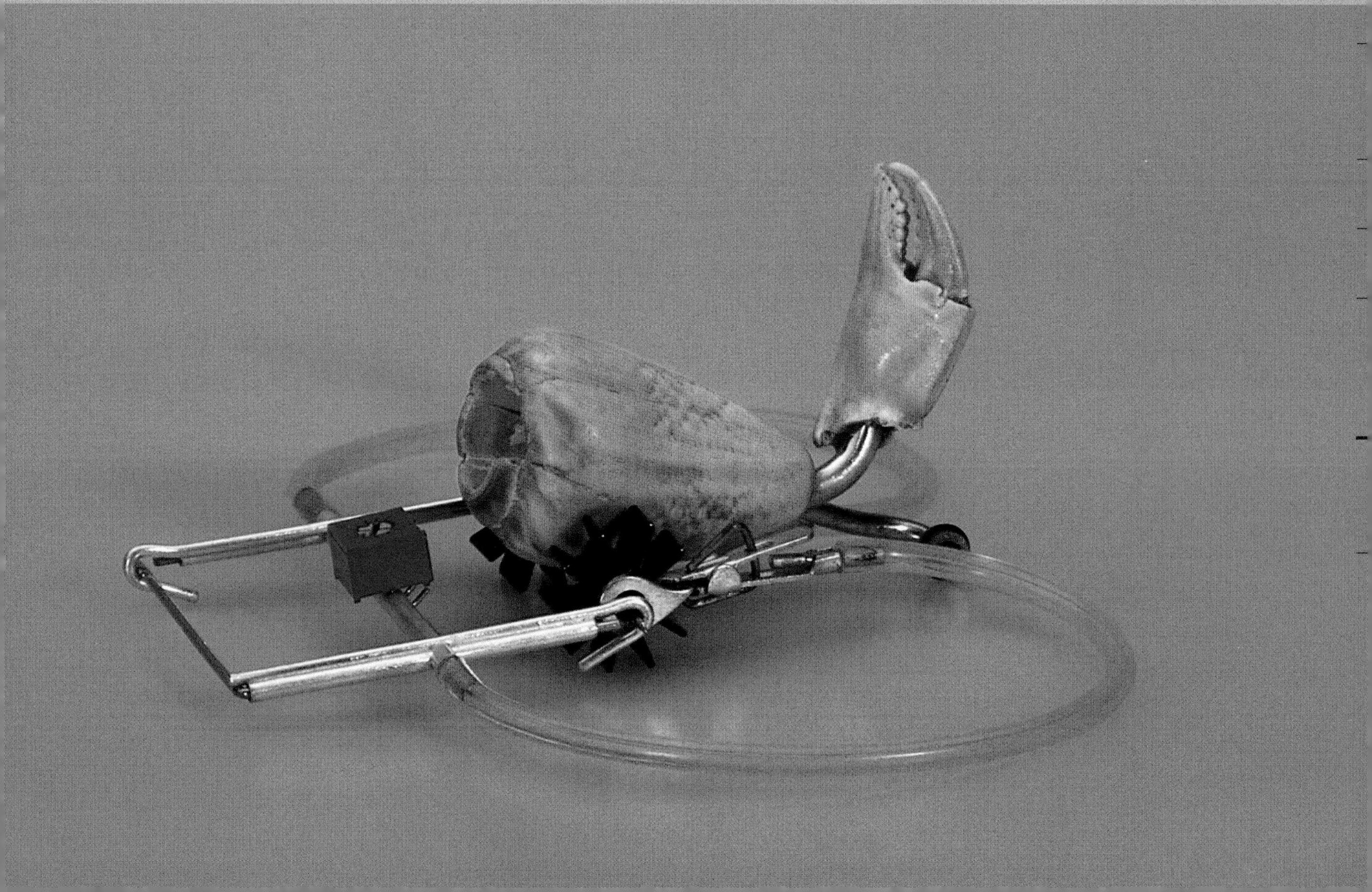

Martin Pittig
2000
Laetitia
Ohrschmuck
Silber, Gold, synthetischer Rubin, Apfelkern, Bördelkappe
Laetitia
ear ornament
silver, gold, synthetic ruby, apple seed, edging cover

Martin Pittig
2000
anima
Anhänger mit Kette
Silber, Kamee, Löwenzahnfallschirme, Bördelkappe, Polycarbonat
anima
pendant with chain
silver, cameo, dandelion parachutes, edging cover, polycarbonate

Martin Pittig
1998
2 von 3
Cyborg
Schneckenhaus, Silber, Latexschlauch, Krebszange
2 out of 3
cyborg
snail shell, silver, latex tube, crab's pincers

schmiedin gemacht, danach – von 1993 bis 1999 – in Düsseldorf studiert. Nach dem Diplom arbeitete ich drei Monate als Technische Assistentin an der School of Goldsmithing, Silversmithing, Metalwork and Jewellery am Royal College of Art in London und war anschliessend freischaffend tätig. Seit Februar 2001 bin ich fest angestellt als Designerin bei der Firma Niessing in Vreden. **Britta Göllner** Ich studiere im 7. Semester. **Claudia Hoppe** Ich bin im 11. Semester und möchte nächstes Semester Diplom machen. **Kerstin Biesdorf** Nach neun Semestern mache ich derzeit mein Diplom. **Heike Tries** Ich bin im 16. Semester eingeschrieben und stecke jetzt ebenfalls mitten im Diplom. Nach der Geburt meiner Tochter Karla war ich drei Semester lang beurlaubt. Seither musste ich das Studium mit der Sorge für meine Tochter in Einklang bringen. **Victor Malsy** Wie haben Sie den Eintritt ins Berufsleben empfunden? War es ein Sprung ins kalte Wasser? **Susanne Winckler** Ich musste mein Studium komplett selbst finanzieren und habe das über Verkäufe meiner Arbeiten, Auftragsanfertigungen und Nebenjobs getan. So war es für mich eigentlich kein Sprung ins kalte Wasser, sondern mehr ein Weitermachen. Ich fand es aber insofern härter, als die Eingebundenheit in die Strukturen des Studiums fehlte. **Anne Mersmann** Bei mir lief es anders. Ich brauchte während des Studiums meinen Lebensunterhalt nicht selber zu verdienen und habe in relativ sicheren Verhältnissen gelebt. Den Traum meiner Studientage, vom Schmuckmachen später einmal leben zu können, musste ich mittlerweile aber etwas modifizieren. Vorher habe ich nie gefragt, was so ein Schmuckstück kosten darf; jetzt, da ich mich damit am Markt behaupten muss, sehe ich mich mit großen Schwierigkeiten konfrontiert. Es gibt viele Firmen, die sich Anregungen von den Hochschulen holen, aber dann in Billigländern produzieren lassen. Damit kann eine freiberuflich tätige Schmuckgestalterin

silversmith, then I studied in Düsseldorf from 1993 until 1999. After graduating I worked for three months as a technical assistant at the *School of Goldsmithing, Silversmithing, Metalwork and Jewellery* at the *Royal College of Art in London*, and then I started freelancing. In February 2001 I took on a full-time job as a designer with the Niessing company in Vreden. Britta Göllner **I'm still studying; this is my seventh term.** Claudia Hoppe **This is my eleventh term. I'm hoping to graduate next term.** Kerstin Biesdorf **I've been studying for nine terms and I'm now preparing for my finals.** Heike Tries **I've been registered as a student at the university for sixteen terms and I'm now also in the middle of my finals preparations. I took a leave of absence for three terms after my daughter Karla was born. Since then I've had to cope with studying and taking care of my daughter at the same time.** Victor Malsy **How was getting started in professional life for you? Was it a leap into the deep end?** Susanne Winckler **I had to finance my course entirely on my own. I managed it by selling my work, doing contract work and taking on part-time jobs – so it wasn't really all that new for me, more a continuation. I did miss being integrated in the structures of the course, however, that made it a little harder.** Anne Mersmann **It was different for me. My financial situation was pretty secure, I didn't have to earn my living while I was studying. As a student my dream was to be able to live from making jewellery, but now I've been forced to modify that a little. I never used to think about how much you can charge for a piece of jewellery, and now that I have to sell my work in the market I find myself facing serious difficulties. There are a lot of firms that collect ideas from the design colleges and then manufacture their products in low-wage countries. Freelance jewellery designers simply can't compete with that. What I really miss**

nicht konkurrieren. Was ich im Berufsleben sehr vermisse, sind der Dialog mit Gleichgesinnten, die Gemeinschaftsprojekte, die problemorientierten Auseinandersetzungen und die Eingebundenheit in eine Ateliergemeinschaft, wie ich sie vom Studium her kannte. Nach Beendigung des Studiums fühle ich mich, trotz Beteiligung an einer Werkstattgemeinschaft, stärker auf mich selbst zurückgeworfen, isolierter. **Elisabeth Holder** Es ist in der Tat mühsam, immer initiativ sein zu müssen, immer aus sich selbst heraus zu schöpfen. Dieses Einzelkämpfertum ist nach wie vor sehr ausgeprägt bei uns Schmuckgestaltern. Ihr habt davon gesprochen, wie sehr ihr den Austausch vermisst, den Diskurs mit Gleichgesinnten, die Mut zusprechen können oder stützend und unterstützend für einen da sind. Vieles wird leichter, wenn sich mehrere zusammentun, wie das Beispiel der Gruppe *elft* zeigt. Die AbsolventInnen der Fachhochschule Düsseldorf hat das gemeinsame Interesse an der immer wieder neu geführten Auseinandersetzung mit gestalterischen Fragen zusammengehalten und sie haben erfahren, dass sie sich in ihrem Tun stärken und bestärken können, um daraus die für den gewählten steinigen Weg als freischaffende Designerin oder freischaffender Designer notwendige kreative Energie zu schöpfen. **Victor Malsy** Haben Sie das Gefühl, dass Ihnen das Berufsleben viele der Freiheiten nimmt, die Sie in gestalterischer Hinsicht während des Studiums genossen? Verlangt das Berufsleben Kompromisse von Ihnen, die Sie eigentlich nicht eingehen wollten? **Susanne Winckler** Ich studierte in erster Linie wegen der Konzepte, der Ideen, das Handwerkliche war von untergeordneter Bedeutung. Vor meinem Studium, während meiner Zeit als Goldschmiedin, hatte ich die unerfreuliche Erfahrung machen müssen, in die Position der Dienstleistenden gezwängt zu werden. Dazu hatte und habe ich nach wie vor keine Lust. Ich empfinde das als eine Zumutung. **Anne Mersmann** Ich möchte mich auch nicht

Uli Biskup
1996
Amphore
Anhänger
Plexiglas, Nylon, Schnur
Amphora
pendant
Plexiglas, nylon, cord

as a working professional is the dialogue with my peers, the group projects, the professional debates and the integration in a craftspeople's community like the one here at the university. Since I graduated I have felt more thrown back on my own resources, more isolated, even though I'm in a workshop cooperative. Elisabeth Holder **Yes, it really is difficult to always have to take the initiative, to draw entirely on your own resources. This loner situation is particularly pronounced among us jewellery designers. You say how much you miss the exchange and discussion with your peers, people who could encourage you, who are there to give you help and support when you need it. Many things become easier when you join forces with others – the *Elft* Group is an excellent example of this. What unites these Düsseldorf University of Applied Sciences graduates and keeps them together is their common interest in the ongoing discussion and analysis of design questions, and they have discovered that the input they give one another can really help them in their work, enabling them to tap the reservoir of creative energy they need to cope with their difficult chosen calling as freelance designers.** Victor Malsy **Do you have the feeling that working as a professional means you lose many of the freedoms, as regards design, that you enjoyed while you were students, forcing you to make compromises that you find difficult or that run counter to your basic principles?** Susanne Winckler **I chose the degree course primarily because I was interested in the conceptual aspects, the ideas; the craftsmanship side was secondary. Before I started studying, while I was working as a goldsmith, I had the unpleasant experience of being forced into the position of being a kind of servant. That is something I never wanted, and that hasn't changed. I find that an affront.** Anne Mersmann **I also don't want to bend my principles for the sake of commercial success.**

Uli Biskup
1997
Wahrheit und Lüge
Zwei Anhänger
Silber, Korallenast, Glasperlen, Schnur, Plexiglas, Nylonschnur, Acrylfarbe
Truth and Lies
two pendants
silver, coral branch, glass beads, cord, Plexiglas, nylon cord, acrylic paint

„Ich mag Dinge, die klar und selbstverständlich sind. Sie sind angenehm zu handhaben und besitzen dennoch eine überraschende Wirkung."
"I like things that are clear and matter-of-fact. They are pleasant to deal with and yet possess a surprising effect."

Nicoletta Camilleri
1997
Palma de Mallorca, Steffi Leyendecker
Postkartenkette
Eloxiertes Aluminium, Stahl, Silber
Palma de Mallorca, Steffi Leyendecker
postcard chain
anodised aluminium, steel, silver

verbiegen, um kommerziell erfolgreich zu sein. Um meinen Gestaltungsideen treu bleiben zu können, würde ich es dann eher vorziehen, mich mit einem Job aus einem ganz anderen Bereich finanziell abzusichern. **Claudia Hoppe** Eventuell könnte man ja zweigleisig fahren, mit einer kommerziellen und einer anspruchsvolleren, künstlerischen Schmucklinie. **Victor Malsy** Bedeutet ‚kommerziell': designorientierte Serienproduktion unter Zuhilfenahme entsprechender Computerprogramme und ‚künstlerisch': von Hand gefertigter konzeptioneller Unikatschmuck? **Susanne Winckler** Nicht unbedingt. Zwar sind Zeichenprogramme – z.B. für technische Zeichnungen – in Schmuckmanufakturen zum Standard geworden, aber für die Ideenfindung hat das Machen am Werkbrett immer noch Vorrang. Erst im nächsten Schritt, bei der Optimierung eines Entwurfs, können die Möglichkeiten, die solche Zeichenprogramme bieten, dann eine Erleichterung sein. Aber Kreativität kommt für mich immer noch aus der Hand, auch beim seriellen Schmuck. **Hilde Janich** Nach den ersten großen Schwierigkeiten habe ich für mich einen guten Weg gefunden, so eine Art Mischform. Einerseits trage ich Dinge nach außen, beteilige mich an Messen und werde mit meinen Arbeiten von anderen vertreten, aber es können auch Menschen zu mir kommen und ein individuell angefertigtes Schmuckstück in Auftrag geben. In diesem Zusammenhang ist der Kontakt zu meinen Kunden ganz wichtig. Nur so kann ich mich einfühlen, und nur darüber können sie ein für sie passendes oder wichtiges Schmuckstück erhalten. Mit Computern hat das gar nichts zu tun. Damit arbeite ich auch gar nicht. Für mich gehört das überhaupt nicht zum Beruf. Das empfinde ich so aus tiefster Seele. Ich habe zwei Hände und ich möchte gerne mit meinen Händen arbeiten. Die Unmittelbarkeit und das Archaische gefallen mir, vielleicht auch als Gegenpol zu der Tendenz der mit den neuen Medien einhergehenden Virtualität und Entkörperlichung.

Nicoletta Camilleri
1997
Australien, Donna Brennan
Postkartenkette
Eloxiertes Aluminium, Stahl, Silber
Australia, Donna Brennan
postcard chain
anodised aluminium, steel, silver

Erinnerung. Widersacher der Zeit. „(...) sie biegt um, was unumkehrbar ist, und holt zurück, was verloren ging."
Remembrance. Adversary of time. "(...) it turns around what is irrevocable and recovers what was lost."
Aleida Assmann, *Zur Metaphorik der Erinnerung* in: *Gedächnisbilder*, hrsg. von Kai Uwe Hemken, Leipzig 1996, S. 29

I'd rather take on a job in a completely different area to have the financial security necessary to enable me to remain true to my own design ideas. Claudia Hoppe **Another possible solution would be to take a two-pronged approach, with one commercial line and a more quality-oriented, artistic jewellery line.** Victor Malsy **Would you say that 'commercial' means design-oriented jewellery products made with the help of computer software, and that 'artistic' is more conceptual, one-off jewellery made by hand?** Susanne Winckler **Not necessarily. Using drawing software is now the standard approach in jewellery factories, for example technical drawing packages, but the physical process of working at the goldsmith's bench is still the most important method when you're coming up with new ideas. Drawing programs are only really a help in the next step, when you're working on optimising your drafts. But for me creativity is still something that comes from working physically with your hands, and that also applies for seralised jewellery.** Hilde Janich **I had a lot of difficulties at first but then I found a good solution for me, a kind of mixed form. On the one hand I work on publicity – I participate in exhibitions and other people also show my work for me – but at the same time people can also come to me and order individual pieces of jewellery. Direct contact with my clients is very important for these jobs, it's the only way that I can really tune in to them and produce a piece that is fitting or meaningful for them. That has nothing to do with computers. I don't use them anyway, they have absolutely nothing to do with my profession. I feel that very strongly, on a very profound level. I have two hands and I want to work with my hands. I like the immediacy and the archaic quality of it, perhaps as a counter to the current tendency towards virtuality and disembodiment associated with the new media.** Claudia Hoppe **Here at the uni-**

Claudia Hoppe An der Fachhochschule habe ich das nicht so erfahren, dass man hier, nur weil es ‚Schmuckdesign' heißt, den künstlerischen Anspruch aufgeben muss. Kunst und Design schließen sich nicht unbedingt aus. **Susanne Winckler** Ich finde es ebenfalls schwierig, Kunst und Design in Opposition zueinander zu setzen. Ich sehe es mehr als ein Spektrum mit fließenden Übergängen, auf dem wir uns bewegen können. **Monika Seitter** Nach einem dreiviertel Jahr der Selbständig-keit stellt sich mir weniger die Frage, ob ich mich mit meiner Arbeit stärker in die Richtung von Kunst oder von Design, Unikat oder Serie bewege, sondern wie ich einen Kundenkreis aufbauen kann. Da haben wir, glaube ich, alle das gleiche Problem. Es reicht nicht, lediglich schönen Schmuck zu machen, man muss ihn auch vermarkten. Für professionelle Fotografen und Grafikdesigner benötigt man viel Geld. Ich versuche deshalb, vieles selber in die Hand zu nehmen und stelle fest, dass das Studium an der Fachhochschule Düsseldorf durch die Nachbarschaft zum Kommunikationsdesign ideale Voraussetzungen für mein unabhängiges Vorgehen geschaffen hat. Nur auf das Problem des Akquirierens und Verkaufens wird man im Studium nicht ausreichend vorbereitet. Sich da etwas aufzubauen, erfordert ungeheuer viel Eigeninitiative. **Susanne Winckler** Ja das stimmt, das kann ich nur bestätigen. Aber ich glaube, dass das den meisten gar nicht bewusst ist. Das müsste im Studium sicherlich viel deutlicher gemacht werden. Die Zusammenarbeit mit dem Kommunikationsdesign bietet hier schon früh vielversprechende Möglichkeiten, um Kataloge und andere Veröffentlichungen zu erstellen. Trotzdem bleibt die Vermittlung unseres Schmuckes für jede einzelne von uns ein schwieriges Thema. **Anne Mersmann** Monika hat erzählt, dass sie alles, was zur Vermarktung gehört, selbst macht. Das habe ich am Anfang auch getan, dann aber sehr bald bemerkt, dass mir ganz wenig Zeit bleibt für meinen Schmuck. So bin ich hingegangen

Nicoletta Camilleri
1999
Ausstellungsstück IV
Sockelring
Silber
Exhibit IV
plinth ring
silver

Nicoletta Camilleri
1999
Ausstellungsstück V
Sockelring mit Abdruck
Silber
Exhibit V
plinth ring with impression
silver

versity I never had the feeling that being involved in jewellery design meant you had to abandon the claim to being an artist, just because it's called 'design'. Art and design aren't necessarily mutually exclusive. Susanne Winckler **I also find it difficult to see art and design as contrary opposites. I see it much more as a spectrum that we can move along as we wish, with fluid boundaries.** Monika Seitter **Now that I've been self-employed for nine months I find that the question is not so much whether I and my work are moving more towards art or design, towards one-off pieces or series production, but rather how I can build up a customer base. I think that's a problem that all of us are faced with. It's not enough to produce beautiful jewellery, you also have to market it. Professional photographers and graphic designers are very expensive, so I try to do as much as I can myself. I've found that my degree course at the Düsseldorf University of Applied Sciences has given me an ideal foundation for this independent approach, among other things because of the links with the communication design department. Selling and canvassing customers are the only things that the course didn't really prepare me for well enough. You need an enormous amount of initiative to get started, to build up a base.** Susanne Winckler **Yes, absolutely, I can really second that, and I also think it's something that most people aren't really aware of. There should be much more emphasis on it in the course. The collaboration with the communication design department provides excellent facilities for making an early start with catalogues and other publications. But even so the process of selling our jewellery is still a very difficult issue for all of us.** Anne Mersmann **Monika said that she handles all the marketing work herself. I did that too initially, but I soon realised that doing it like that left me very little time to work on my jewellery. So I went**

Nicoletta Camilleri
1999
Ausstellungsstück I-III
Sockelring mit Prägung
Silber
Exhibit I-III
plinth ring with embossing
silver

Klaus Müller
1999
Vierbeiniger Stuhl
Edelstahl
four-legged chair
stainless steel
Foto: Achim Kukulies, Düsseldorf

und habe mir bei Fotografen und Grafikdesignern die notwendige professionelle Unterstützung geholt. Im Rahmen dieser Zusammenarbeit wurde mir klar, wie schwierig, aber auch wie wichtig es ist, meine Sichtweise von Schmuck deutlich zu machen. Das ging beim ersten Mal völlig schief, obwohl ich mit der Fotografin zwei Tage lang über die geplante Fotoserie diskutiert habe. Als ich dann die Fotos sah, wusste ich, dass wir völlig aneinander vorbeigeredet hatten. Die Art der Vermittlung ist eben ein ganz zentraler Aspekt. **Uli Biskup** Das trifft auch für den Umgang mit den Käufern von Schmuck zu. Wie anders der Dialog mit Kunden ist und auch sein muss, die ja oft keine Ahnung von Schmuck haben, wurde mir erst nach dem Studium bewusst. Wenn ich mit euch rede, kann ich davon ausgehen, dass wir eine ähnliche Sprache sprechen, dass ich mit meinem gestalterischen Anliegen grundsätzlich verstanden werde. Meinen Kunden muss ich auf einer gänzlich anderen Ebene begegnen. Das ist sehr zeitaufwändig, aber irgendwie auch spannend. Nach dem Studium habe ich mit drei Kolleginnen ein Projekt initiiert, das *Ringsum-Abend* hieß. Wir haben uns in Privathaushalten mit mehreren Gästen getroffen und unseren Schmuck vorgestellt. Wir haben da manchmal stundenlang geredet und erklärt und stießen auf große Neugierde und Aufgeschlossenheit. Dieser direkte Kontakt mit den Kundinnen und Kunden war für mich eine bereichernde Erfahrung, die mich ermutigt hat, den eingeschlagenen Weg weiterzugehen. **Hilde Janich** Solche an Tupperwarepartys angelehnte Projekte habe ich auch ein paarmal durchgeführt und fand, es war eine wirkungsvolle Strategie, um Schmuck zu verkaufen. Wenn eine Gruppe von fünf, sechs oder sieben Frauen zusammen ist, gibt das eine gute Stimmung. So eine kleine Gruppe von interessierten Kundinnen ist ein gutes Forum. Sie regen sich auch gegenseitig zum Kauf an. Das ist ein Weg unter vielen, der begangen werden kann, neben Messe- und Ausstellungsbeteiligungen.

and got the professional support I needed from photographers and graphic designers. Working with them helped me to see how difficult and how important it is to communicate my vision of jewellery clearly. In my first project that went badly wrong, even though I had spent two days discussing the planned photo series with the photographer. When I saw the pictures I realised that we had been approaching the whole thing from completely different tangents. The way you present your work is absolutely crucial. Uli Biskup **That also applies for dealing with jewellery customers. It wasn't until after I had graduated that I really started to understand how different it is to talk to customers who have no idea about jewellery, and how differently you have to deal with them. When I talk to you I can assume that we speak a similar language and that you will understand my basic artistic intentions. I have to approach my customers on a completely different level. That takes up a lot of time but it's also somehow exciting. After graduation three colleagues and I initiated a project that we called *Ring-Around Evenings*. We would meet with groups of guests in private homes and present our jewellery to them. The discussions would sometimes go on for hours, and the people were very interested and open. This direct contact with my customers was a very enriching experience for me, and it gave me the confidence to continue and that I was on the right tack.** Hilde Janich **Yes, those projects are a little like Tupperware parties. I've also done a few of them and I found it was an effective strategy for selling jewellery. When five, six or seven women are together in a group it creates a positive mood. A small group of interested customers like that is a good forum, and they also encourage each other to buy. That's one possible method among many, in addition to participating in fairs and exhibitions.** Susanne Winckler **I find all of these approaches wonderful, they're**

Susanne Winckler Ich finde all die genannten Konzepte wunderbar und sinnvoll. In der Zeit nach meinem Studium beispielsweise habe ich alles komplett über Tausch abgewickelt. Aber wenn ich eine Ausstellung machen oder einen Messestand haben möchte, brauche ich schlicht und einfach Geld. Da reicht das Tauschen nicht. **Victor Malsy** Worin liegen Ihrer Erfahrung nach die größten Unterschiede zwischen einer freiberuflichen Tätigkeit und der Festanstellung in einer Firma? **Susanne Winckler** Als Angestellte bin ich eingebunden in die Firmenphilosophie. In meinem Fall ist es eine Designphilosophie, die ich schlüssig finde und die ich deshalb auch annehmen kann. Sie gibt den Rahmen vor, innerhalb dessen ich mich bewege. Trotzdem kommt dabei etwas heraus, das meine Prägung hat, auch wenn die Herangehensweise eine andere ist. So ist z.B. von vornherein klar, was für eine Art von Schmuckstück entstehen soll, ein Ring oder eine Kette oder was auch immer. Und es gibt eine viel klarere Gliederung in Ideenfindung, Entwurfs- und Entwicklungsarbeit mit exakt kalkulierten zeitlichen Vorgaben für jede einzelne Phase. Hinzu kommt, dass der Kontakt mit den Angestellten in der Werkstatt und dem Vertrieb einen hohen Stellenwert hat. Es bedarf eines ständigen Sich-Rückversicherns, wie die Ideen dort ankommen. Was von dieser Seite dazu gesagt wird, ist letztendlich mitbestimmend für das Endresultat. Das erfordert von mir ein hohes Maß an kommunikativer Kompetenz. **Ulrike Biskup** Eine Festanstellung ist in unserem Beruf allerdings nicht die Norm, sondern eher die Ausnahme. Von solchen Stellen, wie du sie beschrieben hast, gibt es höchstens eine Hand voll in ganz Deutschland. Für die meisten Fachhochschulabsolventinnen stellt sich die Wahl so erst gar nicht. Jede muss ihren eigenen Weg im Rahmen der Selbständigkeit finden. Das ist spannend, aber auch sehr unsicher. In meiner Situation, solange die Tochter klein ist, würde ich das geregelte Einkommen und die garantierten 30 Tage Urlaub

good and effective ideas. In the time after my graduation I did everything through bartering, for example. But when I stage an exhibition or a trade fair stand I quite simply need money – you can't get very far with bartering there. Victor Malsy **In your experience what are the main differences between freelancing and employment in a company?** Susanne Winckler **As an employee I'm integrated in the company philosophy. In my case it's a design philosophy that makes sense to me and so I'm able to accept it. It provides the framework within which I can move. But the result is still something that bears my mark, even though the approach may be different. For example, the jewellery item to be produced – a ring or a chain or whatever – is always clear from the start. And the brainstorming, drafting and development phases of the work are much more clearly organised, with precisely-calculated time frames for each phase. In addition to all this the contact with the staff in the workshop and sales is also very important. You have to keep checking back to see how the ideas are received there. What they say plays an important role in the final result, so this aspect of the work calls for highly-developed communications skills.** Uli Biskup **Full-time employment is more the exception rather than the rule in our profession, however. There are only a handful of jobs like the one you describe in all Germany. Most design school graduates aren't ever faced with that kind of choice. Everybody has to find their own way as a freelancer, within the framework of the self-employed situation. That's exciting but it's also very insecure. For my own part, at least as long as my daughter is still young, I would definitely prefer the regular income and guaranteed 30 days holiday of a full-time position.** Victor Malsy **Do you feel that the degree course provides enough preparation for the demands of being a working professional?** Britta Göllner **I came to university to**

Katja Korsawe
2001
red spring
Halsschmuck
Porzellan, Garn, Lack
red spring
neck ornament
porcelain, yarn, paint

Lockend lauern unerhörte Reize.
Outrageous charms lie temptingly in wait.

einer Festanstellung der Selbständigkeit in jedem Fall vorziehen. **Victor Malsy** Wird man während des Studiums ausreichend auf die Probleme der späteren Berufstätigkeit vorbereitet? **Britta Göllner** Ich kam an die Fachhochschule, um Orientierung zu finden und zu experimentieren. Dazu wird mir hier ein sehr breites Spektrum an Möglichkeiten geboten, innerhalb dessen ich frei wählen kann. Das schließt auch die Entscheidung ein, ob ich mein eigenes Ding machen oder lieber Aufgaben erfüllen möchte. Diese Selbständigkeit ist schon eine gute Vorbereitung auf den Beruf. **Claudia Hoppe** Für mich stellt sich die Hochschule fast als Dienstleister für die Studierenden dar. Und die Lehrenden Elisabeth Holder und Herman Hermsen erfahre ich dabei als ordnende und helfende Instanz. **Hilde Janich** Es ist wirklich so, dass man im Zuge des Experimentierens an der Hochschule lernt, wo der eigene Weg langgeht und wo man eher nicht hingehört. Daraus erwächst auch für später Sicherheit. **Heike Tries** Im Freiraum der Hochschule probe ich den Ernstfall. Als Mutter eines kleinen Kindes ist es für mich organisatorisch ziemlich aufwändig, jede Woche an zwei Tagen hier zu sein. In der Zeit ist es mir dann sehr wichtig, nicht nur nach Plan zu studieren und Scheine abzuarbeiten. Das soll dann auch Freude machen, da möchte ich Themen bearbeiten, die mich interessieren. Was nach dem Diplom kommt, ist noch völlig offen. Ich weiß nur, dass ich ein gesichertes monatliches Einkommen benötige. Mit Kind ist das ja eine völlig andere Situation, als wenn ich alleine wäre **Victor Malsy** Lehrende an Hochschulen sollten Studierende zum Denken anregen. Sie sollten Denk- und Strukturmodelle vorstellen und handwerkliche Fertigkeiten vermitteln, die aber nicht ausschließlich auf den Markt zugeschnitten sind. Welche Änderungen oder zusätzlichen Angebote könnten das Studium in Ihrem Bereich noch effektiver gestalten? **Susanne Winckler** Das Studium als Experimentierfeld zu haben, ist ein Luxus,

Helena Lebá
1998/2000
Klettringe
Klettband, Perlen, Glassteine, Holz
velcro rings
velcro strip, beads, glass stones, wood

Anhängliche Stielaugen zum Vertauschen.
Clinging stalkeyes for interchange.

get orientation and to experiment, and the environment here gives me a very broad spectrum of possibilities for that, within which I am free to choose as I please. That also includes the freedom to decide whether I want to do my own thing or work through preset projects. That independence is a pretty good preparation for professional life. Claudia Hoppe **As I see it the university functions almost as a service provider for the students. And I experience our teachers, Elisabeth Holder and Herman Hermsen, as regulatory and supportive elements.** Hilde Janich **That's really how it is – experimenting at university enables you to find out where your own path is, and where the places are that you don't belong. That builds confidence that you can draw on later.** Heike Tries **The safe environment provided by the university lets me train for the real thing, so to speak. As the mother of a small child it's quite difficult for me to organise my life so that I can be here two days a week. During my time here it's very important for me to not just do things by the book and work through all the standard curriculum requirements. It should be fun, too. I want to work on subjects that interest me. What comes after I graduate is still completely open. I only know that I need a guaranteed monthly income. Having a child is completely different from being on your own.** Victor Malsy **University teachers should encourage their students to think for themselves. They should present intellectual and structural models and provide training in manual skills that are not exclusively geared towards market needs. What changes or additional offerings could make the course of study more effective in your field?** Susanne Winckler **The university as an environment for experimentation is a luxury that I think is absolutely crucial, particularly in our society. In my opinion the students are given a pretty good preparation for their professional lives as far as oppor-**

den ich gerade in unserer Gesellschaft für ganz entscheidend halte. Meiner Ansicht nach sind die Studenten mit dem was sie an Reflexionsmöglichkeiten, strukturellem Denken und gestalterischer Kompetenz mitbekommen, schon ganz gut vorbereitet für die Praxis. Die Dinge, die an der Hochschule ablaufen, müssten aber mehr nach außen, in die Gesellschaft getragen werden. Zum Beispiel über einen verbesserten Tag der offenen Tür. Da könnte die ‚Missionsarbeit' für Schmuck schon mal ansetzen. **Anne Mersmann** Ich habe die Freiheit und Selbstbestimmtheit im Studium immer sehr genossen. Daraus schöpfe ich auch nach dem Studium. Im Nachhinein hätte ich mir aber in den höheren Semestern eine intensivere Zusammenarbeit mit Firmen gewünscht. Oder auch einfach mal die Möglichkeit, einzelne Entwürfe auf ihre Marktfähigkeit hin zu untersuchen. Es wäre ja falsch, sich dem Markt zu verschließen. Messepräsentationen fände ich zum Beispiel gut, weil damit nicht nur Öffentlichkeitsarbeit gemacht wird, sondern die Studierenden direkt überprüfen können, wie die Sachen ankommen. **Susanne Winckler** Was im Studium zu wenig berücksichtigt wird, sind meiner Meinung nach Kommunikations- und Verhandlungstechniken. Diese Bereiche erscheinen mir zunehmend wichtiger. **Monika Seitter** Ja, wir können alle guten Schmuck gestalten, aber wie wir ihn verkaufen sollen, wissen wir nicht. Marketing sollte zukünftig mit in den Lehrplan aufgenommen werden. **Claudia Hoppe** Bei dem Projekt *inpetto* geht es ja schon genau um diese Fragen. Im Studium kommen sie aber kaum vor, weil da gestalterische Fragen im Vordergrund stehen. **Herman Hermsen** Das *inpetto*-Projekt ist hochinteressant, aber es sind nur eine Hand voll Studierende, die daran teilnimmt. Wenn ich so zurückblicke auf meine Lehrtätigkeit der letzten Jahre, fallen mir viele Kursangebote ein, die ausgesprochen praxisorientiert waren und teilweise auch fachübergreifend, *Rechtswissenschaften für Designer*

Helena Lebá,
2000
perla & perlina
Softvasen
Silikonkautschuk
perla & perlina
soft vases
silicone rubber

Verweichlichte Vasen spielen Dame.
Effeminate vases playing at ladies.

tunity for reflection, structured thinking and design skills are concerned. But I do think that everything we do at university could be better communicated to the outside world, to the public at large. For example with a better open day. That could be used as a starting-place for jewellery 'missionary work'. Anne Mersmann **I always really appreciated the freedom and self-determination I had as a student, and that's a source that I can still draw on now, after graduating. However, in retrospect I think I would have liked to have had more intensive collaboration with private companies during the final terms. Or perhaps just the opportunity to test the marketability of individual designs. It would be wrong to ignore the market. I think trade show presentations would be a good idea, for example. In addition to the publicity it would also give students the opportunity to experience directly how their work is received.** Susanne Winckler **In my opinion it's communication and negotiation skills that are not emphasised enough in the university curriculum. These are things that seem to me to be getting more and more important.** Monika Seitter **Yes, we can all design good jewellery but we don't have any idea how to sell it. Marketing should be made part of the curriculum.** Claudia Hoppe **Those are precisely the issues that the *inpetto* project deals with. But they are almost completely absent in the normal curriculum because there the emphasis is on the design side of things.** Herman Hermsen **The *inpetto* project is extremely interesting, but only a handful of students are actually involved in it. When I look back at my teaching experience during the past few years I can think of a large number of courses that were very practise-oriented, and there were also a number of interdisciplinary courses – *law for designers* and things like that. The truth is that despite all the expressions of interest the attendance at these course was often very low. It seems that**

und Ähnliches. Tatsache ist, dass entgegen aller Interessensbekundungen diese Kurse oftmals überhaupt nicht gut besucht waren. Offenbar stehen während des Studiums eben doch eher andere Belange im Vordergrund und die Praxisdefizite ergeben sich erst hinterher. Das uns anzulasten, ist nicht fair. **Britta Göllner** Da gibt es so vieles, was wichtig wäre. Rapid Prototyping, CAD und Grafikprogramme, Marketing, Messebau und Messeplanung. Gestaltung natürlich sowieso. Und Geld muss ich nebenbei auch noch verdienen. Das bekomme ich alles gar nicht unter einen Hut. **Susanne Winckler** Man kann halt nicht alles machen und muss im Studium Schwerpunkte setzen. Rückblickend fällt mir manches ein, das ich hätte belegen sollen. Aber ich glaube nicht, dass man quasi auf Vorrat Erfahrungen sammeln kann für den in der Zukunft eventuell auftretenden Fall X. Man sollte sich auch nicht überfordern während des Studiums, indem man versucht, sich für alle Eventualitäten zu wappnen. Flexibles und individuelles Handeln sind in jedem Fall unerlässlich. **Victor Malsy** Eine Frage an die Studentinnen unter Ihnen: sind Sie Traumtänzerinnen? **Claudia Hoppe** So komme ich mir nicht vor. Ich habe jetzt die Gelegenheit aus der relativ gesicherten Position des Studiums heraus mit Aspekten der Selbständigkeit zu experimentieren und die nutze ich auch. Natürlich sind das dann Eigeninitiativen, wenn ich beispielsweise zusammen mit anderen Studentinnen Ausstellungen organisiere. Niemand hindert mich, eigene Projekte zu verfolgen. Im Gegenteil, das wird unterstützt. Im übrigen plädiere ich dafür, dass die Entwürfe aus den Kursen auch nach außen getragen und auf ihre Tragfähigkeit hin überprüft werden. Zudem habe ich bereits jetzt schon einen Nebenjob, den ich problemlos weiterführen kann. Das gibt mir Sicherheit und ein gewisses Maß an Unabhängigkeit. Ich kann mir auch gut vorstellen, auf einem ganz anderen Gebiet Geld dazuzuverdienen, um bei meinem Schmuck keine

Helena Lebá
2001
Schmuckes Gefäß
Softgefäße
Silikonkautschuk, Metall
Pretty Vessel
soft vessels
silicone rubber, metal

students have other priorities while they are studying and they only notice their practical deficits later on. It's not fair to blame that on us. Britta Göllner **There are so many things that are important. Rapid prototyping, CAD and graphics software, marketing, trade show stand planning and construction, and design as well, of course. And at the same time I also have to earn a living. There's no way that I can manage everything.** Susanne Winckler **There's no way that you can do everything, you have to set priorities when you're a student. In retrospect I can think of quite a few courses I should have taken. But I don't think it's practicable to try to 'stockpile' experiences for every eventuality, so to speak. And it doesn't make sense to overload yourself while you are studying by trying to prepare for everything that might happen. Flexibility and independence are always essential, however.** Victor Malsy **I have a question for those of you who are still students: Are you dreamers?** Claudia Hoppe **I don't feel like a dreamer. My relatively secure status as a student gives me the opportunity to experiment with aspects of what it's like to be a self-employed professional, and I'm taking advantage of those opportunities. Of course, when I organise an exhibition with other students that's always an individual initiative. Nobody prevents me from carrying out my own projects. On the contrary, it's actively supported. But I am definitely in favour of public presentation of the designs created during the courses, to test their viability. In addition I also already have a part-time job that I can easily continue with after I graduate. That gives me security and a certain level of independence. I can also imagine earning my money with a job in a completely different area, so that I don't have to make any compromises with my jewellery.** Kerstin Biesdorf **Some of my works were recently shown at the Silver Triennial and last year I also exhibited at the *Grassi Fair*. You get lots of**

Kompromisse machen zu müssen. **Kerstin Biesdorf** Ich war kürzlich mit Arbeiten auf der Silbertriennale vertreten und habe mich im vergangenen Jahr an der *Grassimesse* beteiligt. Da gibt es viel Anerkennung, aber kaum jemand kauft etwas. Ich hätte mir schon gewünscht, Kontakte zu Firmen zu knüpfen. Es wäre ganz wichtig, bereits während des Studiums Messeerfahrungen zu sammeln oder etwas über den Umgang mit Firmen zu erfahren, zum Beispiel wie Verträge ausgehandelt werden. Das muss ich doch nicht erst alles durch Fehlschläge nach dem Studium herausfinden, oder? **Hilde Janich** Aber derartige Fehlschläge werden dich dein ganzes Berufsleben lang begleiten. Es wird immer wieder vorkommen, dass du in ein Projekt investierst und das Geld dabei in den Sand setzt. Ich schreibe das inzwischen als Lehrgeld ab. Bei der Vielschichtigkeit unseres Berufes ist es gar nicht möglich, alle Erfahrungen schon vorwegzunehmen. **Victor Malsy** Aus unserem Gespräch habe ich gelernt, dass es viel Idealismus braucht, um Schmuck und Gerät ins Gespräch und in das Bewusstsein der Öffentlichkeit zu bringen, und zwar nicht nur in das Bewusstsein einer musealen Öffentlichkeit. Wir hoffen, dass Ihre Ausstellung und dieser Katalog dafür einen Beitrag leisten. Ich bedanke mich für das Gespräch.

recognition at these events but almost nobody sells anything. I've often wished I could establish contacts with private companies. I think it would be very valuable to be able to gain experience with fair participation while you are a student, or to learn something about dealing with companies, for example how contracts are negotiated. I don't think I should have to learn all those things by trial and error after I graduate, should I? Hilde Janich **But you're going to go through that trial and error process for the rest of your professional life. There will always be the odd project where you invest money and then find that you're going to have to write off the whole thing as a loss. Now I just look at these experiences as training expenses. Our profession is so multi-faceted that there's simply no way to prepare for everything.** Victor Malsy **What I've learned from our talk is that a great deal of idealism is needed to increase the awareness of the public – and not just museum-goers – for jewellery and product design. We hope that your exhibition and this catalogue are going to make a contribution to this. Thank you for participating in the discussion.**

Janine Awater
1996
Ritualschmuck für das Loslassen
Bast, Stein, Papier
ritual jewellery for letting-go
raffia, stone, paper

Ritual. Die symbolische Handlung als äußeres Zeichen innerer Wandlung.
Ritual. The symbolic act as the outward sign of inner transformation.

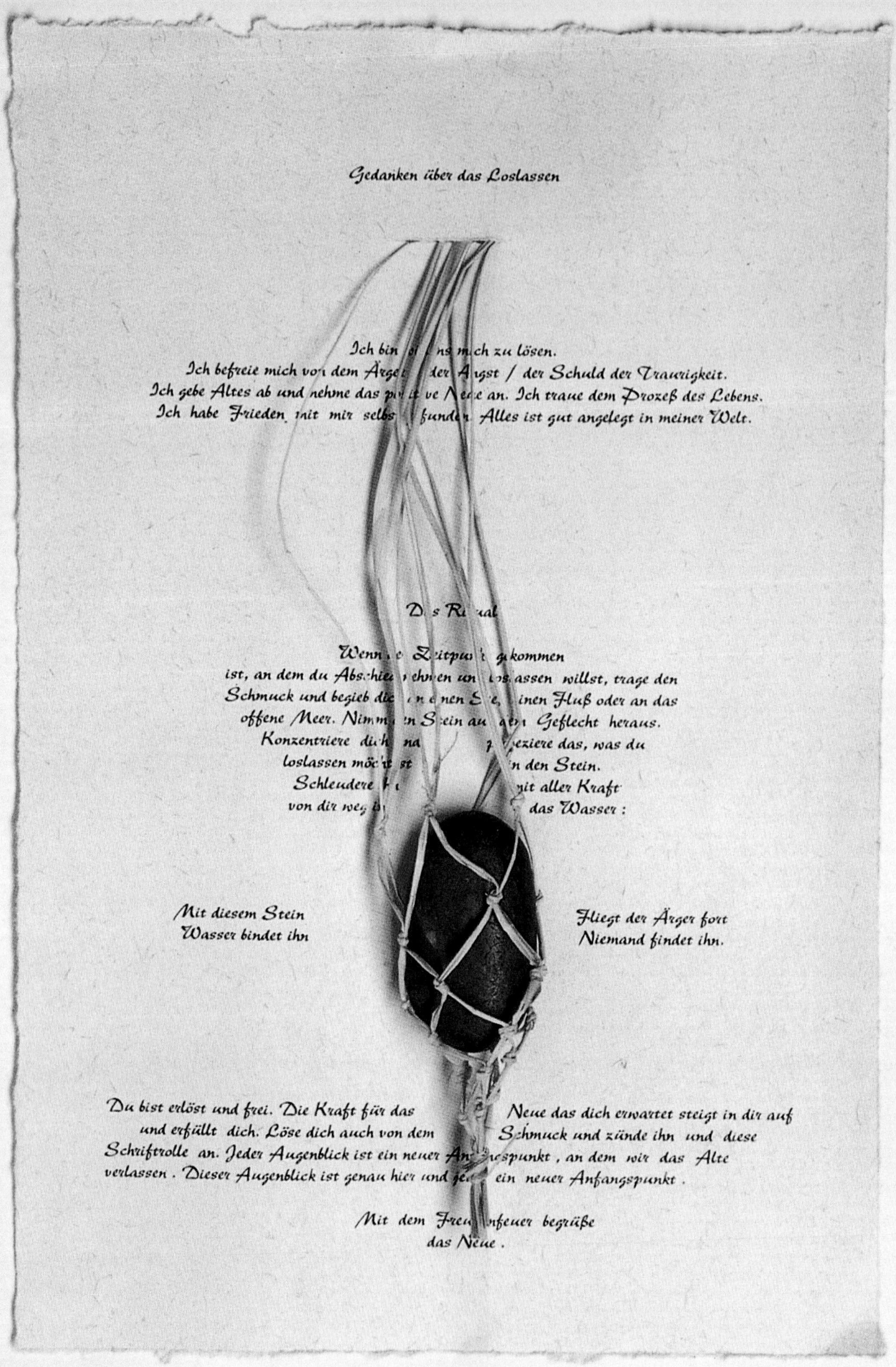

Gedanken über das Loslassen

Ich bin [illegible] mich zu lösen.
Ich befreie mich von dem Ärge[illegible] der A[illegible]gst / der Schuld der Traurigkeit.
Ich gebe Altes ab und nehme das p[illegible]ve Ne[illegible]e an. Ich traue dem Prozeß des Lebens.
Ich habe Frieden mit mir selbs[illegible]funden. Alles ist gut angelegt in meiner Welt.

D[illegible]s Ri[illegible]al

Wenn [illegible] Zeitpu[illegible]gekommen
ist, an dem du Abs[illegible]hie[illegible]ehmen un[illegible]ssen willst, trage den
Schmuck und begieb dic[illegible]nen S[illegible]inen Fluß oder an das
offene Meer. Nimm[illegible]n S[illegible]ein au[illegible] Geflecht heraus.
Konzentriere dic[illegible]na[illegible]eziere das, was du
loslassen möc[illegible]st [illegible]n den Stein.
Schleudere [illegible]it aller Kraft
von dir we[illegible] das Wasser :

Mit diesem Stein
Wasser bindet ihn

Fliegt der Ärger fort
Niemand findet ihn.

Du bist erlöst und frei. Die Kraft für das Neue das dich erwartet steigt in dir auf
und erfüllt dich. Löse dich auch von dem Schmuck und zünde ihn und diese
Schriftrolle an. Jeder Augenblick ist ein neuer An[illegible]espunkt , an dem wir das Alte
verlassen . Dieser Augenblick ist genau hier und je[illegible] ein neuer Anfangspunkt .

Mit dem Freu[illegible]nfeuer begrüße
das Neue .

Janine Awater
1997
Trichter
Anhänger
Feinsilber
Funnel
pendant
refined silver

Janine Awater
1997
Tropfen
Anhänger
Feinsilber
Drops
pendant
refined silver

Veräußerte Formen
innerer Befindlichkeiten.
Licht und Schatten,
Innen und Außen,
Vielschichtigkeit.
Externalised forms of
internal states.
Light and shadow,
within and without,
multi-layeredness.

Lilia Katona
1996
Alice
Silikongefäße
Silikon, Nicki, Edelstahl
Alice
silicone container
silicone, velour, stainless steel

Grenzen durchbrechen.
In die Welt jenseits des Spiegels
eintauchen.
Breaking through boundaries.
Immersion in the world
beyond the looking-glass.

Frauke Matschullat
2000
Schal
Süßwasserperlen, Edelsteine,
Glas, Edelstahl
scarf
freshwater pearls, precious stones,
glass, stainless steel

Behutsam flüchtige Momente von
Kostbarkeit ertasten.
With fingertips gently discerning
fleeting moments of preciousness.

Alexandra Berg-Bode
1995
Kettenhemd
Edelstahl, Silber
chain-mail shirt
stainless steel, silver

Diplomthemen von 2001 bis 1990

Dissertation Topics **2001-1990**

Sommersemester 2001

Anne Kessler Schmuck zum Thema *Wachsen und Wuchern.* Referenten: E. Holder, H. Schulze. **Nicole Langen** Schmuck zum Thema *Naturformen.* Referenten: E. Holder, H. Schulze. **Ursula Magera** Schmuck zum Thema *Naturformen.* Referenten: E. Holder, H. Schulze.

Wintersemester 2000/2001

Babette Egerland Schmuck zum Thema *Volumen und Leichtigkeit.* Referenten: E.Holder, H.Schulze. **Kirsten Grünebaum** *Körperschmuck.* Referenten: E. Holder, H. Schulze. **Ariane Hartmann** Schmuck zum Thema *Wege.* Referenten: E. Holder, H. Hermsen. **Katja Kempe** *Leuchtobjekte für Kinder.* Referenten: H. Hermsen, T. van der Laaken. **Heike Köhler** *Accessoires für das Badezimmer.* Referenten: H. Hermsen, H. Schulze. **Susanne Mayer** *Schmuck oder Produkt für moderne Nomaden.* Referenten: H. Hermsen, E. Holder. **Stephan Schmotz** *Produkte für den zukünftigen Alltag.* Referenten: H. Hermsen, H. Schulze. **Monika Seitter** Zeichnungen und Objekte zum Thema *Die Erschaffung der Welt.* Referenten: H. Schulze, U. Rungenhagen. **Gülten Tapan** *Kleinod Perle.* Referenten: E. Holder, C. Caturelli.

Sommersemester 2000

Anja Heinemeyer Schmuck zum Thema *Oberflächenstrukturen.* Referenten: E. Holder, H. Schulze. **Sylvia Kleine-Börger** *Trauer-Formen: Objekte für den Todesfall.* Referenten: H. Schulze, H. Rogge. **Ina Leppin** Schmuck zum Thema *Ein Hauch.* Referenten: E. Holder, H. Schulze. **Katharina Schwabe** *Taschenobjekte.* Referenten: P. Schudel, E. Holder. **Stefanie von Scheven** *Schmuck zu Geschichten und über Geschichten.* Referenten: E. Holder, H. Hermsen. **Nicole Unterseh** Schmuck oder Objekt zum Thema *Einblicke, Ausblicke, Durchblicke.* Referenten: E. Holder, H. Schulze. **Anke Wolf** *Weggeschichten-Schmuck oder Objekt im Miteinander.* Referenten: E. Holder, H. Schulze.

Wintersemester 1999/2000

Ute Deutz Schmuck zum Thema *Metamorphose.* Referenten: H. Hermsen, E. Holder. **Michaela Huber** Schmuck zum Thema *Scheinwelten und Irritationen.* Referenten: H. Hermsen, E. Holder. **Susanne Krämer** Schmuck zum Thema *Reflexion.* Referenten: E. Holder, H. Hermsen. **Silke Lazarevic** *Schmuck und Gewand – eine Einheit.* Referenten: H. Hermsen, E. Holder. **Anne Mersmann** Schmuck zum Thema *Oberflächen und Strukturen.*

Alexandra Berg-Bode
2000
Medaillon
Silber, Carneol
locket
silver, carnelean

Alexandra Berg-Bode
2000
Medaillonring
Ring
Silber, Carneol, Glas
locket ring
ring
silver, carnelean, glass

Summer 2001

Anne Kessler **Jewellery on the theme *Natural and Rampant Growth.* Examiners: E. Holder, H. Schulze.** Nicole Langen **Jewellery on the theme *Hidden Spaces.* Examiners: E. Holder, H. Schulze.** Ursula Magera **Jewellery on the theme *Natural Forms.* Examiners: E. Holder, H. Schulze.**

Winter 2000/2001

Babette Egerland **Jewellery on the theme *Volume and Lightness.* Examiners: E.Holder, H.Schulze.** Kirsten Grünebaum ***Body jewellery.* Examiners: E. Holder, H. Schulze.** Ariane Hartmann **Jewellery on the theme *Paths.* Examiners: E. Holder, H. Hermsen.** Katja Kempe ***Luminous Objects for Children.* Examiners: H. Hermsen, T. van der Laaken.** Heike Köhler ***Accessories for the Bathroom.* Examiners: H. Hermsen, H. Schulze.** Susanne Mayer ***Jewellery or Products for Modern Nomads.* Examiners: H. Hermsen, E. Holder.** Stephan Schmotz ***Products for Everyday Life in the Future.* Examiners: H. Hermsen, H. Schulze.** Monika Seitter **Drawings and objects on the theme *The Creation of the World.* Examiners: H. Schulze, U. Rungenhagen.** Gülten Tapan ***Gem Pearls.* Examiners: E. Holder, C. Caturelli**

Summer 2000

Anja Heinemeyer **Jewellery on the theme *Surface Structures.* Examiners: E. Holder, H. Schulze.** Sylvia Kleine-Börger ***Mourning Forms: Objects for Bereavement.* Examiners: H. Schulze, H. Rogge.** Ina Leppin **Jewellery on the theme *Just a Breath.* Examiners: E. Holder, H. Schulze.** Katharina Schwabe ***Bag Objects.* Examiners: P. Schudel, E. Holder.** Stefanie von Scheven ***Jewellery For and About Stories.* Examiners: E. Holder, H. Hermsen.** Nicole Unterseh ***Jewellery or object on the theme Insights, Outlooks, Understandings.* Examiners: E. Holder, H. Schulze.** Anke Wolf ***Travel Stories – Jewellery or Object in Cooperation.* Examiners: E. Holder, H. Schulze.**

Winter 1999/2000

Ute Deutz **Jewellery on the theme *Metamorphosis.* Examiners: H. Hermsen, E. Holder.** Michaela Huber **Jewellery on the theme *Illusory Worlds and Confusers.* Examiners: H. Hermsen, E. Holder.** Susanne Krämer **Jewellery on the theme *Reflection.* Examiners: E. Holder, H. Hermsen.** Silke Lazarevic ***Jewellery and Garment – A Unity.* Examiners: H. Hermsen, E. Holder.** Anne Mersmann **Jewellery on the theme *Surfaces and Structures.* Examiners: E. Holder, H. Hermsen.** Britta Schmicking **Jewellery on the theme *Exploration of Japanese Aesthetics.***

Alexandra Berg-Bode
2000
Gitter
Brosche
Silber, Granat, Nylon
Lattice
brooch
silver, garnet, nylon

Heike Baschta
1999
Gefärbte Welt
Anhänger
Spiegelglas, Synthese, Putz, Messing, Faden
Coloured World
pendant
mirror glass, synthesis, plaster, brass, thread

Referenten: E. Holder, H. Hermsen. **Britta Schmicking** Schmuck zum Thema *Reise in die japanische Ästhetik.* Referenten: H. Hermsen, P. Weingärtner-Arnold. **Claudia Wieczorek** Schmuck zum Thema *Verbindungen.* Referenten: H. Hermsen, E. Holder.

Wintersemester 1998/1999

Barbara Schwab *Schmucksysteme und Systemschmuck.* Referenten: E. Holder, H. Hermsen. **Susanne Winckler** Schmuck und Objekt zum Thema *Vergessen und Erinnern.* Referenten: E. Holder, H. Hermsen.

Sommersemester 1998

Melanie Backes-Sitel Schmuck oder Objekt zum Thema *Wüste – wenn das Leben lebendig wird.* Referenten: E. Holder, H. Hermsen. **Kirsten Höcker** Schmuck zum Thema *Zwischen-Raum.* Referenten: E. Holder, H. Schulze. **Malte Meinck** *Narrengestalten, Schmuck mit opalartigem Material.* Referenten: E. Holder, H. Hermsen. **Ortrun Meinhard** Schmuck und Objekt zum Thema *Leben und Tod.* Referenten: H. Hermsen, E. Holder. **Martin Pittig** *Schmuck als Prothese.* Referenten: E. Holder, H. Hermsen.

Wintersemester 1997/1998

Imke Jantzen *Schmuck, abgeleitet von Naturstimmungen.* Referenten: E.Holder, H.Schulze. **Heike Kähler** Schmuck zum Thema *Hülle und Verhülltes.* Referenten: H. Hermsen, E. Holder. **Susanne Leu** *Schmuck als Kommunikationsmittel.* Referenten: E. Holder, G. Pfeifer. **Cordula Möwes** Schmuck zum Thema *Schatten.* Referenten: E. Holder, H. Hermsen. **Susanne Schulze** *Schmuck oder Objekt zum Fühlen oder Riechen.* Referenten: H. Hermsen, H. Schulze. **Birgit Straube** Schmuck zum Thema *Altern ist Reifen.* Referenten: H. Hermsen, E. Holder.

Heike Baschta
1999
Reflektierte Welt
Anhänger
Spiegelglas, Putz, Kupfer
Reflected World
pendant
mirror glass, plaster, copper

Sommersemester 1997

Petra Brenner *Glasbehältnisse zur Bewahrung von Träumen.* Referenten: E. Holder, B. Tendahl. **Ursula Dey** *Schmuck als Ausdruck oder Zeichen einer Freundschaft.* Referenten: E. Holder, H. Schulze. **Anke Günther** Schmuck zum Thema *Linie.* Referenten: E. Holder, H. Hermsen. **Birthe Häusgen** *Schmuck als Träger von Duft.* Referenten: E. Holder, H. Hermsen. **Astrid Heininger** *Schmuck oder Objekt im Spannungsfeld von Illusion und Wirklichkeit.* Referenten: H. Hermsen, B. Tendahl. **Henriette Junkers** *Schmuckobjekte, Geister des Feuers, der Luft, des Wassers,*

Examiners: H. Hermsen, P. Weingärtner-Arnold. Claudia Wieczorek **Jewellery on the theme *Connections.* Examiners: H. Hermsen, E. Holder.**

Winter 1998/1999

Barbara Schwab ***Jewellery Systems and System Jewellery.* Examiners: E. Holder, H. Hermsen.** Susanne Winckler **Jewellery and object on the theme *Forgetting and Remembering.* Examiners: E. Holder, H. Hermsen.**

Summer 1998

Melanie Backes-Sitel **Jewellery or object on the theme *Desert – When Life Comes to Life.* Examiners: E. Holder, H. Hermsen.** Kirsten Höcker **Jewellery on the theme *Inter-Spaces.* Examiners: E. Holder, H. Schulze.** Malte Meinck ***Fool Forms, jewellery with opal-like materials.* Examiners: E. Holder, H. Hermsen.** Ortrun Meinhard **Jewellery and object on the theme *Life and Death.* Examiners: H. Hermsen, E. Holder.** Martin Pittig ***Jewellery as a Prosthesis.* Examiners: E. Holder, H. Hermsen.**

Winter 1997/1998

Imke Jantzen ***Jewellery Inspired by Moods of Nature.* Examiners: E.Holder, H.Schulze.** Heike Kähler **Jewellery on the theme *Wraps and Veiled.* Examiners: H. Hermsen, E. Holder.** Susanne Leu ***Jewellery as a Medium for Communication.* Examiners: E. Holder, G. Pfeifer.** Cordula Möwes **Jewellery on the theme *Shadow.* Examiners: E. Holder, H. Hermsen.** Susanne Schulze ***Jewellery or Object for the senses of touch or smell.* Examiners: H. Hermsen, H. Schulze.** Birgit Straube **Jewellery on the theme *Ageing is Maturing.* Examiners: H. Hermsen, E. Holder.**

Heike Baschta
1995
Felltrichter
Ringaufsätze
Nutriafell, Fuchsfell
Fur Funnel
ring attachments
coypu fur, fox fur

Summer 1997

Petra Brenner ***Glass Containers for Storing Dreams.* Examiners: E. Holder, B. Tendahl.** Ursula Dey ***Jewellery as an Expression or Sign of Friendship.* Examiners: E. Holder, H. Schulze.** Anke Günther **Jewellery on the theme *Line.* Examiners: E. Holder, H. Hermsen.** Birthe Häusgen ***Jewellery as a Carrier of Scent.* Examiners: E. Holder, H. Hermsen.** Astrid Heininger ***Jewellery or Object in the Tension between Illusion and Reality.* Examiners: H. Hermsen, B. Tendahl.** Henriette Junkers ***Jewellery Objects: Spirits of Fire, Air, Water, Earth.* Examiners: H. Hermsen, H. Schulze.** Gereon Klingen ***Censer and Incense Containers.* Examiners: E. Holder, H. Schulze.**

Des Erbstücks neue Kleider.
The heirloom's new clothes.

der Erde. Referenten: H. Hermsen, H. Schulze. **Gereon Klingen** *Weihrauchfass und Weihrauchgefäße.* Referenten: E. Holder, H. Schulze. **Renate Nossek** Schmuck zum Thema *Reihung oder Rhythmus.* Referenten: E. Holder, H. Hermsen. **Helena Pichler** Schmuck zum Thema *Ins Blau hinein.* Referenten: H. Hermsen, B. Tendahl. **Mareile Tinzmann** *Andenkenschmuck: Zwischen Sammlung und Erinnerung.* Referenten: E. Holder, B. Tendahl.

Wintersemester 1996/1997

Ursula Biskup Schmuck zum Thema *Transparenz.* Referenten: H. Hermsen, E. Holder. **Nicoletta Cammilleri** Schmuck zum Thema *Spurensicherung.* Referenten: H. Hermsen, B. Tendahl. **Klaus Müller** *Sitzmöbel.* Referenten: H. Hermsen, H. Schulze.

Sommersemester 1996

Lilia Katona Gefäß zum Thema *Spiegelung.* Referenten: E. Holder,H. Hermsen. **Angelika Knälmann** *Schmuck aus Kunststoff.* Referenten: E. Holder, H. Hermsen. **Daniela Kohl** *Die Verwandlung im Gewand.* Referenten: E. Holder, H. Hermsen. **Katja Korsawe** *Über die Veränderbarkeit der Dinge.* Referenten: E. Holder, H. Hermsen. **Alexander Loose** *Türdrücker.* Referenten: H. Hermsen, K. R'hila. **Jochen Schink** *Schmuck analog zu musikalischen Kompositionstechniken.* Referenten: H. Hermsen, E.Holder. **Bertold Schmidt** *Leuchten, nicht nur für das Schlafzimmer.* Referenten: H. Hermsen, E. Holder.

Wintersemester 1995/1996

Janine Awater *Schmuck als Gedankengefäß.* Referenten: E. Holder, K. R'hila. **Rita Berger-Szuder** *Objekte für Sonne und Wind.* Referenten: E. Holder, H. Schulze. **Monika Ernst** *Vom Wachküssen der Dinge: Gegenstände für die Tischkultur.* Referenten: E. Holder, H. Hermsen. **Nicola Ernst** Schmuck zum Thema *Spannung.* Referenten: H. Hermsen, H. Schulze. **Uta Knoop** *Schmuckobjekte aus Glasrelikten.* Referenten: E. Holder, H. Hermsen. **Bettina Lamberti** Objekte zum Thema *Interaktive Grenzbereiche zwischen Innen und Außen.* Referenten: H. Hermsen, K. R'hila. **Frauke Matschullat** *Schmuck zwischen Zauber und Zier.* Referenten: E. Holder, K. R'hila. **Christiane Schneider** Schmuckobjekte zum Thema *Form und Dynamik.* Referenten: E. Holder, H. Schulze. **Beate Steinfeld** *Schmuck in Hülle und Fülle.* Referenten: E. Holder, H. Hermsen.

Annette Wackermann
1997
Blumenwiese
Schlüsselbord
Aluminium
Flower Meadow
key rack
aluminium

Renate Nossek **Jewellery on the theme *Sequence or Rhythm.* Examiners: E. Holder, H. Hermsen.** Helena Pichler **Jewellery on the theme *Into the Blue.* Examiners: H. Hermsen, B. Tendahl.** Mareile Tinzmann ***Memento jewellery: Between Collection and Remembrance.* Examiners: E. Holder, B. Tendahl.**

Winter 1996/1997

Ursula Biskup **Jewellery on the theme *Transparency.* Examiners: H. Hermsen, E. Holder.** Nicoletta Cammilleri **Jewellery on the theme *Securing Evidence.* Examiners: H. Hermsen, B. Tendahl.** Klaus Müller ***Seats.* Examiners: H. Hermsen, H. Schulze.**

Summer 1996

Lilia Katona ***Vessels on the theme Reflection.* Examiners: E. Holder, H. Hermsen.** Angelika Knälmann ***Jewellery Made of Plastic.* Examiners: E. Holder, H. Hermsen.** Daniela Kohl ***Transformation in the Garb.* Examiners: E. Holder, H. Hermsen.** Katja Korsawe ***On the Changeability of Things.* Examiners: E. Holder, H. Hermsen.** Alexander Loose ***Door Handles.* Examiners: H. Hermsen, K. R'hila.** Jochen Schink ***Jewellery in Analogue to Musical Composition Techniques.* Examiners: H. Hermsen, E.Holder.** Bertold Schmidt ***Lamps, Not Only for the Bedroom.* Examiners: H. Hermsen, E. Holder.**

Winter 1995/1996

Janine Awater ***Jewellery as a Thought Receptacle.* Examiners: E. Holder, K. R'hila.** Rita Berger-Szuder ***Objects for Sun and Wind.* Examiners: E. Holder, H. Schulze.** Monika Ernst ***Of Kissing Things Awake: Objects for Table Culture.* Examiners: E. Holder, H. Hermsen.** Nicola Ernst **Jewellery on the theme *Tension.* Examiners: H. Hermsen, H. Schulze.** Uta Knoop ***Jewellery Objects Made from Glass Relics.* Examiners: E. Holder, H. Hermsen.** Bettina Lamberti **Objects on the theme *Interactive Border Zones Between Within and Without* Examiners: H. Hermsen, K. R'hila.** Frauke Matschullat ***Jewellery Between Magic and Ornament.* Examiners: E. Holder, K. R'hila.** Christiane Schneider **Jewellery objects on the theme *Form and Dynamism.* Examiners: E. Holder, H. Schulze.** Beate Steinfeld ***Jewellery in Wild Abundance.* Examiners: E. Holder, H. Hermsen.**

Summer 1995

Heike Baschta ***The Exceptional in the Series.* Examiners: E. Holder, H. Hermsen.** Alexandra Berg-Bode **Symbolic**

Annette Wackermann
1995
Reiselust
Reiseset für zwei Gourmets
Aluminium, Holz,
Zinn, Edelstahl, Leder
Wanderlust
travel set for two gourmets
aluminium, wood,
pewter, stainless steel, leather

Kulinarisch unterwegs.
On the culinary road.

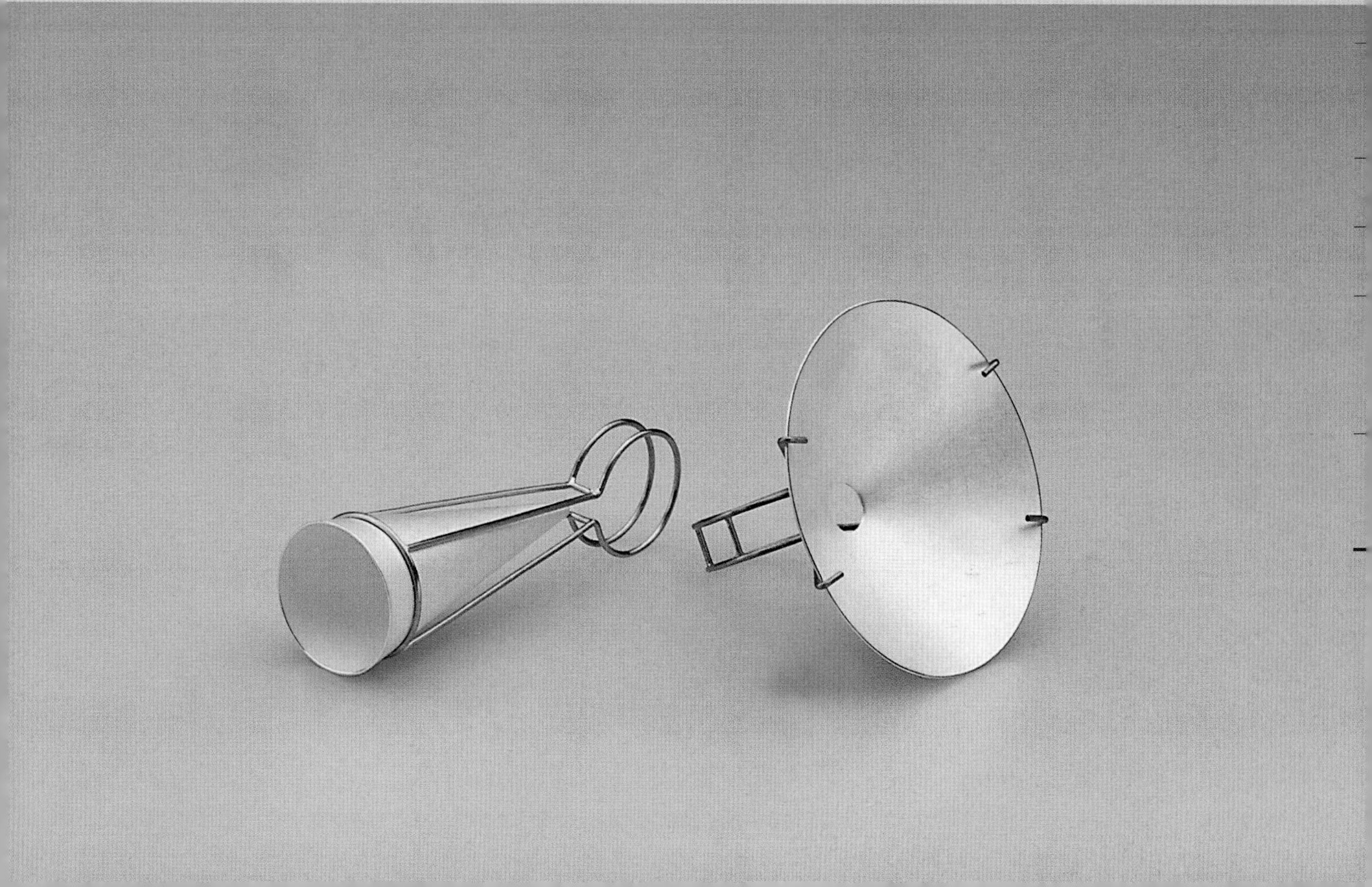

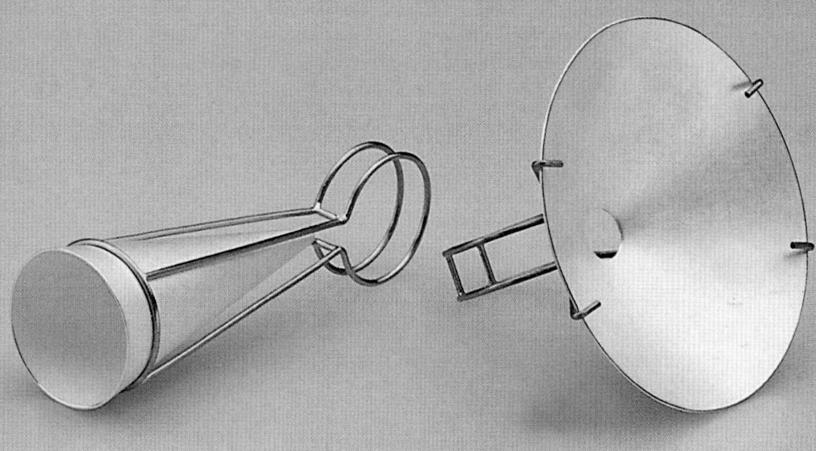

Gabriele Hinze
1994
Gefäß für Gedanken
Anhänger
Feinsilber
Vessel for Thoughts
pendant
refined silver

„Mit meinem Schmuck möchte ich Orte für Gedanken, Befindlichkeiten und Geheimnisse seiner Träger schaffen."
"With my jewellery I want to create places for the thoughts, feelings and secrets of the wearer."

Sommersemester 1995
Heike Baschta *Das Besondere in der Serie.* Referenten: E. Holder, H. Hermsen. **Alexandra Berg-Bode** Zeichenhafter Schmuck zum Thema *Bewegung.* Referenten: E. Holder, H. Hermsen. **Gabriele Hinze** Schmuck zum Thema *Raum.* Referenten: E. Holder, H. Schulze. **Elisabeth Kövari** *Körperschmuck.* Referenten: H. Hermsen, H. Schulze. **Katrin Laville** *Blumenvasen: Der Schritt nach dem Schnitt.* Referenten: E. Holder, H. Hermsen. **Annette Wackermann** *Gegenstände für Reiselustige.* Referenten: H. Hermsen, H. Schulze.

Wintersemester 1994/1995
Petra Eberz *Fünf Personen – fünf Taschen.* Referenten: E. Holder, H. Hermsen. **Pia Iavaroni** *Produkthüllen für dekorative Kosmetik.* Referenten: E. Holder, H. Schulze. **Ina Könnicke-Mader** *Körperschmuck.* Referenten: E. Holder, H. Hermsen. **Margarete Kühles-Marschall** *Boxes.* Referenten: E. Holder, H. Schulze. **Kirsten Schäfer** Schmuck zum Thema *Baumstrukturen.* Referenten: E. Holder, H. Hermsen.

Sommersemester 1994
Petra Borgmann *Gesichtsornament Brille.* Referenten: E. Holder, D. Fuder. **Michael Boy** *Klappmöbel.* Referenten: H. Hermsen, E. Holder. **Susanne Camp** *Schmuck aus täglich anfallenden Verpackungsabfällen aus Kunststoff.* Referenten: E. Holder, H. Hermsen. **Jürgen Dernbach** *Eine Gefäßgruppe.* Referenten: H. Hermsen, H. Schulze. **Marion Funke** Schmuck zum Thema *Sehen und Erkennen.* Referenten: E. Holder, H. Hermsen. **Anja Hannig** *Schmuck als Ensemble.* Referenten: H. Hermsen, H. Schulze. **Ursula Issig** *Besteck.* Referenten: H. Hermsen, H. Schulze. **Caren Meiners** Schmuck zum Thema *Pflanze.* Referenten: E. Holder, H. Hermsen. **Thietmar Schorm** *Multi-Media-Schmuckstücke.* Referenten: H. Hermsen, D. Fuder.

Wintersemester 1993/1994
Thomas Heuschmann *Schmuck aus Metall und Steinen.* Referenten: E. Holder, N. Ferkinghoff. **Claudia Hodapp** *Serienschmuck mit dem Farbmittel Email.* Referenten: E. Holder, I. Beyermann. **Daniela Hundsalz** Schmuck zum Thema *Rhythmus in der Reihe.* Referenten: H. Hermsen, H. Schulze. **Susanne Kolb** Schmuck zum Thema *Wirkung von Kristallen.* Referenten: H. Hermsen, H. Schulze. **Kathrin Nitschke** *Schale als Schmuckobjekt.* Referenten: E. Holder, H. Hermsen. **Claudia Schäfer** *Behältnisse mit einem Kontrast zwischen innen und außen.*

Gabriele Hinze
1995
Lichttrichter
Ring
Silber, Weißgold
Light Funnel
ring
silver, white gold

jewellery on the theme *Movement.* Examiners: E. Holder, H. Hermsen. Gabriele Hinze **Jewellery on the theme *Space.* Examiners: E. Holder, H. Schulze.** Elisabeth Kövari ***Body Jewellery.* Examiners: H. Hermsen, H. Schulze.** Katrin Laville ***Flower Vases: the Cut Following the Cut.* Examiners: E. Holder, H. Hermsen.** Annette Wackermann ***Objects for People with Wanderlust.* Examiners: H. Hermsen, H. Schulze.**

Winter 1994/1995
Petra Eberz ***Five Individuals – Five Bags.* Examiners: E. Holder, H. Hermsen.** Pia Iavaroni ***Product Covers for Decorative Cosmetics.* Examiners: E. Holder, H. Schulze.** Ina Könnicke-Mader ***Body Jewellery* Examiners: E. Holder, H. Hermsen.** Margarete Kühles-Marschall ***Boxes.* Examiners: E. Holder, H. Schulze.** Kirsten Schäfer **Jewellery on the theme *Tree Structures.* Examiners: E. Holder, H. Hermsen.**

Summer 1994
Petra Borgmann ***Spectacles as a Facial Ornament.* Examiners: E. Holder, D. Fuder.** Michael Boy ***Folding Furniture.* Examiners: H. Hermsen, E. Holder.** Susanne Camp ***Jewellery Made of Everyday Plastic Packaging Waste.* Examiners: E. Holder, H. Hermsen.** Jürgen Dernbach ***A Vessel Group.* Examiners: H. Hermsen, H. Schulze.** Marion Funke **Jewellery on the theme *Seeing and Recognising.* Examiners: E. Holder, H. Hermsen.** Anja Hannig ***Jewellery as Ensemble* Examiners: H. Hermsen, H. Schulze.** Ursula Issig ***Cutlery.* Examiners: H. Hermsen, H. Schulze.** Caren Meiners **Jewellery on the theme *Plant.* Examiners: E. Holder, H. Hermsen.** Thietmar Schorm ***Multimedia Jewellery.* Examiners: H. Hermsen, D. Fuder.**

Winter 1993/1994
Thomas Heuschmann ***Jewellery Made of Metal and Stones.* Examiners: E. Holder, N. Ferkinghoff.** Claudia Hodapp ***Serialised Jewellery Coloured with Enamel.* Examiners: E. Holder, I. Beyermann.** Daniela Hundsalz **Jewellery on the theme *Rhythm in the Sequence.* Examiners: H. Hermsen, H. Schulze.** Susanne Kolb **Jewellery on the theme *The Effect of Crystals.* Examiners: H. Hermsen, H. Schulze.** Kathrin Nitschke ***Bowl as a Decorative Object.* Examiners: E. Holder, H. Hermsen.** Claudia Schäfer ***Containers with Contrasting Interiors and Exteriors.* Examiners: E. Holder, H. Hermsen.** Tanja Stockhausen **Jewellery on the theme *Haptic Awareness.* Examiners: H. Schulze, E. Holder.**

Referenten: E. Holder, H. Hermsen. **Tanja Stockhausen** Schmuck zum Thema *Haptische Wahrnehmung.* Referenten: H. Schulze, E. Holder.

Sommersemester 1993
Thomas Binke *Objekte zur Verdeutlichung und Darstellung von Sinneswahrnehmungen.* Referenten: E. Holder, H. Schulze. **Martina Czunczeleit** *Schalenpaare.* Referenten: E. Holder, H. Hermsen. **Bernard Dyllong** *Schalen.* Referenten: H. Schulze, H. Rothweiler. **Claudia Hoffmann-Brune** Schmuck zum Thema *Die vier Jahreszeiten.* Referenten: E. Holder, H. Hermsen.

Wintersemster 1992/1993
Holger Haffke *Lichtobjekte.* Referenten: E. Holder, H. Schulze. **Claudia Lehnert** *Funktionaler Schmuck für die Kleidung.* Referenten: E. Holder, H. Hermsen. **Anne-Pia Orth, Evelyn Vanderloock** *Schmuck unter Berücksichtigung serieller Aspekte.* Referenten: E. Holder, H. Hermsen. **Anke Plöger** *Tischgerät.* Referenten: H. Hermsen, H. Schulze. **Susanne Stifel** Schmuck zum Thema *Landschaft und Landschaftsstruktur.* Referenten: E. Holder, H. Schulze.

Sommersemester 1992
Cordula Fleissig *Schmuck zwischen Ornament und Zeichen.* Referenten: E. Holder, H. Schulze. **Sebastian Hartkopf** *Schmuck als Architektur am Körper.* Referenten: E. Holder, E. Kuhn. **Hilde Janich** *Schmuck zum Thema Schatten.* Referenten: E. Holder, I. Sauer. **Lutz Miosga** *Ketten als Halsschmuck.* Referenten: E. Holder, I. Sauer. **Sabine Schröder** *Schmuck auf der Basis von Gestaltungskriterien des Architekten Frank O. Gehry.* Referenten: R. Assmann, H. Schulze. **Christoph Schröder-Schnee** *Messer.* Referenten: H. Schulze, E. Holder. **Stefanie Wick, Katrin Steidinger** *Christbaumschmuck.* Referenten: E. Kuhn, H. Rothweiler.

Wintersemester 1991/1992
Michaela Gottstein *Schmuck aus planen Flächenelementen.* Referenten: E. Holder, H. Schulze. **Christiane Mindner** Schmuck zum Thema *Reihung und Addition.* Referenten: E. Holder, H. Rothweiler. **Sabine Müller** *Schmuck für Kinder.* Referenten: E. Holder, H. Rothweiler.

Petra Borgmann
1991/92
svelto
Prototyp für ein Essbesteck
Messing, versilbert
svelto
cutlery set prototype
silver-plated brass
Foto: Sibylle Pietrek, Düsseldorf

Summer 1993
Thomas Binke ***Objects that Highlight and Express Sensory Perception.*** **Examiners: E. Holder, H. Schulze.** Martina Czunczeleit ***Bowl pairs.*** **Examiners: E. Holder, H. Hermsen.** Bernard Dyllong ***Bowls*** **Examiners: H. Schulze, H. Rothweiler.** Claudia Hoffmann-Brune **Jewellery on the theme** ***The Four Seasons.*** **Examiners: E. Holder, H. Hermsen.**

Winter 1992/1993
Holger Haffke ***Light Objects.*** **Examiners: E. Holder, H. Schulze.** Claudia Lehnert ***Functional Jewellery for Clothing.*** **Examiners: E. Holder, H. Hermsen.** Anne-Pia Orth, Evelyn Vanderloock ***Jewellery and Aspects of Serialisation.*** **Examiners: E. Holder, H. Hermsen.** Anke Plöger ***Table Utensils.*** **Examiners: H. Hermsen, H. Schulze.** Susanne Stifel **Jewellery on the theme** ***Landscapes and Landscape Structures.*** **Examiners: E. Holder, H. Schulze.**

Summer 1992
Cordula Fleissig ***Jewellery Between Ornament and Symbol.*** **Examiners: E. Holder, H. Schulze.** Sebastian Hartkopf ***Jewellery as Architecture on the Body.*** **Examiners: E. Holder, E. Kuhn.** Hilde Janich **Jewellery on the theme** ***Shadows.*** **Examiners: E. Holder, I. Sauer.** Lutz Miosga ***Chains as Neck Ornaments.*** **Examiners: E. Holder, I. Sauer.** Sabine Schröder ***Jewellery Based on the Design Criteria of the Architect Frank O. Gehry.*** **Examiners: R. Assmann, H. Schulze.** Christoph Schröder-Schnee ***Knives.*** **Examiners: H. Schulze, E. Holder.** Stefanie Wick, Katrin Steidinger ***Christmas Tree Decorations.*** **Examiners: E. Kuhn, H. Rothweiler.**

Winter 1991/1992
Michaela Gottstein ***Jewellery Made of Plane Geometrical Elements.*** **Examiners: E. Holder, H. Schulze.** Christiane Mindner **Jewellery on the theme** ***Sequence and Addition.*** **Examiners: E. Holder, H. Rothweiler.** Sabine Müller ***Jewellery for Children.*** **Examiners: E. Holder, H. Rothweiler.**

Summer 1991
Ursula Döhmen-Schütze ***Jewellery Using Light as a Design Element.*** **Examiners: E. Holder, H. Schulze.** Bettina Fuhg ***Letter Opener.*** **Examiners: E. Holder, H. Becker.** Birgit Gündling ***Bookmarks.*** **Examiners: E. Holder, H. Becker.** Bernd Schermuly **Jewellery on the theme** ***Fragment.*** **Examiners: E. Holder, H. Schulze.**

Petra Borgmann
1994
P.M.
Brille
Aluminium, Stahl
P.M.
spectacles
aluminium, steel
Foto: Sibylle Pietrek, Düsseldorf

Sommersemester 1991
Ursula Döhmen-Schütze *Schmuck mit dem Gestaltungsmittel Licht.* Referenten: E. Holder, H. Schulze. **Bettina Fuhg** *Brieföffner.* Referenten: E. Holder, H. Becker. **Birgit Gündling** *Lesezeichen.* Referenten: E. Holder, H. Becker. **Bernd Schermuly** Schmuck zum Thema *Fragment.* Referenten: E. Holder, H. Schulze.

Wintersemester 1990/1991
Sabine Kaever *Schmuck als Interpretation von Ovids Metamorphosen.* Referenten: E. Holder, D. Glasmacher.
Gudula Roch *Figürliche Schmuckstücke aus der Welt der Mythen und Märchen.* Referenten: E. Holder, H. Rothweiler.

Sommersemester 1990
Georg Plum *Kleinuhren.* Referenten: E. Holder, H. Schulze. **Andreas Wächter** *Kaffeeservice.* Referenten: E. Holder, H. Schulze.

Petra Borgmann
1994
OMEGA
Brille
Pulverbeschichtetes Messing
OMEGA
spectacles
powder-coated brass
Foto: Sibylle Pietrek, Düsseldorf

Winter 1990/1991
Sabine Kaever ***Jewellery as an Interpretation of Ovid's Metamorphoses.*** **Examiners: E. Holder, D. Glasmacher.**
Gudula Roch ***Figurative Jewellery from the World of Myths and Fairytales.*** **Examiners: E. Holder, H. Rothweiler.**

Summer 1990
Georg Plum ***Small Clocks and Watches.*** **Examiners: E. Holder, H. Schulze.** Andreas Wächter ***Coffee Service.*** **Examiners: E. Holder, H. Schulze.**

Petra Borgmann
1994
Dreifach geschichtet
Brille
Aluminium, Stahl, Gummi
Triple-Coated
spectacles
aluminium, steel, rubber
Foto: Sibylle Pietrek, Düsseldorf

Claudia Schäfer
2001
Sternenstaub
Brillantringe
Gold, Brillanten
Stardust
diamond rings
gold, diamonds

Claudia Schäfer
1998/1987
Schatzkugel
Verpackung für Schmuck
Papier
Treasure Sphere
packaging for jewellery
paper

Wenn etwas auftaucht oder verschwindet...
When something appears or disappears...

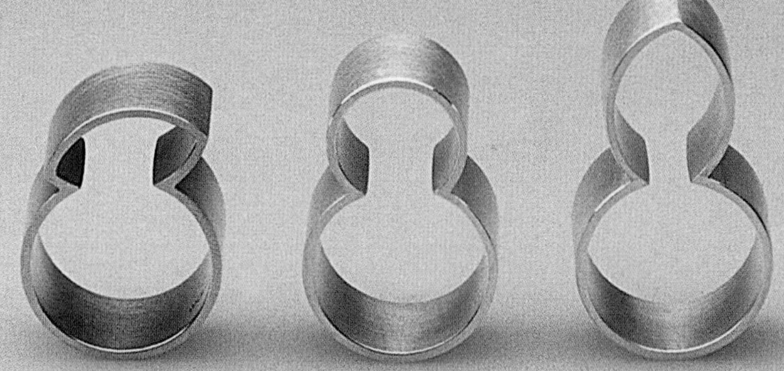

Claudia Schäfer
2000
Easy Going
Armbanduhren
Silber, Stahl, Leder
Easy Going
wristwatches
silver, steel, leather

Martina Czunczeleit
1996
Join I
Ringe
Silber, Gold
Join I
rings
silver, gold

1883 Gründung der Kunstgewerbeschule. **1886-1887** Einrichtung einer Fachklasse für Treiben, Gravieren und Ziselieren. **1888** Wachsmodellieren als Weiterbildungsangebot der Abendschule für Graveure, Gold- und Silberschmiede. **1903-1907** Peter Behrens, Direktor der Kunstgewerbeschule. **1907-1908** Wilhelm Bosselt, Direktor der Kunstgewerbeschule. **1908-1919** Wilhelm Kreis, Direktor der Kunstgewerbeschule. **1909** Einrichtung einer Fachklasse für das Treiben, Ziselieren und Patinieren von Gefäßen. Julius Peyerimhoff ist Fachlehrer bis 1919. **1919** Auflösung der Kunstgewerbeschule. Die handwerklichen Klassen werden der seit 1909 existierenden Fachschule für Handwerk und Industrie zugewiesen, die anderen Klassen der Kunstakademie. **1934** Umbenennung in Meisterschule für das Gestaltende Handwerk. **1947** Einrichtung der Werkgruppe Schmuck. **1947-1948** Dr. Ossenbach, Leitung der Werkgruppe Schmuck. **1948-1952** Erich Frey, Fachlehrer der Werkgruppe Schmuck. **1948-1956** Karl Schollmayer, Leitung der Werkgruppe Schmuck. **1950** Umbenennung des Instituts in Werkkunstschule. **1952-1956** Friedrich Becker, Fachlehrer der Werkgruppe Schmuck. **1956-1974** Friedrich Becker, Leitung der Werkgruppe Schmuck. **1958** Einrichtung der Email-Abteilung. **1958-1965** Lili Schultz, Leitung der Werkgruppe Email. **1958-1966** Margarete Ernst, Fachlehrerin der Werkgruppe Email. **1965-1971** Sigrid Delius, Leitung der Werkgruppe Email. **1971** Übernahme der Werkgruppen Schmuck und Email in den Fachbereich Design der Fachhochschule Düsseldorf. **1974** Zusammenfassung der Fachgruppen Schmuck und Email zum Studiengang Produktdesign mit dem Studienschwerpunkt Schmuckdesign. **1973-1982** Friedrich Becker ist Professor für das Lehrgebiet Schmuckdesign. **1971-1986** Paul-Georg Schminder ist Fachlehrer für Silberschmieden **1976-1989** Sigrid Delius ist Professorin für das Lehrgebiet Schmuck- und Emaildesign. **1982** Umzug des Fachbereichs Design an den heutigen Standort. **1985-1986** Giampaolo Babetto ist Professor für das Lehrgebiet Schmuckdesign **1986** Herbert Schulze wird als Fachlehrer für Silberschmieden eingestellt. **1988** Elisabeth Holder wird zur Professorin für das Lehrgebiet Schmuckdesign berufen. **1991-1993** Herman Hermsen ist Gastprofessor und vertritt die Bereiche Produktdesign und Schmuckdesign. **1993** Herman Hermsen wird zum Professor für die Bereiche Produktdesign und Schmuckdesign berufen. **1995-1999** Professorin Elisabeth Holder leitet als Dekanin den Fachbereich Design. **2001** Studierende und Lehrende des Fachbereichs Design setzen sich erfolgreich ein für den Erhalt des Studienschwerpunkts Schmuckdesign in Düsseldorf. Die von Ehemaligen und Lehrenden anderer Hochschulen, von Firmen, Galerien und Museen geschriebenen Protestbriefe zur Unterstützung ihres Begehrens, den Standort Düsseldorf für Schmuckdesign zu erhalten, füllt ein 214-seitiges Buch (ISBN 3-923669-60-7).

Evelyn Vanderloock
1993
Armschmuck
PVC-Folie, Siebdruck
arm ornament
PVC film, screen print

1883 **Foundation of the College of Arts & Crafts (Kunstgewerbeschule).** 1886-1887 **Establishment of an eveningclass in embossing, engraving and chasing.** 1888 **Wax modelling is added as a further education programme in the evening school for engravers, goldsmiths and silversmiths.** 1903-1907 **Peter Behrens, director of the College of Arts & Crafts.** 1907-1908 **Wilhelm Bosselt, director of the College of Arts & Crafts.** 1908-1919 **Wilhelm Kreis, director of the College of Arts & Crafts.** 1909 **Establishment of a course in embossing, chasing and patination for vessels. Julius Peyerimhoff is head teacher for this course until 1919.** 1919 **Closure of the College of Arts & Crafts. The practical crafts courses are taken over by the Crafts and Industry College (Fachschule für Handwerk und Industrie, est. 1909), the other courses by the Art Academy (Kunstakademie).** 1934 **The college gets a new name: Master Crafts College (Meisterschule für das Gestaltende Handwerk).** 1947 **Establishment of the of the Jewellery Department.** 1947-1948 **Dr. Ossenbach, Head of the Jewellery Department.** 1948-1952 **Erich Frey, Jewellery Department Head Teacher.** 1948-1956 **Karl Schollmayer, Head of the Jewellery Department.** 1950 **The institution is renamed again. New name: College of Arts and Crafts (Werkkunstschule).** 1952-1956 **Friedrich Becker, Jewellery Department Head Teacher.** 1956-1974 **Friedrich Becker, Head of the Jewellery Department.** 1958 **Establishment of the Enamel Department.** 1958-1965 **Lili Schultz, Head of the Enamel Department.** 1958-1966 **Margarete Ernst, Enamel Department Head Teacher.** 1965-1971 **Sigrid Delius, Head of the Enamel Department.** 1971 **The Enamel and Jewellery Departments are integrated into the School of Design at the Düsseldorf University of Applied Sciences.** 1974 **The Jewellery and Enamel Departments are combined to form the School of Product Design with the Jewellery Design Department.** 1973-1982 **Friedrich Becker is Professor of Jewellery Design.** 1971-1986 **Paul-Georg Schminder is head teacher of the Silversmithing Department.** 1976-1989 **Sigrid Delius is Professor of Jewellery and Enamel Design.** 1982 **The Faculty of Design moves to its present location** 1985-1986 **Giampaolo Babetto is Professor of Jewellery Design.** 1986 **Herbert Schulze is engaged as head teacher in the Silversmithing Department.** 1988 **Elisabeth Holder is appointed as Professor of Jewellery Design** 1991-1993 **Herman Hermsen is guest professor, teaching product design and jewellery design.** 1993 **Herman Hermsen is appointed as Professor of Product Design and Jewellery Design.** 1995-1999 **Professor Elisabeth Holder is Dean of the Faculty of Design.** 2001 **Students and teachers from the Faculty of Design successfully campaign to keep the School of Jewellery Design in Düsseldorf. The protest letters supporting the campaign to keep the School of Jewellery Design in Düsseldorf from former students, lecturers at other universities, private companies, art galleries and museums fills a 214-page book (ISBN 3-923669-60-7).**

Evelyn Vanderloock
1993
Halsschmuck
PVC-Folie, Siebdruck
neck ornament
PVC film, screen print

Im Drunter und Drüber mit Leichtigkeit verbunden.
Connected with ease within the topsy-turvy.

Sebastian Hartkopf
2000
Aufmerksamkeitsübung
Doppelringe
Gold
Attention Exercise
twin rings
gold

„lange
sah er ein ding an
bis er einsah,
dass er vorbei sah
und merkte,
dass es kein bild war
sondern ein fenster"
"long
he gazed at it
before he saw
his gaze go past it
and noticed
it was no picture
but a window"
Josef Neuhaus, *Ordnung des Seins, konkrete Kunst in NRW,* Ausstellungskatalog, Gustav-Lübke-Museum, Hamm 1999, S. 62

Sebastian Hartkopf
1992
Broschen
Patiniertes Zink
brooches
zinc with patination

Bücher **Books**
Torsten Bröhan und Thomas Berg, **Avantgarde Design**, Köln 1994 Peter Dormer und Ralph Turner, **The new jewelry, trends and traditions**, London 1985, 1994 Fritz Falk und Cornelie Holzach, **Schmuck der Moderne**, Stuttgart 1999 Freiraum (Hrsg.), **Möbel für kleine Räume: witzige Objekte zum Selberbauen**, München 1997 André Koch, **Struck by lightning**, Rotterdam 1994 Ralph Turner, **jewelry in europe and america, new times, new thinking**, London 1996

Kataloge **Catalogues**
Abschlussarbeiten an nordrhein-westfälischen Designschulen, Karl-Ernst-Osthaus-Museum, Hagen 1992 **A Sparkling Party**, Contemporary European Silverwork, VIZO Crafts Department, Brüssel 1993 **Aspekte von Serie**, hrsg. v. Herman Hermsen, Düsseldorf 1994 **Asymmetrie und Harmonie**, hrsg. v. der Commerzbank Frankfurt und der Gesellschaft für Goldschmiedekunst e.V., Hanau 2001 **20th Century Silver**, Crafts Council, London 1993 **Das neue Besteck**, Deutsches Klingenmuseum, Solingen 1992 **De Keuze van Apeldoorn – Apeldoorn's Choice**, Galerie Marzee, Nimwegen 2001 **Der niedersächsische Staats- und Förderpreis für das gestaltende Handwerk**, Landeshandwerkspflege Niedersachsen, Hannover 1993 **Design Innovations 1998**, Design Zentrum Nordrhein Westfalen, Essen 1998 **Design Innovations 2001**, Design Zentrum Nordrhein Westfalen, Essen 2001 **Design plus**, Messe Frankfurt GmbH, Frankfurt 1996 **26+4 designer präsentieren**, hrsg. v. Herman Hermsen, Düsseldorf 1996 **Dinner for Two**, Stiftung Gold- und Silberschmiedekunst, Schwäbisch Gmünd 1994 **Elisabeth Holder – Zeichen**, Erkrath 2001 **Email international**, Kunstverein Coburg e.V., Coburg 1995 **Email, Schmuck und Gerät**, Magistrat der Stadt Hanau und Gesellschaft für Goldschmiedkunst, Hanau 1998 **Expo Kunststoff**, Verband kunststofferzeugender Industrie, Frankfurt 1992 **insideout**, Katalog zur Ausstellung ‚Neu', FB Design FH D, Düsseldorf 1999 **Jaarlijkse internationale Eindexamententoonstelling**, Galerie Marzee, Nimwegen 2000 **Jewellery meets fashion**, Leipziger Messe, Leipzig 2000 **Jewellery Moves**, National Museums of Scotland, Edinburgh 1998 **Jewellery Redefined**, British Craft Centre, London 1982 **Junges Handwerk Nordrhein-Westfalen** 1992, **Junges Handwerk Nordrhein-Westfalen** 1994, **Junges Handwerk Nordrhein-Westfalen** 1996, **Junges Handwerk Nordrhein-Westfalen** 1998, **Junges Handwerk Nordrhein-Westfalen** 2000, Westdeutscher Handwerkskammertag, Düssel-dorf; 1992, 1994, 1996, 1998, 2000 **Kunst hautnah**, Künstlerhaus, Gesellschaft bildender Künstler Österreichs, Wien 2000 **Liturgiegefäße, Kirche und Design**, Deutsches Liturgisches Institut, Trier 1997 **Made in Holland**, Museum für Angewandte Kunst, Köln 1994 **Maggi Edition, Europäischer Design-Wettbewerb 1995**, Maggi GmbH, Frankfurt 1995 **manu factum 1993, manu factum 1995, manu factum 1997, manu factum 1999, manu factum 2001** Arbeitsgemeinschaft des Kunsthandwerks Nordrhein-Westfalen, Düsseldorf 1993, 1995, 1997, 1999, 2001 **nearly famous**, hrsg. v. Herman Hermsen, Düsseldorf 2000 **Op Art: Eyeglasses by Jewellers**, Oregon School of Arts and Crafts, Portland OR 1994 **Op de huid**, Museum of Modern Art, Arnheim 2000 **Parures d'ailleurs, parures d'ici: incidences, co-incidences**, Carole Guinard und Marie Alamir, Lausanne 2000 **Phänomen Schmuck, Reg. Nr. 21575**, Das Zukunftsministerium, Wien 2001 **Schatzsuche**, Kunstmuseum Düsseldorf, Düsseldorf 1993 **Schmuck '97, Schmuck 2000, Schmuck 2001**, Bayerischer Handwerkstag e.V., München 1997, 2000, 2001 **Schmuck und Gerät**, hrsg. v. der Gesellschaft für Goldschmiedekunst, München/Berlin 1994 **Schmuck und Gerät 1998, Nachwuchsförderwettbewerb**, Bertha Heraeus und Kathinka Platzhoff Stiftung, Hanau 1998 **Schmuck und Gerät 2000, Nachwuchsförderwettbewerb**, Bertha Heraeus und Kathinka Platzhoff Stiftung, Hanau 2000 **9. Erfurter Schmucksymposium**, hrsg. v. Uta Feiler, Bernhard Früh, Rolf Lindner, Erfurt 2000 **Jahrbuch selection '98**, Design Zentrum Nordrhein Westfalen, Essen 1998 **Jahrbuch selection '99**, Design Zentrum Nordrhein Westfalen, Essen 1999 **Jahrbuch selection 2000**, Design Zentrum Nordrhein Westfalen, Essen 2000 **Silbergestaltung, Zeitgenössische Formen und Tendenzen**, hrsg. v. Christianne Weber, München 1992 **Silberstreif. Eine Kunstausstellung**, Neckarwerke Esslingen, Esslingen 1995 **11. Silbertriennale 1995, 12. Silbertriennale 1998**, hrsg. v. Magistrat der Stadt Hanau/Kulturamt, Deutsches Goldschmiedehaus, Hanau 1995, 1998 **Symfonie voor solisten**, Museum of Modern Art, Arnheim 1994 **Talentbörse Handwerk 1993, Talentbörse Handwerk 1994,** Bayerischer Handwerkstag e.V., München 1993, 1994 **Talente '95, Talente '96, Talente '97, Talente 2000, Talente 2002**, Bayerischer Handwerkstag e.V., München 1995, 1996, 1997, 2000, 2002 **Tekens & Ketens**, Threes Moolhuysen, Schiedam 1993 **The Ego Adorned**, Jan Walgrave, Antwerpen 2000 **The Ring**, Rotovision SA, Crans-Près-Céligny 1998 **The Chair**, Christie's, Manson & Woods Ltd., London 1997 **Perlen, eine Schenkung**, hrsg. v. Elisabeth Holder, Düsseldorf 1998 **Perlen, Schmuckstücke**, hrsg. v. Elisabeth Holder, Düsseldorf 1998 **Umsichtig**, Jahrbuch des FB Design der FH Düsseldorf, Mainz 2000 **Wie es Euch gefällt, Schmuckkonzepte frei nach Shakespeare**, hrsg. v. Donna Brennan, Nicoletta Cammilleri u.a., Düsseldorf 1999 **Zeitgenössisches deutsches Kunsthandwerk**, Museum für Kunsthandwerk, Frankfurt/Main 1994

Fachzeitschriften **Magazines**
Art Aurea: Elisabeth Holder, *Mit Schmuck Licht einfangen*, 1/92 **Craft Arts International**: Elisabeth Holder, *Facets of the Standard Cut: Donna Brennan*, Nr. 39 **Design Report**, Rat für Formgebung, Frankfurt: *Comité Colbert Design-Preis 1994*, 11/94; *Thema Schmuck: Spielerisch gehalten*, 5/99 **form 137**: Barbara Grotkamp-Schepers, *Für Fisch und Fleisch... Neue Bestecke für die westliche Eßkultur*, 1/92 **Glashaus**, Internationales Magazin für Studioglas: *Crystallizing Ideas, ein Workshop mit Diana Hobson*, 3/99 **Goldschmiede und Uhrmacher Zeitung**: *Schmuckdesigndüsseldorfpunkt*, 1/92; *Ursula Döhmen-Schütze, Lichtschmuck*, 3/92; *Schmuck aus Kunststoff*, 9/93; *Förderpreis: Christine Lange*, 12/93; *Schatzsuche*, 2/94; Felix Lucas, *Kreativität des künstlerischen Nachwuchses*, 10/94; *Die Kunst der Serie*, 1/96; *Studiengang Produkt-Design*, 2/95; *Ina Könnicke-Mader, Margarete Kuhles-Marschall, Kirsten Schäfer*, 7/95; *Diplomarbeiten SS 95*, 3/96; Herman Hermsen, *26+4*, 1/97; *Diplomarbeiten 1997, Gestaltungswettbe-*

Christine Lange
1992
Landschaft
Armreifen
Edelstahl, Silber vergoldet
Landscape
armlets
stainless steel, silver,
gold-plated stainless steel

Wind, Wasser, Wellen fließen.
Wind, water, flowing waves.

Christine Lange
1993
Doppio
Kette
Gold
Doppio
chain
gold

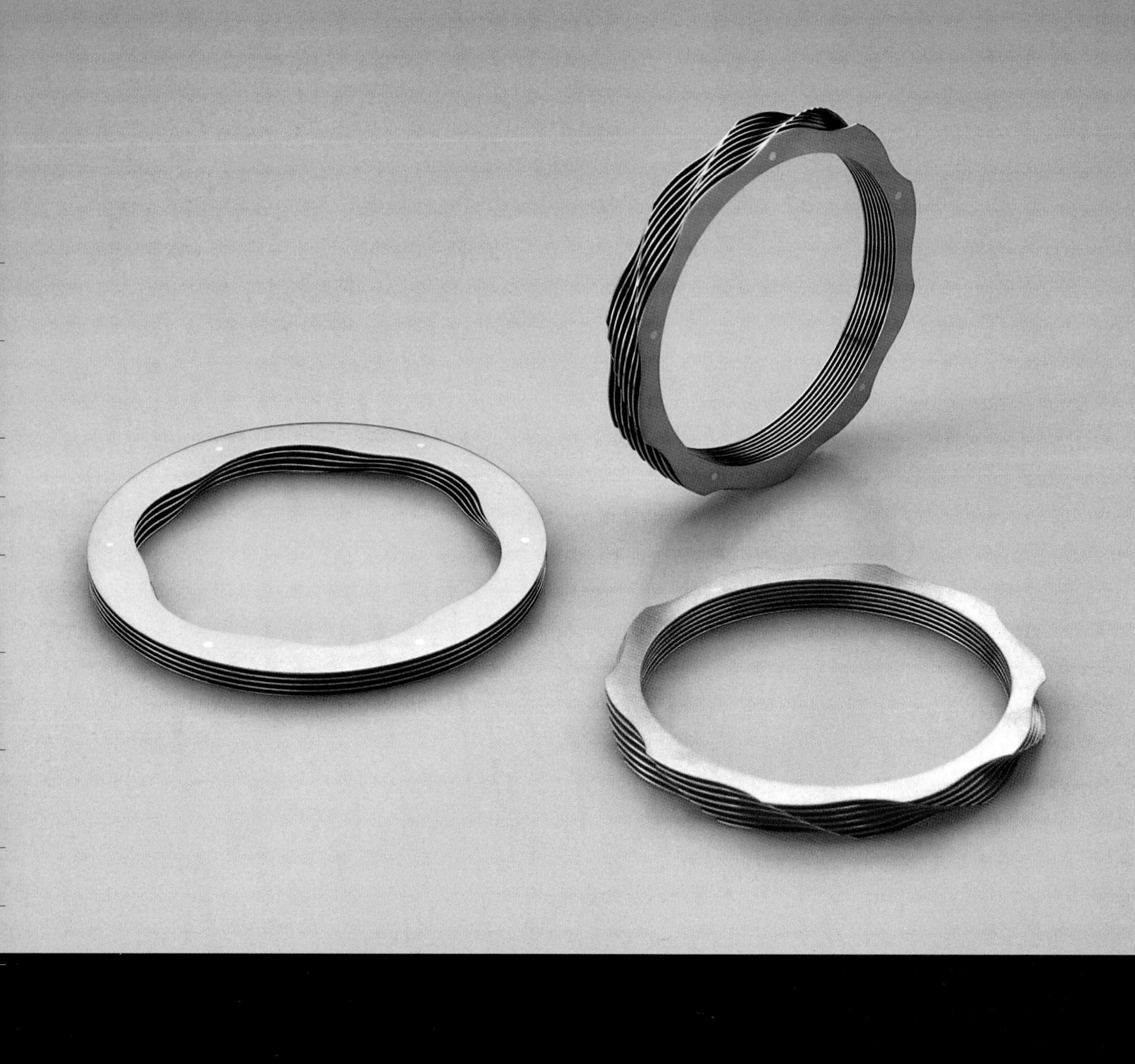

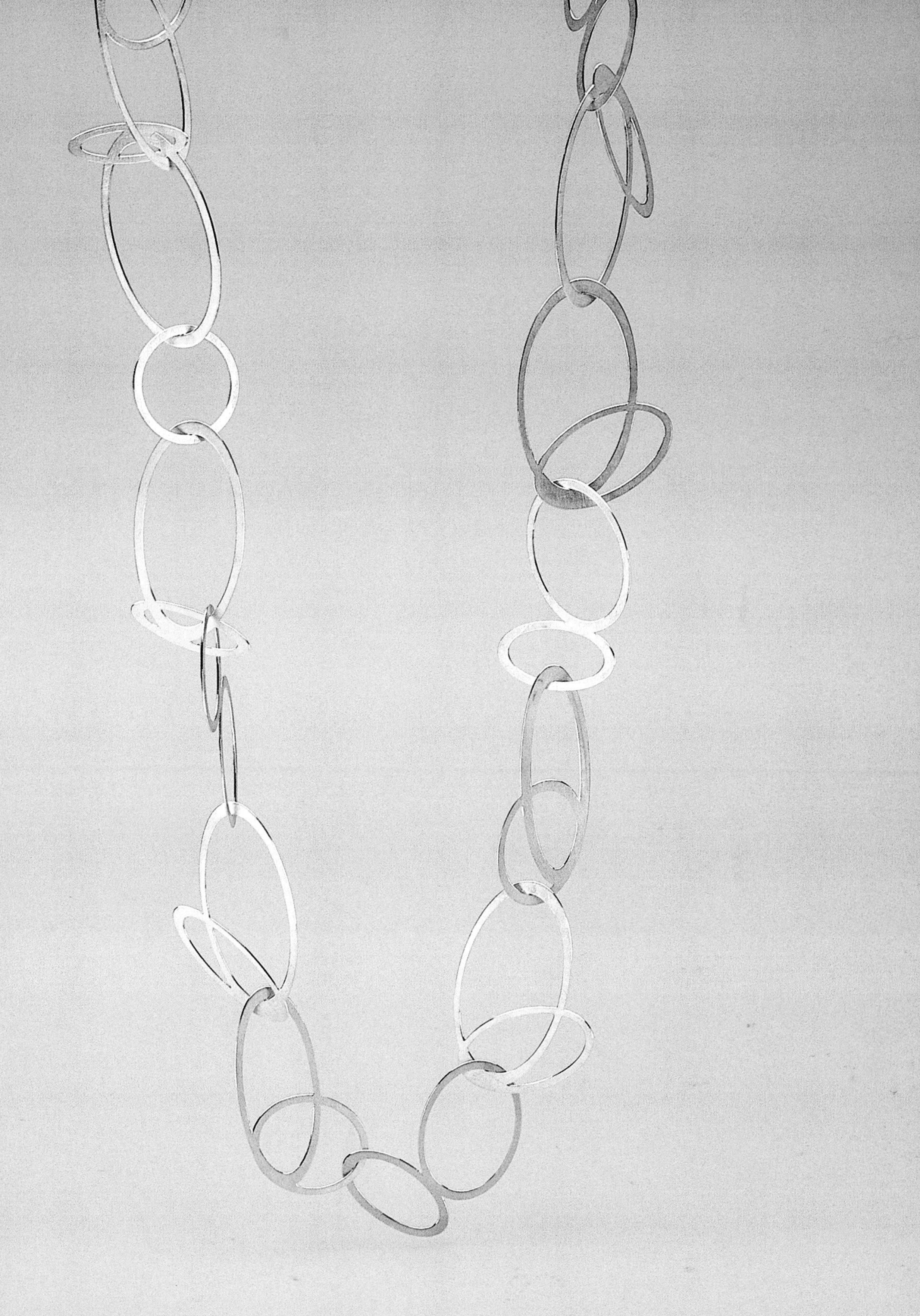

werb: Neue Ideen zum Thema Zuchtperlen, 4/98; *Fachhochschule Düsseldorf, Diplomarbeiten*, 1/99; *Wie es euch gefällt*, 9/99 **Kunsthandwerk & Design**: Elisabeth Holder, *Buchschließen*, 6/93; Uta Meyer, Christianne Weber-Stöber, *Schmuck muss vermittelt werden*, 3/97; Igor A. Jenzen, *Mikrokosmen für die Hand*, 5/97; *Kunststoff-Trilogie, Vom Golde weit entfernt – Schmuckannäherungen an Kunststoff*, 6/97; Elisabeth Holder, *Schmucksymposium Zimmerhof*, 5/98; Jens Rönnau, *In Gebrauch*, 4/2001; Antje Soléau, *Quo vadis manu factum?*, 5/2001; Barbara Maas, *Universelle Zeichen – private Chiffren*, 1/2002; **Metalsmith**: Jan Baum, *Aspects of the Series: 33 European Artists Explore Jewellery as Product Design*, Winter 1996 **Schmuck Magazin**: *Schmuck für die Sinne, ein Projekt der Fachhochschule Düsseldorf in Zusammenarbeit mit der Schmuckmanufaktur Niessing in Vreden*, 3/97; Maria-Bettina Eich, *Hilde Janich, Schmuckgewächse aus Tierhäuten*, 2/98; Maria-Bettina Eich, *Faszination Serienschmuck*, 8/98; Anja Wiederspohn, *Heike Kähler, Eisberge und Gletscher*, 2/2000; *Herrin der Ringe*, 5/2000 **The Gems and Jewellery Magazine**: Subhra Mazumdar, *Unshackling Possibilities*, Vol. 3, Issue 4

Hilde Janich
1992
Die Schatten eines Kreises
Kette
Silber, Gold
The Shadows of a Circle
chain
silver, gold

Hilde Janich
1992
Die Schatten
geometrischer Grundformen
Kette
Silber, Edelstahl
The Shadows of
Basic Geometrical Forms
chain
silver, stainless steel

Hilde Janich
2001
Heuhaufen
5-reihige Kette
Pergament, gefärbtes Nylon
Haystack
chain with 5 rows
parchment, dyed nylon

Filigrane Bahnen.
Strukturen im Chaos.
Delicate trails.
Structures in chaos.

Ursula Döhmen-Schütze
1998
Mehr Licht
Ring
Silber, Gold
More Light
ring
silver, gold

Ursula Döhmen-Schütze
2000
Lichtkästchen
Anhänger
Silber, Gold, Kunststoff
Light Box
pendant
silver, gold, plastic

Licht in Bewegung.
Zarte Bilder
bizarrer Reflexionen.
Light in movement.
Fragile images of
bizarre reflections.

Georg Plum
1990
Winkel 1
Uhrenobjekt
Palladium
Angle 1
watch object
palladium

Georg Plum
1990
Winkel 2
Uhrenobjekt
Silber
Angle 2
watch object
silver

Zeit – Raum.
Trageposition
am Körper.
Time – Space.
Wearing position
on the body.

Georg Plum
1990
Winkel 3
Uhrenobjekt
Silber
Angle 3
watch object
silver

Augenstein, Susanne
1971 geboren in Ulm
1993-96 Ausbildung zur Goldschmiedin
1997-2002 Studium an der FH Düsseldorf
2002 Diplom

Ausstellungen **Exhibitions**
2001 *manu factum '01*, Niederrheinisches Museum für Volkskunde und Kulturgeschichte, Kevelaer; *Identity*, Galerie V&V, Wien

Auszeichnungen **Awards**
1996 1. Preis im Wettbewerb, *Die Gute Form im Handwerk*, Handwerkskammer Rheinland Pfalz, Kaiserslautern
1999 Ehrenpreis im Wettbewerb zum *Marokko-Projekt*, DMF Düsseldorf

Awater, Janine
1965 geboren in Essen
1984-90 Ausbildung zur Goldschmiedin
1990-96 Studium an der FH Düsseldorf
1996 Diplom
seit 1996 freischaffend tätig

Ausstellungen **Exhibitions**
1992 *Junges Handwerk NRW*, Technologiezentrum Aachen
1994 *Vorsicht Schmuck*, Ausstellung der FH Düsseldorf, Creativa in Dortmund; *Aspekte von Serie*, Galerien in Düsseldorf, Wien, Frankfurt/Main, Amsterdam, Nimwegen, Gent und in den USA
1995 *manu factum '95*, Museum für Angewandte Kunst, Köln;
Papierschmuckausstellung, Grafik-Triennale, Prag
1997 *manu factum '97*, Gustav-Lübecke-Museum, Hamm
1998 Organisationsteilnahme mit der Gruppe *elft*, Schmucksymposium Zimmerhof
1999 *7. Deutscher Designers Saturday*, mit der Gruppe *elft* im Kunstmuseum Düsseldorf
2000 Weihnachtsmesse, Museum für Kunst und Gewerbe Hamburg;
Papier, Arbeiten ausgewählt von Hilde Leiss

Auszeichnungen **Awards**
1992 2. Preis für Halsschmuck, Landeswettbewerb *Junges Handwerk NRW*, Technologiezentrum Aachen

Bartesch-Schek, Ingrid
1976 geboren in Großkarol
1997-2000 Ausbildung zur Goldschmiedin
seit 2000 Studium an der FH Düsseldorf

Baschta, Heike
1967 geboren in Köln
1986-90 Ausbildung zur Goldschmiedin
1990-95 Studium an der FH Düsseldorf
1995 Diplom
seit 1995 freischaffend tätig für diverse Firmen der Accessoir- und Schmuckbranche
1995 Eröffnung der Galerie und Werkstatt *Schmucksache* in Zusammenarbeit mit Claudia Steimels und Susanne Stifel
1996 Gründung der Gruppe *elft*
1998 Konzeption und Organisation des Schmucksymposiums Zimmerhof *Zwischen Wunsch und Wirklichkeit: Wie werden Träume wahr?*
2000 Eigenes Atelier für Schmuck in Köln;
Lehrbeauftragte an der FH Düsseldorf;
Gesellschafterin der Firma *team X mas*

Ausstellungen **Exhibitions**
seit 1993 Teilnahme an nationalen und internationalen Ausstellungen
1994 *Aspekte von Serie*, Galerien in Düsseldorf, Wien, Frankfurt/Main, Amsterdam, Nimwegen, Gent und in den USA
1997 *Denn man lebt nicht nur vom Brot allein*, *elft* im Klärwerk Krefeld und der Alten Feuerwache Köln
1999 *Denn man lebt nicht nur vom Brot allein*, *elft* im Kunstmuseum Düsseldorf
ständig vertreten bei Galerie Marzee, Nimwegen
Galerie Gesamtmetall, Frankfurt/Main
Galerie SchmuckProdukt, Essen

Berg-Bode, Alexandra
1965 geboren in Frankfurt/Main
1986-89 Ausbildung zur Goldschmiedin
1989/90 Tätigkeit als Goldschmiedegesellin
1990-95 Studium an der FH Düsseldorf
1995 Diplom
seit 1995 freischaffend tätig
1996 Gründung der Gruppe *SchmuckProdukt*
Gründung der Gruppe *elft*
seit 1998 Werkstattatelier *SchmuckProdukt*, Zeche Zollverein, Essen
1998 Konzeption und Organisation des Schmucksymposiums Zimmerhof *Zwischen Wunsch und Wirklichkeit: Wie werden Träume wahr?*
2001 Konzeption und Organisation das Symposiums *Aspekte von Gestaltung*

Ausstellungen **Exhibitions**
1994 *Aspekte von Serie*, Galerien in Düsseldorf, Wien, Frankfurt/Main, Amsterdam, Nimwegen, Gent und in den USA
1995 *manu factum '95*, Museum für Angewandte Kunst, Köln;
Try out, Galerie Marzee, Nimwegen;
Präsent, Deutsches Klingenmuseum, Solingen und Stadtmuseum Düsseldorf;
Medaillons und andere Geheimnisse, Galerie Lichtblick, Aachen;
cross-over, Krefters Spieker, Ahaus
1997 *Die Leichtigkeit des Seins*, Galerie Cebra, Düsseldorf;
Denn man lebt nicht nur vom Brot allein, *elft* im Klärwerk Krefeld und der Alten Feuerwache Köln
1999 *Denn man lebt nicht nur vom Brot allein*, *elft* im Kunstmuseum Düsseldorf
2000 *Ringe, Ringe, Ringe*, Galerie Hilde Leiss, Hamburg
2001 *Neue Arbeiten*, *elft* bei *SchmuckProdukt*, Zeche Zollverein, Essen

Auszeichnungen **Awards**
1994 2. Preis für Schmuck im Gestaltungswettbewerb *Junges Handwerk NRW*, Technologiezentrum Aachen

Bierbach, Anne-Sybille
1972 geboren in Lüdenscheid
1992-96 Ausbildung zur Goldschmiedin
1997 Tätigkeit als Goldschmiedegesellin
seit 1997 Studium an der FH Düsseldorf

Auszeichnungen **Awards**
1996 Abschluss als Beste der Innung Südwestfalen

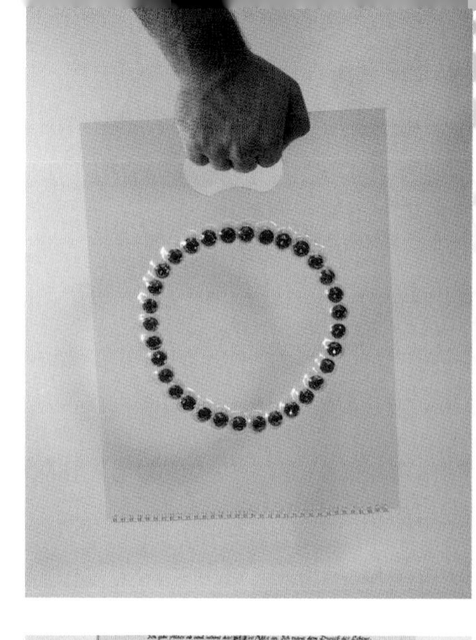

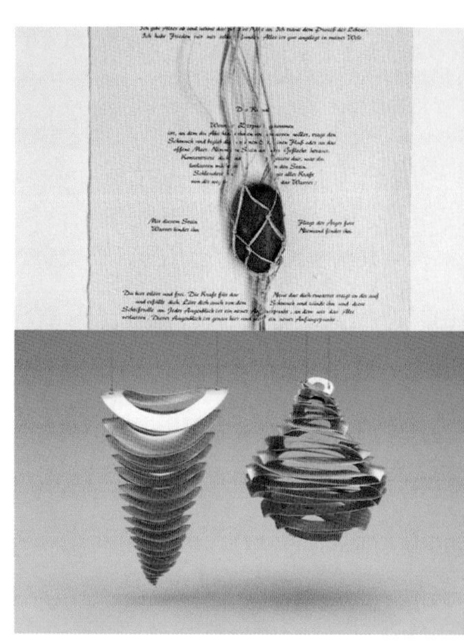

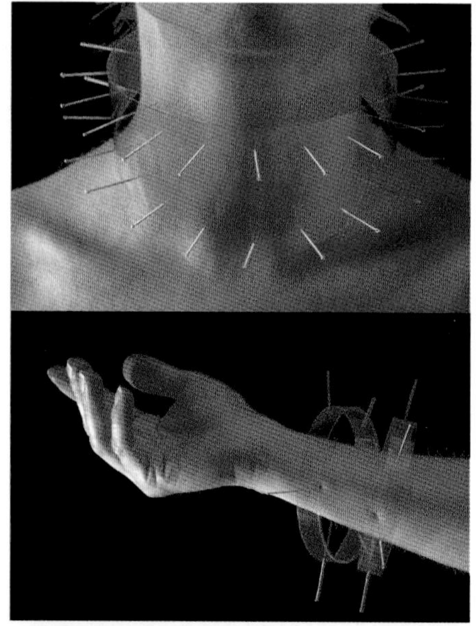

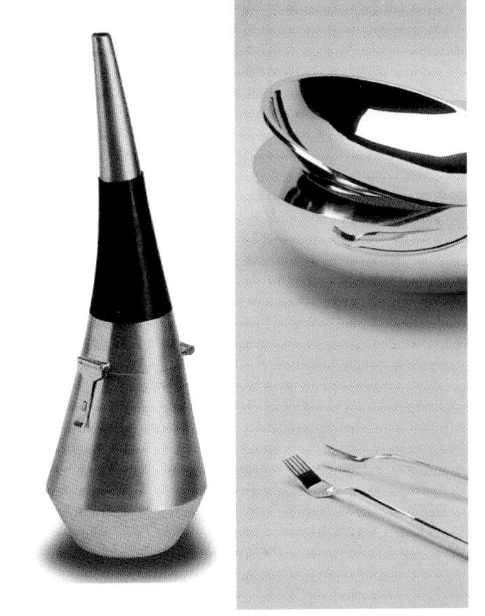

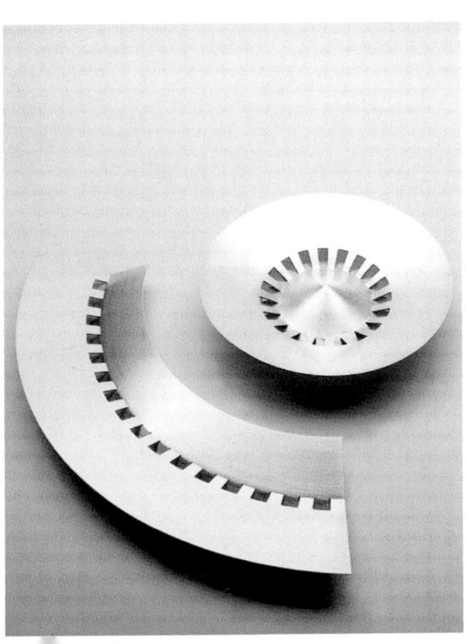

Biesdorf, Kerstin
1973 geboren in Trier
1992-96 Ausbildung zur Gold- und Silberschmiedin
1997 Tätigkeit als Goldschmiedegesellin
1997-2002 Studium an der FH Düsseldorf
2002 Diplom

Ausstellungen **Exhibitions**
2000 *Talente* Sonderschau der IHM, München; *Grassimesse*, Leipzig
2001 *manu factum '01*, Niederrheinisches Museum für Volkskunde und Kulturgeschichte, Kevelaer; *Silbertriennale*, Deutsches Goldschmiedehaus Hanau und andere Orte

Biskup, Uli
1965 geboren in Bergisch-Gladbach
1986-89 Ausbildung zur Goldschmiedin
1989-97 Studium an der FH Düsseldorf
1997 Diplom
1995 Geburt der Tochter Louisa
seit 1997 freischaffend tätig
seit 1999 Fachwerk-Raum für Schmuck, Neuss mit Dorothee Eicker

Ausstellungen **Exhibitions**
1991 *Metall & Licht '91*, internationaler Wettbewerb, Handwerkskammer Koblenz
1993 *Tekens & Ketens*, Amstelveen, Arnheim, Rotterdam
1994 *Aspekte von Serie*, Galerien in Düsseldorf, Wien, Frankfurt/Main, Amsterdam, Nimwegen, Gent und in den USA;
Gestaltungswettbewerb *Junges Handwerk NRW*, Technologiezentrum Aachen
1996 *26+4*, Galerien in Düsseldorf, Nimwegen, Wien, Zürich, Dublin und Den Haag
1997 Ausstellung ausgewählter Examensarbeiten, Galerie Marzee, Nimwegen;
manu factum '97, Gustav-Lübcke-Museum, Hamm
1999/2000 *Wie es Euch gefällt*, Kunstmuseum Düsseldorf und Galerien in Essen, Frankfurt/Main, Nimwegen, Wien und Wuppertal
2001 *Tafel Silber-Transformationen in Schmuck*, Restaurant Canonicus, Düsseldorf

Auszeichnungen **Awards**
1991 Anerkennung für *Metall & Licht '91*, Handwerkskammer Koblenz
1994 1. & 2. Preis, Gestaltungswettbewerb *Junges Handwerk NRW*, Technologiezentrum Aachen
1997 Staatspreis des Landes Nordrhein-Westfalen für das Kunsthandwerk

Borgmann, Petra
1963 geboren in Bochum
1983-87 Ausbildung zur Goldschmiedin
1987 Gaststudium an der Staatlichen Zeichenakademie Hanau
1987-89 Tätigkeit als Goldschmiedegesellin
1989-94 Studium an der FH Düsseldorf
1993 Teilnahme am *mastercourse of silversmithing* mit J. Lemmens und A. Alessi
1994 Diplom
seit 1994 freischaffend tätig
1995 Mitbegründerin des Produktdesignstudios FORMGEBUNG borgmann & durrie;
Zusammenarbeit mit Firmen in Deutschland und im Ausland
seit 2000 Dozentin an der Akademie für Kommunikationdesign, Düsseldorf

Ausstellungen **Exhibitions**
seit 1991 Teilnahme an nationalen und internationalen Ausstellungen

Auszeichnungen **Awards**
1992 Auszeichnung für ein dreiteiliges Besteck *Das neue Besteck*, Deutsches Klingenmuseum, Solingen
1994 1. Preis im Designwettbewerb des Comité Colbert
1999 Sonderauszeichnung für drei Spielobjekte im *Deumer Designwettbewerb*

Boy, Michael
1962 geboren in Balingen
1984-86 Ausbildung zum Goldschmied
1987 Gastschüler an der Staatlichen Zeichenakademie Hanau
1988/89 Tätigkeit als Goldschmiedegeselle
1990-94 Teilzeitarbeit als Juwelenfasser
1990-94 Studium an der FH Düsseldorf
1994 Diplom
seit 1994 freischaffend tätig in den Bereichen Produktentwicklung und Beratung
1995-97 Möbeldesign Studium am Royal College of Art, London, Master of Art

Ausstellungen **Exhibitions**
1993 *Talentbörse Handwerk*, Handwerksmesse München;
A Sparkling Party, VIZO, Antwerpen
1994 *Europa und die jungen Designer*, Sabattini Argenteria, Frankfurt/Main

1995 *manu factum '95*, Museum für Angewandte Kunst, Köln;
Schmuck und Gerät, Deutsches Goldschmiedehaus Hanau
1997 *Drawing the Line*, Art at 100, London
2000 *Impressionen*, Goethe Institut, Neu Delhi

Auszeichnungen **Awards**
1996 Stipendiat des DAAD

Boyaciyan, Alin
1972 geboren in Frankfurt/Main
1994-98 Ausbildung zur Goldschmiedin
seit 1998 Studium an der FH Düsseldorf

Ausstellungen **Exhibitions**
2000 *Junges Handwerk NRW*, Technologiezentrum Aachen
2001 *Grassimesse*, Leipzig

Arbeiten in öffentlichen Sammlungen
Works in Public Collections
Grassimuseum, Leipzig

Brand, Nicola
1972 geboren in Bochum
1991-95 Ausbildung zur Goldschmiedin
1995-97 Tätigkeit als Goldschmiedegesellin
1997-2002 Studium an der FH Düsseldorf
2002 Diplom

Ausstellungen **Exhibitions**
1994 *Schmuckstücke*, Deutsches Elfenbeinmuseum, Erbach;
222 Jahre Zeichenakademie Hanau, Deutsches Goldschmiedehaus Hanau
1996 *Jewellery meets the Future*, MIDORA, Leipzig
2000 *Kunst hautnah*, Künstlerhaus, Wien
2001 *Die Poesie des Funktionalen*, Marianne-Brandt-Wettbewerb, Chemnitz

Braslavsky, Stanislav
1970 geboren in St. Petersburg
1986-89 Ausbildung zum Goldschmied
1989-91 Tätigkeit als Goldschmiedegeselle
seit 1998 Studium an der FH Düsseldorf

Bubel, Bettina
1974 geboren in Ludwigshafen
1995-99 Ausbildung zur Goldschmiedin
seit 1999 Studium an der FH Düsseldorf

Ausstellungen **Exhibitions**
1998 *Email, Schmuck und Gerät*, Deutsches Goldschmiedehaus Hanau
2001 *Grassimesse*, Leipzig

Arbeiten in öffentlichen Sammlungen
Works in Public Collections
Grassimuseum, Leipzig

Cammilleri, Nicoletta
1967 geboren in Dortmund
1987-91 Ausbildung zur Goldschmiedin
1991/92 Studium der Kunstgeschichte an der Universität Bochum
1992-97 Studium an der FH Düsseldorf
1997 Diplom
seit 1997 freischaffend tätig
1999 *Wie es Euch gefällt*, Mitarbeit an Ausstellungs- und Katalogkonzeption
2000 Eröffnung der Galerie *anSchmuck*, Düsseldorf

Ausstellungen **Exhibitions**
1995 Galerie Cebra, Düsseldorf
1996/97 *26+4*, Galerien in Düsseldorf, Nimwegen, Wien, Zürich, Dublin und Den Haag
1998 Galerie Friends Of Carlotta, Zürich;
Galerie Industria, Wuppertal
1999 Zeche Zollverein, Essen
1999/2000 *Wie es Euch gefällt*, Kunstmuseum Düsseldorf und Galerien in Essen, Frankfurt/Main, Nimwegen, Wien und Wuppertal

Czunczeleit, Martina
1962 geboren in Bonn
1984-87 Ausbildung zur Goldschmiedin
1988 Stipendium der Carl-Duisberg-Gesellschaft, Austauschprogramm für junge Arbeitnehmer; Arbeitsaufenthalt in Dublin, Irland
1988-93 Studium an der FH Düsseldorf, Stipendium der Peter-Fuld-Stiftung Frankfurt/Main
1991 Auslandssemester am Wscad College of Art, Farnham/Surrey, England
1993 Diplom
seit 1993 freischaffend tätig
1996 Werkstattgemeinschaft mit Désirée Saadallah und Justus Gröning;
Werkstattgalerie Mir, Offenbach
2000 Schmuckvertrieb Saadallah und Czunczeleit

Ausstellungen **Exhibitions**
1992 *Try out,* Galerie Marzee, Nimwegen
1993 *manu factum '93*, Handwerkskammer Düsseldorf
1993/94 *Tekens & Ketens*, Amstelveen, Arnheim, Rotterdam
1994 *Schmuck Experimente – Perspektiven*, Gedok, Köln;
Aspekte von Serie, Galerien in Düsseldorf, Wien, Frankfurt/Main, Amsterdam, Nimwegen, Gent und in den USA
1994/95 *Schmuck und Gerät*, Wanderausstellung der Gesellschaft für Goldschmiedekunst, Hanau, Budapest, Zons, Erfurt, Hamburg, Schwäbisch-Gmünd
1996 Weihnachtsausstellungen in versch. Galerien
1997 *Variationen in der Form*, Gedok Köln;
Rheingold, Galerie am Turm, Waiblingen;
Erntezeit, Galerie für Schmuck, Biberach;
Jahresausstellung Galerie Aurum, Frankfurt/Main
1998 *Form,* Messe Frankfurt/Main
Harmonie und Spannung, Gedok Köln;
Famous last Jewelery, Friends of Carlotta, Zürich;
Jahresausstellung Galerie Hund, München;
Jahresausstellung Galerie Aurum, Frankfurt/Main;
Steinreich, Galerie für Schmuck, Biberach
1999 *Lust und Lüster*, Galerie für modernen Schmuck, Frankfurt/Main;
Galerie Corniche, Luxemburg
2000 Tresor, Hamburg;
Galerie Hund, München;
Galerie Aurum, Frankfurt/Main;
Galerie Corniche, Luxemburg;
Galerie am Turm, Waiblingen

Auszeichnungen **Awards**
1994 Belobigung im internationaler Wettbewerb des deutschen Elfenbeinmuseums in Erbach

Döhmen-Schütze, Ursula
1961 geboren in Mönchengladbach
1983-86 Ausbildung zur Goldschmiedin
1986-91 Studium an der FH Düsseldorf
1991 Diplom
seit 1991 freischaffend tätig
seit 2000 Mitglied des Deutschen Werkbundes

Ausstellungen **Exhibitions**
1987 *Bijoux de Lumière*, Galerie Noblesse Oblique, Lausanne
1988 *Die ganze Tragweite*, Galerie UND, Düsseldorf
1989/90 *Kämme*, Galerie Marzee, Nimwegen
1991 *Farbe aus Metall – Kunst aus dem Feuer* und *Email jetzt*, Museum für Angewandte Kunst, Köln;
Blickstücke aus Düsseldorf, Stadtmuseum Düsseldorf
1992 *Spiralen*, Galerie Hagen, Hamburg
1994 *Kurzgeschichten*, Schmuckgruppe 7, Volksbank Köln
1998 *Farbe bekennen*, Galerie Schmucksache, Köln
2000 *Best of Selection*, Wanderausstellung des Design Zentrums NRW, Essen
2001 *Parcours 2001*, zu Gast im Atelier von Maria Lehnen, Mönchengladbach

Auszeichnungen **Awards**
1987 Belobigung beim Wettbewerb *Neuartiger Ansteckschmuck*, Industrieverband Schmuck und Silberwaren, Pforzheim

Dufhues, Eva
1973 geboren in Xanten
1992-96 Ausbildung zur Goldschmiedin
1996-2002 Studium an der FH Düsseldorf
2002 Diplom

Ausstellungen **Exhibitions**
1998 *Perlen*, Glasmuseum Wertheim und Museum für Glaskunst, Lauscha
1999 *Nearly famous,* Escola Massana, Barcelona und Galerien in Wien, Düsseldorf und Vorden

NETTO

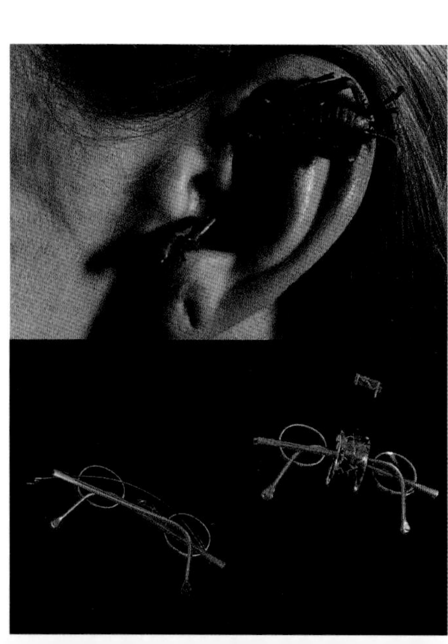

NETTO
NETTO
NETTO

Eckert, Astrid
1971 geboren in Hildesheim
1994-97 Ausbildung zur Goldschmiedin
seit 1997 Studium an der FH Düsseldorf

Ausstellungen **Exhibitions**
2000 *Kleine Dinge für den Alltag*, Handwerkskammer Koblenz

Auszeichnungen **Awards**
2000 1. Preis im Wettbewerb *Kleine Dinge für den Alltag*, Handwerkskammer Koblenz

Egerland, Babette
1964 geboren in Köln
1982/83 Auslandaufenthalt in Seattle, USA
1985-87 Studium der Chemie in Heidelberg
1987-91 Ausbildung zur Goldschmiedin
1991-94 Tätigkeit als Goldschmiedegesellin
1994-2001 Studium an der FH Düsseldorf
2001 Diplom
seit 2001 freischaffend tätig

Ausstellungen **Exhibitions**
1996 *26+4*, Galerien in Düsseldorf, Nimwegen, Wien, Zürich, Dublin und Den Haag
1998 *Nearly famous*, Escola Massana, Barcelona und Galerien in Wien, Düsseldorf und Vorden
2000 Galerie Agnes Raben, Vorden
2001 *manu factum '01*, Niederrheinisches Museum für Volkskunde und Kulturgeschichte, Kevelaer

Auszeichnungen **Awards**
2000 1. Preis im Wettbewerb *Kleine Dinge für den Alltag*, Handwerkskammer Koblenz

Eickhoff, Sigrid
1971 geboren in München
1994-1996 Ausbildung zur Goldschmiedin
seit 1996 freischaffend tätig
seit 1997 Studium an der FH Düsseldorf

Ausstellungen **Exhibitions**
1998 *Junges Handwerk NRW*, Technologiezentrum Aachen
2000 *Junges Handwerk NRW*, Technologiezentrum Aachen
2001 Galerie Flachwerk, Neuss

Auszeichnungen **Awards**
1998 Belobigung für Ring mit Hörnern im Gestaltungswettbewerb *Junges Handwerk NRW*, Technologiezentrum Aachen

Elmer, Gisa
1975 geboren in Wesel
1994-97 Ausbildung zur Goldschmiedin
1997/98 Tätigkeit als Goldschmiedegesellin
seit 1998 Studium an der FH Düsseldorf

Auszeichnungen **Awards**
1997 3. Platz im Praktischen Leistungswettbewerb der Handwerksjugend, Handwerkskammer Düsseldorf

Falzerano, Isabelle
1971 geboren in Frankfurt/Main
1992-96 Ausbildung zur Goldschmiedin
seit 1996 Studium an der FH Düsseldorf

Ausstellungen **Exhibitions**
2001 *Identity*, Galerie V&V, Wien

Auszeichnungen **Awards**
1994 Teilnahme am Wettbewerb *Reflexion* der ZA Hanau

Fischer, Elgin
1968 geboren in Bonn
1991-93 Ausbildung zur Goldschmiedin
seit 1997 Studium an der FH Düsseldorf

Ausstellungen **Exhibitions**
1995 *Köln Gold,* Museum für Angewandte Kunst, Köln
1996 *Junges Handwerk NRW*, Technologiezentrum Aachen
1997 *Märchenhaftes*, Galerie Töller, Aachen
2001 *Colour me beautiful*, Galerie Gesamtmetall, Frankfurt/Main;
Schnapsidee, Galerie Friends Of Carlotta, Zürich
2002 *Passagen*, Galerie 2 Plus, Köln

Flach, Annette
1975 geboren in Morbach
1994-98 Ausbildung zur Goldschmiedin
seit 1998 Studium an der FH Düsseldorf

Göllner, Britta
1973 geboren in Arolsen
1992-94 Ausbildung zur Goldschmiedin
1996/97 Tätigkeit als Goldschmiedegesellin
1998 Gemmologische Ausbildung, Idar Oberstein
seit 1998 Studium an der FH Düsseldorf

Ausstellungen **Exhibitions**
1995 *Silbertriennale*, Deutsches Goldschmiedehaus Hanau und andere Orte

Gosebrink, Verena
1972 geboren in Hilden
1991-95 Ausbildung zur Goldschmiedin
seit 1996 Studium an der FH Düsseldorf

Ausstellungen **Exhibitions**
1997 *Die Mitte der Tafel*, Deutsches Klingenmuseum, Solingen
1999 *Nearly famous*, Escola Massana, Barcelona und Galerien in Wien, Düsseldorf und Vorden
2001 *Grassimesse*, Leipzig

Auszeichnungen **Awards**
1993 Belobigung im Lehrlingswettbewerb der Gold- und Silberschmiede in NRW
1995 3. Platz im Praktischen Leistungswettbewerb der Handwerksjugend auf Kammerebene
1996 Begabtenförderung berufliche Bildung

Halbauer, Melanie
1973 geboren in Bamberg
1991 Praktikum als Theatermalerin und Plastikerin am Stadttheater Würzburg
1992-95 Ausbildung zur Goldschmiedin
seit 1997 Studium an der FH Düsseldorf
2001 Tätigkeit bei der Innenrequisite für einen Kinofilm

Halder, Claudia
1971 geboren in Bülach, Kanton Zürich
1991-95 Ausbildung zur Goldschmiedin
1995-98 Tätigkeit als Goldschmiedegesellin
seit 1998 Studium an der FH Düsseldorf

Ausstellungen **Exhibitions**
1992 *Einer tanzt aus der Reihe*, Berufsschule Essen
2000 *Junges Handwerk NRW*, Technologiezentrum Aachen;
Kleine Dinge für den Alltag, Handwerkskammer Koblenz

Auszeichnungen **Awards**
1995 2. Platz im Praktischen Leistungswettbewerb der Handwerkskammer Düsseldorf
1996 Stipendium Begabtenförderung, Handwerkskammer Düsseldorf
2000 1. Preis im Wettbewerb *Kleine Dinge für den Alltag*, Handwerkskammer Koblenz

Hanselle, Nicole
1973 geboren in Oldenburg
1994-97 Ausbildung zur Goldschmiedin
1999-2000 Studium an der FH Hildesheim
seit 2000 Studium an der FH Düsseldorf

Hartkopf, Sebastian
1961 geboren in Neuss
1982-85 Ausbildung zum Goldschmied
1987-92 Studium an der FH Düsseldorf
1990 Studiensemester am West Surrey College of Art and Design, England
1992 Diplom
seit 1993 freischaffend tätig

Ausstellungen **Exhibitions**
1991 *Rheingold*, Suermondt-Ludwig Museum, Aachen;
manu factum '91, Städtisches Museum Wesel
1992 *Es liegt was in der Luft*, Schmuckmuseum Pforzheim;
Abschlussarbeiten an nordrhein-westfälischen Designschulen, Karl Ernst Osthaus-Museum, Hagen;
Querschnitt, Galerie Marzee, Nimwegen
1993 *manu factum '93*, Handwerkskammer Düsseldorf
1999 *manu factum '99*, Deutsches Klingenmuseum, Solingen;
Sebastian Hartkopf, Herman Hermsen und Dongchun Lee, Galerie Cebra, Düsseldorf
2000 *Asymmetrie und Harmonie*, Commerzbank Frankfurt/Main
2001 *manu factum '01*, Niederrheinisches Museum für Volkskunde und Kulturgeschichte, Kevelaer;
De Keuze van Apeldoorn-Apeldoorn's choice, Van Reekum Museum Apeldoorn

Hartmann, Ariane
1971 geboren in Düsseldorf
1990-94 Ausbildung zur Goldschmiedin
1994-2001 Studium an der FH Düsseldorf
2001 Diplom

Ausstellungen **Exhibitions**
1995 *Maggi Edition für Küche und Tischkultur*, Maggi GmbH, Darmstadt
1998 *PunktUm, Sonderschau der Selection 98*, Zeche Zollverein, Essen;
Perlenflut, Galerie Marzee, Nimwegen
1999 *Nearly famous*, Escola Massana, Barcelona und Galerien in Wien, Düsseldorf und Vorden
2000 *Kunst hautnah*, Künstlerhaus Wien und Galerie V&V, Wien;
Beeld En sieraad, Kunsthaal Hof 88, Almelo

Auszeichnungen **Awards**
2001 2. Preis im Wettbewerb, *Über die Überwindung der Resignation*, Internationale Gemeinschaft für Tiefenpsychologie e.V., Lindau

Heinemeyer, Anja
1967 geboren in Hüttental-Weidenau
1988-92 Ausbildung zur Goldschmiedin
1992/93 Tätigkeit als Goldschmiedegesellin
1993-2000 Studium an der FH Düsseldorf
seit 1998 Betreuung des Projektes *Kölner Dom Schmuck*
seit 2000 eigener Pavillon auf dem Weihnachtsmarkt am Kölner Dom

Ausstellungen **Exhibitions**
1993 *Fünf aus Fünfzehn*, Firma Volmer, Pulheim
1995 *1001 Perle*, Galerie Schmucksache, Köln
1997 *Perlenflut*, Galerie Marzee, Nimwegen
1998 *Perlenrausch*, Krefters Spiecker, Ahaus;
Perlen, Glasmuseum, Wertheim
1999 *Perlen*, Museum für Glaskunst, Lauscha;
Sommerklänge, Galerie Cebra, Düsseldorf;
Nearly famous, Escola Massana, Barcelona und Galerien in Wien, Düsseldorf und Vorden

Hermsen, Herman
1953 geboren in Nimwegen, Niederlande
1974-79 Akademie voor Beeldende Kunsten in Arnheim

Berufliche Tätigkeiten **Career Details**
Seit 1979 freiberuflich tätig als Schmuck- und Produktdesigner
1985-90 Dozent für Produktdesign an der Hogeschool voor de Kunsten in Utrecht
1990-92 Dozent für Produktdesign an der Hogeschool voor de Kunsten in Arnheim
seit 1992 Professor für Produkt- und Schmuckdesign an der FH Düsseldorf
seit 1985 Gastreferent an verschieden Institutionen, und Symposien in den Niederlanden, Deutschland, Großbritannien und den USA;
Jurymitglied in verschiedenen Designwettbewerben in den Niederlanden und Deutschland

Auszeichnungen **Awards**
1993 *Rotterdam Designpreis*, Auszeichnung für Brieföffner *Fontana*, produziert von Designum
1998 *Design Innovationen*, Design Zentrum NRW, Preis für Hohe Designqualität für die *Mäanderringe*, produziert von der Firma Niessing
2001 *Reddot Design Award*, Design Zentrum NRW, *reddot, best of the best*
2002 *IF Design Award* für die Stehleuchte *Charis*, produziert von ClassiCon

Ausstellungen **Exhibitions**
seit 1980 zahlreiche Einzel- und Gruppenausstellungen für Schmuck- und Produktdesign in den Niederlanden, Deutschland, Österreich, Belgien, der Schweiz, Großbritannien, Spanien, Italien, Skandinavien, Tschechien, den USA, Canada, Australien und Japan

Arbeiten in öffentlichen Sammlungen
Works in Public Collections
Bauhaus Archiv, Berlin;
Museum of Modern Art, Arnheim;
Centraal Museum, Utrecht;
Cleveland Contemporary Jewellery Collection;

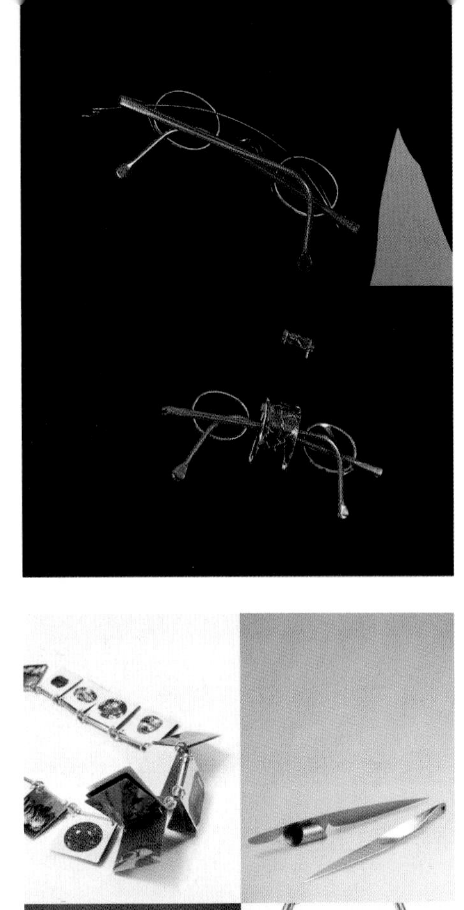

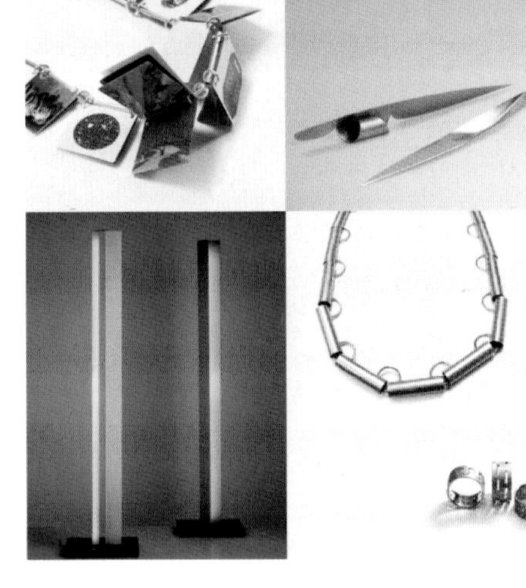

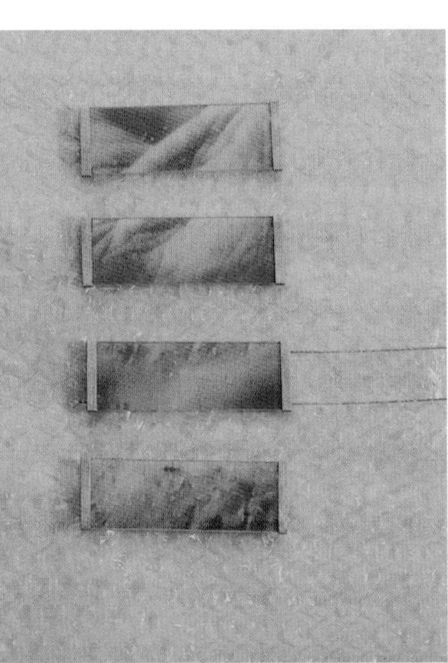

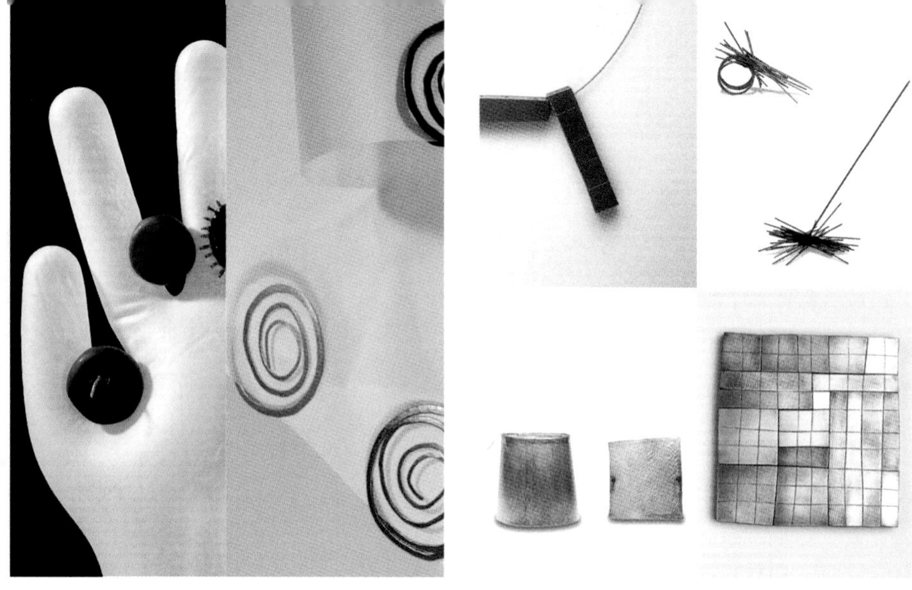

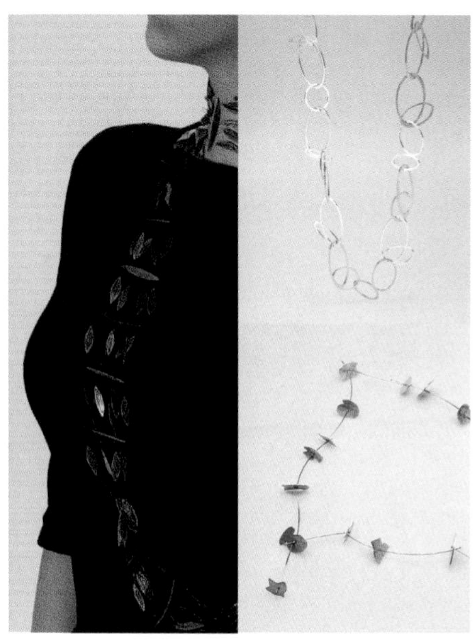

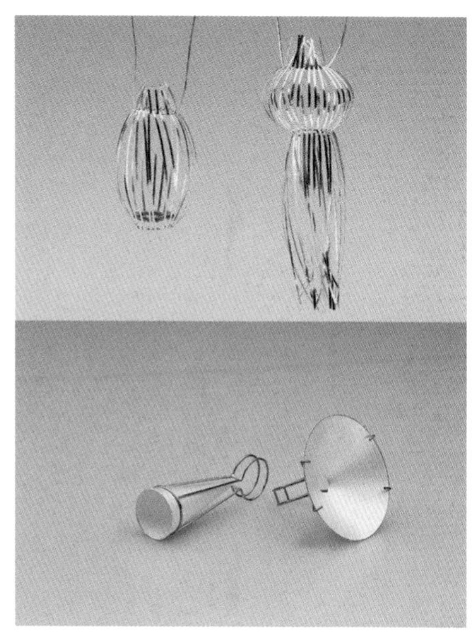

Cooper Hewitt Museum, New York;
Die Neue Sammlung, München;
Haags Gemeente Museum, Den Haag;
Museum des Arts Decoratifs, Montreal;
Museum Boymans-van Beuningen, Rotterdam;
Museum Het Kruithuis, s'Herzogenbosch;
Museum für Angewandte Kunst, Köln;
Museum für Kunsthandwerk, Hamburg;
Museum for Kunsthandverk, Oslo;
Museum of Modern Art, Trondheim;
Rijksdienst Beeldende Kunst, Amsterdam;
Schmuckmuseum Pforzheim;
Stedelijk Museum, Amsterdam;
Van Reekum Museum, Apeldoorn;
Victoria and Albert Museum, London

Hinze, Gabriele
1964 geboren in Essen
1983-87 Ausbildung zur Goldschmiedin
1987-90 Tätigkeit als Goldschmiedegesellin
1990 Sommerakademie Salzburg, Schmuckklasse Johanna Dahm
1990-95 Studium an der FH Düsseldorf
1995 Diplom
seit 1995 freischaffend tätig
1995 Gründung der Gruppe *SchmuckProdukt* mit Alexandra Berg-Bode und Annette Wackermann
1996 Gründung der DesignerInnengruppe *elft*
seit 1998 Atelier in Essen, Zeche Zollverein, Schacht XII

Ausstellungen **Exhibitions**
1994 *Aspekte von Serie*, Galerien in Düsseldorf, Wien, Frankfurt/Main, Amsterdam, Nimwegen, Gent und in den USA;
Kunst, Handwerk Design, Galerie Peschkenhaus, Moers
1995 3. internationale Emailkunstausstellung, Kunstverein Coburg;
Try out, Examensausstellung, Galerie Marzee, Nimwegen;
Medaillons und andere Geheimnisse, Galerie Lichtblick, Aachen;
Präsent, Deutsches Klingenmuseum, Solingen, und Stadtmuseum Düsseldorf
1999 *Zechengold*, Schmuck und Produkt aus NRW, *SchmuckProdukt*, Zeche Zollverein Essen;
manu factum '99, Deutsches Klingenmuseum Solingen
1999/2000 *Wie es Euch gefällt*, Kunstmuseum Düsseldorf und Galerien in Essen, Frankfurt/Main, Nimwegen, Wien und Wuppertal
2001 *manu factum '01*, Niederrheinisches Museum für Volkskunde und Kulturgeschichte Kevelar

Holder, Elisabeth
1950 geboren in Sindelfingen
1966-70 Ausbildung zur Goldschmiedin
1972-74 Staatliche Zeichenakademie Hanau
1974-78 Studium Schmuckdesign an der FH Düsseldorf
1978-80 School of Metalwork and Jewellery, Royal College of Art, MA (RCA)
Stipendium des British Council

Berufliche Tätigkeiten **Career Details**
seit 1980 freiberuflich tätig
1982-85 Dozentin an der Epsom School of Art and Design
1985-88 Lehrbeauftragte und Dozentin an der School of Silversmithing and Jewellery, Royal College of Art, London
1987-90 Externe Prüferin für Schmuck, Middlesex Polytechnic
seit 1988 Professorin für Schmuckdesign an der FH Düsseldorf
1995-97 Externe Prüferin für Schmuck, Edinburgh College of Art, Jurymitglied in verschiedenen Gestaltungswettbewerben

Auszeichnungen **Awards**
1978 Preis der Deutschen Kunsthandwerker im Wettbewerb *Experimentelle Gestaltung;*
Preis im internationalen Wettbewerb *Der Ring;*
2. Preis im Wettbewerb *Der neue Sportpreis*

Ausstellungen **Exhibitions**
seit 1978 Beteiligung an zahlreichen nationalen und internationalen Ausstellungen in Deutschland und Großbritannien, den Niederlanden, der Schweiz, Belgien, Dänemark, Frankreich, Österreich, den USA, Japan und Australien
seit 1979 Zweier- und Einzelausstellungen in Bristol, Brüssel, Düsseldorf, London, Washington D.C., Wien und Zürich

Einzelausstellungen **One Person Shows**
1988 Electrum Gallery, London
1991 Schmuckforum, Zürich
1991 Jewelerswerk, Washington D.C.
2001 *Zeichen*, Galerie V&V, Wien
2002 Detail zwo, Düsseldorf;
Werkstattgalerie Brodhag und Wörn, Berlin

Arbeiten in öffentlichen Sammlungen
Works in Public Collections
Art Gallery of Western Australia, Perth;
Cleveland Contemporary Jewellery Collection;
Crafts Council, London;
Deutsches Goldschmiedehaus Hanau;
Leeds Art Collections Fund, Leeds;
Museum für Kunstgewerbe, Berlin;
North West Arts, Birmingham;
Royal Museum of Scotland, Edinburgh;
Schmuckmuseum Pforzheim;
Stadtmuseum München;
The National Museum of Modern Art, Kioto;
Victoria & Albert Museum, London

Hoppe, Claudia
1972 geboren in Kiel
1992-96 Ausbildung zur Goldschmiedin
seit 1996 Studium an der FH Düsseldorf

Ausstellungen **Exhibitions**
1998 *Herzbrut*, Galerie, Düsseldorf
1999 *Nearly famous,* Escola Massana, Barcelona und Galerien in Wien, Düsseldorf und Vorden
2000 Galerie Elfrink, Düsseldorf
2002 *Passagen*, Köln Galerie 2 Plus

Janich, Hilde
1953 geboren in Hilden
1980-83 Ausbildung zur Goldschmiedin
1983-87 Tätigkeit als Goldschmiedegesellin
1987-92 Studium an der FH Düsseldorf
1992 Diplom
seit 1992 selbständig tätig
1995/96 Schmuckentwürfe für Firma Berolina, Pforzheim
seit 1996 Zusammenarbeit mit Charon Kransen, New York
seit 1999 Zusammenarbeit mit Graziella Folchini Grassetto, Studio GR. 20, Padua

Ausstellungen **Exhibitions**
1993 *manu factum '93*, Handwerkskammer Düsseldorf
1994 *Schmuck Hilde Janich*, Stadtbücherei Hilden
1995 *manu factum '95*, Museum für Angewandte Kunst, Köln;
Sommerschmuck, Einzelausstellung, Galerie Alpha, Würzburg;
Transparent-Pergament, Einzelausstellung, Stadtmuseum Düsseldorf
1996 *Chaines*, Galerie Hélène Poirée, Paris
1998 *Jewellery Moves*, National Museum of Scotland, Edinburgh
1999 *Selection '99*, Zeche Zollverein, Essen;
manu factum '99, Deutsches Klingenmuseum, Solingen;
Gioielli Contemporane, Studio GR. 20, Padua
2000 *Selection '00*, Zeche Zollverein Essen;
Contemporary Decorative Arts, Sotheby's, London;
Einzelausstellung, Galerie Spandow, Berlin

Auszeichnungen **Awards**
1991 2. Preis im Gestaltungswettbewerb *Buchschließen*, Buchbinderei Mergemeier,
1999 Anerkennung beim Wettbewerb *Loving Energy*, Jewellery Network Society, Tokyo

Kähler, Heike
1968 geboren in Burg auf Fehmarn
1988-91 Ausbildung zur Goldschmiedin
1991-93 Tätigkeit als Goldschmiedegesellin
1993-98 Studium an der FH Düsseldorf
1998 Diplom
seit 1998 selbständig tätig

Ausstellungen **Exhibitions**
1994/95 *AufSehen*, Stadtmuseum Düsseldorf
1995/96 *Die Kunst der Serie-Preis der Deutschen Schmuck- und Silberwarenindustrie*, Schmuckmuseum Pforzheim und Präsentation auf der Messe *Ambiente*, Frankfurt/Main
1996 *Junges Handwerk NRW*, Technologiezentrum, Aachen
1996/97 *26+4*, Galerien in Düsseldorf, Nimwegen, Wien, Zürich, Dublin und Den Haag;
Passion and Profession – sieraden toen, nu en straks, Galerie Ra, Amsterdam und Craft Victoria, Melbourne
1997/98 *manu factum '97*, Gustav-Lübcke-Museum, Hamm
1998 *Kontraste*, Galerie für Schmuck, Hilde Leiss, Hamburg
1998/99 Nachwuchsförderwettbewerb *Schmuck und Gerät*, Richard-Küch-Forum Hanau und andere Orte
1999 *20 Jahre Galerie für Schmuck Hilde Leiss*, Galerie für Schmuck, Hilde Leiss, Hamburg
1999 *Jahresmesse Kunsthandwerk 1999*, Museum für Kunst und Gewerbe Hamburg
2000/01 *Triennale des norddeutschen Kunsthandwerks*, Schloss Gottorf und Schloss Güstrow
2001 *in gebrauch*, Kulturforum Burgkloster, Lübeck;
Jahresmesse Kunsthandwerk 2001, Museum für Kunst und Gewerbe Hamburg

Auszeichnungen **Awards**
1991 2. Landessiegerin im Leistungswettbewerb der Handwerksjugend Schleswig-Holstein
1992 Stipendium *Begabtenförderung Berufliche Bildung* des Bundesministeriums für Bildung und Wissenschaft
2001 Alen Müller-Hellwig Förderpreis des deutschen Verbandes Frau und Kultur e.V. Gruppe Lübeck

Karababa, Christina
1972 geboren in Athen
1995-98 Ausbildung zur Goldschmiedin
seit 1999 Studium an der FH Düsseldorf

Kathmann, Karen
1974 geboren in Bremen
1995-98 Ausbildung zur Goldschmiedin
seit 1999 Studium an der FH Düsseldorf

Ausstellungen **Exhibitions**
1998 *10 Jahre Berufskolleg Pforzheim*, Escola Massana, Barcelona

Katona, Lilia
1965 geboren in Meersburg am Bodensee
1988-91 Ausbildung zur Goldschmiedin
1991-96 Studium an der FH Düsseldorf
1996 Diplom

Ausstellungen **Exhibitions**
1994 Gedok Galerie Kunsthandwerk Köln;
Aspekte von Serie, Galerien in Düsseldorf, Wien, Frankfurt/Main, Amsterdam, Nimwegen, Gent und in den USA
1996 *26+4*, Galerien in Düsseldorf, Nimwegen, Wien, Zürich, Dublin und Den Haag
1997/98 *Die Mitte der Tafel*, Klingenmuseum Solingen, Deutsches Goldschmiedehaus Hanau;
Museum für Kunst und Gewerbe, Hamburg
1999 *Herzen*, Euroforum Köln
1999/2000 *Wie es Euch gefällt*, Kunstmuseum Düsseldorf und Galerien in Essen, Frankfurt/Main, Nimwegen, Wien und Wuppertal

2000/2001 *Zierat*, Southwest School of Art and Craft, San Antonio, Texas, Kestner Museum, Hannover;
Galerie Cebra, Düsseldorf; Galerie Beeld & Aambeeld, Enschede

Kempe, Katja
1968 geboren in Krefeld
1993-95 Tätigkeit bei Martina Spätt, Köln
1989-91 Studium der Kunsttherapie in Köln
1995-2001 Studium an der FH Düsseldorf
2001 Diplom

Ausstellungen **Exhibitions**
1997 *Perlenflut*, Galerie Marzee, Nimwegen
1998 *Junge Mode aus Europa*, Lijfstijl 2000, Genk;
Perlen, Glasmuseum Wertheim und Museum für Glaskunst, Lauscha
1999 *Nearly famous*, Escola Massana, Barcelona und Galerien in Wien, Düsseldorf und Vorden
2000 Galerie Cebra, Düsseldorf;
Herzgemenge, Galerie Komplex, Köln
2001 *Licht & Schatten*, Galerie Komplex, Köln
2002 Lichtinstallation bei den *Passagen*, Köln

Kessler, Anne
1972 geboren in Mainz
1993-96 Ausbildung zur Goldschmiedin
1996-2001 Studium an der FH Düsseldorf
2001 Diplom

Ausstellungen **Exhibitions**
1999 *Nearly famous*, Escola Massana, Barcelona und Galerien in Wien, Düsseldorf und Vorden
2000 *Kunst hautnah*, Künstlerhaus, Wien
2001 Galerie Agnes Raben, Vorden

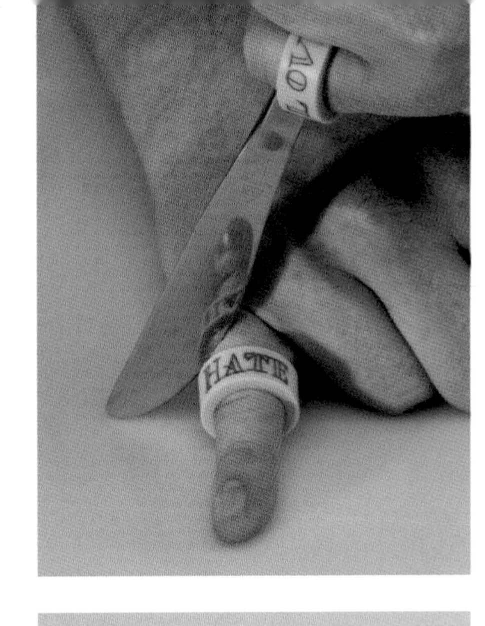
HATE

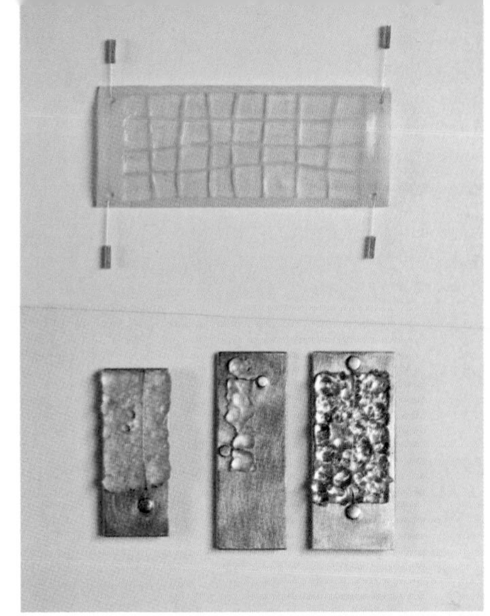

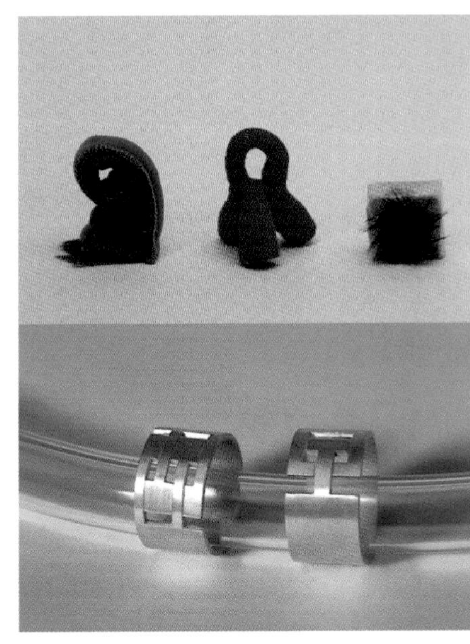

2000

Klein, Stefanie
1971 geboren in Münster
1992-96 Ausbildung zur Goldschmiedin
1996-2002 Studium an der FH Düsseldorf
2002 Diplom

Ausstellungen **Exhibitions**
1994 *Schmuck aus Hohlkörpern*, Schmuck aus Westfälischen Meisterwerkstätten, Münster
1995 *Sternzeichen*, Schmuck aus Westfälischen Meisterwerkstätten, Münster
1998 *offensichtlich*, Ausstellung des Fachbereichs Design der FH Düsseldorf
1999 *Neu*, Ausstellung des Fachbereichs Design der FH Düsseldorf in der alten Paketpost
2000 *Junges Handwerk NRW*, Technologiezentrum Aachen

Auszeichnungen **Awards**
1994 Belobigung im Lehringswettbewerb *Schmuck aus Hohlkörpern*, Münster

Köhler, Heike
1969 geboren in Fulda
1991-95 Ausbildung zur Goldschmiedin
1996-2000 Studium an der FH Düsseldorf
2000 Diplom

Ausstellungen **Exhibitions**
1999 *Grassimesse*, Leipzig;
Neu, Ausstellung des Fachbereichs Design der FH Düsseldorf in der alten Paketpost

Korsawe, Katja
1966 geboren in Dortmund
1988-91 Ausbildung zur Goldschmiedin
1991-96 Studium an der FH Düsseldorf
1996 Diplom
1997-99 Lehrbeauftragte an der FH Düsseldorf
seit 1999 Dozentin an der ASG-Düsseldorf
seit 2000 Werkstatt in Düsseldorf
2001 Geburt der Tochter Zoè

Ausstellungen **Exhibitions**
1994 *Aspekte von Serie*, Galerien in Düsseldorf, Wien, Frankfurt/Main, Amsterdam, Nimwegen, Gent und in den USA
1995 Galerie Cebra, Düsseldorf
1997 *26+4*, Galerien in Düsseldorf, Nimwegen, Wien, Zürich, Dublin und Den Haag;
Talente '97, Handwerksmesse München
1998 *Jewellery meets nature*, Midora Design Award, Messe Leipzig;
Anteprima, Sonderschau der Messe Leipzig;
PunktUm, Sonderschau der *Selection '98*, Zeche Zollverein, Essen
1999 *Jewellery Moves*, National Museum of Scotland, Edinburgh;
Nearly Famous, Escola Massana, Barcelona und Galerien in Wien, Düsseldorf und Vorden;
Wer nicht hören will darf fühlen, Galerie Cebra, Düsseldorf;
Zechengold, Galerie SchmuckProdukt, Essen;
manu factum '99, Deutsches Klingenmuseum Solingen
1999/2000 *Wie es Euch gefällt*, Kunstmuseum Düsseldorf und Galerien in Essen, Frankfurt/Main, Nimwegen, Wien und Wuppertal
2000 Ergebnisse des Schmucksymposiums Erfurt, Angermuseum Erfurt
2000/2001 *Zierat*, Southwest School of Art and Craft, San Antonio, Texas, Kestner Museum, Hannover, Galerie Cebra, Düsseldorf, Galerie Beeld & Aambeeld, Enschede;
Ornaments from here, ornaments from there: incidences, coincidences, Museum für Design und Angewandte Kunst, Lausanne, Gewerbemuseum Winterthur
2001 *Sieraden, de keuze van Almere*, Galerie Marzee, Nimwegen

Auszeichnungen **Awards**
2000 Stadtgoldschmiedin Erfurt, Stipendium mit Arbeitsaufenthalt

Krämer, Maren
1972 geboren in Detmold
1991-95 Ausbildung zur Goldschmiedin
1995-97 Tätigkeit als Goldschmiedegesellin
seit 1997 Studium an der FH Düsseldorf

Kratz, Bettina
1970 geboren in Siegburg
1991-94 Ausbildung zur Goldschmiedin
seit 1996 Studium an der FH Düsseldorf

Ausstellungen **Exhibitions**
1998 *Herzbrut*, Galerie, Düsseldorf
1999 *Herzbrut*, Galerie Rhenania, Köln;
Nearly famous, Escola Massana, Barcelona und Galerien in Wien, Düsseldorf und Vorden
2000 Galerie Elfrink, Düsseldorf
2001 *manu factum '01*, Niederrheinisches Museum für Volkskunde und Kulturgeschichte, Kevelaer

Kutscher, Jan-Marc
1973 geboren in Köln
1993-1995 Ausbildung zum Metallbauer
seit 1997 Studium an der FH Düsseldorf

Lange, Christine
1964 geboren in Eutin
1982-86 Ausbildung zur Goldschmiedin
1987-92 Studium an der FH Düsseldorf
1990 Studienaufenthalt in London am Middlesex Polytechnic, Faculty of Art and Design
1992 Diplom
seit 1992-98 selbständig tätig
seit 1993 freie Mitarbeit für die Firma Niessing in Vreden
1994-98 Mitglied im Arbeitskreis Kunsthandwerk und Design Niedersachsen
seit 1998 selbständig tätig

Ausstellungen **Exhibitions**
1989 *Juwelenschmuck der neunziger Jahre*, Deutsches Goldschmiedehaus Hanau
1990 *Eröffnungsausstellung*, Galerie Treykorn, Berlin
1991 *Design Plus*, Internationale Messe *Ambiente*, Frankfurt/Main

1992 *Es liegt was in der Luft*, Schmuckmuseum Pforzheim
1993 *Die Niedersächsischen Staats- und Förderpreise für das gestaltende Handwerk*, Handwerksforum Hannover
1995 *Industrie Forum Design*, Messe Hannover; *Alen-Müller-Hellwig-Preis*, Burgkloster Lübeck; *Roter Punkt*, *Design-Innovationen '95*, Design Zentrum NRW, Essen
1996 *Golden Girls*, mit Katrin Lucas und Angela Hübel, Grewing Schmuck, Saarbrücken; *Biennial of Industrial Design*, Ljubljana
1999 *Christine Lange + Katrin Lucas*, Barbara Schulte-Hengesbach, Düsseldorf

Auszeichnungen **Awards**
1989 1. Preis im Wettbewerb *Juwelenschmuck der 90er Jahre*
1991 Zwei Auszeichnungen beim DESIGN-PLUS Ideenwettbewerb der Internationalen Frankfurter Messe
1993 Niedersächsischer Förderpreis für das gestaltende Handwerk
1995 Auszeichnung beim internationalen Designwettbewerb *Die zehn Besten des Jahres V*, Industrie Forum Design Hannover; Auszeichnung *Roter Punkt für höchste Designqualität* für die Gestaltung eines Schmucksystems zur Integration von Hörgeräten, Design Zentrum NRW, Essen; Alen-Müller-Hellwig-Förderpreis, gestiftet vom Verband für Frau und Kultur e.V. Lübeck
1996 Goldmedaille für das Schmucksystem zur Integration von Hörgeräten, *Biennial of Industrial Design*, Ljubljana, Slowenien

1998 Galerie Artefakt, München; *Selection '98*, Sonderschau, Essen
1999 *manu factum '99*, Deutsches Klingenmuseum Solingen; Galerie Gesamtmetall, Frankfurt/Main
1999/2000 *Wie es Euch gefällt*, Kunstmuseum Düsseldorf und Galerien in Essen, Frankfurt/Main, Nimwegen, Wien und Wuppertal
2000 *Passagen*, Möbelmesse Köln; *Ringe*, Galerie Hilde Leiss, Hamburg; *Gedok Jahresausstellung*, Handwerkskammer Köln
2001 *Grassimesse*, Leipzig
seit 2001 *Tendence* und *Ambiente*, Messe Frankfurt/Main

Auszeichnungen **Awards**
1995 Auszeichnung für ein Verpackungssystem beim Designwettbewerb der Deutschen Kunststoffindustrie
1996 Sonderpreis beim Schmuckwettbewerb *Die Kunst der Serie* der deutschen Schmuck- und Silberwarenindustrie

Auszeichnungen **Awards**
1994 1. Preis im Gestaltungswettbewerb *Junges Handwerk NRW*, Technologiezentrum Aachen, Kammer- und Landessiegerin im Bereich Gravur
1999 2. Preis für ein Camping-Küchenbesteck, *Designale*, GHM München
2001 Staatspreis des Landes NRW für das Kunsthandwerk

Leithe, Mira Tereza
1975 geboren in Wolfenbüttel
1994-98 Ausbildung zur Goldschmiedin
seit 1998 Studium an der FH Düsseldorf

Auszeichnungen **Awards**
1997 3. Preis im Nachwuchswettbewerb für Edelstein- und Schmuckgestaltung zum Thema *Ringe*, Idar-Oberstein

Magera, Ursula
1968 geboren in Neuenkirchen
1990-93 Ausbildung zur Goldschmiedin
seit 1994 freischaffend tätig
1995-2001 Studium an der FH Düsseldorf
2001 Diplom

Ausstellungen **Exhibitions**
1996/97 *26+4*, Galerien in Düsseldorf, Nimwegen, Zürich, Dublin, Den Haag
1998 *Perlen*, Glasmuseum Wertheim und Museum für Glaskunst, Lauscha
1998/1999 *Silbertriennale*, Deutsches Goldschmiedehaus Hanau und andere Orte; *Nearly Famous*, Escola Massana, Barcelona und Galerien in Wien, Düsseldorf und Vorden
1999 *Perlen*, Glasmuseum Wertheim und Museum für Glaskunst, Lauscha; Angewandte Kunst, Gedok, Handwerkskammer, Köln
2000 *Grassimesse*, Leipzig

Lebá, Helena
1967 geboren in Heidenheim
1989-92 Ausbildung zur Formgeberin für Schmuck und Gerät
1992/93 Studium an der FH für Gestaltung Schwäbisch Gmünd
1993-97 Studium an der FH Düsseldorf
1997 Diplom
seit 1997 freischaffend tätig

Ausstellungen **Exhibitions**
1994 *Dinner for two*, Stadtmuseum, Schwäbisch Gmünd; Museum für Angewandte Kunst, Köln
1996 Schmuckmuseum Pforzheim; *Ambiente '96*, Sonderschau der Messe Frankfurt/Main
1996/97 *26+4*, Galerien in Düsseldorf, Nimwegen, Wien, Zürich, Dublin und Den Haag;
1997/98 Galerie Friends of Carlotta, Zürich

Leppin, Ina
1970 geboren in Essen
1990-94 Ausbildung zur Graveurin
1994-2000 Studium an der FH Düsseldorf
2000 Diplom
seit 2001 freischaffend tätig

Ausstellungen **Exhibitions**
1998 *Silbertriennale*, Deutsches Goldschmiedehaus Hanau und andere Orte; *Perlenflut*, Galerie Marzee, Nimwegen
1999 *Zechengold*, Galerie SchmuckProdukt, Essen
1999/2000 *Nearly Famous*, Escola Massana, Barcelona und Galerien in Wien, Düsseldorf und Vorden; *Wer nicht hören will darf fühlen*, Galerie Cebra, Düsseldorf
2000 *Endexamenswerk*, Galerie Marzee, Nimwegen
2001 Galerie Agnes Raben, Vorden; *manu factum '01*, Niederrheinisches Museum für Volkskunde und Kulturgeschichte, Kevelaer

Matschullat, Frauke
1964 geboren in Hannover
1986-89 Ausbildung zur Goldschmiedin
1990 Sommerakademie für bildende Kunst Salzburg
1990-96 Studium an der FH Düsseldorf
1996 Diplom
seit 1996 freischaffend tätig
1996 Gründung der Gruppe *elft*
1998 Konzeption und Organisation des Schmucksymposiums Zimmerhof, *Zwischen Wunsch und Wirklichkeit: Wie werden Träume wahr?*; Gründung der mobilen Galerie *Rings um*

Ausstellungen **Exhibitions**
1994 *Aspekte von Serie*, Galerien in Düsseldorf, Wien, Frankfurt/Main, Amsterdam, Nimwegen, Gent und in den USA
1995 *Medaillons und andere Geheimnisse*, Galerie Lichtblick, Aachen
1996 *Paare – zwei, die zusammengehören*, Werkstattgalerie Brodhag + Wörn, Berlin

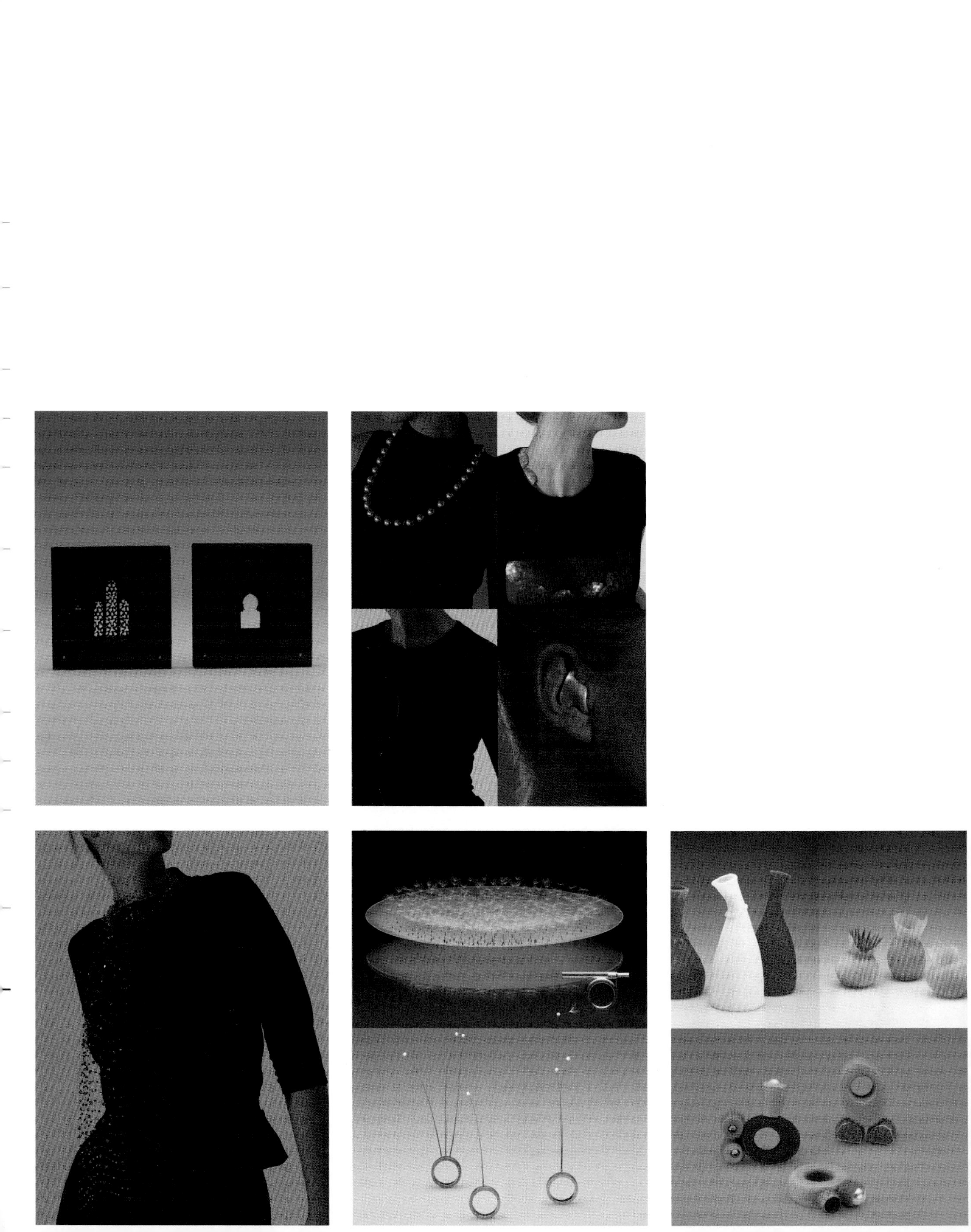

IDENTITET

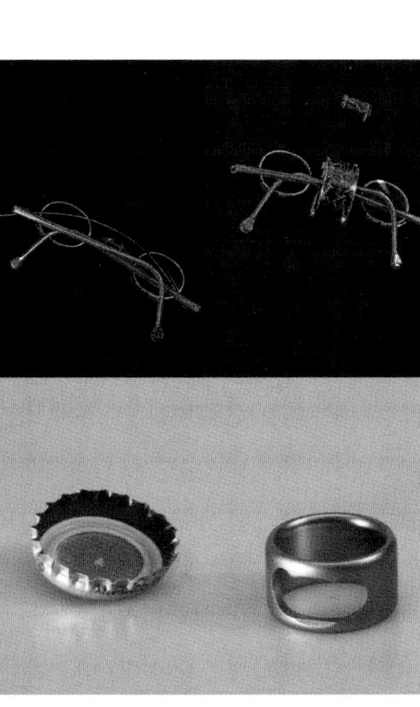

1997 *Denn man lebt nicht vom Brot allein*, *elft* im Klärwerk Krefeld und in der Alten Feuerwache Köln;
Die Leichtigkeit des Seins, Galerie Cebra, Düsseldorf
1998 *Jewellery meets nature*, *Midora Design Award*, Messe Leipzig
1999 *Grassimesse*, Leipzig;
Denn man lebt nicht nur vom Brot allein, *elft* im Kunstmuseum Düsseldorf
2000 *Ringe, Ringe, Ringe*, Galerie Hilde Leiss, Hamburg;
Jewellery meets fashion, *Midora Design Award*, Messe Leipzig
2001 *Neue Arbeiten*, Detail zwo, Düsseldorf

Mayer, Susanne
1971 geboren in Wuppertal
1991-95 Ausbildung zur Goldschmiedin
1995-2001 Studium an der FH Düsseldorf
1998/99 Studienaufenthalt am Edinburgh College of Art
2001 Diplom

Austellungen **Exhibitions**
1999 *Nearly famous*, Escola Massana, Barcelona, Galerien in Wien, Düsseldorf und Vorden;
Kunstpunkte in Düsseldorf;
manu factum '99, Deutsches Klingenmuseum, Solingen
2000 *Kleine Dinge für den Alltag*, Handwerkskammer Koblenz;
Messebeteiligung, Westdeutscher Handwerkskammertag, Köln
2001 Galerie Agnes Raben;
Agnes Raben Moving Galerie, Amsterdam

Auszeichnungen **Awards**
1996 1. Preis im Gestaltungswettbewerb *Junges Handwerk NRW*, Technologiezentrum Aachen
2000 1. Preis im Wettbewerb *Kleine Dinge für den Alltag*, Handwerkskammer Koblenz

Mersmann, Anne
1971 geboren in Lüdinghausen
1990-94 Ausbildung zur Goldschmiedin
1994-2000 Studium an der FH Düsseldorf
2000 Diplom
seit 2000 freischaffend tätig

Ausstellungen **Exhibitions**
1993 *Schmuck in Silber*, Goldschmiedeförderverein Essen
1996 *Tresure*, *3 x neu*, Landesmuseum Volk und Wirtschaft, Düsseldorf
1996/97 Frankfurter Messe
1998/99 *Perlen*, Glasmuseum Wertheim und Museum für Glaskunst, Lauscha
1999 *Nearly Famous*, Escola Massana, Barcelona und Galerien in Wien, Düsseldorf und Vorden;
Neu, Arbeiten des Fachbereichs Design der FH Düsseldorf in der alten Paketpost
2000 *jaarlijkse internationale eindexamententoonstelling*, Galerie Marzee, Nimwegen;
Kunst hautnah, Künstlerhaus Wien, Förderkoje;
Angewandte Kunst, Gedok Köln;
Jewellery meets fashion, *Midora Design Award*, Messe Leipzig
2000/2001 *Hautnah*, amica, Giessen
2001 *Red Bull* Ausstellung, Cube, Essen;
Metamorphosen, Gesamtmetall, Frankfurt/Main
seit 2000 *Inhorgenta*, München;
Tendence, Frankfurt/Main;
Grassimesse, Leipzig

Auszeichnungen **Awards**
1994 2. Preis im Lehrlingswettbewerb NRW, Essen
1998 1. Preis im Gestaltungswettbewerb für Zuchtperlen, Gellner Pforzheim
1999 Sonderpreis für die beste Diplomarbeit in der Fachrichtung Design, Goethe-Buchhandlung, Düsseldorf
2000 Sonderpreis im Designwettbewerb *Jewellery meets fashion*, *Midora Design Award*, Leipzig

Micheel, Ingrid
1976 geboren in Coesfeld
1992-96 Ausbildung zur Goldschmiedin
1996/97 Tätigkeit als Goldschmiedegesellin
seit 1998 Studium an der FH Düsseldorf

Müller, Klaus
1965 geboren in Fulda
1985-89 Ausbildung zum Goldschmied
1989 Tätigkeit als Goldschmiedegeselle
1990/91 Gaststudium an der Staatlichen Zeichenakademie Hanau
1991-97 Studium an der FH Düsseldorf
1997 Diplom
seit 1997 freischaffend tätig
1997-99 Projektweise Assistent für den Künstler John Isaacs, London und den Düsseldorfer Bildhauer Thomas Schönauer;
Beteiligung am Atelier zur Entwicklung von Möbeln
seit 1999 eigenes Atelier in Düsseldorf

Arbeiten in öffentlichen Sammlungen
Works in Public Collections
Nationalmuseum, Madrid

Müllers, Julia
1973 geboren in Coesfeld
1992-95 Ausbildung zur Goldschmiedin
1995-96 Tätigkeit als Goldschmiedegesellin
seit 1996 Studium an der FH Düsseldorf

Austellungen **Exhibitions**
2001 *Identity*, Galerie V&V, Wien

Munkert, Elke
1967 geboren in Nürnberg
1983-91 Tätigkeit bei der Postbank in Nürnberg
1991-94 Ausbildung zur Goldschmiedin
1995-2000 Tätigkeit als Goldschmiedegesellin
seit 1998 Studium an der FH Düsseldorf

Austellungen **Exhibitions**
seit 1998 *Offene Ateliers*, Köln
1999 *Kölsche Domschätze*, Galerie Claudia Schuster, Köln;
manu factum '99, Deutsches Klingenmuseum, Solingen;
Reine Männersache, Galerie Claudia Schuster, Köln
2001 *Bei meiner Ehre*, Mitgliederausstellung des Forums für Schmuck und Design

Auszeichnungen **Awards**
1999 Staatspreis des Landes Nordrhein-Westfalen für das Kunsthandwerk

Niegel, Catherine
1973 geboren in Düsseldorf
1994-97 Ausbildung zur Goldschmiedin
seit 1997 Studium an der FH Düsseldorf

Austellungen **Exhibitions**
2000 *Grassimesse*, Leipzig

Nolden, Simone
1970 geboren in Grevenbroich
1990-94 Ausbildung zur Goldschmiedin
1994/95 Tätigkeit als Goldschmiedegesellin
1995-2002 Studium an der FH Düsseldorf
2002 Diplom
2000 dreimonatige Auslandstätigkeit als Technische Assistentin am Royal College of Art, London

Austellungen **Exhibitions**
1997 *Liturgiegefäße, Kirche und Design*, Deutsches Liturgisches Institut, Trier
1999 *Email – Schmuck und Gerät*, Deutsches Goldschmiedehaus Hanau und Kreismuseum Zons
1998-2000 *Nearly famous,* Escola Massana, Barcelona und Galerien in Wien, Düsseldorf und Vorden
2001 *Grassimesse*, Leipzig

Oeding-Erdel, Uta
1970 geboren in Münster
1990-93 Ausbildung zur Goldschmiedin
1993-95 Ausbildung zur Gestalterin im Handwerk
1994 Tätigkeit im Verkauf
seit 1995 freischaffend tätig
seit 1996 Studium an der FH Düsseldorf
seit 1999 Mitglied der freien Künstlergruppe *Tapezisten*
2000 Mitgründung des Schmuck- und Produktateliers *Freiraum*, Düsseldorf

Austellungen **Exhibitions**
2001 *Auf den zweiten Blick*, Schmuck- und Produktatelier *Freiraum*, Düsseldorf

Auszeichnungen **Awards**
2000 1.Preis im Wettbewerb *Kleine Objekte für den Alltag,* Handwerkskammer Koblenz

Oelschlegel, Anja
1969 geboren in Würzburg
1990-94 Ausbildung zur Goldschmiedin
1994-96 Tätigkeit als Goldschmiedegesellin
1996/97 Mitarbeit in verschiedenen Werkstattgemeinschaften im Raum Köln-Bonn
seit 1998 Studium an der FH Düsseldorf

Ausstellungen **Exhibitions**
2000 *quasi moda*, Aachen;
Grassimesse, Leipzig
2001 *manu factum '01*, Niederrheinisches Museum für Volkskunde und Kulturgeschichte, Kevelaer

Peters, Meike
1972 geboren in Orsoy
1993-96 Ausbildung zur Goldschmiedin
seit 1997 Studium an der FH Düsseldorf

Ausstellungen **Exhibitions**
1999 *Neu*, Ausstellung des Fachbereichs Design der FH Düsseldorf in der alten Paketpost
2000 *Brandneu*, Ausstellung des Fachbereichs Design der FH Düsseldorf in der alten Paketpost

Pittig, Martin
1965 geboren in Gelsenkirchen
1985-88 Ausbildung zum Goldschmied
1990-98 Studium an der FH Düsseldorf
1992 Gastsemester am West Surrey College of Art and Design, Farnham, Großbritannien
seit 1996 Mitglied der Gruppe *elft*
1998 Diplom
seit 1999 Beteiligungen der Werkstattgalerie SchmuckProdukt in Essen

Plum, Georg
1960 geboren in Heinsberg
1979-82 Ausbildung zum Goldschmied
1984/85 Bildhauertätigkeit
1985-90 Studium an der FH Düsseldorf
1987 Auslandssemester am West Surrey College of Art und Design, Farnham, Großbritannien
1990 Diplom
1991-2000 Designatelier in Hamburg; Auftragsarbeiten für: Alfex S.A., Lugano; M&M Uhren, Düsseldorf; Mont Blanc, Hamburg; Niessing, Vreden
seit 2000 Designatelier in Meerbusch

Ausstellungen **Exhibitions**
1987 *Komparativ*, *Zeitgenössisches Metall-Design* Galerie Torsten Bröhan, Düsseldorf
1989 *Silbertriennale*, Deutsches Goldschmiedehaus Hanau und andere Orte;
Biennale der Kunstschulen Europas, Antwerpen;
Aluminium Trilogie, Galerie UND, Düsseldorf;
Goldfinger Galerie Accent, München
1990 *Düsseldorfer Designer,* Galerie Hipotesi, Barcelona;
Juwelenschmuck der 90er Jahre, Deutsches Goldschmiedehaus Hanau
1991 *Aluminium - Metall der Moderne,* Stadmuseum Köln;
Schmuckdesigndüsseldorfpunkt, Messe Düsseldorf;
Rheingold, Suermondt-Ludwig-Museum Aachen
1992 *19 neue 92,* Galerie Leiss, Hamburg;
Schatzsuche, Kunstmuseum Düsseldorf
1996 Einzelausstellung, Galerie Treykorn, Berlin
1992-99 Sonderschau der *Inhorgenta* München
1993-99 Jahresmesse, Museum für Kunst und Gewerbe, Hamburg
1998/99 *Selection*, Zeche Zollverein, Essen

Auszeichnungen **Awards**
1990 Förderpreis für die Abschlussarbeit an Designschulen der Industrie- und Handelskammer Westfalen in NRW
1994 1. Preis für Bestes Einzelstück der Handwerkskammer Hamburg
1995 Museumsankauf, Uhr *Silberwinkel*, Landesmuseum Schleswig-Holstein
1996 *Roter Punkt für hohe Designqualität*, Designzentrum Essen für M&M Uhr *Quarrebogen*
1997 *Roter Punkt für hohe Designqualität*, Designzentrum Essen für M&M Uhr *Steelmate*
1998 Landesprämierung Hamburgdesign und Nominierung Bundespreis Produktdesign für die Uhrenkollektion *Steel Collection*;
Roter Punkt des Designzentrums Essen für M&M Uhr *Herrenchrono*
1999 Ranking: *Design, Industrie Design – Die 100 besten Designbüros*
2000 *Good Design* Award des Chicago Athenaeum für *Alfex*-Uhr *Two Time Bangle*

Arbeiten in öffentlichen Sammlungen
Works in Public Collections
Landesmuseum Schleswig-Holstein
Iyomatsa Museum, Japan

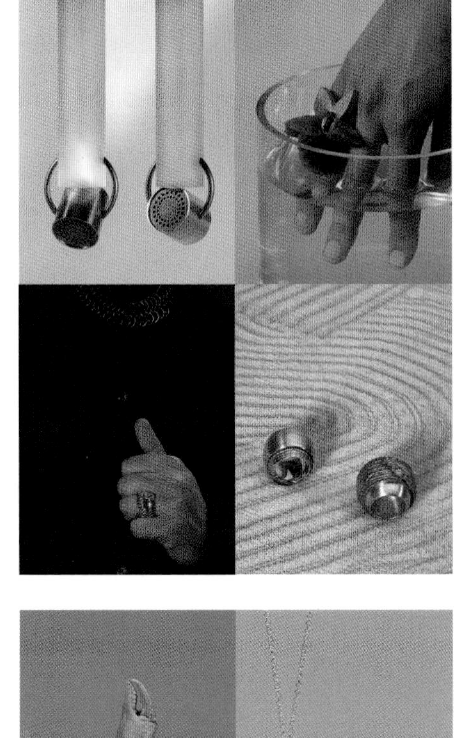

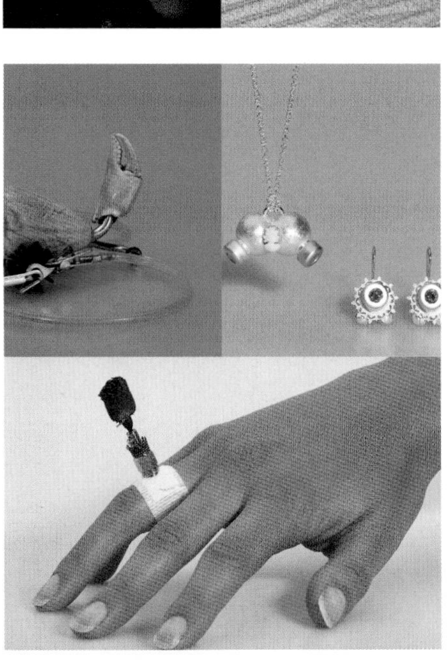

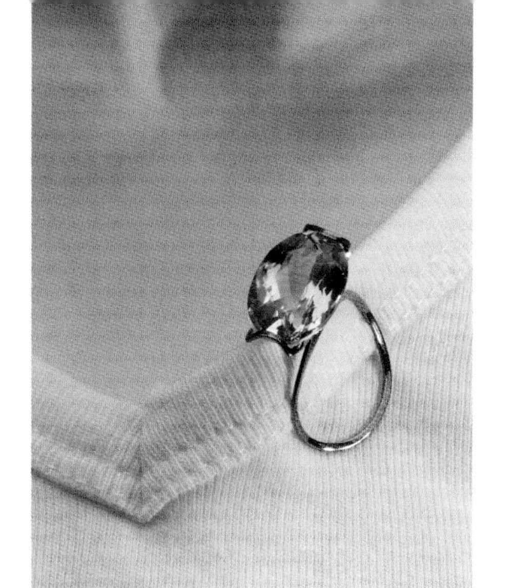
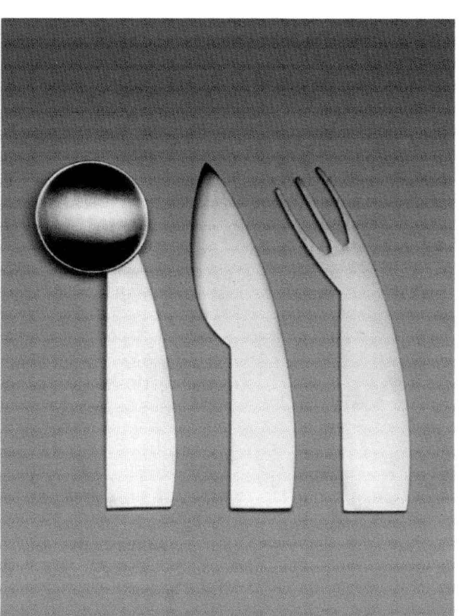
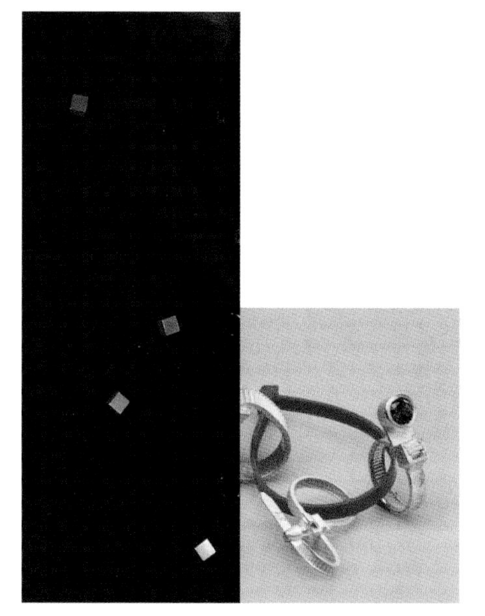

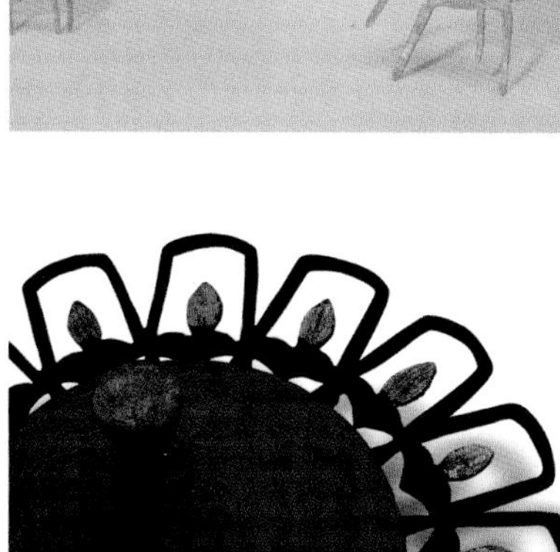

Pukis, Renate
1969 geboren in Kretinga, Litauen
1993-97 Ausbildung zur Goldschmiedin
1997-2000 Tätigkeit als Goldschmiedegesellin
seit 2000 Studium an der FH Düsseldorf

Ausstellungen **Exhibitions**
1997 *Kunst für Amnesty International*, Tuttlingen
1998 *Grün*, Kunstnacht in der Eigelstein-Torburg, Köln

Quaring, Regina
1972 geboren in Kechtna, Estland
1992-96 Ausbildung zur Goldschmiedin an der Staatlichen Zeichenakademie Hanau
seit 1996 Studium an der FH Düsseldorf

Ausstellungen **Exhibitions**
1999 *Nearly famous,* Escola Massana, Barcelona und Galerien in Wien, Düsseldorf und Vorden

Auszeichnungen **Awards**
1996 Kammersiegerin im Praktischen Leistungswettbewerb der Handwerksjugend, Handwerkskammer Wiesbaden

Schäfer, Claudia
1964 geboren in Saarbrücken
1984-88 Ausbildung zur Goldschmiedin
1989-94 Studium an der FH Düsseldorf
1994 Diplom
seit 1994 freischaffend tätig

Ausstellungen **Exhibitions**
1994 *Junges Handwerk NRW*, Technologiezentrum Aachen;
Tekens & Ketens, Museum van der Toogt, Amstelveen;
Aspekte von Serie, Galerien in Düsseldorf, Wien, Frankfurt/Main, Amsterdam, Nimwegen, Gent und in den USA
1995 *Schmuck und Gerät*, Deutsches Goldschmiedehaus Hanau und andere Orte;
manu factum '95, Museum für Angewandte Kunst, Köln
1996 *20 Designers aux Charteux*, Expo, Brüssel;
Design Plus, Sonderschau der Messe Frankfurt/Main
1997 *Metall & Licht*, Handwerkskammer Koblenz;
manu factum '97, Gustav-Lübcke-Museum, Hamm
1998 *Jewelery Willbee Yours*, Galerie Wilbee Alkmaar
1998-2000 *Selection*, Design Zentrum NRW, Essen
1999 *manu factum '99*, Deutsches Klingenmuseum, Solingen
2000 *Ornaris*, Messe Bern;
Asymmetrie und Harmonie, Commerzbank Frankfurt
2001 *Inhorgenta*, München;
manu factum '01, Niederrheinisches Museum für Volkskunde und Kulturgeschichte, Kevelaer

Auszeichnungen **Awards**
1993 1. Preis im Gestaltungswettbewerb für Kleinuhren der Firma M&M, Düsseldorf
1994 1. und 2. Preis im Wettbewerb *Junges Handwerk NRW*
1995 Belobigung im Wettbewerb *Form und Farbe in Bewegung* der Goldschmiede Zeitung
1996 Preis für eine Armbanduhr, *Design Plus*, Sonderschau der Messe Frankfurt/Main

Scheer, Ulrike
1964 geboren in Bad Oeynhausen
1984-88 Ausbildung zur Goldschmiedin
1988-92 Tätigkeit als Goldschmiedegesellin
seit 1992 Studium an der FH Düsseldorf
seit 1996 freischaffend tätig

Ausstellungen **Exhibitions**
1999 *Nearly Famous*, Escola Massana, Barcelona und Galerien in Wien, Düsseldorf und Vorden;
Internationaler Bernsteinkunstpreis, Bernsteinmuseum, Ribnitz-Damgarten
2001 *Zwischen Kunst und Kommerz,* Zwo SchmuckDesign, Hüllhorst/Holsen

Auszeichnungen **Awards**
1998 2. Preis im Gestaltungswettbewerb für Zuchtperlen der Firma Gellner, Wiernsheim

Arbeiten in öffentlichen Sammlungen
Works in public Collections
Bernsteinmuseum, Ribnitz-Damgarten

Schmicking, Britta
1968 geboren in Iserlohn-Lethmathe
1988-91 Ausbildung zur Goldschmiedin
1993 Gastsemester an der Ar. Co Lissabon, Portugal
1994 Gastsemester an der Staatlichen Zeichenakademie Hanau
1994-2000 Studium an der FH Düsseldorf
2000 Diplom
seit 2001 freischaffend tätig

Schulze, Herbert
1953 geboren in Düsseldorf
1969-72 Ausbildung zum Gürtler und Metalldrücker
1974-78 Studium Schmuck- und Gerätedesign an der FH Düsseldorf

Berufliche Tätigkeiten **Career Details**
seit 1978 freiberuflich tätig
1978-99 eigene Werkstatt in Düsseldorf
1982-85 Lehrbeauftragter im Fachbereich Design, FH Düsseldorf
seit 1985 Dozent für Silberschmieden im Fachbereich Design, FH Düsseldorf,
1988/89 Lehrauftrag an der FH für Gestaltung, Pforzheim
1995 Lehrauftrag an der Tallinn Art University, Estland, Jurymitglied in verschiedenen Gestaltungswettbewerben

Auszeichnungen **Awards**
1978 Förderpreis der Stadt Düsseldorf für bildende Kunst;
1. Preis im Wettbewerb *Junges Handwerk NRW*
1980 2. Preis im Wettbewerb *Junges Handwerk NRW*
1989 Staatspreis des Landes Nordrhein-Westfalen für das Kunsthandwerk

Ausstellungen **Exhibitions**
seit 1978 Beteiligung an zahlreichen nationalen und internationalen Ausstellungen in Belgien, Finnland, Großbritannien, Irland, den Niederlanden, Spanien, Tschechien, der UDSSR und Ungarn

Arbeiten in öffentlichen Sammlungen
Works in Public Collections
Bauhaus-Museum, Dessau;
Deutsches Goldschmiedehaus Hanau;
Grassimuseum, Leipzig;
Landesmuseum Oldenburg;
Nationalmuseum, Madrid;
Rheinisches Landesmuseum, Bonn;
Sammlung Torsten Bröhan, Düsseldorf;
Utsunomiya Museum, Japan

Seitter, Monika
1970 geboren in Pforzheim
1990-91 Studium Werbewirtschaft, FHW Pforzheim
1991-95 Ausbildung zur Goldschmiedin
1995-2000 Tätigkeit als Goldschmiedegesellin
1995-2001 Studium an der FH Düsseldorf
2001 Diplom

Ausstellungen **Exhibitions**
1998 *Silbertriennale*, Deutsches Goldschmiedehaus Hanau und andere Orte
1999 Ausstellung zum Wettbewerb des Bundesverbandes der Edelstein- und Diamantindustrie, Idar-Oberstein
2000 *Junges Handwerk NRW*, Technologiezentrum Aachen;
Einzelausstellung, Kunstverein Virtuell – Visuell e.V., Dorsten
2001 *150-Jahre Kö*, Kö-Gemeinschaft, Düsseldorf;
Sonderschau *Form 2000*, *Tendence* Frankfurt/Main

Sommer, Judith
1974 geboren in Düren
1994-97 Ausbildung zur Goldschmiedin
1997-2000 Tätigkeit als Goldschmiedegesellin
seit 1998 Studium an der FH Düsseldorf
2000/01 Gastsemester am Fashion Institute of Technology und Praktikum im Goldschmiedestudio Deborah Aguado, New York City

Ausstellungen **Exhibitions**
1995 *Perlen im zeitgemäßen Schmuckdesign*, Goldschmiedeinnung Köln anlässlich der Handwerksmesse Köln
1996 *Funkelnde Harmonie*, Goldschmiedeinnung Köln anlässlich der Handwerksmesse, Köln

Auszeichnungen **Awards**
1995 Preis im Gestaltungswettbewerb *Perlen im zeitgemäßen Schmuckdesign*, Goldschmiedeinnung Köln und Firma Schuster, Köln
2000-2001 Stipendium der Carl Duisberg Gesellschaft

Stotz, Julia
1974 geboren in Wuppertal
1995-98 Ausbildung zur Goldschmiedin
seit 1998 Studium an der FH Düsseldorf

Ausstellungen **Exhibitions**
1999 *Neu*, Ausstellung des Fachbereichs Design der FH Düsseldorf in der alten Paketpost
2000 *Über unsere Köpfe hinweg*, Protestaktion gegen die Auflösung des Studiengangs Produktdesign der FHD, Galerie Cebra, Düsseldorf;
Brandneu, Ausstellung des Fachbereichs Design der FH Düsseldorf in der alten Paketpost

Auszeichnungen **Awards**
1998 Belobigung, Lehrlingswettbewerb im Gold- und Silberschmiedehandwerk NRW

Straube, Birgit
1964 geboren in Bielefeld
1987 Ausbildung zur Goldschmiedin
1991-93 Staatliche Zeichenakademie Hanau
1993 Meisterprüfung als Goldschmiedin
1993-97 Studium an der FH Düsseldorf
1997 tödlich verunglückt

Ausstellungen **Exhibitions**
1996 *26+4*, Galerien in Düsseldorf, Nimwegen, Wien, Zürich, Dublin und Den Haag

Auszeichnungen **Awards**
1996 3. Preis im Wettbewerb *Junges Handwerk NRW*

Thiemann, Sonja
1972 geboren in Jülich
1992-96 Ausbildung zur Goldschmiedin
1996/97 Tätigkeit als Goldschmiedegesellin
seit 1997 Studium an der FH Düsseldorf
seit 1999 selbständig tätig

Ausstellungen **Exhibitions**
1999 *Neu*, Ausstellung des Fachbereichs Design der FH Düsseldorf in der alten Paketpost
2000 *Brandneu*, Ausstellung des Fachbereichs Design der FH Düsseldorf in der alten Paketpost;
Junges Handwerk NRW, Technologiezentrum Aachen,
2001 *Symposium 2001*, Schmuckmuseum Turnov, Tschechien

Auszeichnungen **Awards**
1996 Landessiegerin des Goldschmiedehandwerks im Praktischen Leistungswettbewerb der deutschen Handwerksjugend, Handwerkskammer Bremen

Tries, Heike
1964 geboren in Bendorf/Rhein
1983-87 Ausbildung zur Goldschmiedin
1987/88 Berufsbildende Schule Mainz, Fachoberschule Technik, Schwerpunkt Gestaltung
1988-91 Tätigkeit als Goldschmiedegesellin
1991-2002 Studium an der FH Düsseldorf
1993 Geburt der Tochter Karla
1995 Wiederaufnahme des Studiums
2002 Diplom

Ausstellungen **Exhibitions**
1997-99 *Perlen*, Glasmuseum Wertheim und Museum für Glaskunst, Lauscha
2000 *Torah Coverings*, Spertus Museum, Chicago
2001 *Identity*, Galerie V&V, Wien

Auszeichnungen **Awards**
2000 Finalistin im Gestaltungswettbewerb *Judging The Book by its Cover – Torah Coverings*, Spertus Institute of Jewish Studies, Chicago, USA

Vanderloock, Evelyn
1963 geboren in Köln
1982-85 Ausbildung zur Goldschmiedin
1986-93 Studium an der FH Düsseldorf
1989 Auslandsemester am West Surrey College of Art and Design, Farnham, Großbritannien
1993 Diplom
1999 Eröffnung der Galerie Tresor

Ausstellungen **Exhibitions**
1989 *Silbertriennale*, Deutsches Goldschmiedehaus Hanau und andere Orte;
Aluminium Trilogie, Teil 1, Galerie UND, Düsseldorf, Stadtmuseum, Köln
1991 *Email jetzt*, Museum für Angewandte Kunst, Köln
1992 *Expo Kunststoff*, Wanderausstellung, u.a. Frankfurt/Main, München, Düsseldorf
1993 *Tekens & Ketens*, Amstelveen, Arnheim, Rotterdam;

Sommerausstellung, Galerie für Schmuck Hilde Leiss, Hamburg
1994 *Aspekte von Serie*, Galerien in Düsseldorf, Wien, Frankfurt/Main, Amsterdam, Nimwegen, Gent und in den USA
1995 *Zehn Schmuckkünstler aus Hamburg*, Expo Arte Smykkegalleri, Oslo;
Weihnachtsausstellung, Werkstatt-Galerie Brodhag+Wörn, Berlin
1996 *Inhorgenta*, München;
Tendence '96, Frankfurt/Main;
Land unter, Einzelausstellung, Galerie So, Freiburg;
Paare – Zwei, die zusammengehören, Werkstatt-Galerie Brodhag+Wörn, Berlin;
Weihnachtsausstellung, Galerie für Schmuck Hilde Leiss, Hamburg
1997 *Inhorgenta*, München;
Tendence '97, Frankfurt/Main;
Water, Den Haag, Waregem, Düsseldorf
1998 *Inhorgenta*, München;
Ambiente '98, Frankfurt/Main;
Tendence '98, Frankfurt/Main;
Steinhart und seidenweich, Werkstatt-Galerie Brodhag+Wörn, Berlin
1999 *Tendence '99*, Frankfurt/Main;
Grassimesse Leipzig

Wackermann, Annette
1966 geboren in Velbert
1985-89 Ausbildung zur Graveurin
1989/90 Tätigkeit als Graveurgesellin
1990-95 Studium an der FH Düsseldorf
1995 Diplom
1996 Gründung der Gruppe *SchmuckProdukt*
1997 Gründung der Gruppe *elft*
seit 1998 Werkstattatelier *SchmuckProdukt*, Zeche Zollverein, Essen
1998 Konzeption und Organisation des Schmucksymposiums Zimmerhof *Zwischen Wunsch und Wirklichkeit: Wie werden Träume wahr?*
2001 Konzeption und Organisation des Symposiums *Aspekte von Gestaltung*

Ausstellungen **Exhibitions**
1995 *Class of '95*, Goldsmiths' Hall, London;
Try Out, Galerie Marzee, Nimwegen;
Präsent, Deutsches Klingenmuseum, Solingen und Stadtmuseum Düsseldorf

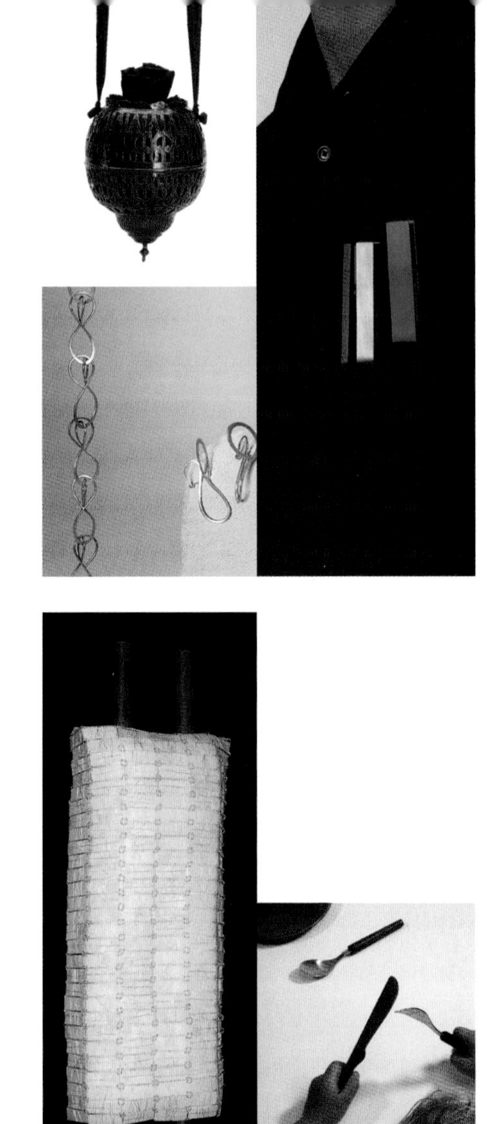

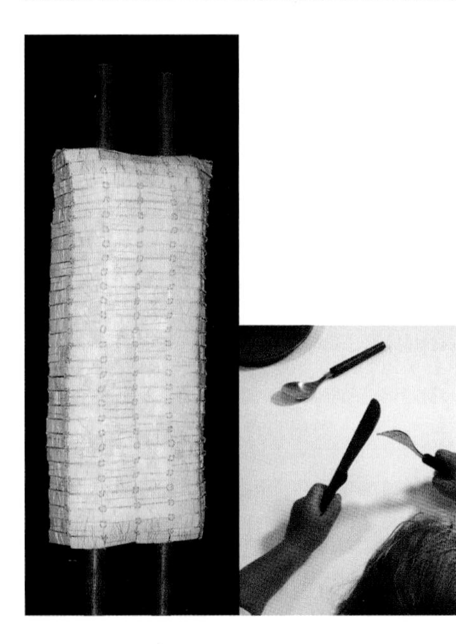

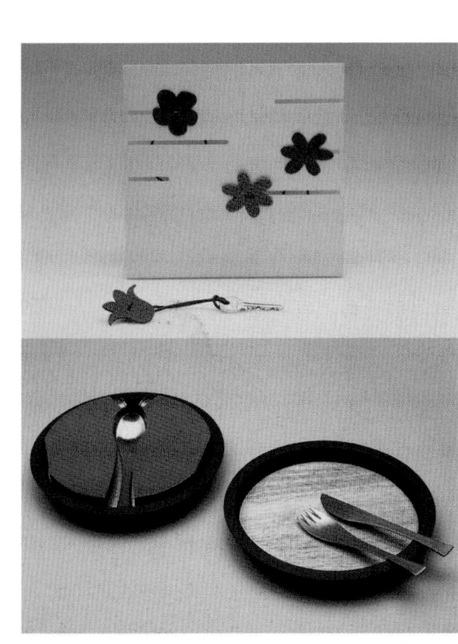

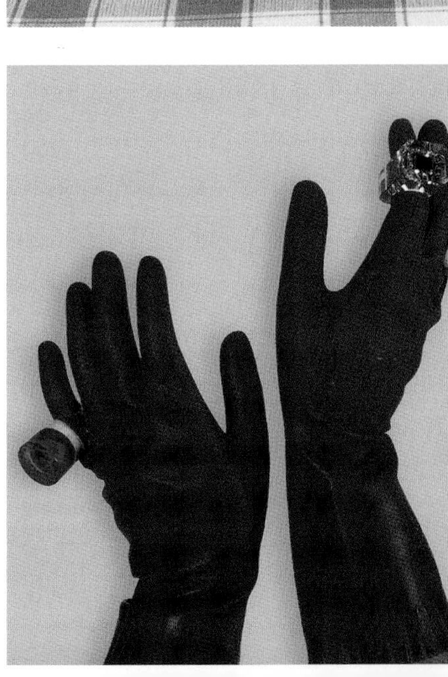

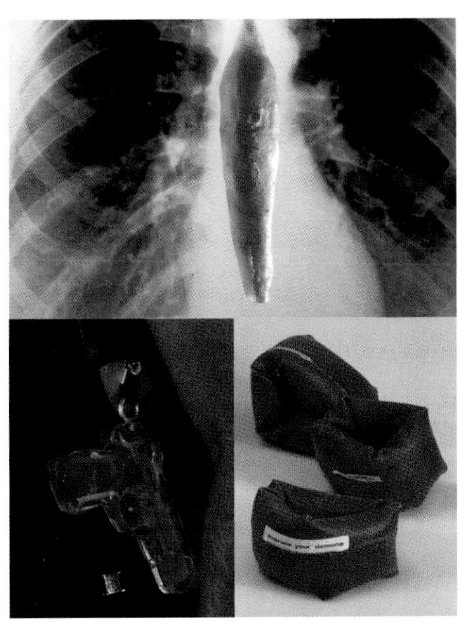
your demons

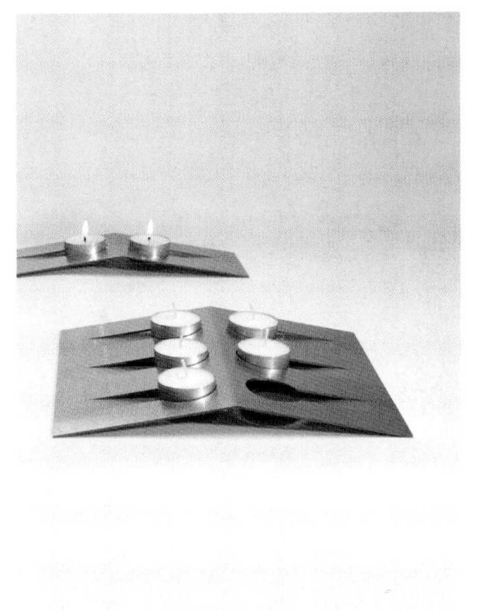

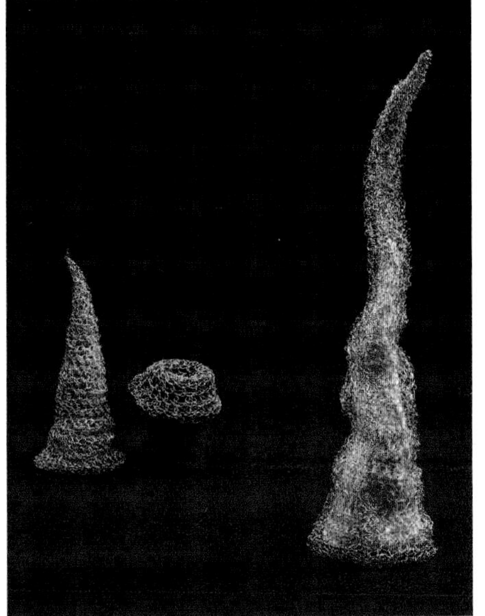

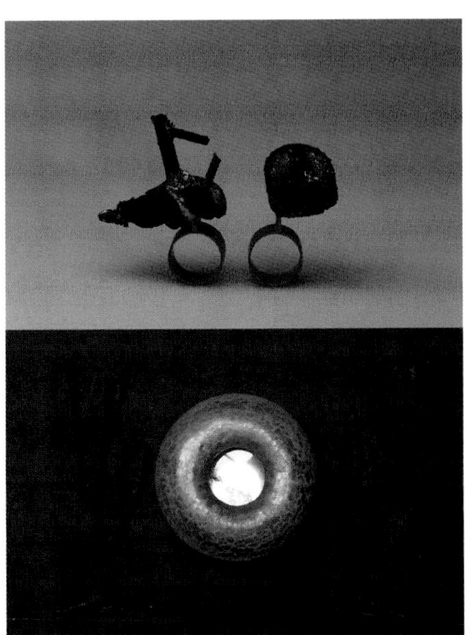

1996 *Talente '96*, Handwerksmesse München; *Metall und Licht*, Handwerkskammer Koblenz; *Denn man lebt nicht vom Brot allein, elft* im Klärwerk Krefeld und in der Alten Feuerwache, Köln
1999 *Zechengold*, Galerie SchmuckProdukt, Essen; *FORMART*, Maschinenhalle Friedlicher Nachbar, Bochum; *Denn man lebt nicht vom Brot allein, elft* im Kunstmuseum Düsseldorf
2000 *Selection 2000*, Designzentrum NRW, Essen; *Best of Selection 2000*, Wanderausstellung des Design Zentrums NRW, Essen; *Ringe*, Galerie für Schmuck Hilde Leiss, Hamburg; *Perspektiven*, Sonderschau der Messe Ornaris in Bern
2001 *manu factum '01*, Niederrheinisches Museum für Volkskunde und Kulturgeschichte, Kevelaer

Wenz, Simon
1974 geboren in Düsseldorf
1994-98 Ausbildung zum Goldschmied,
seit 1998 Studium an der FH Düsseldorf

Ausstellungen **Exhibitions**
2001 *Grassimesse*, Leipzig
2001 *Identity*, Galerie V&V, Wien

Winckler, Susanne
1963 geboren in Bad Oeynhausen
1989-93 Ausbildung zur Silberschmiedin
1993-99 Studium an der FH Düsseldorf
1999 Diplom
1999 Technische Assistenz im Department Goldsmithing, Silversmithing, Metalwork and Jewellery, Royal College of Art, London
2000/2001 freischaffend tätig
seit 2001 Angestellte als Designerin der Firma Niessing

Ausstellungen **Exhibitions**
1996 *26+4*, Galerien in Düsseldorf, Nimwegen, Wien, Zürich, Dublin und Den Haag; *Seerosensafari*, Gruppe ArtiSchocke, Krefeld
1997 Werkschau zum Thema Perlenschatz, Künstlerhof Zollhaus, Willich; *Feuerklirren*, Gruppe ArtiSchocke, Krefeld; *Perlenflut*, Arbeiten vor Ort, Galerie Marzee, Nimwegen
1998 *Perlen*, Glasmuseum Wertheim und Museum für Glaskunst, Lauscha; *allesollensichüppigschmückenaberplötzlich*, eine Schmuckinszenierung, Galerie Taste, Wuppertal
1999 *Perlen*, Glasmuseum Wertheim und Museum für Glaskunst, Lauscha; *Emailschmuck*, Kreismuseum Zons; *Endexamenwerk*, Galerie Marzee, Nimwegen
2000 *Ringe, Ringe, Ringe*, Galerie für Schmuck, Hilde Leiss, Hamburg; Nachwuchsförderpreis 2000, Goldschmiedehaus Hanau
2001 *Schmuck*, Sonderschau der 53. Internationalen Handwerksmesse München und Wilhelm-Wagenfeld-Haus, Bremen

Auszeichnungen **Awards**
2000 2. Preis für die Diplomarbeit, Nachwuchsförderpreis 2000 der Bertha Heraeus und Kathinka Platzhoff Stiftung

Wink, Christiane
1972 geboren in Frankfurt/Main
1993-96 Ausbildung zur Goldschmiedin
1996-2002 Studium an der FH Düsseldorf
2002 Diplom

Ausstellungen **Exhibitions**
1995 Sonderschau auf der Messe *Ambiente*, Frankfurt/Main
1997 *10th Cloisonné Jewelry Contest*, Ginzo La Pola Gallery, Tokyo Yamanashi
1998 *11th Cloisonn Jewelry Contest*, Syosenkyo Shippo Museum
1998/99 Galerie Friends of Carlotta, Zürich
2000 *Nearly famous,* Escola Massana, Barcelona und Galerien in Wien, Düsseldorf und Vorden
2001 *14th Cloisonné Jewelry contest*

Auszeichnungen **Awards**
1997 Preis im Gestaltungswettbewerb *New Idea for Materials Integration*, *10th Cloisonné Jewelry Contest*, Japan Shippo Conference, Tokio, Japan

Wöhlke, Nina
1977 geboren in Sinsheim
1996-99 Ausbildung zur Goldschmiedin
seit 1999 Studium an der FH Düsseldorf

Ausstellungen **Exhibitions**
1998 *Schmucktriebe*, Deutsches Goldschmiedehaus Hanau und Escola Massana, Barcelona
1998/99 *Email, Schmuck und Gerät*, Deutsches Goldschmiedehaus Hanau

Wolf, Anke
1959 geboren in Gevelsberg
1978-82 Ausbildung zur Goldschmiedin
1982-1989 Tätigkeit als Goldschmiedegesellin
1989-2000 Studium an der FH Düsseldorf
2000 Diplom
seit 2000 freischaffend tätig

Ausstellungen **Exhibitions**
1997 Werkschau zum Thema *Perlenschatz*, Künstlerhof Zollhaus, Willich; *Perlenflut*, Arbeiten vor Ort, Galerie Marzee, Nimwegen
1998/99 *Perlen*, Glasmuseum Wertheim und Museum für Glaskunst, Lauscha
2000 *jaarlijkse internationale eindexamententoonstelling*, Galerie Marzee, Nimwegen
2001 *manu factum '01*, Niederrheinisches Museum für Volkskunde und Kulturgeschichte, Kevelaer

Auszeichnungen **Awards**
2001 Staatspreis des Landes Nordrhein-Westfalen für das Kunsthandwerk

Wir bedanken uns für die Hilfe und großzügige Unterstützung bei der Realisierung dieses Katalogbuchs
We would like to express our thanks for all our sponsors' generous help and support with the production of this publication

Fachhochschule Düsseldorf University of Applied Sciences
www.fh-duesseldorf.de

Museum für Kunsthandwerk Leipzig / Grassimuseum (Interim)
www.grassimuseum.com

Handwerkskammer Düsseldorf
www.hwk-duesseldorf.de

Deutsches Goldschmiedehaus Hanau
www.museen-hanau.de

Kestner-Museum Hannover
www.hannover.de

Headline Layoutsatz Service GmbH, Bremen

Agfa Deutschland Joachim Weber, Köln

Veld Laser Innovations Lohnfertigungsbetrieb für industrielle Laserbearbeitung
www.veldlaser.nl

Wolfgang Clement Ministerpräsident des Landes Nordrhein-Westfalen
www.nrw.de

C.-F. Dau Berlin
www.Dau-Berlin.com

Engels Goldschmiede, Ahaus

Dr. Ulrich Freiesleben Diamantmanufaktur, Münster
www.freiesleben.de

Galerie Cebra Anemone Tontsch, Düsseldorf

Galerie Grosche Schmuckwerkstatt, Castrop-Rauxel

Gellner GmbH & Co. KG Wiernsheim
www.gellner.com

Pur Atelier für Schmuckgestaltung, Nettetal
www.Pur-Atelier.de

Schiefer & Co. Edelmetall-Scheideanstalt (GmbH & Co.), Hamburg

Barbara Schulte-Hengesbach Galerie und Goldschmiede, Düsseldorf

Volksbank Düsseldorf Neuss eG

Anke Wolf Stolberg

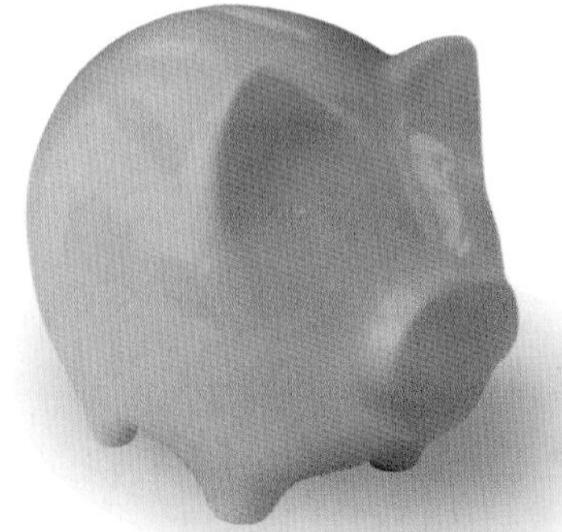

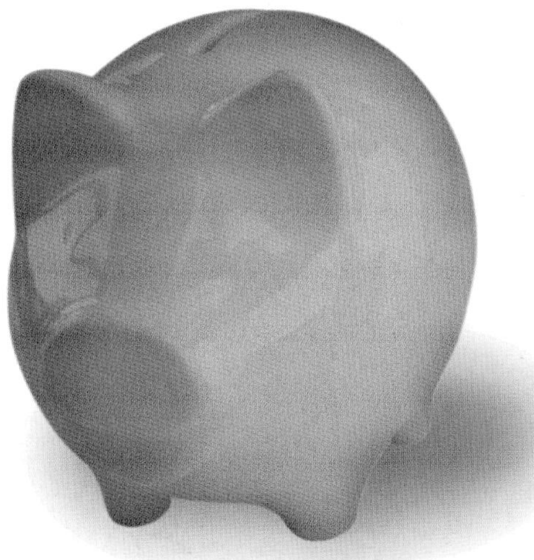

Impressum Credits

Katalogbuch Exhibition Catalogue

Idee und Konzept Idea and Concept
Prof. Elisabeth Holder, Prof. Herman Hermsen, Dipl. Des. Herbert Schulze

Herausgeber Editor
Fachhochschule Düsseldorf, University of Applied Sciences

Redaktion Editiorial Work
Prof. Elisabeth Holder, Janine Awater, Elgin Fischer, Gudrun Görl, Maren Krämer, Elke Munkert, Anja Oelschlegel, Julia Stotz

Autorinnen und Autoren Authors
Dipl. Des. Heike Baschta, Köln; Prof. Herman Hermsen, Arnheim; Prof. Elisabeth Holder, Erkrath; Dr. Barbara Maas, Mühlheim; Dr. Wolfgang Schepers, Hannover; Dipl. Des. Herbert Schulze, Linnich

Englische Übersetzung English Translation
Timothy M. Green, Brühl

Gestaltung Design
Konzept Markus Brand, Junghwa Kang, Meike Peters, Minja Töniges **Typografie** Olivier Arcioli, Ethel Strugalla **Realisation** Olivier Arcioli, Markus Brand, Michaela Burger, Junghwa Kang, Natascha Miteva-Efremova, Meike Peters, Ethel Strugalla, Sandra Tenbrink, Bärbel Wesberg

Fotografie Photography
Konzept Nora Hartmann-Küster, Natascha Miteva-Efremova, Ethel Strugalla, Bärbel Wesberg **Realisation** Olivier Arcioli, Markus Brand, Michaela Burger, Nora Hartmann-Küster, Junghwa Kang, Natascha Miteva-Efremova, Meike Peters, Ethel Strugalla, Sandra Tenbrink, Bärbel Wesberg, Julia Stotz, Catherine Niegel, Gudrun Görl, Elke Munkert, *inpetto*-Team **Fotomodelle** Cyrus Abbaszadeh, Simone Holzberg

Betreuung Consultants
Prof. Victor Malsy, Dipl. Des. Herbert Schulze, Prof. Gerhard Vormwald

Fotonachweis Photo Credits
Dirk Hansen, Köln; Walter Klien, Düsseldorf; Ans Dekker, Arnheim; Frank Kanters, Arnheim; Sibylle Pietrek, Düsseldorf; Herbert Schulze, Linnich; Fotostudio Hans Döring, München; HP Hoffmann Agentur, Düsseldorf; Achim Kuklies, Düsseldorf

Druck Printing
Rung-Druck, Göppingen
Papier Paper
Galaxi Keramik, 115g
Schrift Type
LT Syntax light und medium 7,3pt und 9pt
Reproduktionen Lithography
Headline Layoutsatz Service GmbH, Bremen

BuchseitenöffnerLesezeichenInhaltsverzeichnis PagecutterBookmarkIndex
Konzept Markus Brand, Junghwa Kang, Meike Peters, Minja Töniges **Realisation** Markus Brand, Meike Peters

Die Deutsche Bibliothek – CIP-Einheitsaufnahme

Ein Titelsatz für diese Publikation ist bei der Deutschen Bibliothek erhältlich
ISBN 3-89790-174-9

Ausstellung Exhibitions

Idee und Organisation Idea and Organisation
Prof. Elisabeth Holder, Nicola Brand, Elgin Fischer, Gudrun Görl, Maren Krämer, Elke Munkert, Anja Oelschlegel

Gestaltung Design
Prof. Herman Hermsen, Prof. Elisabeth Holder, Stanislav Braslavski, Anette Flach, Britta Göllner, Karen Hüttner, Karen Kathmann, Sabine Lang, Eilean Somnitz

Konzept und Realisation Conception and Production
Prof. Elisabeth Holder, Prof. Herman Hermsen, Dipl. Des. Herbert Schulze und Studierende des Studiengangs Produktdesign

Leihgeber Exhibit Lenders
Design Archiv Torsten Bröhan, M&M Uhren GmbH, Düsseldorf; Gebr. Niessing GmbH & Co., Vreden; Renate und Dominikus Straube, Bielefeld; Rita Klemmayer, München

Plakate und Einladungskarten Posters and Invitation Cards
Konzept Olivier Arcioli, Natascha Miteva-Efremova, Sandra Tenbrink, Bärbel Wesberg, Ina Watermann
Realisation Olivier Arcioli, Natascha Miteva-Efremova, Sandra Tenbrink, Bärbel Wesberg

Wir danken für Rat und Tat Thanks for Help and Advice
Axel Appel, Ulf Gräber, Karl-Heinz Janke, Dagmar Teske, Katharina Will, Alice